Sport in the Global Society

General Editor: J.A. Mangan

SITES OF SPORT

The study of built environments such as gymnasiums, football stadiums, swimming pools and skating rinks provides unique information about the historical enclosure of the gendered and sexualised body, the body's capabilities, needs and desires. It illuminates the tensions between the globalising tendencies of sport and the importance of local culture and a sense of place.

This collection uses spatial concepts and examples to examine the nature and development of sporting practices. At at time when the importance of spatial theories and spatial metaphors to sport is being increasingly recognised, this pioneering work on the changing landscape of sporting life will appeal to students of the history, sociology and management of sport.

Patricia Vertinsky is Distinguished University Scholar and Professor of Human Kinetics at the University of British Columbia, Canada. A social and cultural historian of the body she has published widely in the fields of gender, health, sport and physical activity. She is past-President of the North American Society of Sport History and Vice-President of the International Society of the History of Physical Education and Sport. Among her books are *The Eternally Wounded Woman: Women, Doctors and Exercise in the Late Nineteenth Century*, and *Disciplining Bodies in the Gymnasium: Memory, Monument and Modernism*.

John Bale obtained degrees from the University of London and currently shares his time teaching and researching between Aarhus University, Denmark and Keele University, UK. He has been a visiting professor at the University of Jyvaskyla, Finland, the University of Ontario, Canada, and the University of Queensland, Australia. Among his books are *Sport, Space and the City*, *Landscapes of Modern Sport*, *Kenyan Running* (with Joe Sang) and *Sports Geography*.

SPORT IN THE GLOBAL SOCIETY

General Editor: J.A. Mangan

The interest in sports studies around the world is growing and will continue to do so. This unique series combines aspects of the expanding study of *sport in the global society*, providing comprehensiveness and comparison under one editorial umbrella. It is particularly timely, with studies in the political, cultural, anthropological, ethnographic, social, economic, geographical and aesthetic elements of sport proliferating in institutions of higher education.

Eric Hobsbawm once called sport one of the most significant practices of the late nineteenth century. Its significance was even more marked in the late twentieth century and will continue to grow in importance into the new millennium as the world develops into a 'global village' sharing the English language, technology and sport.

Other Titles in the Series

SITES OF SPORT

Space, Place, Experience

Editors

PATRICIA VERTINSKY
University of British Columbia

JOHN BALE
Aarhus University

Routledge
Taylor & Francis Group

LONDON AND NEW YORK

First published in 2004 in Great Britain by
Routledge
11 New Fetter Lane London EC4P 4EE

Simultaneously published in the USA and Canada by
Routledge
29 West 35th Street, New York, NY 10001

Routledge is an imprint of the Taylor & Francis Group

British Library Cataloguing in Publication Data

A catalogue record of this book is available from
the British Library.

ISBN 0-7146-5343-8 (cloth)
ISBN 0-7146-8281-0 (paper)
ISSN 1368-9789

Library of Congress Cataloging-in-Publication Data

A catalog record of this book is available from
the Library of Congress.

Printed in Great Britain by MPG Books Ltd, Bodmin, Cornwall

Contents

Illustrations

Series Editor's Foreword

'As regards space', wrote Bertrand Russell, 'the modern view is that it is neither a substance as Newton maintained, and as Leucippus and Democritas ought to have said, nor an adjective of extended bodies, as Descartes thought, but a system of relations.'[1] This is appreciated by the editors and contributors to *Sites of Sport*. Systematic human relationships are explored in, for example, gymnasiums, swimming pools, ice-rinks, school playgrounds, mountains and beaches. These are all locations replete with possibilities for the consideration of sport and human relations and the manner in which models of masculinity, consumption and performance set in spatial contexts have defined these relations.

Whatever arguments are advanced, and however persuasively, about the sameness of contemporary sites of sport, it remains a potent reality that locations have their strong particularity which press on the senses, and thus 'flash upon the inward eye' again and again in bliss of reflective solitude. Sports sites possess their idiosyncratic identity, capture unforgettable moments, have a special resonance: smell, touch and nostalgia do make a place out of a sterile space! The human imagination is exercised in sports sites with extraordinary creativity. *Sites of Sport* reveals, by way of merely one example, that ice-skating 'grew in the intersection of climate, landscape and technology' – to which can be added class and gender, and involved multifarious illustrations of human relationships – on ice. School sportsfields arguably furnish the most remarkable illustrations of sites of sport, pressed into the service of the most extreme of human demands – militarism and its claimed virtues of self-sacrificial abnegation, glorious heroism, carefree courage and docile conformity. More could certainly have been made of this in *Sites of Sport*, but then comprehensiveness is seldom achievable in a single volume.

Enough has been written above to demonstrate the attractive possibilities of the study of sites of sport and human relations. *Sites of Sport* provides many more. It has blazed a trail for others to follow.

J.A. MANGAN
IRCSSS
De Montfort University (Bedford)
September 2003

Introduction

JOHN BALE and PATRICIA VERTINSKY

The significance of space and place as central dimensions of sport is well recognized by scholars who have addressed questions of sport from philosophical, sociological, geographical and historical perspectives. Sport contests are often talked of as 'struggles over space', and the very notion of 'representative sport' invokes the centrality of places, which, through sport events, are represented at local, regional and national levels.[1] Yet there is a tendency in at least philosophical and some geographical writing, to privilege space over place and to present the normative 'landscape' of sport as one of 'placelessness'. Paul Weiss, for example, suggests that an 'ideal' situation for sport to take place is one which seeks to eliminate external factors such as weather, topography and, by inference, spectators.[2] And the idea of an ideal model of the milieu for sport has been presented as a sanitized 'non-place', drawing on ideas from geographer Edward Relph and post modernists Paul Virilio and Jean Baudrillard.[3] Such a site has been likened to an isotropic plane, a sterile space, de-populated to ensure no home advantage is induced by spectator interference. It has been suggested that the long-term trajectory is that sport sites are, indeed, becoming increasingly rational, a quality encouraged by the laws of sport which insist on playing areas being the same – exactly the same – as all others of their type. The broad prediction, therefore, is that places for sport are being – and some would say, should be – replaced by sport spaces. These would amount to what the architect Le Corbusier might have termed 'machines for sport'.[4]

This book seeks to emphasize the continuing significance of place in sport, to emphasize the sight as much as the site. The distinction between place and space has been drawn in various ways. From an architectural perspective, Christian Norberg-Schultz observed that 'spaces where life occurs are *places*' and that a 'place is a space which has a distinct character'. Hence, the idea of *genius loci*.[5] The humanist geographer Yi-Fu Tuan likewise notes that 'space is formless'; places, on the other hand, have 'unique faces'.[6] From their uniqueness springs 'a sense of place' which creates sites possessing meaning and memories.

In the chapters that follow, authors from a variety of backgrounds address what they perceive to be the significance of different kinds of sport places. Several of them elaborate on our summary observations about space and place noted above (for example, Fusco, chapter 11, and Pronger, chapter 10). In commissioning these essays the editors made it clear that no rigorous pre-scriptions would be provided for authors. There is, therefore, no 'pattern' in the essays: each sport and its associated places is dealt with dif-ferently. Essays range in scale from the locker room and gymnasium to moun-tains and beaches. The essays celebrate the variety of locations and sites used for sport. At the same time, it is possible to detect tendencies for control and contestation. There is evidently variety in the landscapes of sport; there are also tensions and problems, notably the tension between space and place. We earlier noted the term 'sense of place' and we hope that some of the essays communicate such 'sensuous geographies'; we know that others tell of ten-dencies for control and surveillance, of conflict and power.

Patricia Vertinsky's opening chapter draws attention to the importance of context and social relations in analysing places designed for sport and physical culture. She explores the meanings of a 'sense of place' and de Certeau's notion of 'space as a practised place' by examining the making of a gymnasium and its effects upon social relations and disciplinary knowl-edge. Local gyms and sporting sites, she suggests, have tended to be neg-lected as sites of study, yet they reflect particular notions of the training and education of the body while their various orderings of space embody con-structions of race, place, gender and identity. Using spatial concepts she illustrates how a War Memorial Gymnasium in Western Canada in the post-war years became a partner in a dialogue with the bodies of students and bodies of memory and how its unique architectural and spatial arrangements became a particular setting for movement and social interac-tion arrangements. Her selection of the War Memorial Gymnasium was prompted by the fact that it was also a prize-winning example of modernist architecture which affected understandings of what fitted where, how the academic landscape was articulated for teaching and learning, whose knowledge was seen to be legitimate and how the boundaries of disciplines were formed and defended. Architectural space, including sporting and physical culture arenas such as gymnasia, was thus not neutral and trans-parent but deliberately attempted to express stereotyped gender roles in its spatial arrangements.

Feminist scholars have complained that built landscapes have been remarkable in their desire to confine, control and exclude women and this chapter focuses upon the issue of gender in relation to the masculinizing effects of the ordered, functional spaces of modernist design which reflected the architecture of modern sport training and the masculine culture in which the spatial rules of sport had been defined and developed. Modernist design in a Foucauldian sense thus became one of the major disciplinary means of power by which modern bodies were to be produced. As a site of lived relationships the gym marked out ordered spaces through which certain bodies were encouraged to move and relate in prescribed ways or be excluded from the action, so it was hardly surprising that the female body soon became estranged from the spaces of the gymnasium.

As noted earlier, in the humanist literature on places (in and out of sport) allusions are often made to a 'sense of place' or *genius loci*. These concepts suggest that there is more to watching a sport event than the sport itself. In chapter 2, Chris Gaffney and John Bale seek to identify the senses that might contribute to 'senses of place' in the context of modern sport. Their chapter starts by suggesting that the long-term tendency in sport spaces is to erode particularity and to move toward 'sameness' or 'placelessness' in the sport environment. Crudely put, pre-modern 'natural' landscapes of sport have been replaced by late-modern synthetic simulations, 'drained of lived experience' as Caroline Fusco notes in chapter 11. Gaffney and Bale explore the tension between place and space in the context of the modern soccer stadium. Drawing on the work of humanistic geographers, notably Yi-Fu Tuan, and on research undertaken in the USA and the UK, the authors draw attention to the many senses that are stimulated at a soccer match. The sense of sight is strongly privileged in modern society and we generally talk of going to 'see' or 'watch' a game of football. However, in the stadium, sound, smell, touch and nostalgia are evoked, making a place out of what is potentially a sterile space. The sensory geographies that are experienced in sport environments make attendance at the stadium much more than simply watching a game.

In chapter 3, Thierry Terret provides us with a broad historical overview of the emergence of pedagogical spaces to teach schoolchildren how to swim. Focusing mostly upon France, he shows how swimming pools have traditionally been the product of a consensus arising from several competing desires for use. Where education was concerned, disciplinary and safety concerns were tantamount, leading to techniques for teaching swimming strokes on land or suspending pupils over and in the water on cables and ropes. Hygienic regulations eventually led to the general standardization of water treatment and the increased management of bathers in the 'modern' swimming pool, which was typically a small rectangular pool with calm and transparent water. Terret goes on to show how, in the second half of the twentieth century, school standards for swimming pools took precedence over other sporting and recreational needs and the school swimming pool became thoroughly standardized to conform to the requirements of teaching, discipline and safety. Individuals have increasingly obtained more freedom in the water

– they can swim and act in a space which is still well delimited but less
Cartesian and symmetrical. The rectangle, as a resolutely disciplinary geometrical model, has been partly replaced by more functional and attractive
designs. On the other hand, school norms are still there to adjust the organization of lessons and provide discipline where necessary.

Mary Louise Adams's study of ice-rinks and the development of figure
skating is also concerned with sport spaces as sites for the production and
maintenance of social relations based on class and gender, but she is
primarily interested in the way in which the enclosure of previously outdoor
(public) activities became an exclusionary process that separated activities
from each other and divided people along class and gender lines. Early
skating, she suggests, grew in the intersection of climate, landscape and
technology. Different landscapes led to different kinds of skating which
were also influenced by the type of skates available and the prevailing
social mores. Skating outdoors made class differences and gender restrictions visible, especially as skating clubs developed, controlling access and
circumscribing practice.

It was figure skating that precipitated the invention of artificial ice and
indoor rinks with its focus on technique and controlled precision – skating
as science rather than art, suggests Adams. Contrasting styles of skating that
developed in different countries, she shows how spacious outdoor rinks suf-
fered from the vagaries of the weather while the circumscription of space in
indoor rinks affected movement and skill.

With advances in technology, the encroachment of commercialism and
the promotion of female ice skating stars through Hollywood and the media,
ice rinks became less exclusive and figure skating became a popular activity
for girls. Yet rinks, she says, like other contested social spaces, continue to
have regulatory effects such that access to ice time has become a politically
charged issue in places such as Canada where male hockey players vie for
practice time with female hockey players, and also with the figure skaters
and the general public.

The school playground is the focus of chapter 5 by Sarah Thomson. The
playground has traditionally been viewed as a place of release, where children may engage in sport in both its pre-modern (disport) and modern (sport
as game) sense. Here the playground is presented as anything but a place of
play. Indeed, Thomson uses the metaphor of the classroom to make explicit
the significance of control in the primary school playgrounds that form the
focus of her research. They are contested places over which a large number
of agencies impose considerable discipline and control. They are read by
Thomson as places, not of play but of constraint. In a risk and litigious
society the playground can all too readily become a site for the construction
of Foucauldian 'docile bodies'. Thomson identifies the various ways in
which the playground is, in effect, an outdoor analogue of the school class-

room and, as a result, a mechanism for denying children's freedom to 'play'.

Charlotte Macdonald's portrayal of marching spaces follows nicely from Thomson's discussion of the role of the enclosed playground in schooling bodies. While marching spaces are more often identified as military and ceremonial spaces, they have also served as sporting places. In chapter 6 Macdonald shows how closely coordinated formation marching became a major competitive summer sport for girls in New Zealand in the decades spanning the cold war years. Marching, she points out, presents a vivid example of the way body cultures have come to define space, and space has been used to define and allow certain body cultures to flourish. This was certainly the case for girls and young women in New Zealand who claimed entry to public spaces and held the public's gaze with their highly practised, carefully orchestrated routines and decorative, short-skirted uniforms. As they wheeled and strutted, with military precision but showing plenty of leg, they disrupted gender identity in a number of ways – displaying a sexualized girlishness on the one hand and a sense of team play, good conduct and order on the other. In her cleverly argued piece, Macdonald shows how marching teased at definitions of military and civilian, masculine and feminine, traditional and modern in a post-war society insecure about its position in a changing world order and anxious about the social order among its own citizens. In this respect, the spectacle of rows of energetic and neatly marching girls and young women in straight lines was an appealing reassurance of order.

Tara Magdalinski's focus is Homebush Bay, the Olympic site for the Sydney 2000 Olympic games, and in chapter 7 she shows how Australian organizers tried to promote the spectacle as 'the Green Games' in a natural paradise fashioned for the natural (clean, healthy, drug-free) athlete. Taking up Bale's argument that sportscapes are always subject to interpretation as 'mythical' landscapes projecting a particular set of images, she shows how Homebush was imbued with iconic meanings that extended beyond the bounds of the Olympic site and encompassed not just an athletic but also a national typology in its image. Her analysis provides an insight into the ways that the Olympic site produced meanings about the Australian landscape, contributing at one and the same time to a reaffirmation of the traditional elements of Australian identity and confirming broader Olympic ideals and philosophies. Efforts to represent Homebush as a natural paradise were, not surprisingly, complicated by the fact that the site was a toxic waste dump, the result of decades of unfettered pollution by heavy industry. Also problematic was the need to represent the site as a pure and natural location for athletes whose bodies were uncontaminated by drugs and technologies of change. Below the surface of Homebush, she says, throbbed a level of toxicity, whilst athletic bodies were contained in a skin that elided the degree to which the human form has been chemically manipulated in its pursuit of sporting glory. The irony was that few recognized the fundamental contradiction in admiring the architectural achievements of the built environment at the Olympic site while simultaneously rejecting the same built quality of the Olympic athletes.

Douglas Booth, in chapter 8, focuses his attention on the beach as an environment for sport and recreation. Long regarded as a liminal space, the beach, for Booth, is seen as a contested geographical site. He particularly addresses the tension, in Australian beach culture, between surf lifesavers and surfers. He demonstrates how the rules of beach behaviour have not only changed over time but have been subject to delicate changes in the hegemony of beach usage. Initially, the beach was claimed by the lifesavers who defined the rules and discipline of beach behaviour. The rise of surfing as an hedonistic reflection of 1960s counter-culture led to confrontation with the established and conservative lifesavers. Eventual rapprochement was achieved by the institutionalization of surfing, a further example of respectability being brought about though sportization.

In chapter 9, Peter Donnelly addresses mountains as sacred and dramatic places that have been transformed into sites where humans attempt to defy gravity, on the one hand, and utilize it on the other. A wide range of sports have colonized mountain environments, ranging from mountaineering itself to white-water rafting and downhill skiing. As Donnelly points out, however, the first modern use of mountains was for scientific rather than sporting endeavour. Mountaineering, he suggests, brought together aestheticism, science and imperialism (mountaineering arguably being the imperial sport par excellence). The formal sportization of mountaineering came with the establishment of records, bureaucracies and the various other characteristics that Allen Guttmann has identified as typifying modern sport.

In chapter 10, Brian Pronger presents a novel way of reading sport as a focal point for the 'landscape' (in its broadest sense) of pornography. The massive presence of pornography in western culture has readily colonized the world of sport. At the same time, however, it should be recognized that many of the body practices of sport contain implicitly sexual connotations that, if practised outside sport, would be recognized immediately as sexual in nature. It should not be so surprising, therefore, that the physical landscape of sport today provides a background for many pornographic representations porn drawing on mainstream sport. The early part of Pronger's chapter elaborates on the sensory dimensions of the sport landscape. He proceeds to note that the recognized spaces of sport (locker rooms, showers, the field itself) may be used and represented in non-traditional ways, reinforcing the point that various landscape elements of the sport environment may not be as mono-cultural (nor hetero-sexual) as they first seem. It is the

erotic transgression of sport places, and how the sportscape becomes sexualized and eroticized, that forms the broad theme of this chapter.

Caroline Fusco, in chapter 11, deals with the ubiquitous sport place of
the locker room. Although often depicted as mere spaces, clinically
sanitized and depersonalized, Fusco argues that locker rooms are highly
territorialized spaces where 'the abject' create social spaces and a human
presence. Far from being in a 'safe' and 'secure' space, the fear of bodily
pollution is communicated in both explicit and implicit ways. Drawing on
the work of geographers, anthropologists and cultural theorists, Fusco sees
the apparent boundaries of the locker room as being permeable and always
present. Despite pressure towards sanitization, dirt and pollution transcend
the boundaries of any 'pure', fully 'modern', locker-room space. Fusco's
essay is made powerful by her autobiographically informed approach.

Roberta Park returns us to the gymnasium in the final chapter, using the
building of Harmon Gymnasium at the University of California, Berkeley,
in 1879 as a starting point for an examination of Berkeley as a site for the
oldest, continuous physical education major programme at any American
university. The hundred-year span of this programme, which was disestablished in 1997, provides an unparalleled opportunity to examine the rise and
fall of physical education programmes in higher education, and Park shows
how the changing nature of sport facilities on the campus both stimulated
and reflected changing attitudes toward the physical education of the body
and the ever-burgeoning demands of competitive sport. Located in the
Harmon Gymnasium, the first Department of Physical Culture announced
in 1888 that it was not the purpose of a college gymnasium to make athletes.
When the Harmon gym was pulled down in 1997 and replaced by the
Walter Haas Jr. Pavilion, spectatorship of competitive athletics had
triumphed and there was no room for physical education either in its spaces
or in the academic curriculum – this despite a Senate review that showed
Berkeley's AB degree in physical education as an intellectually rich and
diverse human biology major reflecting liberal education at its best.

1

Locating a 'Sense of Place': Space, Place and Gender in the Gymnasium

PATRICIA VERTINSKY

With the continued acceleration of globalization, the contexts in which we think about sport and physical culture, and the narratives we have woven about the places and spaces of our sporting past, are all coming under question as we try to understand a world we have not experienced before.[1] We have become increasingly aware of the artificiality of the boundaries and centres that hitherto dominated our thinking about the world so that among the effects of globalization is increasing uncertainty about what we mean by a 'sense of place' and how we relate to the changing landscape of sporting and recreational life in our personal and professional lives. How, in the face of massive global movements, homogenization and the commodification of the landscape can we retain any sense of local places and their particularities? Should we try to reassure ourselves that one of the crucial roles played by sport may be that of delineating and confirming a 'sense of place', and a more secure sense of embodiment, of specific and lived space?[2] Is a heightened sense of place an essential aspect in addressing the difficulties of time–space compression?[3]

That 'sense of place', reminds Clifford Geertz, has been so thoroughly absorbed into our particular ways of seeing the world, and of the stories we tell ourselves about ourselves, that it is helpful to reflect anew upon the meanings of places of sport and physical culture we have seen or imagined in our historical and comparative studies, and the nature of the spaces (of sporting practices) that we have inhabited, transformed or been excluded from.[4] Karl Raitz invites us to think of sport places as a kind of theatre in which the behaviour of those who participate or watch alter both the nature of the activity and the place where it is practised.[5] The sport place, like the theatre, shapes the play, while also providing a context for different experiences and social interactions within and beyond it. In his many studies on sporting space, Henning Eichberg reminds us too that sport has always, to some extent, been determined by place and space, and that it has itself produced specific forms of place and space.[6]

Michel de Certeau's sense of 'space as a practised place' (for example, when the street, geometrically defined by urban planners, is transformed into a 'place' by walkers) is helpful in discussing sporting places and spaces.[7] Reversing the customary assumption that place is a structured space, space can be conceived of as an outcome, the product of an activity, which has a temporal dimension.[8] Place, then, is constituted by sets of relations which cut across spatial scales. In other words, places touch the ground as spatially located patterns and forms of behaviour and are defined, maintained and altered through the impact of unequal power relations.[9] From this perspective, different sporting places can be distinguished from each other through the operation of the relations of power that construct boundaries around them, creating spaces with certain meanings in which some relationships are facilitated, others discouraged. Places are made through power relations, which construct the rules, which define the boundaries; these boundaries are both social and spatial. They mark belonging and exclusion – who belongs to a place and who may be excluded – as well as the location, site and nature of the particular sporting experience. Thus, says Doreen Massey, the spatial organization of sport places 'is integral to the production of social relations and not merely its result. It is fully implicated in both history and politics'.[10] And, since we live our lives in and through places, and in and through the body (for the body is the place or the site of the individual), the ways in which we live our body/place relationships are necessarily political too. 'Bodies and places are woven together through intimate webs of social and spatial rules that are made by and make embodied [sporting] subjects.'[11]

This chapter explores the meanings of a 'sense of place' and 'space as a practised place' by examining the making of a gymnasium and its effects upon social relations and disciplinary knowledge. It will show how the fortunes of individual sporting places or buildings cannot be explained by simply looking within them, but must be viewed as open and porous networks of social relations subject to a variety of influences within the context of the time. My intent, therefore, is to demonstrate that 'what gives a place its specificity is not some long internalized history but the fact that it is constructed out of a particular constellation of social relations, meeting and weaving together at a particular locus'.[12] First, however, I want to review the development of a spatial focus through some of the critical literature about space and place that complicates notions of a 'sense of place' and draws attention to the importance of context and social relations in analysing places designed for sport and physical culture.

The 'Spatial Turn'

In reiterating that 'a sense of place' 'carries the resonance of homestead, location, and open space as well as a position in the social hierarchy', Dolores Hayden notes that 'place is one of the trickiest words in the English language, a suitcase so overfilled one can never shut the lid'.[13] This suitcase has bulged even more since concepts of space and place have taken on such importance among scholars of the social sciences and humanities and been further problematized in a globalizing world. Along with the 'cultural turn' within the social sciences as a whole (which can be roughly equated to the postmodern turn), has been a 'spatial turn'. With the reassertion of space in social and cultural theory, an entire spatial language emerged for comprehending the contours of social reality.[14] All of a sudden, the language of space and place was everywhere claiming to be central to the maps of meaning that constitute cultural experiences.[15] Paul Gilroy called it the 'spatial focus' where identity is hedged about with spatial metaphors.[16] Michel Foucault liberally borrowed from the lexicon of space to posit a correlation between forms of subjectivity, discourse and the material effects of three-dimensional space:

> The great obsession of the nineteenth century was … history … with its themes of development and suspension, of crisis and cycle … with its great preponderance of dead men … The present epoch will perhaps be above all the epoch of space … We are at a moment when our experience of the world is less that of a long life development through time, than that of a network that connects points and intersects with its own skein.[17]

These new historical analyses of space and place have encouraged scholars of sport and physical culture to look much more closely at how forms of popular culture such as sport have been worked out in particular places through the production and maintenance of social relations and the distribution of power.[18] Spatial metaphors have been particularly useful for focusing upon the underpinnings of concrete, tangible, embodied practices. They have encouraged us to shift our scrutiny from the study of social life in its totality and the use of the meta-narrative, to the study of social life in all its plurality and particularity.[19] We have begun to focus more closely and critically upon the practice of everyday life, the ordinary man, woman and child in their everyday physical culture and sporting pursuits in 'the expression of the ubiquitous and the local'.[20] After all, everyday life, for most, is very much a local affair.

While the place-bound nature and localization of everyday life seems indisputable, Anthony Giddens (a sports fan who wrote his master's thesis on the social history of soccer) has argued that one of the consequences of modernity has been the separation of space from place and the severing of face-to-face interactions.[21] Giddens claims that distant places and events have become as familiar or more so than nearby influences, and are easily integrated within the frameworks of personal experience (a soccer fan, for example, may be more at home and identify more closely with distant World Cup events than his or her local club). Economic and social identities are thus uprooted as new systems of communication and power reach over the nation state and create nodes in a network society.[22] With this decline in the sense of local attachment, people may suffer a partial and a cultural separation from their own 'sense of place', their traditions and their personal history. For Giddens and his followers, place tends to disappear, leading to what John Bale characterizes as 'placeless' sporting landscapes, mass produced and international in style where different locations both look and feel alike and in which distinctive places are experienced only through superficial and stereotypical images.[23] This is so, he explains, because in the case of many organized sports like football, swimming, basketball and track and field, standardization, quantification and record-keeping have made it necessary for the spatial parameters of the immediate physical environment to be as identical as possible, regardless of global or local location. Thus, says Karl Raitz, 'we get monster cookie-cutter concrete stadiums with plastic seats set along standardized fields covered with plastic turf' – a blight upon our games.[24] Such places, whatever we think of them, are close to what Lefebvre has called 'abstract space', where all differences between global and local space are erased.[25]

Paradoxically, of course, this situation can make the elaboration of place-bound identities *more* rather than *less* important. Indeed, it can be argued that globalization leads to cultural differentiation, not homogenization, maintaining rather than undermining cultural difference and the importance of place and particularity.[26] There are many signs of a continued, even intensified, sense of locality around the world. While mobility cannot be denied, places – local attachments – remain significant.[27] After all, argues Robertson, doesn't MacDonald's alter its menus to suit local tastes – and don't tourists go to different places to seek out local sights?[28] Bale too recognizes the ambiguities of modernity and globalization. He admits that the modern sports landscape is by no means immune to local resistance, with the result that a sense of place cannot be totally replaced by space. Global influences can reconstruct rather than destroy localities. Indeed, points out Eichberg, no sporting place can be characterized by a single image of a fixed and bounded piece of territory, observing a softening of the harsh configurations of modern sports places by pointing to new forms of ecological and feminist architecture, a return to the open air and a growth in alternative sports. 'The prevailing notion of sport', he suggests, 'is only one way in which the moving, physical body can be configured in modernity' and experience a 'sense of place'.[29]

Clearly, in a global society, the places and spaces where we pursue our disciplines, our professions, and our sporting and recreational pursuits have very different 'power geometries' (that is, the shape and structure of the space in which our lives and physical activities are given meaning) than a century or even a decade or so ago.[30] It is here we see how the historian's craft can be described as delineating the shape of time. A hundred years ago, exclusive claims to places such as the men's golf club, the football field, the professions, institutions of higher education and the military drill-hall were all attempts to fix the meanings of particular places (and repositories of knowledge) by staking claim to them, enclosing them and controlling the activities within them through the use of particular power discourses.

In the obvious gendered example, the long-standing perception that women were the weaker sex and medical shibboleths about female frailty allowed late nineteenth century physicians, educators and sportsmen to rationalize women's exclusion from sporting places and define the home as the limits of female activity.[31] Home was a female place, a space of senti-ment and duty, a place of constraint from which vigorous sport, competition and power were banished. It was men, after all, who initially formed the organizations, which drew up the spatial rules of sports, defining the spatial limits, and which separated the sport place from the landscape.[32] The enclo-sures of sporting spaces served to reinforce hierarchical boundaries between who was to count as an athlete and who was not – and to perpetuate the exclusion of women through masculinist discourses which constructed women's bodies as certain kinds of entities with certain properties, spatial capabilities and proper places.[33]

Using the methodologies of the new spatial turn, a number of historians and comparative scholars have focused their research upon the nature of these and other related discourses and attempted to rethink the unity of space and place in different terms – to show, for example, how men's exclu-sive claim to higher education and sporting clubs and activities in the nine-teenth century was not a natural or God-given sanction but a constructed, manufactured and sometimes invented argument constituted by and reflec-tive of the dominant patriarchal organization of space and place in Western culture. In particular they have pointed out that space is not the unchanging backdrop against which life is played out.[34] Nor can place ever be posed as a source of stability and an unproblematic identity. 'Simply put', says David Harvey, 'those who command space can always control the politics of place, even though it takes control of some place to command space in the first place.'[35]

'Practised Space as a Place' – The War Memorial Gymnasium

The ability to influence the production of space is an important means to augment social power.[36] One way to analyse the production and processes of 'space as a practised place' is to look at power struggles as they appeared in the planning, design, construction and use of particular buildings for sport, training and the pedagogy of physical education. Says Camille Wells, 'most buildings can be understood in terms of power or authority – as efforts to assume, extend, resist or accommodate it'.[37] Hence the idea that a place (or building) has a single essential identity is immediately exploded. A woman's 'sense of place' in a football stadium, for example the spaces in which she has been accustomed to move and her connections with others inside and outside the stadium are often quite different from a man's.[38] It is from this perspective that I want to explore issues of space and place within and around a unique modernist building for sport and physical education: the War Memorial Gymnasium at the University of British Columbia (UBC) in Canada, built just after the Second World War to commemorate Canadian soldiers who gave their lives for their country (see Figure 1.1). Local gyms and sporting sites, unlike Olympic sites and famous baseball stadiums, have tended to be neglected as a site of study. They are often seen as too commonplace and ubiquitous to make meaningful study, yet they reflect particular notions of the training and education of the body while their various orderings of space embody constructions of race, place, gender and identity.[39]

Examining the design and production of space in this place where physical education knowledge was constructed and purveyed, citizenship values embodied, sporting identities formed and relationships developed can be a more evocative and revealing approach to the social history and compara-

FIGURE 1.1

UBC's Million Dollar Gymnasium on the day of its official opening ... the gym is the largest in any Canadian university. *Totem*, 1951, p.54. (University of British Columbia Archives)

tive study of physical education and sport than any written records. Spatial readings can illustrate what Raphael Samuel in 'Theatres of Memory' calls memory's shadows – 'those sleeping images which spring to life unbidden and serve as ghostly sentinels of our thoughts'.[40] Spatial concepts can illustrate how this memorial gymnasium became a partner in a dialogue with the bodies of students and bodies of memory. They can infuse our everyday understanding of what fits where, how the academic landscape is articulated for teaching and learning, whose knowledge is seen to be legitimate and how the boundaries of disciplines are formed and defended.[41]

From this place – this million-dollar gym, dubbed a 'palace of sweat', and Canada's largest and most modern gymnasium in the 1950s – emerge important stories of sport and social contest. Over the five decades of its existence the gymnasium provided a 'sense of place' to students, faculty, staff and the local community as the changing face of knowledge and popular culture demanded accommodations, shifting spatial arrangements and acquiescence or resistance to views on how the Canadian body should be remembered and educated. We can see how the gymnasium, designated a war memorial, evolved into an arena of contested spaces and functions around gendered, racial and sexualized bodies, as well as bodies of knowledge and the shape of disciplines. One can reconstruct the intense struggles around disciplinary paradigms as UBC reached to accommodate Franklin Henry's vision of the academic discipline of physical education and then fractured around splintering sub-disciplines and the different priorities of professional development, performance and scientific laboratory work.[42] Organizational units were created and destroyed in response to internal conflict, the changing scene of higher education and athletics, leadership styles, and shifts in student and faculty supply and demand. We can develop telling narratives around the inclusion and exclusion of people or groups, modes of physical culture and sports activities, and a million formative moments in the lives of those who were enabled (or not) to explore the limits of their bodies and minds in its shifting spaces. Just as Eichberg has drawn conclusions about the patterns and dynamics of physical culture from historical changes in sports architecture so we can trace the power geometries – the effects of multiple configurations of space and social relations within and around the War Memorial Gymnasium – which provided a certain 'sense of place' in higher education in the second half of the twentieth century.[43]

Architecture, Modernism and the Gymnasium

As much as the War Memorial Gym was about physical education and student recreation, it was also about the profession of architecture …

and as much as it was about student's bodies it was also about the architectural body.[44]

Architecture builds, over and over, philosophically endorsed ideas of home, city, place – inscribing them in space much as a scribe records the words of an absolute ruler. From this viewpoint, architecture is a deeply conservative force that keeps what is philosophically, politically and ideologically 'proper' in place.[45]

Whilst the War Memorial Gymnasium provided a unique 'sense of place' to many people for a number of reasons, particularly compelling to the observer (and meaningful to the gym's occupants and their activities) was its architectural design. Architecture functions importantly as a potential stimulus for movement, real or imagined. Hence, the unique architecture and spatial arrangements of the War Memorial Gymnasium at UBC became an incitement to action, a particular setting for movement and social interaction.[46]

[Gym], body and mind are in continuous interaction, the physical structure, furnishing, social conventions and mental images at once enabling, molding, informing and constraining the activities and ideas which unfold within its bounds.[47]

The original architectural design, a Collegiate Gothic-style gymnasium to match other buildings on campus (see Figure 1.2) was rejected early in the design process by critics at the University who contended that 'twentieth century recreation for twentieth century men and women was unrelated in function and spirit to a fifteenth century architectural form'. It was, reported the University's *Graduate Chronicle*, 'an anachronism as applied to a gymnasium and to a university devoted to the discovery of truth and to the training of minds and bodies fit for leadership in the tasks of today and tomorrow'.[48] Clearly the editors had in mind a particular approach to physical culture and sporting excellence, which was to be expressed from outside and within, and it included a desire to memorialize in a 'modern' way the courageous struggles of local soldiers lost in both World Wars.

This post-war moment of anxiety over traditional design was precursor to an era of enthusiasm over what would be called 'high' modernism – and an important wing of this movement appealed to the image of rationality incorporated in the machine. The eclipse of history by memory profoundly influenced modern commemorative architecture, and modernism, in its flight from tradition and history, pursued rational utility over past traditions. Modernist architects saw the past as a distraction that required forgetting rather than remembering, though one could suggest that this notion of modern did not so much imply an erasure of the past as an encryptment

FIGURE 1.2

University of British Columbia launches campaign for $500,000 War Memorial Gymnasium. Architect's original gothic design. (*Daily Colonist*, Victoria, BC, 2 Feb. 1946)

of certain uncomfortable narratives – in some sense a desire for *not* having had a past and therefore being less subject to the malaise of nostalgia.[49] Certainly, the ruling ideology of the immediate post-war years was forward looking and progressive as Vancouver modernist architects sought to adopt European modernist efforts to improve society through new applications of science, technology and the arts.[50] The modernist ethos promised to address urgent social questions as well as personal architectural aspirations through the conception of the modern architect as a forward-looking social engineer focused on equity, economy of form and construction, and community-building values.[51] According to the University's President, Norman Mackenzie, modern functional design would bring beauty, utility and health to the campus.[52] His appointment of Frederic Lasserre, mountain climbing aficionado, former Navy officer and apprentice of Tecton,[53] as Head of the new School of Architecture was directed toward that goal. Modern, said Lasserre with an approving nod to the values of youth and progress, meant honestly expressing the needs of today through the frank and economical use of structure and materials.[54] With Ned Pratt, university-retained architect and former Olympic medal winning rower, the new gym took shape[55] and the University was pressed to adopt a courageous stand for modernist architecture – a style that was to act as a metaphor for the modern bodies produced within it.

To the modernist architects of Vancouver at mid century, including Arthur Erickson, the new gymnasium's design was a superb statement of modernist values – a lucid resolution of structure, plan and aesthetic.[56] Even before it was completed the *Alumni Chronicle* claimed that it was 'probably the finest building the University has yet built on campus and one of the finest college gyms on the continent'.[57] Its architects received a national award for the 'simple dignity and imaginative quality of its architectural design' and the gym was voted the best of all recreational buildings erected in Canada since the end of the war.[58] The focus was on light and space, the design hard-edged with stark lines, flush walls, right-angled corners and bold geometric patterns.[59] In particular, the dominant machine ethic was very apparent: hygienic and simple, stripped of ornament and reference to the past – memorializing yet erasing in one fell swoop.

'Architects designing in their own image, often centralize their own experiences of space and marginalize and negate the experiences of others.'[60] The places they create are palpable territories of social activities and meanings.[61] And, on closer examination, the new 'brutalist' architecture (as some called it) was deeply masculine in its biases, projecting the notion that what it means to be masculine is, quite literally, to embody force, to embody competence, to occupy space, to have a physical presence in the world.[62] Based upon the conceptions of French modernist architect, Le Corbusier – one of the most influential architects of the twentieth century – with his adherence to straight lines and Newtonian view of the body as a machine, a gymnasium logically had to be a machine for training the body and the shape of the gymnasium had to reflect this function. Thus the behaviour-shaping possibilities of built form became starkly evident. Form shaped space and in turn, space gave shape to social relations. Man, said Le Corbusier, was a geometric animal, a closed system, a surrogate machine in an industrial age.[63] And the machine, in Freudian terms, represented all that was male: activity and power.

> We must invent the modern building like a giant machine ... the house of cement, iron and glass, without curves or ... ornament, rich only in the inherent beauty of its lines and modelling, extraordinarily brutish in its mechanical simplicity.[64]

Claiming that his buildings were simply machines for living in, Le Corbusier assigned to them a gendered distinction as male – revealing his desire for forms of spatial perfectibility premised on a pure body type conceived of as the youthful, normal, and classical body.[65] As an architect he liked to demonstrate his aversion to women through design, showing the mastery of the feminized body as colonized territory. Hence his buildings were specifically designed with an eye to those who respected order, governance, and dominance over unruly (womanly) nature with its curved lines and jagged edges (the power of the straight line always being superior to the curve).[66] The relationship to the ground on which the gym was built was oppositional, using pillars to impose order on an unruly and curvaceous landscape. Even the windows were carefully placed to frame the landscape outside, allowing man to analyse and control it visually. A window is a man, said Le Corbusier. It stands upright and allows the gaze of domination over the exterior world.[67] It was masculine territory, a citadel, in Le Corbusier's words, in which a man could feel secure.[68]

Most of the behavioural clues to gender boil down to how we occupy space, both alone and with others, and bodies in space raise all sorts of questions about the space and place they occupy.[69] In describing the configurations of modernity, Le Corbusier succinctly expressed the architecture of modern sports training and the masculine culture in which the spatial rules of sport had been defined and developed. Such a spatial configuration was related to a sportified, geometric, enclosed sense of space associated with a distinctively male version of nationality and a functional image of sport as a planned and regulated activity.[70] 'The human being steps straight ahead', he said, 'because he has an aim. He knows where to go, he has decided on one direction, and he strides resolutely forward … The right angle is necessary and sufficient for action because it serves to determine the space in a completely equivocal fashion.'[71] When sport and functionalism went hand in hand, the most appropriate shape for a gymnasium was (and still is) rectangular (with standardized and mechanized spaces), incorporating the geometrical logic of Foucault's panopticon, drill-hall and prison with their central perspective and view of power.[72] Modernist design, in a Foucauldian sense, thus became one of the major disciplinary means of power by which modern bodies were to be produced, for the human body was the site at which all forms of repression were ultimately registered.

Modernism reified a passion for large geometric spaces and perspectives, for uniformity and the power of the straight line, and Le Corbusier always thought big – big buildings, big open spaces, big urban highways. Upon observing the widespread gothic style of gymnasium architecture on North American campuses he determined that such spaces could never be considered appropriate for athletic development in higher education. They were, he said, 'caged, chlorotic and spiritless – not in any way helpful in building supermen'.[73] In his eyes, every modernist project was a gymnasium of sorts where the modern body was regulated in measured spaces, with light, air and space arranged for training, ordering and recreation. Not everyone, however, was granted equal access to the symbolic realm of modernism and its ordered and functional spaces, and, as we shall see, the female body soon became estranged from the spaces of the War Memorial Gymnasium.

Gender in the Gym – A Process of Exclusion

> One's relationship to the social world and to one's proper place in it is never more clearly expressed than in the space and time one feels entitled to take from others; more precisely, in the space one claims with one's body in physical space.[74]

The modernist ethos, apparent in the stark clean cut lines of the prize-winning architecture of the gym, was complemented in the spaces created for learning activities, sports training and athletic competition. The techniques of athletic training and the disciplinary knowledge of physical education, as well as particular sets of social relations, became inexorably etched into the spaces of the War Memorial Gym as the various influences of the Department of Physical Education, the Athletic Directors, the student body and the external world of intercollegiate athletic competition impacted on life and people's 'sense of place' in the gymnasium over the next five decades.

When Fred Hume, local historian of UBC Athletics Hall of Fame, wrote nostalgically about the War Memorial Gym in the athletic department's student newspaper he pointed out with pride that:

> Over the years War Memorial has been the scene of many events and activities. But most of all it has been 'home,' giving us that special feeling when rival players claim how difficult it is to beat the 'Birds' when in the confines of the War Memorial. A tribute to those who gave their lives serving Canada, an example of what community initiative and participation can produce, the palace of sweat has been home to numerous heroes and champions – War Memorial remains centre stage at UBC.[75]

But while the gym gave a real sense of home to some, that 'sense of place' called home has also been the focus of much work by feminists who have seen 'home' as a site of disenfranchisement for women – just as the sporting arena has been so often.[76] Social distance does not always imply geographical distance, says Linda McDowell, and occupants of the same Cartesian spaces may live in very different 'places'.[77] The War Memorial Gym was not a place for everyone and it was certainly *not* always home to many female students, athletes and staff who were excluded in the early years from the working and emotional spaces of the gym (except for the secretarial and janitorial work, that is, where women occupied a subordinate service role). Nor was it home to many gay and lesbian athletes, students and coaches who felt (and may still feel) pressed to hide their sexuality in the locker rooms, at team gatherings and even in the boardroom. In the postwar period mannish athleticism was increasingly linked with lesbianism, stigmatizing women athletes and coaches, and forcing many to remain misfits or shadowy figures under a cloud of sexual suspicion. Gay athletes who loved sport learned to heed the code, 'play it, don't say it'.[78] After all, says Elspeth Probyn, sport highlights the fact (and anxiety) that bodies do something, and Gilles Deleuze concurs, warning that 'on ne sait pas ce que peut un corps' (we just do not know what a body can do).[79]

Even before the gym's completion in 1951, women fared badly in relation to the allotment of spaces for changing rooms, offices and the physical
activities deemed appropriate for them, and the dramatic difference in space
and facilities for women's and men's affairs generally has remained to this
day. Difficulties first arose during the construction of the gym when a short-
fall in the budget compromised the original design. In spite of the pleas of
the female Director of Athletics to retain facilities for the large numbers of
female students, the dance studio, a small second gymnasium, the squash
courts and most of the women's changing rooms were eventually sacrificed
on the recommendation of the male Director, himself a former Olympic athlete. 'Dear Ned', he wrote to Ned Pratt, the university architect and fellow
sportsman, 'I recommend that accommodations for women be kept to an
absolute minimum in the interests of economy and administrative efficiency.'[80] Although one student in three was female in 1950, and women
students had lent equal support in fund-raising for the new gym, little effort
was made to include them in the building as anything other than spectators
of the men's sporting competitions or as cheerleaders to enhance the spectacle. Their performative role confined, women spectators confirmed the
association between looking and consuming that was such a crucial part of
the spectacle of modernism.[81]

The actual construction of the gym also highlighted issues of race and eth-
nicity in respect of 'which' Canadian soldiers were to be memorialized and
'whose' bodies were to be educated in the spaces of the gym. The President
of the Alma Mater Society felt compelled to complain to the university-
retained architects about the ban on hiring 'persons of Asiatic or African
descent' to work on the construction of the War Memorial Gymnasium. It
was, they noted, particularly offensive in light of the number of Chinese
Canadian soldiers who fought and gave their lives for Canada during the war.

With the opening of the new gym, the women's physical education faculty was soon moved back to the old gym, which became known simply as
'the women's gym'. It was small, solid and traditional, matching the collegiate neo-gothic style of most other buildings on campus (see Figure 1.3).[82]
And across campus, the War Memorial Gym was soon known simply as
'the men's gym'. It was the kind of classic situation that Elizabeth Grosz
comments on where men build a world for their own purposes and in doing
so they take up all the space themselves. After all, a proving ground for
masculinity can only be preserved as such by the exclusion of women from
their activities, and this has been all too apparent in the world of sport.
Women are thus contained within a building which they did not build, and
which was not built for them, and the result is a homelessness within the
very home itself.[83]

Feminist scholars have complained how built landscapes have been
remarkable in their desire to confine, control and exclude women. Built

FIGURE 1.3

The Old 1929 Gymnasium becomes the Women's Gym. *Totem*, 1950, p.13. (University of British Columbia Archives)

environments have participated in the construction of gendered identities, often reflecting received wisdom about gender roles and reproducing the flawed logic of simplistic binary oppositions in the conception, allocation and meaning of spaces for male and female activities. Furthermore, feminists working in architecture have begun to challenge the underlying assumptions of rationalist modernist design. Architectural space, they realize, including sporting and physical culture arenas such as gymnasia, was not neutral and transparent but has deliberately attempted to express stereotyped gender roles in its spatial arrangements. From the beginning, the spaces of modern sport facilities such as gymnasia were sexed spaces involved in the construction of sexed bodies. In schools and colleges, gymnasiums were initially seen as a useful tool for securing discipline among particular groups of students and for sanctioning new styles of behaviour in a place set apart for sport and exercise.[84] They were starkly evocative of the ways in which gender boundaries could be policed through access to facilities within, their design and placement, prescribed curricula, attitudes of coaches and teachers, and administrative and legal policies. When resources permitted, many educational institutions built separate gymnasia for men and women, though all too frequently the women's or girls' gym was smaller, more poorly equipped and lacking in spectator space.[85] Furthermore, of all the disciplines, physical education with its central focus on the body was the most strongly influenced by echoes of Rousseau's view of biology as the root of gender assignment and as justification for separate educational/physical and sporting arrangements based on male power and dominance and female frailty and constraint. Through sex-coded activities, physical educators were able to mark and patrol the borders between masculinity and femininity.[86] Hence perceived physical differences and abilities formed a bedrock on which physical education programmes were constructed as well as the spaces in which they were conducted – and they proved remarkably resistant to change.[87]

As the War Memorial Gymnasium was being designed and built in the early 1950s, spatial re-mapping in the world of physical education had barely begun. The story of women's experiences in the women's gym until its demolition 20 years later to make way for an amplified Faculty of Arts is recounted elsewhere, as well as their struggles around control of the physical education curriculum and the imposition of women's rules basketball. The price of the autonomy they came to enjoy within their separate sphere was the acceptance of polarized and rigid sex roles, the loss of seniority of the Director of Women's Physical Education and the diminishing of their role in the affairs of the School of Physical Education, solidly entrenched in the modernist spaces of the War Memorial Gymnasium.

Conclusion

> To at least some extent, every real place can be remembered, partly because it is unique, but partly because it has affected our bodies and generated enough associations to hold it in our personal worlds ... and of course the real experiences of it, from which memory is carried away last much longer.[88]

Sport, one might say, is the body's playground, but as a site of lived relationships the gymnasium marked out ordered (and not necessarily playful) space/s through which certain bodies were encouraged to move and relate in prescribed ways or be excluded from the action. The physical education curriculum, that for more than a decade was compulsory for all students, showed that sports and games favoured for girls and women tended to impose artificial limits on their potential, while those for male students were designed to develop potential in the form of strength, leadership skills and competitive power.[89] Competitive sport especially, like warfare, is historically a masculine phenomenon (even though women can and do participate in this historical expression of masculinity). Brian Pronger notes, 'boys (and men) raised on competitive sport learn to desire, learn to make connections according to the imperative to take space away from others and jealously guard it for themselves'.[90] Basketball, for example, which was from the beginning a central activity in the War Memorial Gym, is a sport where the quest to forcefully take and maintain physical territory by bodily invasion is central to the game.

Thus the spaces of the gym echoed a particular (albeit changing) version of masculinity, constructed through the shared male camaraderie of the basketball, wrestling and other male teams, and the predominantly male coaches, athletes and faculty who came to develop close personal links that extended across time and through many other organizational roles in the university at large and beyond. Athletics prepared them for participation in the 'larger republic beyond the gym and the campus by fostering the faculty of organization, executive power and the qualities that enabled men to control and lead other men'.[91] Their 'sense of place' and belonging is celebrated at flamboyant annual fund-raising gatherings and fostered through the Hall of Fame activities, spectator privileges at sporting events and influential social networks, albeit now fraying with age.

If places can be conceptualized in terms of the social interactions which tie them together, then it is important to reiterate that these interactions are not static – they are processes subject to the winds of change in a globalizing society. Relph's *genius loci*, his 'sense of place', cannot be designed to order.[92] It may be, suggests Doreen Massey, that we must continually rethink our 'sense of place' in progressive ways – to see place more as a process than a fixed and historically bounded entity, and to encourage a 'sense of place' which is outward-looking, non-exclusionary and adequate to this era of time–space compression.[93] This, in turn, allows a sense of place, which is extroverted and includes a consciousness of its links with the wider world.[94] The project ahead, says Grosz:

> ... is to return women to those places from which they were dis- or replaced or expelled, to occupy those positions ... partly in order to show men's invasion and occupancy of the whole of space as their own ... and partly in order to be able to experiment with and produce the possibility of occupying ... new spaces which in turn help generate new perspectives, new bodies, new ways of thinking.[95]

In a world economy that looks very different from the way it did in the mid-twentieth century, different kinds of social relationships and power are now being stretched out in space. Increasingly fewer of these relations are contained within the gym itself but reach, instead, beyond its walls, linking that place to places beyond. 'To live is to leave traces', writes Walter Benjamin,[96] but there are fewer moving bodies and more machines in the gym today as technology has moved into the laboratories and classrooms and they have both encroached upon the playing spaces. Women have sought redress from the constrictions of space available to them, and global

communication and the Internet, as well as requirements of equity and mul-
ticulturalism, have transformed the spaces of the learning environment and
affected the nature of knowledge about the moving and sportive body. The
widening of spatial horizons could herald the possibility of many more
liberating effects.[97] The past is now *not* a land to return to in the simple
politics of memory but one of imaginary landscapes in imagined worlds.[98]
Clearly there is no single 'sense of place' which everyone shares when
gymnasiums are brought to mind – we each build our own and create our
own theatres of memory by reading and experiencing sporting landscapes
in very personal and often contradictory ways.

Sensing the Stadium

CHRIS GAFFNEY and JOHN BALE

Introduction

In his book, *Sport: A Philosophic Enquiry*, Paul Weiss presents a normative model of the sports place. He argues that ideally the sports place should have 'a normal set of conditions', where there is no wind, no interference and no surface irregularities – 'in short no deviations from a standard situation'.[1] Mirroring Weiss, it has been suggested more recently that to satisfy the norms of achievement sport, the ideal stadium would be characterized by 'placelessness' – a plane surface without spectators, communicated tele-visually to an audience which constitutes an absent presence.[2] This, it must be admitted, is (for fans, at least) a dystopian dream, yet there is more than a suggestion that the world of sport is moving towards a landscape of anaes-thesia.[3] This essay seeks to explore one basic question. What would be lost if the aesthetic/sensory experiences derived from attending a stadium were replaced by the anaesthesia of the sporting non-place? Drawing mainly on ideas developed by the Chinese-American humanistic geographer, Yi-Fu Tuan,[4] we seek to explore ways in which our various senses are stimulated when attending stadium events.[5] For convenience, we take the game of soccer as a source for most of our exemplifications, which come from the USA and the UK. However, our general ideas could be applied to most sports and the places in which they take place.

Experience of life events is a complex matter. The interpretation of stimuli through the bodily senses combines with individual histories, dis-positions, preconceptions and other contextual processes to form 'experi-ence'. Over time, the accumulation of experience helps to shape who and what we are as individuals. We are nothing but what we have experienced. The more individuals repeat the form of experience in a particular place, the more heavily that place and that type of experience will figure in the con-struction of the individual. As Tuan notes, 'experience is a cover-all term for the various modes through which a person knows and constructs a reality'.[6] The construction of reality then is contingent upon experience. We would claim that in many cultures a stadium – a universal architectural form of the modern city – is the place where the 'most people' have the 'most common experience' most frequently. As almost the full spectrum of experiential modalities can be found in the stadium it is important to examine the stadium experience as a vital element of both constructions of reality and constructions of identity.

The Feeling of Place

A dynamic description of how and why people identify with place is the subject of a well-established literature. The ideas are not abstract, however. People are attracted and repelled by certain spaces and places for a myriad of reasons. The experience of a place will always be compounded of feeling and thought, the essence of being human. It is well known what humans 'think' about soccer and one only has to pick up a daily paper to see the intellectual processing of different sports in any culture. The sensory aspect (feeling) of the stadium experience is harder to relate to a general audience. Or as Yi-Fu Tuan says:

> It is a common tendency to regard feeling and thought as opposed, the one registering subjective states, the other reporting on objective reality. In fact, they lie near the two ends of an experiential continuum, and both are ways of knowing.[7]

In order to understand the whole of experience it will be useful to examine how the senses are engaged to produce 'feeling' at the stadium.

The Senses

Our primary means of experiencing events is through our somatic (bodily) receptors. Extra-somatic (technological) means of altering somatic stimuli also influence experience. Our sensual experience of the stadium, rooted within place (seats, sections, sides, ends, boxes, etc.), rooted within space (the stadium), within a larger place (the city), within ever larger spaces (region, state, nation, hemisphere, globe, solar system) contributes to the idea that all the senses are geographical; each contributes to one's orientation in space, to an awareness of spatial relationships, and to the appreciation of the qualities of particular places, which include those currently experienced (through residence or visiting) and those removed in time.[8]

There are, of course, senses that are created through thinking (fear, paranoia, etc.), or extraordinary abilities (ESP), or training (dance, movement, timing, etc.) Some of these peripheral senses will necessarily enter the discussion of senses that affect the experience of the stadium.

Sight

There is little doubt that the sense of sight is the most important sensory receptor for humans. It is difficult for those with the ability to see to fully comprehend a world without sight. Sight is the reflection of the world. Our entire processes of building on the physical earth are visual. Indeed, 'landscape is explicitly produced for visual consumption. Moreover it is self-consciously produced.'[9] The stadium rises out of the earth and helps to create the visual landscape of the city. As it relates to the stadium, sight reflects several processes of seeing – each following from the other.

First is the appearance of the stadium upon the cityscape. The stadium is a massive building, in most cities the largest single container of crowds. There are few construction processes as complex as those involved in the building of modern stadiums. From space and seats and washrooms for tens of thousands of people, to retractable roofs, to 50 x 80 ft television screens suspended hundreds of feet in the air, stadiums are massive undertakings. The movement from modern to postmodern architecture in stadiums has seen the movement of lights from towering stanchions to their inclusion within the frame of the stadiums itself. This has had several effects. It has increased the overall size of the stadium structure. Postmodern stadiums are massive in size, even though their carrying capacity is not increased proportionately. They fill the eye more completely as an individual scans the cityscape. They are also ambiguous in the sense that they merge their functions as sports facilities with provision for banqueting, accommodation (hotels), rented offices, museums and merchandizing. The former monofunctional soccer stadium has given way to a multi-functional business facility. The first impression the visitor gets when visiting Old Trafford, Manchester, is that of a hypermarket rather than a 'football ground' which invites the word 'tradium' rather than 'stadium'. Even though the structures have increased in overall size, they have actually decreased in height, which has served to limit the appearance of the stadium on the skyline of the city. From the outside, some stadiums may 'look' little different from other urban containers. The light stanchions can no longer be seen from miles away and the only visible product of a night game is the noise of the crowd and the lightening of the sky projected from a mystical bowl.

Second, the interior of the stadium is constructed in such a way that spectator 'sight lines' are unimpeded. 'There isn't a bad seat in the house' reflects the idea that each individual should have a clear, direct view of the action. This is not always the case in early modern stadiums where support beams frequently obstructed the view.

Third, the stadium façade makes an important statement regarding the stadium's place in space and time. Stadiums, as important pieces of architecture, are constructed to be visually consumed. Additionally, whether or not a stadium is completely enclosed reflects a certain character. At some stadiums, such as Wrigley Field in Chicago and Celtic Park in Glasgow, people can see into the stadium from surrounding buildings. Totally encircled and domed stadiums further serve to divorce the stadium experience from the reality of the world around it. This increasing territorialization and commodification turns public space into private space and offers a more particularized and individualized means of visual consumption.

Fourth, seeing thousands of other people gathered together in the same place at the same time to partake in a common experience gives one a sense of extended valuation. One feels something when looking at a crowd of which one is a part. The crowd 'looks at' its self and 'reacts to' its self, which creates an ever-changing experience of its self.

Gaze

Buildings are thought to be able to look out across a city. Penthouses are located on the top floor so people can look out across the city and cast their gaze on the huddled masses below. Prior to the twentieth century, the constructions of balconies for upper-class houses in France and the development of balconies in English theatres were also constructed with the gaze in mind. The desire to 'gaze but not be touched, participate in the crowd yet be separate from it'[10] continues to feature in the construction practices of stadiums today. The modern stadium's version of balcony building, luxury suites, also asserts the power of the panopticon.[11] The one-way reflective glass prevents the crowd from knowing whether or not any one is in the luxury boxes, looking out at them. They are thus under continual surveillance by the corporations and upper classes who purchase the rights to this panoptic gaze. Additionally, the increasing presence of video surveillance at stadiums, especially in Europe, has added to the gaze of the state in and around the stadium.

Sound

Sound occupies space and gives fullness to experience. Sound connotes volume, distance and meaning. Tuan observes that 'the world of sound would appear to be spatially structured, though not with the sharpness of the visual world ... People are subconsciously aware of the sources of noise, and from such awareness they construe auditory space.'[12] The noise of

100,000 people projects itself into space, a collective construction produced and sustained by individual energies. The noise begins as a murmur and builds into a roar as each struggles to be heard above the crowd. As the ball rushes towards goal, the roar becomes louder, the goal is nearly missed and the collective exhalation of breath can be heard and felt throughout the stadium. In soccer the noise of the stadium is not interrupted by officialdom. In tennis, the crowd engages in turn-taking, being quiet when requested by the umpire and tending to cheer only when a point is scored. The noise of the soccer stadium crowd, though, is historically specific. In the early twentieth century it was felt that shouting and screaming was offensive and requests were made for noise to be eliminated from football grounds.[13]

People make different sounds in the stadium than they do in the car park, or even in the refreshment queue. In North American culture it is generally considered rude to shout out or make loud noises. There is a place and time where one can occupy as much space as one wants with one's voice: the stadium (though in certain sections of the stadium shouting, urging and screaming would be as out of place as in polite society). The sounds of the stadium are particular to the stadium and can create intense feelings as well as physical discomfort. Shouting and singing at the top of one's voice for several hours can result in physical discomfort, extending the experience of the stadium in a corporeal way.

There is an animalistic passion in the way people create noise in the stadium. There is frequently no apparent thought involved; people spontaneously and collectively react to visual stimuli and shout things they would be embarrassed to hear their children repeat. In a more personalized context it could be construed as verbal assault. In the stadium's noise, the premodern and pre-rational culture of common people is tied together with post-modernity's suspension of the demand for meaning and depth in expression. Screaming 'Smash Him!!!' or 'You Suck Ref!' as observed in soccer in the United States, and in various, cruder forms in Britain, has no essential meaning, save that it ties one more personally to the action on the field and contributes to the general noise of the stadium.

In the more developed stadium cultures of Europe and Latin America, the noise of the stadium is orchestrated to a very high degree. Chants and songs are as much a part of the stadium experience as the game itself. There are very few sensory experiences as powerful as the collective harmony of 50,000 people. Choreographed songs and chants are as much a part of the ritual of sport as the introduction of teams, the pre-game festivities or half-time refreshments. In the United States, we are familiar with the emotion generated by the singing of the national anthem or 'take me out to the ball-game'. Hockey venues are known for organ music, American football games for half-time music shows, and children's games for screaming parents. Stadium, and specifically soccer, cultures in the United States are beginning to develop into entities of sound. As a result, one hears television commentators speaking about the crowd being 'in good voice', meaning that songs and chants are a continual part of the game experience and can be heard throughout the stadium.

At Foxboro Stadium, the songs and chants generated for both New England Revolution games as well as US National Team games originate in a specific section of the stadium known as the Fort. In the Fort, located at the north end of the stadium (the traditional Kop location), spectators stand for the duration of the game and collectively raise their voices throughout. This chorus is heard by the players, who draw inspiration from the sense of collective encouragement (as evidenced by the post-game applause of the players towards the spectators in the Fort – not towards the expensive and relatively silent seats). The 'atmosphere' of the stadium experience is heightened by the collective noise generated. Because 'sound itself can evoke spatial impressions',[14] the stadium seems fuller when there is more noise. Sound serves to dramatize spatial experience. The more sound there is, the more emotive the experience and it cannot be denied that the soundscape of soccer often contributes to the well-known home-field advantage.[15]

Currently, a major problem facing Major League Soccer is that the stadiums in which the teams play are too large. This frequently results in empty stadium space that cannot be filled with the sound of those present. The cavernous feel of Foxboro Stadium, the Rose Bowl and the Cotton Bowl is in part due to the absence of sound reverberating through space. In smaller stadium spaces such as Crew Stadium in Columbus, even small crowds can fill the stadium with their collective voices, sometimes amplified by musical instruments such as drums and trumpets. Sound is a vital component in the development of a sense of place. The absence of a fullness of sound can make a stadium feel empty, even though there are tens of thousands of people in attendance.

One of the primary elements of stadium architecture is the development of acoustics. The creation of sound systems in stadiums is a highly technological process. Hundreds of thousands of dollars are spent on sound systems. Designing acoustics in such a large space is no easy matter since each fan hears sound from multiple speakers, which must be placed so that all the sound arrives within thousandths of a second. Many fall short of this ideal and much of the output is incomprehensible though far from inaudible. The degree to which the acoustic design of a stadium influences the overall experience is a matter for further investigation. Indeed, the ways in which different people within the stadium both generate and experience sound as well as the ways in which sound affects individual experience of the stadium could be the focus of extended research.

The sounds of the stadium are as varied as the places within the stadium. The press box, the luxury box, the terraces, the expensive seats, the bathrooms, the locker room and the concession queue all have varied qualities and decibels of sound. The examination of the particular spatial qualities of sound in the varied spaces of the stadium is a subject for further study but we should not be deluded into believing that the sound of the stadium is always benign. The malignant sound of racism and sexism may also be present.[16] The ways in which sound helps to define the stadium experience are as complex as the stadium itself. Without sound, the stadium is empty.

Touch

The containment of thousands of people in stadium space has a certain feel to it. One does not experience the crush of humanity in stadiums in the United States as it is sometimes experienced in Latin America and Europe, but the immediate proximity of dozens of others implies a limited sense of spatial freedom. This sense is partly conveyed through the skin, which is 'able to convey certain spatial ideas and can do so without the support of the other senses, depending only on the structure of the body and the ability to move ... The skin can convey a sense of volume and mass.'[17] The feeling of compressed humanity can be comforting or troublesome, depending on the individual. The cultural constructions of individual and public space are also important in that 'space and spaciousness carry very different meanings in different cultures'.[18]

The constraints to movement imposed on the individual by the close proximity of large numbers of people are significant. One cannot move quickly without impinging on another's space. One sometimes has to struggle to maintain personal space in the stadium. One develops a heightened sense of the extent of one's body and its relationship in space to others. One is firmly rooted in place; this helps to focus attention on the action.

Ironically, there is more freedom of movement when people are standing together on the bleachers than there is for the individual cramped into a plastic chair. Generally speaking, the upper classes are contained by their own device while the proletariat have individual freedom within the larger body of the crowd. The generalized restriction to movement in stadiums supports Tuan's idea that:

> movements such as the simple ability to kick one's legs and stretch one's arms are basic to the awareness of space. Space is experienced directly as having room in which to move. Moreover, by shifting from one place to another, a person acquires a sense of direction.[19]

As discussed above, the presence of large numbers of people heightens one's sense of corporeal self. 'In postmodern somatic culture, the body is seem as a sign of the self: it constitutes identity.'[20] The relationship of one's body to the crowd in stadiums has changed over time. This can be seen in the changing architecture of European stadiums, which are increasingly being modelled on those of the United States. In discussing the loss of individual space at English soccer matches in the 1980s, Bill Buford speaks of being carried with the crowd in the terraces.[21] He explains the experience of being on the terraces as one in which the individual does not have total freedom of movement. The stands were so tightly packed that one could be transported great distances without physical effort. The crowd surges and tumbles on its own, there is a total collapse of personal space and identity. Such haptic experiences are recorded by Buford: 'There was no waiting; there was also no choice, and this particular mad rush of people actually lifted me off my feet and carried me forward. I had no control over where I was going.'[22]

The individuals create the crowd, and the crowd consumes them. The major stadium disasters of Europe in the 1980s were caused by the crush of crowds against barriers erected to save them from themselves. This in turn has led to a change in stadium architecture in Europe, which has created a much different experience of one's body in stadium spaces. Additionally, where and how one sits (or stands) in the stadium influences the experience of the stadium. Whether one is sitting on metallic bleachers or in a plastic seat, one could eliminate all the other senses and identify one's location in space. Conversely, the feel of a padded seat in a luxury box generates a much different experience. In a comfortable seat one is more relaxed and by extension more passive about an event. One is also afforded the ability to move about the box without impinging upon others' space. It is as if one has gone to the theatre or movie for entertainment. This contrasts sharply with Buford's experiences of English matches where a:

> shot on goal was a felt experience. With each effort, the crowd audibly drew its breath, and then, after another athletic save, exhaled with equal exaggeration. And each time the people around me expanded, their rib cages noticeably inflating, and we were pressed more closely together ... You could feel the anticipation of the crowd on all sides of your body as a series of sensations.[23]

The ways in which one's body is contained in stadium space have a significant impact on one's experience of the stadium.

Smell

Like Proust with his *madeleines,* there's nothing like the smell of an old ballpark. It can't and won't be recreated by well-ventilated, airy, and large new facilities, and probably it's best for the weak-stomached that it's not.

But there's also nothing more evocative to the memory of a place than its smell.[24]

Smell evokes memories and transports us through time and space. Smell is a powerful and sometimes overwhelming component of experience. The stadium is a rich tapestry of smell and is a critical yet subtle element of experience. The smells of different parts of the stadium evoke different responses in people. The stench of the urinals can induce nausea while the smell of smoke coming from the next seat can provoke cravings, or discomfort and annoyance. It can also evoke nostalgia. One soccer fan commented that whenever he sensed cigarette smoke in the open air he was immediately reminded of the past times he had on the terraces at Easter Road, home of the Scottish club Hibernian.[25] The smell of burning flares can induce panic or euphoria. The odour of thousands of tightly packed bodies can be oppressive or familiar. For players, the smell of the locker room is a powerful source of emotion and anticipation. Boot polish and muscle ointments can help to stimulate adrenal glands and signify that action is at hand. The smell and taste of sweat and blood signify that the battle has been engaged, while that of dirt and grass recall long hours of training and sacrifice.

It would be possible to travel through the varied spaces of a stadium and catalogue their smells. The press box, for instance, has a certain sanitized, institutional smell to it. Cologne, perfume, and cigar smoke no doubt predominate in the directors' suite, while spilled beer, stale cigarette smoke and body odour pervade the terraces. On leaving the stadium, we find the parking lot smells of exhaust and signifies the journey home. The stadium and its environs are in part spatially defined by the presence or absence of particular smells. These smells can produce powerful imagery, as noted by one supporter of D.C. United:

> There's a feel and a smell to RFK which evokes sultry nights, sudden thunderstorms, and echoing empty corners where you can isolate yourself and meditate while watching the game to the almost hypnotic non-stop chanting of the bouncing Barra Brava. Those sensations are the feel and smell of Home.[26]

Taste

Taste is closely related to smell and peripherally affects the stadium experience. The tastes of the stadium are part of the larger ritual processes of stadium events. Similar to carnivals and holiday celebrations (at least in the United States) hotdogs, hamburgers, nachos, smoke, and beer are the staples of the stadium diet. The smell of a tailgate cookout combines with the taste of a pre-game burger and beer to invoke a sense of carnival and release from the workaday world. The consumption of large amounts of red meat and beer is commonplace at the stadium and helps to fuel the energy of the crowd. The taste on the tongues of the masses are only as diverse as the menu at the concession stand. This common sensory experience helps to create a ritualized experience that is not particular to any one stadium.[27] Stadiums throughout the world stimulate the palates of their patrons in a very limited way. The particular tastes of the stadium are anticipated and savoured, however, and are hopefully a departure from habitual patterns of consumption.

Sixth Senses: History, Belonging to a Crowd

The experience of the stadium is not bounded by sensory stimuli. Nor are our senses limited to the five enumerated above. The traditional conception of the five senses is somewhat limiting. The ways in which we experience, interpret and react to the world necessitate much more than sight, smell, sound, touch and taste. Senses of humour, timing, rhythm, place and space (among others) are all part of the stadium experience. The individual and the crowd probably use upwards of 15 senses during any given game though we must admit that the exploration of the full range of stadium-related senses remains to be undertaken. We identify the senses additional to those outlined above, as sixth senses, in that they are not fully intellectualized nor fully somatic, but lie somewhere in between. Each of these sixth senses adds to the individual and collective experience of the stadium and helps to inform action, response, emotion and understanding.

Sense of History Every stadium event is a historical experience. People know when and where to gather to participate in a particular event. Historical documents (programmes) are produced, memorabilia are purchased, and sometimes even bits of the stadium are taken home as mementoes.[28] After the event, history is documented in the papers, popular opinion is expressed on the radio and the action is replayed on television. Each popular treatment of the events of the stadium heightens the sense of historical import. As we see all too frequently in the United States, events like the Super Bowl are unable to live up to the media pre-constructions of historical value (labelled 'hype'), and the game itself is considered boring or trivial event though it is a typical exhibition of the sport.

Particularly intense or meaningful stadium events are talked about for years and can be seminal moments in a person's life. The more such important events happen in a stadium, the more sacred the stadium will become – even developing a sense of religiosity. The pilgrimages of fans to certain stadiums such as Old Trafford (Manchester) or Anfield (Liverpool) is well documented.[29] They are almost 'sacred places', inducing in fans what Tuan has termed 'topophilia'[30] – a love of place. In New England, the degree of reverence individuals have for Fenway Park far exceeds either the perform-ance history of the Red Sox or the actual physical condition of the stadium. The construction of collective history in the stadium produces memories, which

> are often organized around artifacts and particular spaces such as buildings, bits of landscape, rooms, machines, walls, furniture, what-ever. It is these spaces and objects that structure people's capacities to reminisce, to daydream about what might have been, or to recollect how their lives have intersected with those of others.[31]

Thus the sense of belonging to processes which extend both forward and backward in time are contained within the stadium and help to foster the sense of shared purpose, historical process, and cultural belonging.

The sense of historical continuity as well as the sense of participating in history is a powerful component of the stadium experience. The stadium can be read as a historical text, not only in terms of the events that have transpired but in architectural terms as well. To a large extent the collective energies, dreams, and aspirations of large segments of the population are posited and deposited in the stadium. Although the individual events may be trivial (one baseball game out of 162 in a season), it is the collected his-tory of place that implies a much deeper and specific meaning for thousands upon thousands of individuals. History is one of the ways in which collec-tive identity is both formed and maintained. In the stadium, there is a peri-odic creation and recreation of a pre-constructed historical paradigm. The cyclical nature of sport and the repetitive course of historical events are not insignificant. These processes create a larger experiential context for indi-viduals, groups and communities. Indeed it is by:

> demonstrating through routine and repetitive action that one belongs to a certain place, in a certain time; that is to say, one is specific in a temporal spatial 'historicity'; one creates history rather than just being created by history; and history is created by the body substantial. The crowd may be an historic product, yet, in its crowding together – such as at the stadium it dismisses the product-likeness and recreates it(self), not as mere distributed nitwits, but as an historic being making its presence known and making a great fuss about it.[32]

Sense of Belonging to a Crowd This has several factors influencing it. There is the sense that one is privileged to be inside the stadium. One might even feel sorry for those watching at home or in the sports bar just across the street. One has to spend an increasing proportion of one's income to attend stadium events. With this comes a sense of getting what one has paid for. If the quality of the play is poor, as at so many New England Revolution games, the fans will not feel as if they have received their money's worth and will have a more negative impression of the stadium experience. Additionally, if one has gone to the stadium with a family, the cost can be staggeringly high for a few hours of entertainment. The experience can take on more implied meaning because one has paid upwards of 200 dollars for tickets, food and transportation for the family. The event takes on additional importance because it cannot be repeated often. The more one has paid, the more one tends to value a certain thing. Thus, in the stadium one senses, sometimes very acutely, the economic import of the experience. For events that have greater cultural significance, such as the World Cup, one has to plan well in advance of the event to get tickets. The demand for tickets to culturally important stadium events far exceeds the supply, which raises the price for tickets, adding to the sense of entitlement and privilege within the stadium and a sense of belonging denied to those outside the stadium.

Connected to the practical sense of crowd life is the communal sense of a crowd. There is a certain feeling that comes with enmeshing one's self with thousands of other people, whether it be in the parking lot, moving en masse to the turnstiles, or participating in the wave. Crowds are historical entities, but they do not often happen spontaneously. A thorough study of the history of crowds is beyond the scope of this paper but would be very interesting. For instance, Urry, in his examination of stadiums and modernity considers

> How travellers and visitors (who can also be identified as local visitors to a familiar place viz. Stadiums) relate to the diverse sounds and sense impressions of a crowd of strangers remains one of the defining conditions of the modern experience, involving an array of technologies, memories, and selective use of the range of human senses.[33]

The ways in which individuals identify themselves as both part of and separate from the crowd would also be the basis for a fascinating psychological study. The ways in which a crowd functions as a powerful spatial entity moving to, in and from the stadium could occupy years of research. As Buford notes in his description of life among English soccer hooligans:

> The history of the behaviour of crowds is a history of fear: of being a victim, of losing property, of a terror (and of *the* Terror) so powerful that it needs a name – to be accounted for, distorted into intelligibility, made safe. The history of the behaviour of crowds is one of the

explanations. It has given us the politics of violence and its sociology. It has provided us with the models of revolution and the ego-ideal.[34]

Also of interest are the ways in which our relationship and identity with crowds can change in a matter of minutes. The relationships between individual and collective space both inside and outside the stadium are expressed perfectly by Tuan:

> Inside a packed stadium other humans are welcome; they add to the excitement of the game. On the way home, driving along the clogged highway, other humans are a nuisance. The stadium has a higher density of people than the highway, but is on the highway that we taste the unpleasantness of spatial constraint.[35]

In short, the senses of belonging not only to history but to a larger collective entity are vital components of the stadium experience. These sixth senses combine with the somatic senses to give a feel to the stadium.

Conclusion

Nearly all the senses are engaged in the stadium and combine with knowledge to form experience. The stadium is a unique container of collective emotion and energy which produces experiences that are as varied and complex as the individuals who periodically visit them. The stadium experience can totally remove individuals from their concerns about the outside world. Stadium events can be overwhelming, as Buford found at a Third Division game in England where 'the match had succeeded in dominating my senses and had raised me, who had never given a serious thought to the fate of Cambridge United, to a state of very heightened feeling'.[36]

The experience of the stadium is a combination of sense and thought. Stadiums and the events that occur within them cannot be fully understood unless one experiences it. The emotion of hearing the orchestrated (or not) voices of thousands of people cannot be fully communicated through media. Indeed, the full import of a stadium experience cannot be known until later, since

> An object or place achieves concrete reality when our experience enables us to know a place intimately, yet its image may lack sharpness unless we can see it from the outside and reflect upon our experience.[37]

The historical nature of stadium events is available for the price of the daily paper, which allows those who witnessed the event to expand their understanding of the historical event they helped to create and those who weren't at the stadium to participate in the collective history.

While it is true that 'stadium life arguably involves an orchestrated staging of embodied emotions – both for those who are "there" and for those who receive its images through the media/sport production complex',[38] it is also true that:

> To experience is to learn; it means acting on the given and creating out of the given. The given cannot be known itself. What can be known is a reality that is a construct of experience, a creation of feeling and thought.[39]

The realities of the stadium are as complex as life itself. Hopefully the ways in which we sense the stadium will come to be part of the larger discussion about the ways in which stadiums and the events which transpire within them help to shape individual, group, community and national constructions of identity. The postmodernist Jean Baudrillard has read the stadium of the future as an empty arena. The world could watch on television 'a pure form of the event from which all passion has been removed'.[40] This would seem to satisfy Weiss's criteria for the ideal sportscape. But would it be worth it?

Educative Pools:
Water, School and Space in
Twentieth-Century France

THIERRY TERRET

As a social institution the school has always been bound by two requirements: to make the process of learning more effective, and to limit its loss
of control over students. Whatever the era and its dominant ideologies, pedagogical success and disciplinary normalization were but two aspects of the
same political goal – the regulation of human behaviour in society. While
every area of schooling was concerned, physical education was seen as a
particularly efficient tool since body education was its main preoccupation.

Among the various strategies traditionally used by schools, the management of space has probably been one of the most important. Its linear
arrangement and government resulted in the control of students' behaviour[1]
through the organization of classrooms,[2] the arrangements of furniture, and
the spatial organization of people and their movements.[3] Generally, the
organization of school space was planned

   a) to induce a favourable student attitude toward work, and restrict
      movement in non-functional spaces,
   b) to control inappropriate behaviour such as chattering and idleness
      while moving students into a more favourable position to listen to
      the teacher, and finally,
   c) to eliminate any 'risks', including those concerning body practices.

In addition, teaching space has been arranged to carefully control each student's thinking. Cartesian, linear, symmetrical space refuses the curved
inconsistency of non-straight lines and condemns those who are not
straightforward and disciplined in their behaviour and their vision of the
world. Traditionally, a principle of normality emerged from linear,
Cartesian space and transformed the spatial arrangements of the school into
a particular model of social organization. It aligned the strict planning of
distances between students in the classroom, as well as in the gymnasium,
with the idea of a society where each individual was an identical unit with

the same rights and duties. Student personalities were expected to disappear as a result of the principles of standardization and normalization resulting from this organization of space.

Some school practices, however, were set into spaces which were not standardized. Such was the case of swimming. Integrated into the very first French programmes of physical education at the end of the nineteenth century, swimming still remains a part of the curriculum today, though with different aims. Whatever the purposes, however, from hygiene to safety, sport or recreation, swimming always required particular conditions for its enactment. How, then, could the needs of the school be adapted to the particular constraints of water spaces?[4] Historically, how did the school succeed in managing the contradictions between the role of the class or gymnasium as a privileged space for rationality, and the medium of water, whose characteristics were, on the surface, unfavourable to teaching and disciplinary work?

Apart from the specifics of the physical environment, and the question of teaching in it, the standardization of water spaces holds a special interest for the history of swimming pools.[5] Swimming pools were very popular in ancient times, but over the centuries slowly became socially discredited, and considered inappropriate. During the Middle Ages, submerging in water was suspect for two reasons: first, for fear of the penetration of liquids into the body through the skin, which was seen as a kind of invasion of evil (like the plague);[6] and secondly, from the nature of bathing practices themselves, which were increasingly less tolerated by the Church, which associated them with the pleasures of the body such as drinking and sex. Thus, steam rooms and other such establishments gradually disappeared until the Renaissance when baths taken for the cure in houses and spas began to be perceived as beneficial to health. By the end of the eighteenth century in Europe, this perception had grown to provide a strong hygienic concern for all pedagogical uses of water.

FIGURE 3.1
HISTORICAL NORMS OF AQUATIC SPACE

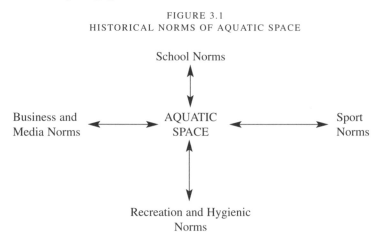

On the other hand, in their organization and architecture, swimming pools were always, and still are, the product of a consensus among several competing desires for use. Across various times and cultures, swimming pools have been subject to the diverse demands of sport, school, hygiene, recreation and commerce, some temporarily dominating others.[7]

Negating the Uncertainties of Water (1880–1914)

At the end of the eighteenth century, thanks to Rousseau and the newly perceived importance of nature and hygiene (and its implications for body control), the number of public pools increased in many large cities in England, France, Italy, Belgium and Germany. By 1773 there were nine in Paris and this number increased to 78 within a few years, before declining to about 30 in 1880.[8]

England, however, led the way. In 1846, within the context of the increasing regulation of public health and the transformations brought about by the industrial revolution and new moral attitudes, an act was passed by the English Parliament to facilitate daily access to hygiene for the working classes.[9] This law required local authorities to support the establishment of public baths, and was based on a growing concern for health which had been largely brought about by the cholera epidemics of 1831 and 1832. Moreover, in 1838, the 'Poor Law Commission' put forward the notion that although costly, public health measures could result in savings later on. Lastly, in 1842, Chadwick published his important report on the sanitary living conditions of the working population in which he laid out a hygienist policy. Four years later, petitions were circulated in London in favour of providing washing facilities for the working classes.[10]

The Act of 1846 was a clear contribution to the larger process of regulating public health, which led to the establishment of baths, pools and washhouses. The financial commitments were left to municipalities in the form of subsidies, or concessions to water and grounds for private contractors. Even before the 1846 Act people had begun to build aquatic spaces. The first public baths opened in Liverpool in 1828, as a result of urgent requests from the population.[11] The success of this new venture stimulated competition and thus supported a great diversification of facilities. For these reasons, English baths were not established to conform to a standard model. There were various models for different populations, including women and boys, and the most popular included washing facilities, though the range was vast. Some had tubs and showers, others were true swimming pools, some favoured cold water, others hot.[12]

Due to the success of these first establishments and the development of swimming as a popular sport and recreation in the 1860s (as well as increased attention to the pollution of rivers in industrial cities which made bathing dangerous), Parliament voted in 1878 to build swimming baths with covered pools as well as public baths. Thus, the convergence of political, economic and social interests generated the development of an important network of aquatic facilities. The annual report of the Amateur Swimming Association for 1904 listed 570 baths in the country. In 1912, 460 cities had 800 baths, of which 600 were swimming pools; 700 were open to the general public.[13] The integration of leisure, hygienic and commercial objectives for the provision of these pools lead to various effects, of which three stood out. Firstly, the desire to measure sport performances favoured the standardization of aquatic spaces. Secondly, this new market contributed to the development of a body of professionals who supervised and taught swimming. Finally, pools in England became a reference, and sometimes a model, for other countries or, more modestly, for municipalities and industrialists wishing to build their own swimming pools.

For a long time such establishments remained relatively rare in Europe. In France the English influence was slight before the First World War, and the French also had to deal with pools that had been built in the first half of the nineteenth century. These facilities often consisted simply of tubs with a number of services attached such as living rooms, smoking rooms and hairdressers. Some accommodated aquatic activities like swimming and these were generally built close to rivers where water could be easily taken up and renewed. Some were built on the rivers themselves, using boats with special flat-bottoms arranged for bathing.[14] Lifesavers were sometimes employed in these private establishments, some teaching swimming for money. These facilities on rivers were often exclusive to the upper classes, men as well as women, but they would soon attract a larger public. Tepid and warm baths were favoured by the nobility, while swimming schools proved popular among the middle class. Unpretentious installations – sometimes providing only sticks and a cloth for bathing – became available to the working class.[15] The law supporting the building of these facilities (which also tried unsuccessfully to prevent bathing in rivers running through cities) determined the authorizing of such spaces in the cities.

In fact, Europe increasingly invested in new aquatic facilities after 1880 (with notable differences in the frequency and degree of investment across nations). As the market for swimming pools developed, this supported the building of new kinds of baths and pools. These were now set apart from rivers with water sometimes being heated by steam engines, or with water already used in nearby factories. This process of building pools developed energetically in the places where climatic conditions could limit outdoor water activities (England, Germany, Belgium). In contrast, the countries in the south of Europe experienced a weaker growth in the network of aquatic facilities (Spain, Portugal, Italy and France). Designs varied too, but the main goals remained generally the same: to provide water spaces for 'natural' hygienic practices (hygiene then being understood more as the prevention of disease than as cleansing the body) and, possibly, for 'utilitarian' purposes.[16] This explained why small gymnasiums, saunas, tubs, showers and massage rooms often complemented the bath itself.

In France it was the middle class that generally used these new swimming pools as they became increasingly attuned to new ideas about health and the importance of physical exercise and nature. This sometimes had a direct effect on architecture. Some of the new pools were built with very long (up to 100 m) and very narrow baths (10 m), or with variable depths (65 cm to 3 m) in order to look like a river. Some pools had rocks and waterfalls, which simulated a natural environment.[17] Some had balconies which made exhibitions and water festivals possible. Thus, by the end of the nineteenth century, the variety of swimming pools available gave an obvious priority to commercial, recreational and hygienic goals with little reference to schools and sport standards.[18] Moreover, they remained restricted to certain places. In France, for example, swimming pools were found mainly in Paris and in the north of the country, with some other 'natural' baths arranged on docks, lakes or rivers. These facilities were never really planned for teaching swimming, but rather for hygiene and recreation. The industry of swimming pools was only beginning.[19] Technological innovations were still precarious and many municipalities preferred to invest in public washhouses, with less expensive equipment.[20] In the first French *Encyclopaedia of Sports* published in 1905, Paul Augé had to admit that the majority of swimmers were still obliged to bathe in rivers.[21]

Thus, when schools tried to integrate the teaching of swimming into the compulsory curriculum there was a need to find suitable open water. This, of course, meant taking risks, since the competence of the teachers in this area was extremely poor. Most of them were gymnasts, firemen or soldiers looking for extra salary.[22] Anxieties involved concern for the bodies of the students who came into contact with the numerous uncertainties of water (algae, currents, opacity of water and so on). Other risks related to teaching, since bodies were not totally visible in the water, and the anxiety and the irrationality of the reactions and attitudes of some students made their behaviour in the water a problem. It was all too distant from the disciplinary requirements of schools which reacted by adopting various strategies such as the negation of water space, or a return to a more individual use of space and form of teaching.[23]

Both official programmes[24] and most handbooks broke up the teaching of swimming into a phase of elementary strokes taught on the ground followed by a more operational phase in the water, though the focus was generally upon the former.[25] In this way, as 'a gymnastic art', swimming could escape the uncertainties of water.[26] Those students staying on firm ground could behave in an orderly fashion and the master could maintain his gaze over the group. In the schoolyard or in the classroom, at tables and benches, everyone was located at a specific place and in conformity with the traditional management and disciplinary use of school space. Teaching swimming challenged this approach. Consider, for example, the particular case of primary schools on the French coast. The authorities here recommended learning about the vocations of sailors and fishermen by visiting boats and focusing upon the concepts of geography, natural history and commercial navigation or the fishing industry. Swimming lessons, a practical necessity for these vocations, were inaugurated in the schoolyard and complemented by a theoretical approach to 'hygiene concepts for sailors' and 'the utility of swimming'.[27] It was not that the rejection of aquatic space for teaching meant a negation of water itself. In certain cases, the swimming lesson, reduced to its hygienic and medical functions, was transformed into a series of collective body ablutions in basins or washhouses. When bathing in the river was impossible, 'ablutions (were) advised instead'.[28]

Other solutions existed too, which resulted in compromises in the use of aquatic space. Since teaching in water was not very compatible with the characteristics of traditional teaching, individual teaching methods were seen as an answer. The students were placed in shallow water, free from particular instructions, but under the supervision of the teacher. The master, who reproduced, with cable and stick, the traditional ways of teaching bargemen, then took those who showed some aptitude individually. As Doctor Mangenot testified in 1892: 'a swim Master is in each compartment to help those who would be in a bad situation, and also to teach and control the movements of those who have a special aptitude to swim'.[29] A photo of a class group in the *Progrès Illustré* of 16 July 1896 showed clearly the contrast between the free behaviour of the whole group of students and the rationality of the teaching lesson experience by a single individual suspended on the end of a rope. The school recreated an individual space where each student in turn was controlled by a cable connected to the master. However, disciplining within aquatic space still remained problematic because a single teacher could not deal with the requirements of teaching a whole immersed class.[30]

This problem reinforced requests to build swimming pools where the water was calm, clear and clean, and the ground was flat and safe. Teachers and sportsmen agreed, for once, to ask municipalities to undertake such projects and to denounce the conditions they had to deal with in the large cities.[31] Antoine Poulaillon, for example, joined with the swimming clubs of Lyon in 1904 to request that the public authorities remove all obstacles to the building of public swimming pools and centralize efforts to create a site for bathing in open water.[32] These wishes started to be achieved only after the First World War, when swimming pools multiplied in France and schools were obliged to take up new approaches to the teaching of swimming.

The Creation of Individual Water Spaces (1918–45)

After 1918 in France, the new swimming pools differed from older ones in several respects. First, the impetus to build came from various places, from municipalities and industrialists who wanted to offer hygienic and recreational arrangements to their employers, or from entrepreneurs who were attracted by potential financial profits. The number of aquatic facilities expanded as social demands increased for sport, but also for leisure since people increasingly sought places to swim and bathe in open water. Secondly, the period was characterized by a reaction to over-urbanization and a new desire for natural surroundings, which resulted in perceptions of the swimming pool as 'a beach'. The official journal of the French swimming federation, *Natation*, summed this up by taking the title *Eau-Sport-Soleil* in the 1930s. Thirdly, swimming pools (like stadiums) progressively became an issue during election campaigns for political groups who wished to affirm an avant-garde image and to be better positioned in the regional or national political scene.[33]

In these circumstances, new facilities had to respond to more diverse needs than before, though sport standards dominated. Indeed, from 1908, with the creation of FINA (Fédération Internationale de Natation Amateur), the process of standardizing swimming pools accelerated and became more international. Limitations remained for a simple reason. In the majority of European countries, sport – including swimming – had not reached a sufficient degree of popularity vis-à-vis other physical activities, in particular gymnastics. Thus, throughout the 1920s in France, some municipalities remained unsure about what dimensions to highlight when building a swimming pool. It explains too why swimming leaders continued to insist on building pools and also to ensure that municipal councils considered the sport's rules and its requirements concerning the dimensions of pools (rectangular and with a length of 25 m or, more rarely, of 50 m) and the quality of water.[34] Press campaigns were initiated by sportsmen who proposed detailed architectural projects for new swimming pools and a model was gradually imposed which made aquatic space a place for swimming races and training. To be sure, not everybody shared such a point of view and, in the 1920s, many still believed that swimming should first, and exclusively, be taught for safety purposes. However, the need for better racing provisions soon led to the conclusion that clubs which had better pools and training conditions were more successful than those who still used open water.

Leisure bathers were always present, though apart from some exceptional facilities like the one at Wannsee close to Berlin which had 1.2 km of beach for a potential of 50,000 people per day, these bathers generally had to adapt to spatial conditions which were mainly designed for sport. Even the old swimming pools had to be modified, since footbridges spanning the baths, or waterfalls flowing out of rocks, made it impossible to practice water polo or competitive swimming.

The growing flow of bathers had an increasing influence during the 1940s and the 1950s, resulting in a whole series of less visible – but quite important – changes in aquatic environments. During these years a new phase of hygiene regulation in swimming pools and aquatic facilities resulted in the general standardization of water treatment. Medical controls and testing for infection and germs intensified. Industrial technology was used to equip the existing network of swimming pools with more powerful filters, and access to the baths became the point at which control of microbes and germs could be organized.[35] The test for colon bacillus infection, for example, became compulsory in France in 1947.[36] More generally, the 'management' of bathers resulted in a new focus: toilets, footbaths and showers were physically repositioned to become crossing points to the pool which were impossible to circumvent.

France had started to build swimming pools in earnest during the interwar period, partly for political and hygienic reasons but also in reaction to the pressures of sport and leisure. This resulted in two types of facility – those with the status of a 'beach' incorporating recreational equipment, less depth, and frequently unusual architecture; and those which answered the requirements of sport, as specified by FINA, and were more uniform (baths were 25 m, 33.33 m, or 50 m long, rectangular, with calm water, etc.).[37] In 1935, no less than 118 cities had 169 aquatic facilities approved by the French swimming federation (outdoor and indoor swimming pools), of which many conformed to the description of the 'modern swimming pool': 'small dimensions (25 m x 12 m maximum), a rectangular bath, and limpid and transparent water'.[38] What was significant was that all these spaces were organized along recreational or sporting principles, but rarely for teaching purposes.[39] This was probably one of the reasons (along with teachers' poor competencies) why swimming pools remained so little used by schools, for it would have been necessary for schools to refer to swimming as a sport, a consideration that did not exist in any of the European countries.[40]

Consequently, the development of school swimming did not result in the creation of new spaces but in the temporary transformation of existing spaces. The traditional rectangle of the pool was a given base which had to be artificially divided to allow the teaching and management of groups. Technology thus assisted the teachers to make the swimming pool conform to school space standards and solve the problems of teaching a group. From now on, half a class could simultaneously be taught in water under the supervision of a single master. The innovation came from Tourcoing, in the north of France, where Paul Beulque had developed a series of experiments aimed at a collective educational system for teaching swimming in water. Admittedly, Beulque had not given up the land-based teaching phase, but the new approaches ruptured previous models such as the free bath and individual teaching. Using the principles of both the 'éphydrosphère', invented in 1850 by Doctor Blatin, and the horse-gear as imagined by P.L.A. Lechevalier in 1851,[41] and by adapting them to water, Beulque built a complex apparatus which enabled him to control several students at a time by keeping them at the end of a moving cable, see Figure 3.2. The unit was composed of a pontoon placed transversely over the pool (for the teacher), two transverse cables which suspended the individual, and finally horizontal cables with pulleys which allowed the students to move.[42]

The physical delimitation of space benefited both teaching efficiency and the instrumentalization of the body. Indeed, the disciplinary dimension was necessary, since 'if the study of the movements of swimming on land presents no difficulty, it is not the same when the students are set in water'.[43] Beulque's apparatus resulted in a squaring of the water space and the organization of individual subspaces where each student was confined by a rope. There was some freedom because the teacher had a whole group to supervise, but it was in fact only slightly more effective because water compartmentalization favoured both group supervision and the individualization of teaching. The system, just as that of Trotzier later on, was in reality only a transfer of the model of gymnastics teaching to an aquatic environment.

The innovation, however, was appreciated and was well received since Beulque's system was adopted as the national method of swimming

FIGURE 3.2

Paul Belques's Méthode de natation. (Tourcoing, 1922)

teaching by the French federation of swimming.[44] It was still recognized as a good method after the Second World War by Monique Berlioux[45] and by Emile Schoebel in his *Précis de natation scolaire*.[46] Another recommendation of Beulque was to collect 'water falling on the roof of the school, or on that of the church (and to) send it to a small bath (10 m x 6 m x 1 m) built with a floor and four walls of cement'.[47] Such proposals made new achievements possible. Since 'the collective lesson appear(ed) to be difficult in a bath with no low depth,'[48] a specific space for teaching had to be planned while the pool was being conceived, leading to a clear transformation in general attitudes towards swimming pool architecture.

The Invention of a Space for Teaching (1945–70)

In Europe in general, and in France in particular, the economic priorities of the immediate post-war period were not favourable for the construction of sport facilities, and especially not for swimming pools.[49] After 1960, however, there was an increased demand for leisure in a new consumer society and the status of swimming pools changed as they became a part of the welfare state. Their architecture, which had focused on sporting criteria to this point, now responded to new demands. The preceding generation of swimming pools did not disappear, but new innovations were introduced in a period which was the richest ever known for the construction of new sport facilities.[50]

First, huge 'cathedral swimming pools' were built. These large facilities accommodated both swimming races and water leisure norms. There were often several pools of different lengths, some covered, others outdoors, with spectator terraces for performances, exhibitions and sports meetings. Various services were provided, from bar–restaurants to solaria. These establishments, often built as a sign of local prestige, became a financial drain on many municipalities. Simultaneously, numerous small swimming pools of 25 m were built in response to a new call from school physical educators who needed pools appropriate for both sport and the teaching of swimming.

The need for pools with differentiated uses was not new, of course.[51] In 1890, people had requested shallow baths for men or for women (and sometimes for horses),[52] but hardly for 'beginners'. During the inter-war years pools had been divided off into specific parts for 'teaching' or for 'instruction' as well for races, as in Toulouse in 1926[53] and in Villeurbanne in 1932.[54] Specific pontoons for teaching beginners were also often used in rivers.[55] But the general standard was for a small swimming pool with a progressive depth.[56] After the Second World War, as the needs of sport facilities became clearer, the desirability of a distinct and specific aquatic space for beginners was recognized.[57]

The main characteristics of these separate baths for teaching were their low depth and small size. The establishment at Villeurbanne, for example, was 18 m × 5.50 m; the main bath was 50 m × 18 m. Teaching baths could be independent from the main bath or located in physical contiguity with it. They were rectangular, to facilitate a symmetrical and rational management of learner groups and to allow a single person to supervise the whole space. As pedagogical water spaces they were safe, easily controlled, and amenable to group discipline, and the traditional breaststroke was easy to teach because of the low depth. Thus schools were finally successful in defining a clean and specific space for teaching swimming.

During the 1960s, school standards for pools took precedence over other sporting and recreation needs. Thanks to the regulations and programmes for sport facilities launched by the French High-Commissioner Maurice Herzog, a series of official texts and projects were made available. In 1964, Mr Gerville-Réache, president of the safety sub-commission within the Haut-Comité des Sports, issued a report on French swimming pools stating that all facilities should provide a space of at least 1.50 m between the teaching pool and the swimming pool.[58] The following year, several texts were published on teaching swimming at school, in which very precise criteria were set regarding supervision and group management.[59] Pools for teaching were distinguished from shallow water pools, deep water pools and open water pools. In all cases, however, space was regulated according to the quality of the ground and depth and transparency of water, along with a maximum number of students per teacher (from 8 to 25 according to conditions) and a maximum surface of 5 m^2 per student. Similar texts for primary schools followed in 1971 and 1972, with the number of supervisors being proportional to the surface area of the water.[60] Thus the school swimming pool wasthoroughly standardized to conform to the requirements of teaching, discipline and safety.

In 1951, the equipment department (lead by J.B. Grosborne, an engineer and one time top-level swimmer)[61] of the Secretariat for Youth and Sports authorized a private company, the Société d'Études de Spécialités (SES, see Figure 3.3), to sell collapsible floating 'bath schools'.[62] These provided rectangular zones for teaching. Each of these floating bridges, called '*domineaux*', measured 3 m × 1 m and was 0.5 m in height. Various accessories could be fixed on them: armbands, ladders and brackets, and each final structure created a water space from 12.50 m × 6 m with a depth of 0.75 m to 1.40 m; it could also be enlarged to meet the sport competition standards (25 m × 12.50 m) of the French swimming federation in 1953.[63]

Students could stand up anywhere in the *domineaux*, they could be easily seen and controlled, and groups of 18 children could be taught simultaneously. Students were easily able to achieve their diploma with a simple 'there and back swim' (25 m).[64] As the advert from SES indicated, 'the

FIGURE 3.3

BASSINS-ECOLE DE NATATION, PREFABRIQUES, DEMONTABLES, TYPE PF/14

Photo MARTINE

Vue d'ensemble du Bassin Ecole type PF 14, installé au Centre Scolaire de la Ville des MUREAUX (S.-et-O.)

Plan d'eau : 12,50 x 6,25 · Profondeur régulière de 0,70 à 1,40

Technical document from the company SES, 1955. (Private archives)

children are safe, the monitors teach easily, and the parents are quiet'.[65] The city council of Meaux, for example, expressed its satisfaction with the fact that 'for the masters, the equipment is excellent and allows rational and efficient teaching for both groups and single pupils'.[66]

On the basis of such teaching and disciplinary effectiveness, the construction of this equipment was subsidized up to 50 per cent by the Ministry of Education, the other half being met by the municipalities. Some were built in Meaux, Poitiers, Semur in Auxois, Durtal, and elsewhere,[67] but their success remained limited until a second technical innovation was proposed to further separate teaching space from the larger aquatic environment.[68]

During the 1970s, with the creation of the *bassins d'apprentissage mobile* (BAM)[69] required by the Haut Commissariat aux Sports, equipment became less expensive, lighter (cloth tank) and more flexible for various uses. It looked like a covered and heated swimming pool with a perimeter of 16 m × 8 m, which contained a bath 13 m × 6 m and 1.10 m deep.[70] The unit was transportable by trailer and could be installed in a few days. The first BAM was inaugurated in April 1970 in Isle-sur-Sorgue (Vaucluse). Planned for small cities (up to 15,000 inhabitants), 50 of them were used in France until 1975, the bath being placed within a school (generally for a year). Thanks to new policies for sport facilities buildings provided by the Fourth and Fifth National Economic Plans, 832 swimming pools, including

168 indoor pools, were built.[71] It was now deemed necessary to continue the effort 'to cover the territory with a sufficiently dense network so that all schoolboys could be initiated into swimming',[72] while waiting for othe,r more stable, solutions.[73]

In all these cases, the small size of the pool restricted both commercial and sport uses. It is true that racing swimmers and leisure bathers had access, but its small dimensions resulted in strict, Cartesian time planning. Priority was given to the schools during the day, to the sporting public at the end of the afternoon and during the evening, and to the leisure public for a few half-days per week (or, in certain cases, at the same time as the swimmers).

Aquatic Spaces for Action (1970–90)

From 1967 on, however, these facilities were called into question, thanks to the approach to sport taken by physical educators in France, which resulted in a new arrangement to keep spaces well adapted for teaching while seeking for greater flexibility among sports.[74] The Department of Youth and Sport launched a competition for 'economic and convertible swimming pools' in order to reconcile teaching, recreation and sport.[75] Four hundred architects worked on the project and, at the beginning of the 1970s, a final selection lead to the building of swimming pools called '*Tournesol*' (Sunflower), '*Caneton*' (Duckling) and '*Iris*' (Irises) within the framework of the State programme for 'one thousand swimming pools'. Nearly 60 per cent of these facilities were built in French towns of 20,000 to 40,000 inhabitants between 1970 and 1977.

The dimensions of these new pools were generally smaller than the very prestigious swimming pools built during the inter-war period, and the new facilities were also less well adapted to teaching groups and their manage-ment due to their size (25 m × 15 m) and greater depth. Some teachers expressed nostalgia for the small teaching baths 'with ideal conditions' of the past,[76] but new approaches to child psychology and education were calling into question the use of heavy brackets and disciplinary equipment. Old and new swimming pools had consequently to be rethought as a medium where pedagogy could find new ways of controlling student space while exploring the aquatic environment.

Swimming masters and teachers now had to reconsider their use of space to accommodate circuits and workshops in their teaching. Raymond Catteau, leader of the constructivist swimming movement in France, sug-gested that 'the need for establishing circuits (appears) to help those who have a certain level to attain'.[77] These 'learning circuits' were functional spaces organizing the activity of the students in certain ways. Beginners

were relatively free within physically specified limits (lines, pole, etc.) or in
the framework of teaching instructions. Thus, the general goal seemed more
pedagogical than disciplinary. But circuits were in fact a subtler device and
thus more effective. As part of 'a pedagogy of attraction', encouraging individual exploration, the spatial organisation changed the rational squaring of
water space into a 'management of the medium'.[78] This imposed trajectories
and attitudes upon the students and made the omnipresent master less necessary. Each individual became his/her own space manager within the limits
of their needs. The students were self-controlled, with clear effects on both
discipline and quality of learning. Such organisation was even clearer in the
case of specific workshops, each of them being rigorously associated with
a special function or pedagogic goal. Any incorrect behaviour could be
adddressed immediately by intervention of the teacher. Space was now a
means of physically delimiting the students' behaviour and attitudes. In
other words, aquatic space management moved progressively from
body control to action while simultaneously reinforcing its control of the
action itself.

This pedagogic work was still in progress in non-directive methods like
the 'aquatic garden' experiments led by Alain Vadepied in Evron at the
beginning of the 1970s. The structure he planned was a 'territory' for a
child's first experiment. Its depth went from 0 to 50 cm and there were
places marked by coloured buoys for jumping and diving as well as a longer
and deeper area to practise skills.[79] Here space was conceived as a recreational 'medium' to stimulate the child's imagination and interest in attractive objects.[80] However, even if the children were entirely free to move
around confidently in each workshop area, spaces were still designed
according to teaching and safety rules.[81] While traditional spaces were
called into question, the critics were concerned more with their form than
the principles used by the teachers. Thus, the activity of the students 'would
be guided' according to their level of development while at the same time
underlined by hierarchical teaching objectives. In the video 'Nager, réussir
et comprendre',[82] for example, the organization of space clearly depends on
a definition of children's developmental stages. For children from 3 to 6
years old, the goal was to build a repertoire of aquatic skills, exploiting a
workspace composed of well-delimited spaces which favoured different
ways of getting in and around the water. For children from 7 to 8 years old,
the project was to master deep-water immersion, using 'life spaces'.
Carpets, watermarks, oblique or vertical poles determined different zones
for different skills, including holding one's breath under water. It also pin-
pointed where each task should take place, thus ensuring the disciplinary
management of the whole group. Children from 9 to 11 years old were
invited 'to solve problems' in order to improve their effectiveness in water.
Here, the organization of space was rectilinear and Cartesian, and looked

like the waterlines of the traditional swimming pool where students move from one wall to another on a fixed itinerary. Between the limits fixed by the waterlines, the teacher could easily check and control the progress of pupils, and failure to respond appropriately would be immediately sanctioned by exclusion from the aquatic space.[83]

Teaching Space and Recreational Space (1990–2002)

In the past 12 years, traditional swimming pools have been subject to numerous changes in response to changing pedagogical approaches. In the domain of sports training, space has remained Cartesian since lines and rectangles ensure control of the swimmers (time, distances). This pertains not only to swimmers belonging to the Olympic federations, but also to sportsmen involved in triathlons, diving clubs, and even firemen.

Where the teaching of swimming is concerned, space has been arranged differently according to both pedagogical orientations and the level of the students. Generally, the younger the child (including babies), the more liberal the teaching and the more open the space. In contrast, when the pedagogical method is more traditional and the level of swimming higher, the use of 'in line' activities is favoured.

With aquatic leisure, one finds three forms of practice corresponding roughly to three ideal types of swimmers and bathers that we might call 'ascetic', 'sensitive' and 'communicative',[84] all more or less supported by a strong neo-hygiene orientation. Health today is seen as a physical, psychological and social process, which implies a more complete vision of the self. The 'ascetics' tend to be practitioners of aerobics, physical culture and jogging. They go to the swimming pool to stay in good shape and do not hesitate to engage in energetic physical work such as distance swimming in line. They remain in the water only for the duration of this self-organized training, which differs from traditional sport training by its individual nature. The 'sensitives' look for another type of pleasure in water. Sensitive to the aesthetic dimensions of movement they listen to their bodies, motionless or moving. They favour relaxation and well-being in their choice of activities, resulting in specific water space investments. They often use small perimeters, in circles or in line, and integrate the space outside the pool into their territory of action, such as solariums and showers. The 'communicatives' use water less as a medium for swimming than as a social environment. They go alone or in groups to the pool to enjoy and benefit from the presence of others. The beach and the solarium, along with the bar and the restaurant, have become important spaces for discussion and exchanges, or for games of seduction, in particular among young adults. Water has become a vector for games, leading some bathers to avoid sustained effort in favour of challenges (spontaneous races), exploits (dives), and the search for recreational and emotional situations (pyramids, breath-holding, and so on).

Thus the 'ascetic' like the traditional architecture of swimming pools because they prefer calm water where they can pursue endurance activities. The 'sensitive' and 'communicative' are more open in their choices of aquatic spaces and less inclined to favour designs which reflect the historical domination of sport and teaching models. They like water which is alive – noisy, warm and recreational – as opposed to the cold and standardized conditions of water spaces for races and performance. Such rejection of the former conditions has resulted in a series of remarkable transformations in aquatic space over the past decade or more.

The adaption of the existing network of swimming pools has been a problem for numerous municipalities wishing to adjust their public facilities to new leisure practices. Faced with material and economic constraints, these adjustments have often been reduced to the addition of shutes and floating objects made available to bathers. Traditional institutions were the more frequent users of these swimming pools: 38 per cent were schools and 34 per cent were various associations and clubs,[85] while the general public represented only 28 per cent of users. More specifically, new fitness and gym clubs, as well as public structures, have begun offering various courses of aquatic fitness (aquabuilding, aquastretching, aqua jogging, aqua dance ...) during which people, particularly women, exercise and rediscover the virtues of water.[86] In Paris, for example, half of the municipal and private pools were offering aqua gym in 1997.[87] The success of such practices, emanating largely from the USA, resulted in the building of small swimming pools close to dance studios, bodybuilding gyms or gymnasiums. In the Lyon metropolitan area, more than three-quarters of fitness clubs now have a small pool.[88] In the Rhône Department as a whole, aquatic exercise can be found in 71 per cent of the large fitness centres, although in only 25 per cent of the small ones.[89] In some cases, this new use of aquatic space has lead to a reconsideration of deep water as a medium for therapeutic and psychological exercise.[90]

The emergence of these new recreational forms has resulted in a new generation of leisure swimming pools and aquatic parks. Leisure swimming pools are relatively small (around 4,000 m²), while aquatic parks can far exceed that. Both have appeared in Europe simultaneously. As commercial structures, the parks were often built on the Mediterranean coast (for example in Cap d'Agde, near Montpellier in 1983) before being established closer to the large cities and leisure centres (Aqualands, Aquaboulevards, Forest Hill, Wallibi). Leisure swimming pools appeared in Germany in the 1970s with 60 'Freizeitbäde', then in the United Kingdom after 1974.[91] Other North European countries took up this fashion at the end of the 1970s (Scandinavia and Belgium), with southern Europe following later.

These last structures were designed for leisure purposes so the choices made in terms of space were basically different from those of traditional facilities.[92] The pools integrated numerous sub-spaces; the lines were curved and the depth was generally shallow. They favoured moving water (waves, fountains, waterfalls) instead of cool water and promoted the bather's movement, using shutes, tunnels, and rivers with buoys. These swimming pools were made for friendship, recreation, and to provide novelty to the users. The focus on friendship and consumption resulted in much used 'annexes', which were seen as important as the bathing itself: cloakrooms, toilets, lawns, beaches, restaurants, bars, places to move and places to stay. Feelings of relaxation were promoted through the use of hot showers, attractive jacuzzis, beaches, solaria and saunas. Elements of adventure in the water were cultivated too. Commercial owners sought all kinds of new ways to make their pools attractive – and they were not necessarily linked to swimming. Swimming pools sometimes became places of spectacles along with movies, art exhibitions, concerts and dance shows. School usage, being less profitable, had to adapt by changing the pedagogical use of space. Even the edges around water were reappropriated by teaching strategies, as shown by a recent study.[93]

Today, the majority of the pools available for teaching swimming employ the principle of circuits (around or in the basin) or workshops. The choices can be recreational (especially in primary schools) or formal when it is simply a question of using lines to divide the pool into long rectangles (in theory 2.50 m × 25 m).[94] More generally, one still has to divide the pool into sections in order to separate the various activities during the same lesson and ensure safety for those who cannot swim.[95]

Conclusion

Open water was a medium which doubly disturbed the social order. It presented a physical risk to the swimmer or the bather due to the uncertainty he or she had to contend with, and a moral risk since it made the regulation and control of students more difficult. This is why political, sport and school institutions always stressed closed, cool and delimited spaces.[96] Over the last century, public and private aquatic space has focused upon hygienic, sport and/or recreational points of view, obliging schools to constantly adapt their pedagogical strategies and pool arrangements in order to maintain discipline and promote efficient learning.

On the one hand, individuals have obtained more and more freedom in the water. Today, they can swim and act in a space which is still well delimited but less Cartesian and symmetrical. The rectangle, as a resolutely disciplinary geometrical model, has been partly replaced by more functional designs. On the other hand, school norms are still there to arrange the organization of lessons and provide discipline where necessary. As the management of aquatic space has become more complex, and teaching methods more active, there are fewer constraints and more focus upon student motivation and play. Discipline has become subtler, exploiting the attractive and unexpected dimensions of creative new pool designs.

Admittedly, these transformations of school norms were not only a refinement of the instrumentalization of student's bodies, they were also a consequence of pressure from sport and leisure interests. If sport and school needs converged, they became radically dissociated soon after. The same result can be said about the relationships between recreational space and school space, even if the link between them seems strong today. At a time when sport is in question in France, when physical education has to better integrate new leisure activities[97] and when pedagogical concern is focused on safety in physical activities,[98] will aquatic leisure space be compatible with teaching requirements? Shutes, for example, do not have the rigour of corridors encircled by floating lines, and artificial waves can change the relationship of the bather to the water. These waves, however, are neither wild nor natural. They are anything but anarchic. Under the control of a computer, which determines their number, size and force, they provide an image of tamed nature. Finally, the history of aquatic spaces may be understood as a history of convergent disciplinary strategies to instrumentalize the bodies of swimmers and bathers.

Freezing Social Relations:
Ice, Rinks, and the Development of
Figure Skating

MARY LOUISE ADAMS

Once there was simply ice: on lakes, ponds, rivers, canals. It froze or it didn't. The ice was hard or it was slushy. It bore or it broke. People skated for fun, they skated to get somewhere, or they waited in vain for freeze-up. Skating was a winter pastime, pursued out of doors in cold climates.

It might seem that this goes without saying. Surely skating is to winter and ice as sailing is to summer and wind. Here, in Canada, the frozen pond is a key signifier of our national claims on winter and northernness, of our identity as a wholesome, hardy people. Rosy-cheeked children play shinny against a prairie sky, a city skyline, a ridge of pines. Cold winds are vanquished by the swoosh and cut of a blade, the thwack of a frozen puck on a stick. A national fairy tale. For some Canadians the story actually rings true. But most Canadian skaters – and many Canadians do not skate – find our ice indoors, in ugly, cinder block buildings where the air stinks of old hockey gear and the black rubber floors are flecked with frozen spit. In such rinks we skate the whole year round; we are no different than skaters in Spain or Australia or Israel. On artificial ice, in climate-controlled buildings, skating is no more tied to winter than is basketball.

Artificial ice has made figure skating and hockey into global industries. Figure-skating shows regularly tour Southeast Asia and Latin America. Professional skaters find jobs on cruise ships that travel between Caribbean ports. Ice hockey associations exist in Argentina, Hong Kong and the United Arab Emirates. The building of ice rinks is itself an international industry as developers export their designs and technology. In such a context, skating marks capitalist affluence more than northern hardiness – much as it did when the technology for indoor ice was invented in England in the late nineteenth century.

Early skating was something else. It grew in the intersection of climate, landscape and technology. In this chapter I sketch a brief, idiosyncratic social history of the skating rink. My route through this story follows the development of figure skating in Britain. More than any of the other ice sports (speed skating, barrel jumping, skate sailing, curling, hockey), figure skating precipitated the invention of artificial ice and indoor rinks, the first of which appeared in Britain in the late nineteenth century. Prior to this, figure skaters (and their predecessors) helped to launch the notion that even outdoor ice – a quintessential symbol of public, open space – was something that could be parcelled up and roped off.

As I knit this narrative together, my primary concern lies with the social meanings ascribed to skating spaces and how these were shaped by and helped to shape the social identities of various skaters. I am particularly concerned with skating spaces as sites for the production and maintenance of social relations based on class and gender. As geographer Doreen Massey has written, the 'spatial organization of society ... is integral to the production of the social, and not merely its result. It is fully implicated in both history and politics.'[1] In this case we are talking about the history and politics of physical activity and sport, of the organization of labour and technology that makes sport possible, and of gendered and classed styles of movement. We are talking also of the politics of exclusion and access and of the social identities they shore up. To think of ice rinks in terms of the 'spatial organization of society' is to think of them as implicated in – rather than just the setting for – a broad net of human activities and relationships. Ice rinks are not simply the stage upon which class or gender inequalities play out, rather they help to structure them. Moreover, social relations of class and gender are among the conditions that made ice rinks possible. The space of the rink is not simply that which can be measured in square meters, it is also symbolic and, hence, ideological and political.

Skating rinks are just one example of many that show how spaces regulate identities and behaviour. We see this process every day as we walk past coffee shops peopled only by men, or past bars that prohibit the entry of children. In some cases the boundary one crosses into such a space is official – as with the bar where young people are legally restricted from entering. In other cases the boundary is social – while women are not prohibited from entering a café filled with men, few feel comfortable doing so. Such informal boundaries are most obvious in enclosed spaces where the people and behaviour on one side of the door are different from those on the other. Yet informal boundaries also exist in the open: on beaches, city streets, and frozen lakes and ponds. The fact that such informal boundaries are flexible and permeable does not negate their role as a vector of power, as one of the many banal ways that inequity is constructed and maintained in everyday practices.

Skating as Elegance and Freedom – For Some

Early skaters used bone or wood to propel themselves over frozen waterways. Such skates were used for centuries in North America, in Scandinavia and England, and in other parts of northern Europe until iron skates were developed by the Dutch around the fourteenth century. Sharpened metal blades have distinct edges that grip the ice, allowing for stronger pushes and more speed. Skaters can change the direction of their forward or backward motion by leaning to the inside or outside of the blade. It is the edge of the blade cutting into the ice that gives each stroke its distinctive sound and requires the curving step that is the basis of all modern skating. Until the early 1800s, a long gliding step on the forward outside edge – known in England as the Dutch roll – stood as the height of skating's technical development.

In Holland skating developed as both amusement and transportation. Paintings from the fifteenth and sixteenth century show canals crowded by people of all classes – men and women, adults and children. As one English observer writes:

> these instruments [skates], indeed, are indispensable to the Dutch in the winter season; and are used by men, WOMEN, and *children*, constantly. The women skate to market with provisions, and *children of five or six years old* and upwards, accompany them, not lazily hanging at their backs or on their arms, but each little skater with *winged feet* flies after its mother, and carries a little basket of eggs, or other articles along with it. *Interesting scene!*[2]

The easy integration of skating into everyday life seems to have been unique to Holland, as was the democracy of the iced-over canals. Apart from a few attempts to use skates in the military, skating evolved throughout the rest of Europe and North America as a form of recreation, albeit one with class- and gender-specific histories.

Seventeenth- and eighteenth-century skaters were tied to the landscape in obvious ways. If there was no ice, there was no skating. If the river was long, and the ice was solid, skaters might run races or use their skates to travel quickly and easily from one village to the next. On ponds where there was no distance to capture their imaginations, skaters explored the technical possibilities of the blade on the ice. Different landscapes led to different kinds of skating and these became associated with the people who practised them. In the Fen District of England, for instance, where the still flat water froze in great smooth stretches, it was mostly, but not exclusively, male farm labourers who invented courses and formats for racing on skates. In London and other big cities, skating was a pastime of young boys and of

well-to-do men. While the boys played games on frozen ditches or canals –
on any bit of ice they could find – the gentlemen practised a sedate and dig-
nified style of gliding on the small ponds and lakes in urban parks and
estates. This 'gentle art' was the style of skating that would eventually turn
into figure skating. The product of elegant and noble manners, it became a
popular court entertainment, honed at ice balls and masquerades and at
other aristocratic gatherings across the continent.

With few exceptions, Marie Antoinette being one, the practitioners of
the gentle art were men. Women, bundled in fur robes, were more likely to
be pushed about the ice in carved wooden sleighs. Paintings of the ice festivities held during the Congress of Vienna – a negotiation among European
rulers over the borders of a post-Napoleonic Europe (1814/15) – show cos-
tumed male skaters and swan-shaped sleighs carrying elegant women.[3] In
Russia the first skating club, founded in 1865, even had a special department of 'chaise' skating. It is not clear why so few women outside Holland
skated. Some skating writers suggest that feminine skating would have been
considered too liberated, or immoral.[4] Others say women were afraid of
breaking through the ice[5] or that female clothing made skating impractical.[6]
Whatever the reason, skating authors were unanimous in their calls for
women to don skates and take to the ice.

As a combination of art, exercise and social event, skating fit somewhere between the categories of walking and dancing, both of which were,
within limits, considered appropriate for upper-class women. But, unlike
dancing, skating often took place before crowds of curious onlookers in
public parks. And, unlike walking, competence in skating was hard won.
Only skaters of the highest noble ranks would have been able to practise
their art in private. What gentlewoman could suffer the humiliation of
falling before men and women of lower classes?

Elegant skating, like skill at dancing or refined table manners, was a
means through which the highest classes constructed their social identities.
But while dancing skills and table manners were displayed primarily to other
upper-class people – as a way to mark shared membership of that class –
skating was on display to anyone who happened to pass by the skater's frozen
pond. In this sense skating made class differences visible. Huge homes, servants and fine carriages did the same thing, of course. But while the ability to
own a fine carriage could seem a simple question of wealth, the ability to
skate in an elegant fashion could seem a question of inborn physical ability.
Rich people and poor people, even now, learn to move their bodies in different ways. They walk differently, they sit differently, they have different sets
of physical skills. These different styles of moving can make it seem that
there are actual physical differences between upper- and lower-class people,
that richness or poorness are inherent rather than the product of social and
economic practices. The notion that people of different classes are funda-

mentally different kinds of people helps to naturalize class disparities – and it makes economic inequality seem inevitable. Bodies and the movements they make are tremendously powerful representations of ideology. The rough-housing of boys – 'street Arabs' as one British writer called them – on a frozen ditch, and the studied gliding of top-hatted men in London's finest parks, sent different messages to the onlooker. And those messages were not just about skill on skates (see Figure 4.1).

FIGURE 4.1

From the first book on skating. (Robert Jones, *A Treatise on Skating*, 1772)

Skating on urban ponds and canals, upper class men put their elegance on display, performing and producing class difference along with their turns and edges. Not for them the vulgar pursuit of speed for its own sake. As Robert Jones wrote in the first published text on skating, 'an easy movement and graceful attitude are the sole objects of our attention'.[7] What other choice was there on tiny urban ponds, far too small for racing? In Jones's time, grace was an essential characteristic of upper-class masculinity. Grace was a matter of deportment, manners and appearance. In skating it was expressed by a man's posture, his bearing and the attitude of his poses. But grace was not simply aesthetic, it was also a spiritual quality. The art of fine skating allowed men to transcend normal human limitations and to feel closer to nature. Skating was likened to the flight of birds or to the feeling of a boat under sail. Scenery and fresh air added to the sheer physical pleasure of gliding and to the experience of a speed and freedom of movement previously unknown. To open his book *L'Art du patinage*, Parisian writer George Vail borrowed the following paean, published by the French poet Alfonse Lamartine in 1857:

> To be carried with the speed of the arrow, and with the gracious swoops of the bird in the air, on a surface that is smooth, brilliant, resonant and treacherous; to print with a simple lean of the body, and, in this manner to describe, guided only by the rudder of the will, all the curves, all the inflections of the boat on the sea, or of the eagle hovering in the blue sky, it was, for me, such a drunkenness of the senses, and a voluptuous exhilaration of the mind that I can no longer reflect on it without emotion. Even horses, which I love very much, do not give to the rider the delirious melancholy that the great frozen lakes give to skaters.[8]

While Lamartine's prose was certainly not typical of English writers, his sentiments were.

At the end of the 1700s, German romantic poets used the freedom of skating as a metaphor for liberation from social constraints. Skating historian Matthias Hampe argues that in Germany skating did not emerge among the aristocracy as it did in England, France, Austria and Italy, but among the middle classes. He says it was literature and poetry, rather than the prestige of nobility, that made skating acceptable.[9] Until the end of the eighteenth century skating was deemed appropriate only for small boys and lower class people. Praising the bond between skaters and nature, and the potential of skating to develop both body and mind, poets like Goethe and his friend Friedrich Gottlieb Klopstock recast skating as important to the emancipation of the middle class, as morally uplifting and practical. They helped make it possible for German men, at least, to take to the ice without fear of social judgement.

In the outdoorness of skating lay much of its appeal. The beauty of the winter environment, the courage of the skater against the cold, the healthful effects of fresh air, the open space: these were summoned by writers to elevate the value of skating above that of other exercises pursued in more pedestrian environments. The fact that one could never take the presence of ice for granted nor count with any certainty on its longevity – a season could pass with one's desire to skate unsated – only intensified skating's pleasure and gave a certain aura to its afficionados. Ironically, for all the romantic rhetoric, it was less the exhilaration of skating out-of-doors than the logistics of it that brought skaters together in the first organized clubs (see Figure 4.2).

Negotiating the Elements

The world's first skating club was founded in Edinburgh in the mid 1700s; the exact date is not known. Skating on the 'picturesque' loch at Duddington, club members found congenial company while they worked on the development of their art – no simple feat when the loch could go several years in a row without freezing. All members were men of excellent social standing and able skaters. New members were vetted for social compatibility and were required to demonstrate their ability on skates by performing a circle on each foot and jumping over three hats

FIGURE 4.2

Vienna Ice Skating Club – late eighteenth century. (Bilarchiv, ONB, Vienna)

stacked on the ice. Women were not admitted until 1910 and then only through family ties:

> There can be few more animating sights than a meeting of the Skating-Club there [on the lake] on a clear bright winter's day during a season of hard frost – enhanced as it is by the singular beauty of the locality, with the overhanging hill, the ancient church on the margin, and the fringing woods of the Marquis of Abercorn and Sir William Dick Cunningham.

So wrote the author of an 1865 history of the Club.[10] While the location may have been beautiful, aesthetics alone could not guarantee good conditions for skating. Annual suppers for members included toasts to 'John Frost', the 'patron saint of the Club'. Just as important, but less recognized, was the small band of labourers that maintained the club's ice. According to a letter written by the club's treasurer, at least one good frost in 1814 was 'of little avail from want of funds to clear the ice …'[11] Far be it for gentlemen skaters to sweep the snow themselves.

Of course once having paid for the clearing of the ice, members of the club had then to pay for the clean ice to be protected from boys or others who might damage it. The club employed labourers and watchmen who were both overseen by a paid officer. It was the task of the officer to report on the condition of the ice to the club's secretary or treasurer every evening. If the ice was indeed suitable for skating the officer would post notices around the city the next morning or deliver a note to the home of each member. No need, therefore, for gentlemen skaters to venture out needlessly into the cold.

Similar concerns motivated the founding, in 1830, of what would become Britain's most prestigious nineteenth-century club: The Skating Club in London. An invitation sent to potential members made no mention of the shared pleasures of skating but described an organization that would provide 'notice of when the ice will bear, in what place all probability the Members will meet to have the ice properly swept and watched, a convenient booth for putting on skates, keeping great coats, &c., &c., &c'.[12] The club, like others that followed it, provided a structure for gentlemen skaters to hire out the work that made skating possible. Depending on the weather that work could be considerable. On the lake at Wimbledon, for instance, home of the Wimbledon Skating Club, an extravagant area of 20 acres was cleared for the exclusive use of figure skaters, curlers and bandy players. After a heavy snowstorm, the Club might employ up to 170 men to clear the ice with 'scows and snow boxes'. In the 1890s the average cost of a snowstorm to the club was one pound per minute.[13] During one series of heavy snowstorms, 100 men worked constantly for 10 to 12 days to keep the ice clear.[14]

As sport historians routinely point out, the play of the few depended on the work of many. The wealth and leisure of the upper classes depended on the labour of employees or tenants as well as on an economic and political system shaped by and for the upper classes. On a far more practical level, the games and pastimes of the rich depended quite directly on the work of people less well off than themselves: people who would maintain the stable or riding course, who would wax the rowing shells, who would sweep the rink and mind the coats. Henry Vandervell and T. Maxwell Witham wrote about the particularly cold winter of 1860/61:

> The well-known words, 'Ave a pair on, sir? Skates on, sir?' invited the promenaders in the London parks in every direction, and it was apparent that thousands of the humble classes were getting their daily bread in a most inclement season by ministering to the wants of the skater.[15]

For almost forty years, members of The Skating Club had permission of the Ranger of Woods and Forests to skate on a section of the Serpentine, a small lake in London's Hyde Park, and to erect a marquee on the bank. But when the weather was cold and the untutored skating masses descended, club members found it hard to protect their space:

> All attempts to carry out those beautiful figures which give such delight to the on-lookers were frustrated, and many of the strongest members of the Club, well-bruised all over, departed in disgust to other parts of the Serpentine, or more frequently to the outskirts and environs of the metropolis.[16]

Beyond the infringements on their private ice, the gentlemen skaters were horrified to think that unknowing spectators might confuse the awkward and unskilled hordes with bona fide club members. To stave off such mis-identifications, the club adopted a small silver skate as a badge and any member who appeared on the ice without it could be fined. Complaints about the club's privileged access to a piece of London's best ice were much harder to stave off.

In the late 1860s, the gentlemen skaters finally constructed a rink for their sole use on the flooded archery pitch of the Royal Toxophilite Society in Regent's Park. After the opening of the new private rink, measuring 150 yards long by 50 yards wide, club membership was much sought after. Worried about crowding on the new but limited ice surface, members voted in 1870 to restrict the total membership to 120 gentlemen and 20 ladies. They also instituted skating tests as a means – beyond existing requirements for sponsorship and a formal balloting system – of screening applicants.[17]

With their new ice and new procedures, members of The Skating Club were transforming an exercise synonymous with personal freedom and unencumbered space into a carefully circumscribed practice. Skating as they organized it became increasingly exclusive in terms of class background and level of skating skill – the two being closely related – even as it opened up a tiny bit for upper-class women.

Sport theorist Henning Eichberg draws on the work of the French historian Philippe Ariès to argue that the enclosure of previously outdoor activities was an exclusionary process that was as much about separating activities from each other as it was of dividing people of different social rank.[18] Eichberg is concerned mostly with enclosed indoor spaces like training halls or indoor riding arenas. In the case of The Skating Club, the members did not yet have the option of fully enclosing their pastime, although entrepreneurs in Canada had begun to build enclosed structures over natural ice in the late 1850s. It would be a few more decades before skating in Britain could be an indoor pursuit. Nevertheless the aristocratic skaters did what they could with the technology available to them, removing themselves, their distinctive style of skating, and the knowledge of how to perform it, to private grounds. Historian Dennis Brailsford argues that nineteenth-century sports clubs were fundamentally about exclusivity.[19] And while figure skating was not generally considered a sport in the 1870s, it was in many ways organized like one, with clubs promoting a shared body of technique and emphasizing the achievement of physical skills. Yet knowledge and performance were probably not – as any number of historians could remind us – the main reason for joining a sports club: 'the company came first'.[20] And in this regard too skating was sportlike.

Published in 1909, the history of The Skating Club makes no mention of when the first women members were admitted. However, the provision of 20 spaces for ladies in 1870 suggests that at least some women were skating before this time. In North America and in parts of Europe, the number of women skaters rose dramatically in the 1860s with the development of new kinds of skates that were easier to use and more comfortable to wear, and with the removal of skating from frozen lakes and rivers to the much safer flooded fields in urban areas. Women in London may have been motivated to skate by similar factors. But, for those who wished to join The Skating Club, desire to skate was not enough: women's access to the club was mediated through fathers or husbands who were members. No woman could join on her own accord, no matter how high her social standing or how proficient her skating. Gentlemen members permitted the number of women using their rink to grow only slowly. It took until 1894 to get the number of women members to 50, an increase so great that it necessitated the enlargement of the women's club room.[21]

From Freedom to Control

By the second half of the nineteenth century, the term 'figure skating' had been adopted in Britain and referred to a sombre form of skating that was developing in clubs like The Skating Club. In the 1800s, technically minded skaters spent most of their time practising their edges and developing various turns that could link the four basic edges together (forward-inside, forward-outside, backward-inside and backward-outside). Whereas skaters in the early decades of the century had been very concerned about the artfulness of their movements or the position of their arms and heads, later skaters were far more interested in the science and precision of their technique. Freedom, once a primary enticement for skaters, was replaced by control. And the individuality in skating – the ability to move any which way across a wide-open surface – was replaced by conformity in a new form of skating called 'combination skating'. Combination skating was figure skating's answer to Victorian team sport. Combined figures were skating movements performed in strict unison by groups of four or more skaters. An orange on the ice marked the centre of the figure. The skaters would position themselves symmetrically around it and on the command of their leader they would perform turns and other moves towards and away from the orange. In order to minimize deviance from the unison of the group, all extraneous movements, say of the hands or arms or free leg, were prohibited. A skater was forbidden even to bend the knee of the skating leg – a feat that contemporary skaters would find all but impossible.

While this kind of skating still required large ice surfaces, the space was used geometrically – each skater was limited to his or her particular corner of the larger figure. When done well – with the strictest control – combined skating must have been a tremendous sight, but it would hardly have inspired comparison with birds on the wing. It would have resembled more the internal workings of a clock or the smooth fit of cogs in a machine. Combined skating matched well the sensibility of the times. It was a skating decidedly right for Victorian men: publicly unexpressive, formal, stiff. It was skating as science rather than skating as art (see Figure 4.3).

This English style of skating, as it came to be called, contrasted with more expressive styles on the Continent and more intricate styles in North America; British skaters considered it far superior to either of these. Scottish writer George Anderson, writing under the name 'Cyclos', spoke favourably of the new institution of Canadian ice rinks – 'large sheds enclosed against wind and snow, and lighted with gas, so that the skater can follow his pastime comfortably, day or night, in all weathers except thaw'.[22] But while the extended time of practice and quality of the ice led to a more 'finished performance', he wrote, 'the circumscribed space has greatly dwarfed the bold sweeps and circles in which the British skater most delights, and has substituted small turns and intricate twists, such as the

FIGURE 4.3

A Club Figure: Skating in the English Style at the turn of the century.

"grape vine", which though difficult of attainment, and in themselves very pretty, are not, at least in British opinion, the finest style of skating'.[23] The complicated moves developed by Canadian skaters were, in part, a product of the limited space in the new enclosed rinks, but they were also a product of a lesser requirement for regal appearances and unwavering control. To put it simply, upper-class British skaters would never have consented to be seen moving their bodies as the Canadian men did. 'Bold sweeps' were about all they could do if they needed to hold their bodies straight and square. The 'finest style of skating' stayed well within the bounds of British gender and class ideologies and their requirements for how upper class men's bodies could look and move.

For all their need to be in control, British skaters had no control over the weather. During the last two decades of the nineteenth century there were on average 18 skating days a year at the Wimbledon Skating Club. Three winters during the period had no ice at all, 6 winters had an average of more than 40 days, and one exceptionally cold year had 53 days of skating.[24] While this longest season might have been fine for pleasure skaters, keen figure skaters found the limitations on even this season frustrating. As skating developed technically, a few weeks of practice was too little to achieve the highest levels of skill. Skaters needed more ice.

Those with enough time and money found it in Switzerland. In the late 1870s, English skaters began travelling to Davos and St Moritz in the Swiss Alps, where they could practise on outdoor ice for three or four months every winter. The first Davos Skating Club, founded by English skaters, opened in 1880 and, despite its continental location, became affiliated with the National Skating Association of Great Britain (NSA), which had been formed the previous year. In the Swiss resorts the outdoor rinks, constructed by hotel employees, were enormous, and the ice, apparently, flawless.[25] Special reservoirs were built at some height above the rinks to generate sufficient water pressure to sprinkle the ice and 'patient laudable men sit up all night watching the thermometer to see if it is safe to offer water to the delicately-nurtured crystal'.[26] Writer E.F. Benson claimed that the 'construction and renovation of these rinks … ranks among the fine arts'.[27] And a good thing too. Some members of the NSA claimed that the requirements for merit tests had been set so high they could only be met by those who spent the winter practising on fine ice on the continent. It is not surprising that skaters who spent much time in the Swiss resorts were instrumental in raising the technical standards and stylistic direction of English skating. Their achievements became the goal of all skaters, even those who only had access to natural ice at home. The comparisons must have been painful.

Back in England, the demand for figure skating ice and the emerging pastime of waltzing on skates prompted the invention of artificial, indoor ice. The first indoor rink opened in Chelsea in London in 1876. With a tiny ice surface – 40 feet long by 24 feet wide – the rink was not open to the public and operated on paid subscriptions from noblemen and gentlemen.[28] But its tiny size made it impractical and the venture was short-lived. A rink in Manchester was another short-lived experiment while one built in Southport managed to survive for a decade. The Southport Glaciarium, much larger than the earlier rink in Chelsea, was credited by some writers for having saved both the art of figure skating and the National Skating Association from a string of mild winters in the early 1880s. The rink was advertised in the first Official Handbook of the NSA as 'The only real Ice-Skating Hall in the World, The Figure Skaters' Paradise, open in all seasons, Spring, Summer, Autumn and Winter. Admission 6d.!!'[29]

To say the Glaciarium was a paradise was a bit of stretch; certainly skating at the rink was nothing like skating out of doors. Space was limited, the ice was crowded and, most important, ventilation was bad. Skaters laboured through dampness and mist as they perfected their figures. Miracle or not, artificial ice seemed distinctly unhealthy; skating on it was skating as technique only, it was not skating as feeling. The new rinks were no competition for the open air ice of Davos or St Moritz and wealthy British skaters continued to overwinter on the continent well into the twentieth century.

By the 1890s, rink technology had advanced to allow for good indoor ice in favourable skating conditions. Spectacular ice palaces opened in major cities across Europe. Three London rinks opened in the mid 1890s. At the

Niagara Hall rink the ice covered a circular area of about ten thousand square feet, the ventilation was, apparently, excellent and the 'atmosphere in the hall is in no way injurious to health'.[30] A second rink known as the National Skating Palace helped London secure hosting rights for the 1898 World Figure Skating Championships. Without the indoor ice, the International Skating Union (ISU) would never have risked an event in London's mild climate. The National Skating Palace and the Niagara Hall rink were both open to the public, a situation that was good for finance and for waltzing as an evening's entertainment, but bad for figuring. By contrast, a third rink opened in Knightsbridge for the exclusive use of the Prince's Skating Club (see Figure 4.4), the subscriptions to which must have been enormous. Figure skaters needed clean ice where they could lay out their designs and practise their combination figures. In indoor facilities they were gluttons for space, a situation that combined poorly with the tremendous costs of running the new palaces.

They were not simple structures, these rinks, even the public ones. As American skater Maribel Vinson wrote home to her family in the 1930s:

> It *is* so nice to skate where comfort is not sacrificed ... When I think of everyone at home skating in that barn-like arena [in Boston]! It may be better for carnivals, but for every-day practice, give me the warm dressing rooms, the lounges, reading rooms, writing desks, and glassed-in restaurants of the English rinks.[31]

FIGURE 4.4

Prince's rink in London. (Postcard from the World Figure Skating Museum)

Most of the rinks open to the public remained decidedly bourgeois if not upper class into the twentieth century. To keep rink culture at an appropriate standard, skating texts routinely included instructions on proper behaviour for those new to the pastime (no smoking on the ice, no shirt sleeves for men, no gossiping on the ice). Nevertheless, the tie between figure skating and elegance started to unravel in the late 1920s with the encroachment of commercialism. Developers and promoters started a small boom in rink-building as they tried to cash in on the popularity of the young Sonja Henie and the increasing acceptability of commercial entertainments. Rinks opened in smaller towns and cities with too few posh skaters to support them. In London the new Richmond ice rink could easily accommodate a thousand skaters – impossible for them all to be the 'right kind of people'.

It was commercial rink operators and not the National Skating Association nor the many British skating clubs that brought figure skating to the middle classes. In doing so they shifted the meaning of the activity, changed what could be read from the rapidly evolving technical innovations. Commercial rink operators hired professional coaches – some from Europe or North America. It was no longer necessary to find a sponsor to gain membership at an exclusive club in order to learn how to figure skate. By the 1930s the accessibility of skating widened again when three-time Olympic champion Sonja Henie starred in a series of Hollywood films. In her ten films Henie brought skating to the broader public, many of whom, in an era without television, would never have seen figure skating before – they wouldn't have had access to the spaces where it took place. Henie brought skating to the media, among the least exclusive of public spaces. And, with her huge popularity and financial success – she remains one of the most financially successful female athletes in history figure skating ice and figure skating clubs evolved into spaces for girls and for the production of a sparkly, bubbly femininity, the legacy of their aristocratic roots remaining in the image of the ice princess that has been the norm in women's figure skating for almost 80 years.

Over the course of the twentieth century indoor ice rinks have grown up all over the world.[32] They are no longer the exclusive playgrounds of the upper classes, although there are certainly some that are – most of which, I would hazard to guess, are owned by private clubs and are used exclusively for the training of figure skaters. Women and girls, of course, find their place on the ice now and not just during the time set aside for figure skating. Clearly some of the earlier social relations that led to the roping-off of rinks and to the way they were used have changed. Yet rinks, like other contested social spaces, continue to have regulatory effects. In Canada, where there are more rinks per capita than anywhere else in the world, they are generally public, state-owned facilities rather than commercial enterprises, and access to ice time is a politically charged issue. Who gets more hours:

Just Another Classroom?
Observations of Primary School
Playgrounds

SARAH THOMSON

The Idyllic View

The school playground is one of those places that we immediately associate with children. Arguably, the primary school playground is one of the sacrosanct territories of childhood because it is perceived as a space that, at given times, is governed on children's own terms. Traditionally this space is set apart for children and their activities. Ask any adult to cast their mind back to their school experiences and often, amongst their anecdotes, will be some personal reminiscences about the playground. When we first walk into a contemporary British primary school playground at playtime what are our initial impressions? At first glance children dominate the playground, frequently out-numbering the adults. The whole arena appears eclipsed by children. The chief impression is one of frenetic activity combined with a high level of noise. The superficial picture is one of confusion, of excited, generally exuberant children energetically playing games. Although the observant outsider might see, amongst the chaos, occasional desultory and sedentary behaviour, overall the playground is noisy and appears undisciplined, disorganized and chaotic.

To the passer-by, a school playground full of children signifies a break from learning. Institutionally the playground space represents an area set aside for childish activities, implying an engagement with children, an acknowledgement of their ways, habits and needs. The general picture that emerges is a happy one; supposedly this is a place where the 'lore and the language' of the child dominates.[1] Blatchford supports this view and notes that in the playground 'pupils are relatively freed from the attention of adults and the structure of the classroom'. Playtime, he says, is a time 'when pupils can find freedom and a social life independent of the classroom, where the rules of conduct are more their own, and where activities stem from their own initiative'.[2] The space, he argues, offers children an opportunity to occupy a more private place than that of the classroom. Certainly, it is a common assumption that the playground is the one area in school where children can express themselves more freely than they can in other parts of the school site. It is generally perceived as providing them with an environment where *they* dictate the activities. Furthermore, the playground is portrayed by teachers and others as a place for children to 'let off steam' and 'recharge the batteries'.[3] The site, when fully occupied, appears to express the vigour and unselfconsciousness that is the epitome of child-hood. One would assume, therefore, that children would have the dominant use and shaping of this space, particularly at breaktime.

Why Bother about this Space?

Children today have few private *open* spaces in which to play, particularly in public areas. Parents 'swayed by a plethora of anxieties concerning their children playing in unsupervised public spaces limit the opportunities for their children to play outdoors'.[4] Children's outdoor free time is becoming a highly structured activity. Instead of coming home and playing in the garden, the street or the local park/playground, after-school outdoor activities are becoming more rationalized.[5] Thus the chances to play in this type of environment are diminished and the school playground might be the only large *outdoor* setting where children can play informally with others. Clearly the school playground not only offers children the opportunity to meet together on their own terms: it is one of the few spaces where children can meet with their peers *en masse*, devise their own activities and express themselves more freely than they can in other parts of the school site.[6] It provides young children with one of the first opportunities to manage an open space for themselves, physically and mentally occupying the space in their own way. It might offer them a place where their physicality is unre-strained. Certainly, for children this space defines the margin between work and play. This space, therefore, represents an area that provides children with some freedom from the restraints and disciplines of the classroom, and offers them an area where they are temporarily free from the rules and reg-ulations of adults and the classroom. The school playground, then, has the illusion of being a space where children rule, where their desires are upper-most. In essence the school playground space should form a context for behaviour that is fundamentally different from the context of adult behav-iour and is in marked contrast to the regime of the classroom. My own research on playgrounds suggests that this is not always the case.

Ways of Seeing the Playground

In contrast to the idyllic view presented above, one can see how the envi-ronment of the playground is used for both the explicit and implicit controlling and monitoring of the bodies that occupy it. Foucault notes that during the eighteenth and nineteenth century, power extended, not only to regulate institutions such as the school, but also to 'gaze' on and control the body.[7] Moreover, as Sack points out, 'human territoriality' (the segmentation of space as a source of power) is a 'powerful and pervasive element in our lives'. Territoriality, he notes, is a way of 'displacing attention from the relationship between the controller and the controlled. Thus, territory appears to be the agent doing the controlling'.[8] The school playground, then, offers adults and their agents both the territory and the opportunity in which to exercise forms of control over children. Underlying the benevolent appearance of the playground lies a site that acts as a template for the formation and maintenance of the 'techniques of power' over children.[9] Rather than the playground providing an open, free space in which to play, the evidence suggests that there is very little freedom in the playground because the child has a limited choice about what s/he does in this space. Although Blatchford maintains that the playground provides pupils with the freedom that they cannot find in the classroom,[10] the image of children playing freely in an uninhibited, unconstrained way in the primary school playground is hardly a true reflection of the practice of the playground. Their freedom is only a relative freedom from the physical boundaries and constraints of the classroom. In many respects, it is just a change of venue, an exchange of one educational surrounding for another. Since Sutton-Smith notes that 'children's play in schools is of an increasing domesticated and organized variety',[11] we have to ask whether the idyllic image of playtime at school is realistic? The image described in the opening paragraph, when decoded, might create a new interpretation of school playground life; it might reveal systems of control that are not obvious at first glance and expose the duplicity of some of its practices and purposes. How, therefore, does the school playground 'measure up to what might be conceived as a children's environment'?[12]

For children the joy of school is 'being with friends and trying to play as much as possible'.[13] For teachers, their job in school is largely 'to keep children from doing just that'. Teachers generally have to 'settle down children'.[14] The discourse of the school as a site, and particularly the classroom, as a place of 'spatial discipline'[15] and how it effects the reconfiguration of children's bodies has been covered extensively.[16] Yet to date this broader debate has focused predominantly on the question of the classroom.

A close study of the daily routines of the playground space might uncover the 'ideological position of the educational organization'.[17] The study of the playground's design and an investigation of the ordering of its activities offers a view into the physical, mental and ideological characteristics of pupils' and teachers' daily lives in school.[18] If we question the organization of the symbols, contents and activities of the playground and look at the messages that they send, what can we learn about its policies and practices? What can we learn from the way this site is managed? In this respect therefore, I want to argue that the school playground space, one that is often considered the epitome of childish freedom, is just another room within the school institution. Moreover, it is one that serves the same purposes of those inside the building. Using as clues a number of signs, symbols and actions that I have collected from my observations of the playground, I will illustrate how the operation of the playground makes it an enclosure that is remarkably similar to that of the classroom.

The Sample and the Setting

The research on which this chapter is based derives from detailed ethnographic observations of three primary schools located in the Midlands in England. They were located respectively in urban, suburban and rural settings and were administered by three different educational authorities. Playtimes at lunchtime, morning and afternoon, where applicable, were observed over a period of several weeks, throughout all the seasons. The fieldwork consisted of observing several hundred children and their accompanying supervisory staff. Supporting the observational data is a number of semi-structured interviews with teaching staff, midday assistants and representatives of various agencies. As part of my research, it was important to obtain a detailed description of the physical aspects of the playgrounds. To do this and as an aide-memoire, I took photographs at the beginning and the end of the study. I also kept a record of all the physical aspects of the playground design, plus a list of contents such as furniture and play equipment, decoration and any architectural anomalies such as service boxes and manhole covers. This part of the research provided detailed studies of the children's play environment. From these descriptions I was able to develop several key themes which are relevant to this work.

Just Another Room?

Can the school playground be viewed as just another room set within the confines of the school? What signs can be extrapolated from the daily routines and design of this space to provide evidence to support this statement? Historically, paternal philanthropists interested in mass education such as Robert Owen, Samuel Wilderspin and David Stow were very significant in not only influencing the design of playgrounds but also in outlining and organizing the pursuits and behaviour expected within this space. These early innovators of primary school design influenced the architecture of school buildings and playgrounds intended for the mass education of the lower orders. All three men viewed the playground as a useful enclosure. Robert Owen, for example, declared in 1812:

> The time (when) the children will remain under the discipline of the play-ground and school, and will afford all the opportunity that can be desired, to create, cultivate and establish those habits and sentiments which tend to the welfare of the individual and of the community.[19]

Equally, Stow saw the playground as an 'uncovered school' in which to establish discipline and monitor and train children's behaviour.[20] In 1823 Wilderspin also referred to the playground as the 'uncovered schoolroom'.[21] Both are clearly explicit in their suggestions that the playground is to act as an 'open-air classroom'.[22] Physically the playground has many of the conventional constructs of a room. A room is a 'space that is or might be occupied by something; part of a building; enclosed by walls or partitions'.[23] Normal convention has it that a room usually has walls, a floor, doors, windows and a ceiling. Moreover, frequently something or someone occupies the room.

The Conventional Constructs of a Room

A Room is ... Enclosed by Walls British primary school playgrounds usually consist of an area surrounded by some sort of boundary. In most instances these consist of hedging, fences, railings or brick walls, and they frequently contain items of furniture such as benches and dustbins. Kelly (1994) describes school playgrounds as 'empty spaces between buildings and perimeter walls'.[24] In the case of the three schools in this study, all three playgrounds were bounded on at least one side by a set of railings (in one instance the railings consisted of 12 ft-high, pointed, wide, steel uprights). There appears to be an increased sensitivity about the potential dangers facing school children in the playground. Head teachers have had to contend with a growing level of anxiety about children's well-being and safety at school. Tragedies such as the Dunblane shooting in 1996 and the Wolverhampton machete attack in 1997 have heightened their concerns with school safety. Consequently there is a drive to surround school playgrounds with a more substantial form of perimeter and this has led to some playgrounds becoming more like a cage than an open landscape. One of the schools in my study is in the middle of a dispute with local residents because the head teacher wants to make the perimeter of the playground more secure and more substantial. The neighbours are disputing the planning application because their view will be blocked, maintaining that the area will be devalued as a result of the new fencing.

A Room has ... Partitions In addition, all three schools have a least two sides encircled by the brick walls of the school building. In every case, one of the walls overlooking the playground contained the window of the head teacher's office, so that the head was able to supervise what was happening in part of the playground.

> Head teacher: People say you are not really that well supervised around here. But if you think that when you are sitting here in the staff room you can see what is going on and you only have to hear a squeal and you are straight up. So this area is covered, that area is covered, similarly the front area is covered by the members of staff out there and around so really we have got a fairly good coverage of what is going on.

One head laughingly commented to me about the view from his window and admitted that it gives him some covert viewing: 'they don't know that I can see them, it is my little spy hole, this window'. At another school, the midday assistants remarked that when they were supervising the children at playtime they were aware that the head teacher watched them through her office window: 'she is watching us, always watching us.' In two cases, the windows of the staff room also looked out into the playground. Thus the construction of the playground is very similar to that of a room, in that walls and windows surround it. In this case those at the windows are looking out at the children, rather than the children gazing out through the window. Moreover, taking into consideration the number of midday assistants on duty, in conjunction with the other watching members of staff, there is as much surveillance – both explicit and implicit – as that of the classroom, in some cases more so. In many respects, the air of surveillance is as notable as that within the classroom. During my observation of playtime activities, I was challenged by a child with the statement 'I know what you are doing you are inspecting us.' It makes one conscious of how aware children have become to scrutinization, and how they almost accept it as part of their whole school experience, including that of playtime. These examples nicely illustrate Foucault's panoptic view and techniques of surveillance and its ever-widening arc.

The Ceiling One might argue that the playground could not be a room because it does not have a ceiling. However, the metaphor of 'covered' is obvious in the language used by the head teacher, quoted above, when he is justifying his policy of supervision. Whether the term 'covered' is used intentionally or even knowingly within this context, the underlying image is one of children being unable to rise above the boundaries set by the staff, be they physical or abstract. There is also a 'ceiling' on what behaviour is allowed and a prescribed set of safety procedures that affords them a protective shelter. A 'lid' is kept on the children's behaviour by the lunchtime supervisors, thereby setting metaphorical and physical limits above which the children are unable to rise. Such limits are as confining as physical roofing imprisoning the children within the confines of their playground.

The practices of leaving this playground room are worth considering, since if it was a space of freedom children should be able to enter and leave at will. But the rules of leaving the playground during the timetable period of breaktime are stringent, to the extent that it could be argued that the occupants were locked in the playground. Some studies have shown that children, given the choice, would rather stay inside during playtime.[25] Certainly many of the teachers interviewed throughout the study echoed the girls' desires to stay inside at playtime: 'the girls are happy to sit and talk. I had a year group last year who used to ask "could we stay in and practise a dance?", "can we stay in and help you tidy up?" They don't want to go out in the cold.'

Nevertheless, whatever the weather, the children have to go outside and stay out. Entering the school building during playtime is definitely discouraged and children are censored for doing so. I watched children running inside to get a drink and the staff chastising them for going indoors. Comments taken from my observation notes illustrate these aspects of control: 'children are going in and out of the door into school and occupying the entrance corridor that leads to the lavatories. The midday assistant tells them off and sends them back outside.' Those who wanted to visit the toilet had to gain permission to leave the playground. I observed one child asking to go to the toilet and the head teacher replied that the child could not have permission, until the word 'lavatory' was used instead of 'toilet'. This is similar to needing a privileged password to gain entry.

A Room is ... a Space One of the common assumptions made about the playground relates to its flexibility in relation to other zones of the school site. Yet, rather than being flexible, the whole area of the playground is a rigid place just like that of the classroom. In fact, some areas of the playground are more restricted and just as prescriptive as that of the classroom. In the classroom there are certain areas that children are discouraged from occupying. One place not considered a communal space, for example, is the area behind the teacher's desk and chair, or the area immediately in front of the blackboard. In the playground, quite often several areas are off limits or out of bounds or are designated for specific activities. One school in the study had two playgrounds divided by fencing and in these playgrounds only certain age groups were allowed to play. Another school instructed its pupils that there was an imaginary line drawn across the playground area, the intention of which was to segregate the year groups from each other.

The children rarely transgressed this hypothetical line. If they did, the supervisors on duty blew a whistle to draw their attention to this transgression. More alarming was the action of children who would point out to each other how they had transgressed this space.

All three schools banned the children from running on the adjacent grass playing fields, except in the summer. In addition, two of the schools had designated no man's lands where children were not allowed to enter or meet each other. Prescriptive areas were the zones designated as 'quiet areas' where children were ordered to walk, not run. I overheard one head teacher say 'please do not run, this is our quiet playground, this is the sensible playground'. One school had fenced off a small area of the tarmac and replaced it with a small lawn and a flowerbed, to which was added garden seating. To enter this space at playtime special permission was required and the children were told that this space was for sitting in and for 'behaving nicely in'.

'A Room ... Might be Occupied by Something' All the playgrounds had some form of furniture. In most instances, it was furniture intended for sitting and there were particular regions designated as seating areas.

> Head teacher: We have also cordoned off this area around here [an area at the back of the school building, adjacent to the staff room window] which is meant to be a quiet area. We are currently raising money to have planters purchased and seating, additional seating for the children to sit on, they go and sit and chat ... That will then, hopefully, give us two or three areas where children can play ball games or sit quietly; they play quiet games out to the front of the school.

The benches were in a fixed spot anchored by chains, and if the children attempted to stand on them or jump off them they were remonstrated with. Quite often, I saw the children during their imaginative play, attempting to change the purposes of the seating. They changed them from areas of seating into 'prisons', 'dens' or 'cages'. However they were frequently admonished by those supervising them for not 'playing nicely' on the furniture. The purpose of the seating was always so that the children could sit down quietly. Another school in the study had money set aside to increase the number of benches placed in its playground so that the children had a greater opportunity to sit quietly.

Other items of furniture that are an essential requisite of the playground are the dustbins. Great emphasis is placed on the picking up of rubbish and the cleanliness of the playground. I observed 'girls given tongs to pick up rubbish, and to use to fish in the dustbin for crisp packets which had vouchers on. Vouchers mean free equipment for schools.' Occasionally these dustbins double as goal posts, but this activity is discouraged.

The Floor Often the 'black topped'[26] surface of the playground serves a similar use to that of the classroom blackboard. It contains inscribed instructions telling the children what to play: for instance, painted lines denoting games of hopscotch, dots, snakes and ladders, circles and squares.

> Head teacher: There are more pictorial lines on the playground for the children to walk on, play on …

> Interviewer: You think more lines are a good idea, do you?

> Head teacher: Yes I think it is those kind of things that create a playground, games, the squares, the snakes for them to follow, those kind of things that the children enjoy doing, you can see that, by them being put to good use at different times.

At this particular school, I never did see them playing with the painted snake in the infant playground. Nor did I observe the children in the junior section playing hopscotch or twister on the painted marks in the playground. Perhaps this lack of activity reflects a self-consciousness towards these markings. It recalls the words of Yi-Fu Tuan that 'a successfully designed playground is one in which the children are conscious only of their own kinaesthetic joy and the potential field for action. In such a setting, they are barely aware of the environmental design and equipment that make their activities possible.'[27] Some schools, though none in this study, paint murals on the external walls that enclose the playground. Again, this emulates artwork that is hung in the classroom. A professional artist or a teacher frequently paints these murals, yet if a child were to paint or draw on the walls or the tarmac without permission this would be viewed as graffiti. Moreover, research carried out by Learning through Landscapes (LTL) suggests that children are not nearly as enamoured by painted lines and murals as adults tend to think.[28] Finally, on the walls of one of the school playgrounds in the study, there are several painted metal signs issuing instructions to the children. One says 'The never, never club' and 'Say no to strangers'.

A Site of 'Gainful Activity'

The whole site of the playground could be viewed as a room for constructive learning. The engagement with constructive learning is paramount and exemplified because the activities of the playground are defined as either useful or time-wasting. McKendrick and Bradford argue that the 'time for play is being squeezed, at the behest of gainful activity'.[29] Certainly, it appears that adults quite often appear to have taken ownership of children's games. Games encouraged in the school playground are quite often insti-gated and monitored by the adults who govern, process and organize these games into packages, which they deliver to the children in an artificial format. South Somerset Museum in England is running a project in con-junction with Ash Primary School, Somerset, which involves a playtime scheme where they teach the children old traditional games, such as skip-ping and hopscotch. The government stated that it 'was looking to expand this scheme'.[30] In addition, a head teacher from Stoke-on-Trent proclaimed that 'children are being taught the time-honoured playground games because the games are there to make sure children do not idly waste away their time. Rather than having everybody chasing around, it is good to have them playing together.'[31] The ownership and administration of the chil-dren's games by adults suggests that the mastering of most of the games presented by teachers and others to children often has very little to do with spontaneous creative play. The mastery of the games by children is instru-mental to the teacher's goals and the institution's desired outcomes. Sutton-Smith suggests that this type of control is part of 'the experimental manip-ulations of childhood'.[32] Certainly in most of the cases I observed, the play activities encouraged were defined and regulated by the staff and tended to serve a useful rather than a playful purpose.[33] The Opies and Blatchford both make the point that 'over the past few decades many of the games and rhymes' of the school playground have 'become part of the mainstream cur-riculum in the early years'.[34] From this perspective, it would be easy to meld the activities of the playground into the activities of the classroom. There is little definition between the two areas.

Body Language

In the playground I saw many examples of how teachers and supervisory staff perceived children's natural behaviour as unacceptable, and watched them as they restructured and organized it in a similar way to that of the classroom. There was an expectation of propriety in the playground as well as the classroom. Language was often corrected and if a child swore, used a rude word, or told a poor joke in the hearing of an adult, s/he was always admonished. I watched one incident where a child pretended that he had a loose tooth, which meant that he acquired a lisp and said 'shit' instead of 'ship'. This performance was carried out with great hilarity in front of a new member of lunchtime staff.

Clothing and the way it was used also obsessed the supervisory staff. If cardigans, jumpers or coats were used to mark out football pitches and goal posts, this was forbidden. None of the staff could bear to see children lying on the ground while playing; they always told the children to get up as their clothes might get wet or dirty, or that they (the child) would get too cold. If the children looked dishevelled or chose to wear their coats as capes then, quite often, they were advised to put their clothes on 'properly'. Ostensibly with a concern for children's bodily welfare, children were told not take their clothes off or to put their clothes on. A great joy for the children during summer time was to take off their shoes, particularly when playing hand-stands and cartwheels. However a member of staff invariably rushed across and advised the children that they might cut their feet.

Lining up in 'tidy lines of twos' governed ends of playtime procedures. 'Let's show this lady how neat and tidy we are and stand in a nice straight line.' By using these strategies, staff members are able to maintain an appropriate bodily demeanour similar to that expected inside school. In this way staff are able to dictate how pupils should deport themselves in this space, teaching them to accept that appropriate behaviour for the play-ground must not be too dissimilar to that of the classroom.

Forms of Resistance

Nevertheless, while watching playtimes I was able to observe signs of what might be considered children's acts of resistance towards the school ethos, discipline and manipulations of childhood behaviour. Frequently children tended to ignore all the prescribed places and activities and gather in the corners of the playground where they could not be seen. Often in these places the children were observed playing with sand, grit, twigs, stones, insects and leaves. Here they were using their own imagination and initia-tive about what they did in the playground. Manhole covers and service boxes were another great source of fun. Boys and girls frequently sat, stood or jumped off the service boxes when the teachers and the midday assistants were not looking. Manhole covers were used as dens. Games of football terminated by the confiscation of the one and only football would restart with the kicking of stones, wallets or rolled up gloves. At one school one of the walls had a large sheet of metal attached and one of the favourite pas-times was to run at this sheet of metal and bang it as loudly as possible with the intention of frightening the staff on duty. Boys and girls would flout the rules by jumping on and off the field of grass bordering the tarmac; they would throw grass cuttings at each other in the summer and use over-hanging branches of trees as swings. Shoe-throwing contests became pop-ular at one school; at another, spitting the furthest reigned for a while. These examples highlight some of the ways in which children successfully reclaim some control over what goes on in the playground and what they do with their physicality.

Conclusion

A recurrent theme throughout my study has been the reconstruction of play-ground space and its activities in accordance with adults' wishes. James suggests that the playground may become 'an artificial device created by adults to keep the young in their place'.[35] Because of the external demands of prescriptive agents, school governors and parents, teaching and supervi-sory staff are feeling increasingly vulnerable at school and there appears to be a conflict between the needs of children and adults in the playground. Children allowed to play freely and unchecked will occupy and use play-ground space in very different ways. Children in this space wish to express themselves, to be spontaneous, to test their abilities and can tolerate a greater degree of flexibility, noise and chaos than adults appear to be able to tolerate – at least in schools. On the other hand, teachers, ancillary staff and the agencies responsible for the management of the playground, such as The Health and Safety Executive, Office for Standards in Education, and the Local Education Authorities, prefer an orderly atmosphere with a focus upon organized, restrained, productive, safe activity. My research reveals that there is significant evidence to suggest that the concerns of the latter are gaining ascendancy over the former.

This chapter has reviewed the way the playground can be 'read' and conceptualized. It has highlighted the way adults reconfigure the space through their management and organization of the activities and the occu-pants in the playground. Although there is a fluidity about the playground as it changes its use and serves different purposes, for instance physical education, sports or fire drill, and as a dropping-off and collecting point at each end of the school day, and most of all for playtime activities, there is a real inflexibility about its administration. Arguably, the playground is just another annex used for maintaining the daily routines of the school. This is because adults and other agencies have transgressed the boundaries of this space and contrived to manipulate and dominate it.

From one perspective the playground can be seen as a 'battleground' with 'both sides striving to capture the high ground'.[36] Yet in many respects, pupils have been forced to relinquish their right to a free and spontaneous self-governed playtime and this has had the effect of transforming the chil-dren's play site into another educational arena. Consequently, this has led to the erosion of one of the most established arenas that divide childhood from adulthood. The 'confined character' of the playground, plus the rules and surveillance of those who monitor it, 'constrains the freedom and flow of spontaneity'.[37] The management and domination of playtime by adults and the agencies that they represent has meant that our children seem to have lost yet another area of control in a space where one would have thought they would have had considerable autonomy. In many respects, there is very little that is liberating about breaktime at school.

Putting Bodies on the Line: Marching Spaces in Cold War Culture

CHARLOTTE MACDONALD

Marching and drill have long been the means by which men have been made into soldiers, individuals forged into a group, order and authority imposed on disparity. Spectacles of might and grandeur have been conjured from the highly orchestrated movements performed by precisely arranged ranks of people wearing identical (and often elaborate) uniforms; an impression that has commonly been deployed to demonstrate the power, prestige and status of a ruler, a regime or an organization. Straight lines, common movements executed on command, an exactitude in gait and posture, all make up the marching spectacle. As such, marching spaces are more often identified as military and ceremonial spaces than as sporting spaces. But marching has not only been confined to this realm in the twentieth century. From the mid 1940s to the 1970s, closely coordinated formation marching became a major competitive summer sport for girls and young women in New Zealand. In doing so it inverted several central categories of meaning, exposing tensions and competing interests in cold war culture. Competitive formation marching made drill a civilian rather than a soldier's routine, an activity for females rather than males, and a pursuit for sporting glory rather than state duty. Such disruptions and the spaces in which they occurred were not without challenge.

On 25 February 1958, page 3 of the *New York Times* carried the story of a 'fierce controversy' raging in distant New Zealand. What was in contention was girls' competitive marching. Likening marching to a 'cult' rather than a sport, critics condemned it as 'unnatural, unfeminine and ungraceful'; an activity in which participants moved in a style that resembled the goose-steppers and 'the strutters of dictatorships'.[1] What made it worse in the critics' eyes was marching's obvious popularity and high public profile. Just days before the story appeared, the national championship team, the Scottish Hussars, had taken a leading part in a prestigious civic ceremony welcoming Her Majesty, Queen Elizabeth, the Queen Mother, to Auckland at the beginning of her tour of the country (see Figure

6.1). Objecting to the choice of a marching team to represent the best of New Zealand's national life and femininity, critics were also troubled by the attraction which marching teams held for spectators. What element in the national psyche, they asked, causes 'New Zealanders to love the unlovely spectacle?'[2] Supporters, much greater in number than the critics, were quick to jump to marching's defence, asserting the 'clean, physically beneficial' character of the sport. Precision marching, they pointed out, promoted health, good posture, pride in appearance, friendship and team loyalty 'at a time when juvenile delinquency and street-corner lounging were causing concern'. Moreover, marching displays were attractive, giving enjoyment, and drawing the admiration of large numbers of people.[3]

The 1958 controversy was short-lived but, as a popular display sport, marching continued to enjoy a prominent space in public attention, especially in the decades spanning the cold war years. Running against the tendency for highly orchestrated formation marching to be discredited in the wake of the excesses of fascist regimes of the 1930s, marching became codified and highly organized as a sport for girls and young women in New Zealand in the immediate post-war period. In this form it occupied a cultural space where competing claims over the value and meaning of girls' marching, the body of 'the marching girl' (as participants were universally described[4]) and the character of the society which claimed the sport as uniquely its own, were fought out. Broader tensions between order and freedom, sexuality and discipline, geopolitical loyalties (British ties and sentiment versus US power in the world and the Pacific), tradition and modernity, and ritual and invention also underlay debates about this particular marching space.

In a recent discussion of drill and dance across a long span of human history, William H. McNeill proposes the term 'muscular bonding' to describe the experience of stepping out in time. He identifies a common, and beneficial, psychological response to this kind of body culture, one that has constituted a more significant part of 'human sociality' than is currently acknowledged.[5] Marching presents a vivid example of the way body cultures could come to define space, and space could be used to define and allow certain body cultures to flourish. As a display activity marching occupies public space – usually prominent and often privileged public space. Girls and young women claimed entry to this space through competitive formation marching as it developed and flourished in New Zealand in the mid twentieth century. Occupying such a position makes this phenomenon of marching a particularly rich subject for examining the enduring tensions in women's sport in negotiating the difficult terrain between spectacle for male gaze, athletic achievement and the creation of an autonomous female sporting realm. In this case that realm was additionally one in which the female participants could command the high level of public attention usually enjoyed by prominent male sports players. While New Zealand's competitive formation marching does bear some resemblance to other kinds of formation performances, such as cheerleading or American drum majorettes, it is quite distinct from them, having a very different evolution and purpose.[6] Competitive marching developed independently rather than as auxiliary activities or curtain raisers to other sporting events, matches or organizations. Marching was shaped from its beginning as a competitive sport. It was not to be done just for the sake of entertainment but for the purpose of competitive performance.

The history of the sport of marching roughly coincides with the decades of the cold war. Emerging in an organized form in 1945, flourishing in the 1950s and 1960s, by the 1980s the sport was fading fast and in the 1990s survived only in a few small pockets in attenuated form (notably in epic-scale public performances, including the annual Edinburgh Military Tattoo and similar 'show spectaculars'). It is now virtually extinct. While attempts were made to export the sport – principally to Australia and Great Britain – it remained largely a New Zealand phenomenon. In girls' marching there is an example of a localized variation on twentieth-century marching spaces. The subject provides a rich vein for the study of sport and space. Precision marching was dedicated to putting order on parade. In the sport of marching, *order* became a popular *sporting* goal for women and girls in the 1940s to 1960s. In the larger context the public display of order presented by girls' marching teams serves as a metaphor for wider conflicts of meaning in the post-war world. The chapter situates the sport of marching in the culture of the cold war, focusing particularly on what Elaine Tyler May has argued in relation to the United States as the 'symbolic connection' between anxieties about sexuality, gender and social order with 'the insecurities of the cold war era'.[7]

The sport of marching had its origins in New Zealand in the 1920s and 1930s. Groups of young women made appearances performing mass displays, often including an elaborately rehearsed marching on and off the field at the beginning and end of sports and show days. Some of these were shop, office and factory teams from business house sports competitions, others came from YWCA or church groups. But these were occasional and localized events with widely varying competitive bases rather than regular activities. Marching received a boost with the advent of widescale military training in the Second World War. Parade ground drill became routine for many people. Men with military experience but beyond the age for active service were co-opted into training positions with ancillary organizations: the home guard, women's auxiliaries and civilian groups eager to contribute to the war effort. Girls' marching received additional impetus from several women officers working in the Physical Welfare and Recreation Branch established in 1937 within a department of central government. Keen to increase participation by women and girls in sport, these officers saw marching as an ideal summer sport requiring little in the way of equipment or specialist facilities. They actively assisted in bringing the regional groups together in 1945 to form a national structure.[8] Within a short time marching as an activity was transformed into a sport with an organizational structure, a common set of rules, a national championship, a hierarchy of grades, judging panels and criteria, and a common set of conditions for competition.

Teams comprised ten members arranged in three columns of three, plus a leader who directed movements with whistle commands. Teams wore uniforms of their own choosing though guidelines were set that these were not to be too costly. The overall purpose was to produce a display of precision marching to a set march plan with judging according to a finely graded points schedule. From the foundation of the New Zealand Marching Association at a national level in 1945, girls marching quickly attracted a large number of competing teams participating in local, regional, island and national championships. Marching teams soon became regular features of annual and holiday street parades in towns and cities throughout the country. In numbers it rivalled tennis as the leading summer sport for girls

FIGURE 6.1

Simultaneously applauded for precision display and condemned for unfeminine 'strutting', members of the champion Scottish Hussars marching team step out on the Auckland Domain, New Zealand, as part of the Civic Welcome for the Queen Mother, February 1958. (National Publicity Studios Archives New Zealand, Alexander Turnbull Library, National Library of New Zealand, Wellington)

and young women through the 1940s and 1950s. By 1951 over 80 district marching associations had been formed; this was in a country with a total population of just under 2 million (2.4 million by 1961).[9]

For the first ten to fifteen years the judges, coaches and office holders in the sport were all men – many of them military or former military officers.[10] With pride rather than apology it was noted in 1951 that marching, 'though a girl's sport, is run for girls by men'.[11] The expertise of men as judges and coaches was perceived as elevating the status of the sport and ensuring competitors strove to attain the highest possible standards. The stature of competition and activity was also enhanced by the presence of politically powerful men at key championship events – the Prime Minister and leader of the major opposition political party were regular attendees at national championships. In 1941, at an early display, the Governor General (as the monarch's representative head of state) passed between lines of a guard of honour formed by girls' marching teams at Athletic Park in Wellington.[12] Participants were mostly 11–15 year old girls and young women aged 16–20 years, though pressure from younger would-be participants led to the establishment of a 'midget' grade for 7–11 year olds. Members of more successful teams were likely to stay on in older ages – into their early 20s, but the number of women who continued marching after they married was, in these years, very small. Those women involved in the sport, mostly mothers of girls in the teams, were kept occupied as makers of uniforms, managers and chaperones accompanying their 'girls' to competition as well as to practice sessions.

From the outset the marching routine was highly ceremonial and regimented. The style of uniforms reinforced the element of pageantry, with preferred designs echoing nineteenth-century British regimental styles (see Figure 6.2). Key elements were long-sleeved and high-collared tunics with prominent buttoning and braid, accentuated epaulettes, waist belts in contrasting colours, often with lanyards; hats were integral elements of the outfit with busbys, cockades, and high-fronted berets plus chin straps particularly popular styles.[13] Uniforms followed anachronistic styles but invested them with a modern meaning through colour (mauves, yellows and pinks) and in the young female bodies on which they were worn. Skirts were short and often pleated, the aim being to give maximum freedom and display to the legs, with white boots (and usually white gloves) drawing attention to the movements of feet and hands. Great efforts were made to achieve exemplary levels of presentation, with special care taken to ensure a team's uniform appearance despite the varying height and dimensions of those wearing them (skirt length, tunic length, sock length and hat angle were amongst the many details appraised by judges). The only exposed part of the body, the legs, were painted with tanning lotion to produce an even appearance.

FIGURE 6.2

Wearing thistles as emblems on their berets, members of the Balmoral marching team perform in December, 1953. The leader's lanyard carries a whistle to signal commands. In the later 1950s and 1960s uniforms became more structured (tunics with high collars rather than blouse tops) and accessories more elaborate – tasseled epaulettes, contrasting belts, double rows of brass buttons and vee-shaped braid on sleeves were all popular. (Alexander Turnbull Library, National Library of New Zealand)

Bodily appearance and movement defined a space as well as performance in a space that came to be designated as 'marching space'. March plans featuring wheeling, countermarching, echelon formations, quick time and slow time, diagonal march, independent file movement and various combinations of these were all practised endlessly on sports grounds and performed there and in street parades.[14] The style of marching emphasized movement in the shoulders and knees with swinging arms leaving the body trunk to maintain an upright stance, creating the effect of a single plane for the whole team of marchers. The movements required to perform formation marching were highly angular and rigid. They also required a rectilinear space in which to be performed. Straight lines, exact right angles, half, quarter and full turns were all calculated, practised and performed on spaces bounded by straight lines, intersecting diagonals, and 90 and 45 degree angles (see Figure 6.3). Each section of the body was intended to produce an echo of the exact angles achieved by the group stepping in formation: chin held parallel to the ground, head swivelling in precise angles to give a salute or in advance of a 'wheel' movement, the body held at exact right

FIGURE 6.3

An early marching team performing at a local agricultural show day, 1931. As girls' marching became organized as a competitive sport in the following decade teams of ten became the standard. (J.R. Wall Collection, Alexander Turnbull Library, National Library of New Zealand)

angles, arms and legs swinging in the same plane as the body. The eyes were to hold a level forward focus. To move as a single body was the goal – the body culture of straight lines, of orchestration, of linearity.

Compared with other women's sports and physical activities, marching was a severe aesthetic. Its abrupt geometry and command-directed movements created an impression of rigid formality rather than flexibility, grace or litheness. While promoters of marching emphasized the deportment, presentation and grooming skills of the sport, it was hardly the kind of everyday posture or dress that young women in the 1940s to the 1960s were likely to emulate outside the competition parade ground. And at the core was the competitive goal, promoting rivalry between females over appearance. An extreme degree of control and precision was required to achieve the exact length and height of step, swing of arm, closing of hands to expose the right hand knuckles, facial expression, etc. While a sense of rhythm and some fitness was required to execute the routines, it was not really a test of muscular strength or endurance but rather of memorizing moves and achieving a high level of control. The skill was in following routine, suppressing individuality.

In this sporting form, as well as in its military form, marching space easily lent itself to national meaning. Marching space could also be national space. As an indigenous activity girls' marching came to have a representative significance. In the 1950s in particular, marching teams commonly featured in presentations of national culture. The civic welcome to the Queen Mother in 1958 was just one of these and typical of the period in its show of loyalty to Britain and royalty (see Figure 6.4), yet indicative that such links required more emphatic articulation in the face of declining real power and security in the British connection.

When the prize-winning Blair Athol team toured Britain in 1952 they were much more than sporting representatives: the finesse in their demonstrations was designed to impress the value of marching as a sport on their hosts and encourage emulation. Girls' marching was a cultural addition to New Zealand's contribution of primary produce exports (meat, wool and butter) to post-war Britain's reconstruction project. More importantly, the New Zealand girls' marching teams – on tour in Great Britain *and* in New Zealand – made a powerfully symbolic parade of the historic and enduring ties between the old country and the new. The choice of Scottish and English regimental and aristocratic nomenclature (Scottish Hussars, Kensington Guards, Lochiel, Grenadier Guards, Balmoral, Blair Athol), regalia (busbys, tartans, etc.), music and march plans indicated a direct

FIGURE 6.4

Pomp and ceremony completed, members of the 1958 Scottish Hussars team were reported to have 'chatted' with the Queen Mother at the conclusion of the Welcome. Prominent feather cockades adorn the marcher's berets while medal panels worn across the front of the tunics testify to the participants' competitive achievements. (National Publicity Studios Collection, Archives New Zealand, Alexander Turnbull Library, National Library of New Zealand)

borrowing of traditions.[15] But in the performance by young women was signalled a demonstration of how innovation on tradition was possible in a
former colony, now an independent but unquestionably loyal ally. Britain
was still referred to commonly as 'the Mother Country', leaving the possibility for New Zealand to adopt the personification of loyal daughter.

In the immediate post-war years marching served to reaffirm the place
of Great Britain to New Zealanders in the face of a rapidly shifting world
order. The old ties of empire and British greatness may have faded but the
cultural links were reinforced, gaining particular impetus through the
unprecedented popularity of the royal family following young Queen
Elizabeth the Second's ascension to the throne.[16] As David Cannadine has
argued, the place of ritual and pageantry was never as important to the
British monarchy as in the period when real power was at its lowest ebb.
Royal ceremony and tradition flourished in the era of monarchical weakness.[17] Marching spaces of the kind created in New Zealand became a place
for inventing a tradition, an element of national culture displaying the particular tensions of the country's situation in a post-war world order – caught
uncomfortably between ties to Britain and a new recognition of the USA as
the major defence power for a country located in the south Pacific.

While a 'young' and loyal nation might be construed as a female subject, women's formation marching inverted the usual identification of
marching space as militarist and thereby masculine space. Gender identity
was disrupted, but the disruption can be read in a variety of ways. As a
simple inversion, the presence of young women on the parade ground could
have simply confirmed the prevailing definition of this space as a masculine domain. A female incursion into such space served to heighten the masculinist definition by making women appear ridiculous, exceptional, temporary and non-serious, if not burlesque, imposters; an instance in which
the inversion underlines the hegemonic meaning. Alternatively, if post-war
marching by young women and girls is placed within an argument which
sees the Second World War as expanding the scope of women's citizenship
in political, economic, social and cultural terms, then it can be read as
allowing women a peacetime role – of a solely symbolic kind – in
defending the state. Whichever meaning was taken, competitive marching
certainly represents a complication to any blanket application that the post-
war decades were about the emergence of a hyper-femininity or reassertion
of domestic femininity.

Marching teased at definitions of military and civilian, masculine and
feminine, allowing these to be entangled and oddly combined. Versions of
hyper-masculinist military marching performed by scantily skirted young
women created a captivating spectacle of exaggerated gender dichotomy.
Public performance presented a powerful place for the representation, if not
resolution, of gendered identities and meanings.

The success of marching in the post-war era can be attributed to the way in which it presented an improbable but acceptable set of connections between military preparedness and gender identity. Girls and young women marching to military routines both 'normalized' the military impositions which had become an intensely familiar part of life of the war years and at the same time rendered them innocuous. Marching was full of the accoutrements of power and symbols of authority, yet was performed by girls and young women who were the antithesis of power or authority. The bodies of girls and young women were far removed from the trained combat forces or technical engineers of modern warfare. At the same time, military preparedness among a group least likely to be drawn into direct combat acknowledged that the war zone was pervasive when attack by atomic weapons was the anticipated form of future warfare. The archaic uniform styles, the short skirts and white boots marked 'marching girls' as purely decorative and unmistakably feminine elements in a parade. Yet the discipline required to execute the moves *did* suggest that, if needed, these young people would be able to step forward and 'do their bit' if national security was threatened.

While geographically remote, the impact of the cold war was felt directly in New Zealand at political and defence levels, as well as in more diffuse social and cultural patterns. A high level of insecurity pervaded the late 1940s and early 1950s. Peacetime conscription was introduced in 1949 bringing military service to a country that had little tradition of maintaining a regular defence force, relying instead on voluntary call-up at times of need. As this occurred Labour Prime Minister Peter Fraser confirmed New Zealand's commitment to send fighting units in the event of war breaking out again in Europe – as it had done in 1914 and again in 1939. In 1950 New Zealand forces fought in Korea and in 1951 New Zealand, along with Australia, signed a defence treaty with the United States (known as the ANZUS Treaty) in order to add the buttress of security in the Pacific to its existing defence arrangements with Great Britain. In the 1950s New Zealand forces served in Malaya, Borneo and Singapore, before becoming involved in Vietnam in 1964 (the numbers were small but the political support was significant; it was the first war in which New Zealanders did not fight alongside British troops).[18]

Marching teams were never expected to perform a directly defensive function, but like other uniformed youth movements of the mid twentieth century they were regarded as providing initial experience for young people in learning to value a sense of group identity, belonging and pride.[19] The development of marching as a team sport for girls and young women was part of the general proliferation of female sporting opportunities in the mid twentieth century but its distinctive characteristics were derived from the circumstances of the Second World War. Wartime demands which drew women into economic production as workers, into direct war service in armed force auxiliaries, and under the broad ambit of civilian life constrained by wartime priorities, led to their inclusion in national life to a greater degree than had been recognized previously, and with it came enhanced status as citizens. That enhanced status found the strongest symbolic expression in the prestige associated with service and occupational uniforms worn during the war years. Marching survived beyond the war as a legacy of this symbol of expanded citizenship. On the one hand, marching carried into the post-1945 era the sense of female potential and capacity that women had demonstrated during the war years. On the other hand, it rendered that form of expanded citizenship into an acceptable form for the return to 'normal' peacetime existence by shaping a form of femininity which emphasized an orderly, decorative and appearance-oriented identity, highly differentiated from a masculine identity. It was also a femininity that admitted a sexual component but placed it in an overwhelming framework of control that allowed observation from afar, and denied individual engagement or individual expression, thereby containing its power. The female body was admitted to be feminine and sexual, but could not be viewed individually or allowed expression individually. The message was control.

In the uniforms worn by marching girls the two rather contradictory elements of military preparedness and a decorative (almost flirtatious) femininity came together. The incongruities of the military-style upper half of the body with the feminine lower half presented a kind of sartorial oxymoron. Much of the popular appeal to contemporary spectators came from this spectacle of improbably juxtaposed signs. Among the minority who viewed marching with distaste or outright hostility, the incongruities carried burlesque or more sinister overtones of authoritarian or fascist groups' preference for displays of gross inequalities in power. To these people, a tiny but at times vocal minority, there was something unhealthy, at the very least, in older men exercising power of command and judgement over groups of pubescent girls. For the promoters of the sport, however, eager to recruit participants, and the thousands of spectators who watched marching parades and competitions, the marching teams' uniforms were strong attractions.

Compared with the predominantly dull and unshapely school and sports uniforms and outfits prescribed for girl guides and girls' brigade members which were worn by the majority of girls in the 1940s, 1950s and 1960s (boxy and unfashionable gym frocks), marching uniforms were original and held a certain allure. Highly coloured, modern in fabric and associated with a degree of glamour or 'snazz', they were emphatically decorative and dramatic. They signalled 'smartness' and 'importance' rather than either the drabness of other uniforms, or the feminine softness of pastel shades, floral patterns and curvy styles characteristic of 1950s female clothing. They could almost be seen as costumes for a pageant rather than unexciting uniforms imposed by authoritarian figures such as school mistresses or Guide commissioners. Being part of a marching team opened up the possibility of dressing up rather than being forced into an expectation set by a distant authority. The sense of importance bestowed by the wearing of marching uniforms was reinforced by the marching drill, the whistle commands, pipe and band music and the setting of the public parade in which teams featured prominently. Being on display, being watched and admired in this way held considerable attraction. Uniforms were also highly important in defining the space in which a particular body culture was performed, as well as in asserting the group presence.

The adoption of similar marching uniforms across all grades had the effect of obscuring the distinctions of age. A 'marching girl' could be anyone from age 8 to 28. The uniform, the team identity and the regimented movement combined highly contradictory elements of the short skirts of childhood with the tunics, elaborate hats, commands and strong movements of adulthood. The kind of femininity conveyed was one which suggested that females – of any age – were both girls and women, innocent and knowing, sexual objects and untouchable. If marching uniforms and their wearers were not at all intended to be taken seriously as military auxiliaries, they conveyed a sexualized girlishness along with an impression of good conduct and order.

The form of military dress incorporated in the marching uniforms did not threaten the authority or legitimacy of contemporary armed forces. It was archaic compared with the utilitarian style and khaki and subdued colours adopted by twentieth-century forces. The contrast with the uniforms worn by women's auxiliary forces in the Second World War are also striking. The Second World War women's uniforms were generally modified forms of male battle dress where the alterations were carefully negotiated in order to ensure that male ranking and status was not compromised by the women's service. The generally drab and concealing women's Second World War uniforms were perceived as endangering the gender identity of their wearers by being 'too masculine', or by having a 'desexing' effect. Marching uniforms were carefully contrived declarations of their wearers' femininity.

Beyond that femininity, the marchers' appearance, for all its elaborateness and exemplary appearance, was surprisingly devoid of wider ideological content. Order and a uniform appearance existed largely as a goal in isolation. Removing military parade drill to the sportsground, and to performance by young women, changed its meaning, placing it in the ostensibly politically neutral world of play rather than politics. As a sport, marching focused wholly on order, appearance and conformity in executing precise movement. It was physical activity devoid of *explicit* ideological meanings and symbols: team members did not carry insignia of national, territorial, religious or political groups, nor did they salute flags or figure-heads, swear oaths of allegiance or enter into a shared code of behaviour. Unlike other contemporary youth movements such as Girl Guides and Brownies, Boy Scouts and Cubs, Girls and Boys Brigades, or YM and YWCAs, marching team uniforms and routines were not invested with broader significance signalling adherence to a broader movement or purpose (to be good citizens, to do good turns, to perform service to others, to develop loyalty to queen or country). In competitive marching, stepping in line became highly reified.

In the pursuit of the physical achievement of precision movement and the defence of marching against detractors overwhelming value was placed on order and conformity as goals in themselves. These formed criteria by which marching teams' routines were judged in an elaborate array of points allocated to stages in the march plan, to the leader and each member of a team. But the model of order they presented was also one imbued with moral and social value.

The discipline required of individual marchers was defended as a desirable training. The order achieved through team practice and expertise was also the order and discipline that individual team members could, and were expected to, exercise over themselves. Being a successful member of a marching team required an exercise of will power, of inner control.[20] Despite team effort, team success relied on a very high level of individual discipline, performance and concentration. Self-discipline meant turning up at practice, remembering numbers of steps and moves, wearing uniforms correctly, moving arms, legs, hands and holding the head and body correctly. Successful marching was, to a degree, dependent on mastering discipline *over* the body. Individual expression was to be suppressed, team cohesion and uniformity was uppermost. The well-kept body signalled a 'good character' and a good citizen. The pubescent body was to be shown to be under higher control. It was not a wild entity, a subject to forces beyond its control, but was to be kept under restraint.

The female sport of marching, in instilling and displaying order and bodily control, was in diametric opposition to the prevailing function of sport as promoted for boys and young men at this time. As a physically combative sport, rugby union football, the predominant game in New Zealand, was seen as highly beneficial as a cathartic outlet. Playing sport, and rugby in particular, was regarded as an excellent way to channel excess energy, sexual or social, which might find unacceptable (illicit or even illegal) expression if not vented on the sports field. In this sense a certain degree of giving way to disorder on the sports field ensured the maintenance of order away from it.[21]

Girls' marching attracted strong support from individual adults and influential organizations for its capacity to teach discipline and order through proper conduct. When called to defend the sport against criticism that marching was over-regulated and unsuitable for girls, supporters most often pointed to the value in girls and young people learning 'discipline'. In a literal sense this referred to the exacting movements and routines of the march plan, but it also referred to the broader sense of discipline learned through belonging to a team, learning to subordinate individual will and being subject to instruction and the strictures of team discipline, leaders, coaches and managers. Order achieved over the body, and over the sexually maturing pubescent body, as well as a broader sense of social order, all served as rationales for recruitment into marching.

Such arguments held strong appeal in the face of disturbing evidence of social and sexual disorder lurking beneath the prosperous and otherwise apparently placid surface of 1950s suburban life. Three notorious incidents involving the country's 'youth' rocked certainties about the level of social cohesion and moral order, stirring anxieties that cold war insecurities in the wider world might also be eroding the domestic fabric of the society (as has also been argued in the American setting[22]). The first was the violent murder of a Christchurch woman in a premeditated attack by her daughter and her daughter's close friend in June 1954. The two girls were aged 15 and 16 at the time of the incident.[23] Between the murder and the time the case went to trial came alarming revelations that teenagers in the Hutt Valley (an area of large suburban development on the margins of the capital city, Wellington) were indulging in high levels of sexual promiscuity in public places, especially after school and on weekends and evenings. The fears of an underlying social malaise unleashed by the Hutt Valley revelations were taken very seriously by the government of the day, which proceeded to instigate a major inquiry into the allegations, chaired by a senior judge. A copy of the resulting report (the 'Mazengarb Report') was delivered to every household in the country.[24] A year later social peace was dealt a further shocking blow by the sensational shooting of a young woman by a 19-year-old youth outside a city milk bar, this time in Auckland. After this time those referred to as 'milk bar cowboys' were no longer considered simply rather annoying idle layabouts but represented a more menacing presence.

There was clearly a fear that beneath the breaches of social order was the prospect of widespread sexual disorder. The reaction to such a threat was not so much one of moral outrage (though there was some of that), but rather a suspicion that, if not stemmed firmly, there was the prospect of deeper pathology or chaos. The response was not to deny sexuality but to channel and order it; in this setting it was women's responsibility to regulate 'how far a man could go' and to exercise self restraint while encouraging and upholding heterosexual conventions and interest during the years between sexual maturity and marriage. In this sense the contradictory elements within femininity encompassed in marching were perfectly in congruence. Discipline over the body was an important model to instil.

As well as these sensational events, there were also the lower level pervasive changes in style and culture signalled by the advent of (and alarmed reaction to) rock and roll music, including New Zealand's answer to Elvis Presley – a man named Johnny Devlin, whose sobriquet was 'the Satin Satan' – and the release of the James Dean film *Rebel without a Cause*.[25] Rather differently (being more local in cause), but equally unsettling, was the appearance in the main cities, Auckland pre-eminently, of young Maori who had moved to the towns from country areas as part of what was referred to at the time as 'urban drift' (in fact it was one of the fastest urbanizations of a population in twentieth-century history).[26] Many of these young Maori men and women found themselves discriminated against in finding houses and jobs, and in trouble with the law. The cities, long associated with dangers as well as excitements, became the location for what came to be termed 'Maori problems'. Social order, including gender, generational, racial and class relations, was under threat from a number of directions.

There was an underlying fear among some sections of society that the newly grown suburban areas full of state housing were places where pathological social patterns were breeding, or where healthy ties between young and old, men and women, young men and women, etc., were failing to take hold. New houses and roads had been built – the structure of a new community, but not the necessary fabric; the intangible but essential sinews of social order and institutions had failed to take root.[27] A new form of social order would have to be built, and sports, amongst them the healthy modern activity of marching, could be one of those forces for binding a community together. In this marching could claim success, though it was one the Association itself played down. The majority of marching participants were drawn from the less affluent new suburbs in the major cities and the low to middle sections of provincial towns.

The demise of marching from its heyday in the late 1940s to the 1960s was the consequence of a number of interconnecting factors. Public parades and the prestigious status of uniforms had lost a good deal of popular appeal as television took over as entertainment, and informal and dissident attire became youthful fashion. Official endorsement for the sport faded and the cultural resonances – especially the links with Britain – became less important to a generation which regarded itself as independent in culture rather than off shore Britons. Rival sporting codes and more interesting and varied outdoor pursuits drew participants away from what was increasingly seen as a rather arcane and overly regulated activity. Through the 1970s and beyond, marching teams gradually ceased to exist in many parts of the country. Increasingly, they came to be seen as subjects of curiosity rather than ordinary parts of New Zealand life. While a very small number of teams were competing in the 1990s, the most successful team, Lochiel, survives as an entertainment rather than a sporting group.

Girls' marching, though transient and local, was a highly successful sport. For several decades the model of young women performing orderly routines in a military but feminine manner was one which attracted popular public support and official legitimacy. Marching space was transformed into sporting space. It was a space constituted by a set of sharply defined relations: between male directors and female subordinates; between adults and young people; between judges and competitors; between autonomous individuals and those identified by group. But there was also in the relation of performers and spectators the double-sided relation of the gaze.

Whether in competition or on public parade, teams were under the scrutiny of judges (mostly male) and the community en masse. The gaze was not returned directly. But perhaps there were ambiguities in the exchange. That this was a one-way power relationship can be questioned. Do the marching teams represent an example of the submission of the female body, in this case, a sexualized youthful body, to the judging, possessing eye of men? Or was there, in the ordered, semi-authoritative and publicly parading performance of the marching team girls and young women, a position of power and a measure of enjoyment. They could occupy centre stage, drawing admiration without the complications of individual engagement. Was this, for both sides – performers and spectators – an enjoyable or at least accepted place in which gender, class and social tensions could find expression?

In the broader ambit of cultural space, the sport exemplified the desire for order in a post-war society in which security and freedom, civilian and military, individual and the group, sexual and gender identities had all been thrown into new dimensions. The straight line was an appealing, and strong, expression of order. It also takes a good deal of effort to achieve and sustain in a column of humans moving in concert. Marching gave a reassurance, if only ephemeral, that some certainties were within reach.

Acknowledgements

Generous thanks are due to Linda Borish, who convened the panel and offered a commentary on the first rehearsal of some of these ideas at the NASSH Conference in 2000, and to my fellow panelists: Gerd van der Lippe, Annette Hofmann, Patricia Vertinsky, Manuela Hasse and Roberta Park. The financial assistance of the Faculty of Humanities and Social Sciences, Victoria University of Wellington, and excellent research assistance of Derek Clear, are also gratefully acknowledged.

Homebush:
Site of the Clean/sed and
Natural Australian Athlete

TARA MAGDALINSKI

When Sydney was awarded the 2000 Olympic Games in 1993, its success was, in part, based on its commitment to an 'environmentally friendly', 'athletes' games', an event that was unpolluted and unpolluting.[1] The extensive marketing of Sydney relied on images that presented Australia as a wild landscape with extremes of both climate and geography: 'Australia. A country of contradictions. Vast and uncrowded. Modern and highly urbanized ... Parched red desert and endless golden summer grasses. Lush primeval green rainforest adjacent to sparkling sandy beaches. Rugged blue mountains and dazzling white snowfields.'[2] At the same time, the emphasis on environmental restoration was mirrored in attempts to reclaim a lost Olympic innocence and to ensure the legitimacy of the athletic contest. Such a pristine location was considered an appropriate site for the Games, predicated as they are on 'healthy' bodies engaging in wholesome play. To this end, the Sydney Olympics were promoted as the 'Green' Games at the same time that Australian sporting authorities assured the public that stringent doping controls would be applied. Consumers were thereby reminded that the natural/Olympic environment was being recovered whilst the sporting results were guaranteed to be the sole outcome of an athlete's pure bodily performance.

The representation of 'natural' bodies competing in 'natural' activities in a 'natural' landscape was primary to the Sydney 2000 Olympic Games. Within the official Sydney Organizing Committee for the Olympic Games (SOCOG) image guidelines, related merchandising and the televisual media, the Australian landscape played a dominant role in Olympic promotional activities. Australia was popularly conceptualized as an environmental paradise in which healthy play could be guaranteed, and the vocal, national stance against 'unnatural' intrusions into elite athletic competition meant that Sydney could provide the requisite assurances that the Games would remain pure and untainted on a number of levels. Within the production of these landscapes, the relationships between the body, the Olympic site and the Australian nation were revealed. What is important in this analysis is the way that the construction of an uncontaminated athletic body was mirrored in the manufactured 'nature' of Homebush Bay, which in turn was represented as a microcosm of the national environment.

I argue here that the discourses surrounding Homebush Bay as a remediated environmental site had a dual function: spectators were reminded that Australian Olympic authorities had constructed an Olympic site in/as a broader natural paradise, whilst implementing a stringent process to restore the 'natural' athlete to his or her rightful place. It is clear that this process rests on assumptions about the integrity of sporting performance and the naturalness of competitors, which negates the obvious 'construction' of sporting abilities through training and other bodily modifications. At the same time, assurances about 'natural' competition bespeak an underlying confidence in the notion of 'fair play', an ideal central to 'Olympism' but one that ultimately ignores the structural elements of competition, achievement and success. This chapter thus examines the role of 'nature' and the 'natural' in our understanding of athletes and athletic bodies, and how the conception of the natural athlete is replicated in the site of the athletic event as well as extended to reflect the validity and authenticity of the national project. By focusing on Homebush Bay and the Sydney 2000 Olympics, it is possible to identify a metonymic relationship between the athletic body and the Australian nation for which it stands. At the same time, both the nation and the body are reproduced in assurances about the cleanliness of the Homebush Bay site.

Analysing the relationship between space, sport and the body in this context reveals a plethora of cultural assumptions about the nature of 'nature'. The presence of natural bodies in a natural site was a paramount concern in not only Olympic advertising but among the sporting fraternities themselves, and the success of the event hinged on selling the Games as a return to traditional values that eschewed extreme bodily modifications. 'Nature', as embodied in the 'natural athlete' or the 'environment', thus became central to an understanding of not just the Sydney Games, but of modern sport itself. Neil Smith argues that 'the authority of "nature" as a source of social norms derives from its assumed externality to human interference, the givenness and inalterability of natural events and processes that are not susceptible to social manipulation'.[3] The success of sport rests upon the pure physical performance unaffected by any kind of external interference. The body, in this instance, is isolated from social construction, alone in its pursuit of physical proficiency. The irony here is that neither the body, the site nor the nation are free from manipulation: each are subject to both discursive and physical interference and interpretation.

By contrast, the notion of landscape embodies the 'natural' world as well as its interaction with human influences. Paul Groth states that 'cultural landscape studies focus most on the history of how people have used *everyday* spaces … to establish their identity, articulate their social relations, and derive cultural meaning'.[4] An analysis of Homebush Bay provides an insight into the way that the Olympic site produced meanings about the Australian landscape, contributing thereby to the reaffirmation of traditional elements of Australian identity, at the same time that it confirmed broader Olympic ideals and philosophies. Although nature is privileged in the sporting world, the relationship between nature and culture is more revealing and as such I use the concept of 'landscape' to denote a geographical realm (Homebush Bay) as well as a bodily terrain (athletes). Landscape, in this sense, refers neatly to the organic 'natural' quality of both body and site, while remaining cognisant of their cultural constructedness. Nadia Lovell further suggests that 'landscapes are inscribed onto bodies through the mutual positioning of humans within nature and nature within society'.[5] Thus, both spaces and bodies represent surfaces onto which a multitude of meanings can be mapped.

In his analysis of sporting landscapes, John Bale argues that 'sportscapes' are always subject to interpretation as they are 'mythical landscapes, projecting a particular image, sometimes with an explicit purpose in mind'.[6] What is important about Bale's assertions is that the meanings embodied in a sportscape are as much a construction as the venue itself. His revelation that sportscapes are ideologically informed proves instructive, for after all it is the mythical Olympic landscape that is central to this chapter. Homebush Bay provides an excellent example of the way that athletic spaces can be imbued with iconic meanings that extend beyond the bounds of the stadium and encompass not just an athletic but a national typology in their image. Indeed, the environmental ideology embodied in the Homebush Bay site was promulgated through the surveillance and regulation of Olympic bodies.

Building a Natural Landscape: Homebush Bay

Selling the 2000 Olympic Games as the 'Green Games' linked athletic bodies through sport to a mythology that regards the 'Australian spirit' as intimately connected with the bush and thus with the natural/national environment. For over two centuries, the landscape, and people's interaction with it, has been at the centre of non-indigenous Australia's search for a distinctive identity.[7] The Olympic vision promulgated by the Sydney Bid team was of Australia as a natural and unpolluted environmental paradise, an 'ancient and mysterious land',[8] where the youth of the world could gather to play without the threat of contamination. This ideology was celebrated in an Opening Ceremony that depicted Australia's natural landscape conquered and tamed by European progress, an integral part of the nation's 'pioneering legend',[9] as well as in the official corporate 'image' of the Sydney Olympics, which confirmed the presence of clean, pure, natural bodies in clean, pure, natural sites:

> In the cities, parks, forests and valleys, seas, lakes, rivers and pools, athletes relentlessly train. Fresh oxygen powers through their blood. Pure water quenches their thirst. A clean environment provides them with their most precious asset – the opportunity to excel.[10]

Despite representing Sydney and, by extension Australia, as a pristine environment, the Olympic site at Homebush Bay was built on a toxic waste dump, the result of decades of unfettered pollution by heavy industry. Although the level of environmental degradation was known prior to the Games (indeed staging the Olympics was integral to the Bay's 'regeneration'), the event remained steadfastly and popularly 'green'.

The restoration of Homebush Bay sought not only to develop 'environmentally sustainable' sporting facilities but also to rejuvenate the surrounding 'natural' habitats, thereby providing a 'legacy' for the people of Sydney. The city's civic boosters and local councils had identified the Olympic Games in the early 1970s as a vehicle to promote the city's profile on a 'world stage', presenting Sydney as a centre for Asia-Pacific commerce and a destination for tourists. Originally targeting the 1988 Olympics to coincide with the Australian bicentennial celebrations, the New South Wales State Government initially selected a potential site in Sydney's eastern suburbs. After protests from affluent residents, however, it was determined that Homebush Bay would serve the government's Olympic strategy instead.[11]

Homebush Bay was an ideal site. It was located in the heart of Sydney, close to public transport, and was a state-owned parcel of land, which meant that the construction of a sporting precinct did not require the repossession of parkland and homes, as had been suggested in the previous proposal.[12] Whilst it was a suitable location for sporting facilities, the site's history as variously an abattoir, brickworks and munitions dump meant that the ground was unstable as well as highly polluted. According to Greenpeace, around 9 million cubic metres of waste were dumped in the area, which filled over 160 hectares of natural wetlands in both Homebush and Wentworth Bays. Homebush Bay subsequently became the only waterway in Australia where fishing is banned as a result of the high levels of dioxin poisoning.[13] Despite the significant outlay required to remediate Homebush Bay, its waters were portrayed in Bid documents as 'serene' and 'glistening', and the site was ratified as the venue for a future Olympic Games.

Sydney's bid for the 2000 Games was launched amidst a growing awareness of the potential links between sustainability and sporting endeavours, as well as at a time when environmental issues were gaining greater exposure through the world's media. The International Olympic Committee (IOC) was under enormous pressure to adopt environmentalism as a 'third arm' of the movement's philosophy of Olympism, along with sport and culture. The Albertville 1992 Winter Olympics had been soundly criticized for the destruction wreaked upon the pristine Alpine village in France, and protesters insisted that the Lillehammer Games of 1994 be organized according to 'green' principles.[14] Environmental advocates increasingly pointed out that sporting and leisure pursuits, particularly those designed to take advantage of the 'outdoors', were having a devastating effect on natural areas, both in terms of actual physical degradation as well as the polluting effects of large numbers of participants and spectators.[15]

Sydney Olympic Bid Limited (SOBL), the company established to bid for the Games, quickly recognized the expediency of relying on 'green' rhetoric, and what was originally dubbed the 'Athletes' Games', also acquired the 'Green Games' epithet. After winning the bid in 1993, many of the environmentally sustainable initiatives that had been proposed were shelved in favour of more cost-efficient construction methods and materials.[16] Whilst the proposed 'eco-village' all but disappeared, the perception of the Green Games remained, reinforced by a plethora of 'environmental fact sheets' on the web pages of the Olympic Coordination Authority, SOCOG, and a host of other Olympic-related organisations. In addition, the image of the Green Games was strengthened by SOCOG's relentless imagery of the unparalleled beauty and purity of the Australian landscape.

Landscape and Australian Identity

The desire to showcase Australia's natural beauty as part of the Olympic bid is not without precedent. Since European occupation, the Australian land has been interpreted in radically different ways. Europeans had long imagined a 'Great South Land', an antipodean 'Other', whose landscape was regarded after settlement as variously a 'pastoral Arcadia, as a bushland for utopian reverie, and as refuge for romantic escapists', each of which contributed to the presentation of Australia as 'an unproblematic exotic essence'.[17] By the late nineteenth century, writers, poets and artists, influenced by an emerging nationalism, sought to define 'Australianness' and saw a distinctive national identity embodied in an outback lifestyle that was narrated as quintessentially Australian.[18] Harsh and uncompromising, the land was represented as a virgin territory in need of conquering, taming and modifying, and popular images of the outback portrayed a hostile environment, ready to swallow the intrepid explorer should he (and it was always a he) stand still even for a moment.[19] The landscape has thus provided a point of reference for Australians, a means of distinguishing themselves from both the imperial centre and other colonial territories and as a way of forging an identity based on their responses to the challenges of the outback.[20] Since the late nineteenth century Australians have celebrated their native flora and fauna as a marker of difference and as a source of national collective identification[21] and these versions of Australia find resonance in contemporary tourist campaigns that reproduce an image of the nation as an exotic refuge, an empty land full of geological and climatic wonders.

Confirmed by the success of movies such as *Crocodile Dundee*, the Australian landscape has come to dominate the popular global conception of Australia and, as such, the concept of a green, environmentally friendly Olympic Games was not far removed from many of these oft-displayed images. In North America and elsewhere, images of a rugged outback sparsely peopled with laid-back Aussies are coupled with images of the rainforest, Great Barrier Reef and coastal and tropical regions. Australia represented a *terra nullius*, a land largely empty of people but replete with expansive and varied terrains, open to consumption by both tourist and tele-visual voyeur. These images contributed to a popular understanding of Australia by global audiences as an environmental paradise and were reinforced by Olympic advertising, tourist strategies and popular entertainment, such as *Survivor II: The Australian Outback* or *The Crocodile Hunter*.

The primacy of the landscape in constructing a suitable national vision of Australia was evident at the Opening Ceremony of the 2000 Olympic Games, where the spectacular diversity of Australia's flora and fauna was gradually tamed under the yoke of industrial progress. From the ethereal Barrier Reef to the harsh landscape destroyed by fire and the re-emergence of flowers and bushland thereafter, Australia's topography was stylized and inhabited with appropriate iconic beasts. Thomas Dunlap reveals that traditionally Australian flora and fauna was used to delineate the nation from its northern hemisphere counterparts.[22] More recently, however, as native plants and animals are increasingly globalized (one can buy wattle in Berlin or see koalas in San Diego), indigenous cultures are used to represent national difference and distinction.[23] Thus, Aboriginal Australians in the Opening Ceremony appeared together with other national 'natural' emblems and were thereby confirmed as mere 'inhabitants' of the bush. Indigenous Australians were embedded in this natural realm and featured as part of an ancient land, an historic people 'linked to the dawn of man'. Yet

after thoughtfully 'moving aside' to facilitate European occupation, indigenous Australians had little role to play in the ceremony. Akin more to the
kangaroo than the white settler, their status as a distinctive 'feature' of the
Australian landscape reaffirmed the status of the 'Great South Land' as an
empty space.

The montage of images and sounds, voiced over by James Earl Jones,
presented at the start of the Opening Ceremony on US network NBC set the
immediate tone for the international consumer of the Sydney Olympics:

> Terra Australis incognita. The unknown Southern land. An island con-
> tinent where all around the sea pummelled the shore with a beautiful
> fury. With beaches guarded by towering rocks carpeted by the whitest
> sands, a place where there was a reef more than a thousand miles long,
> sheltering a jungle of underwater life, a place where geography was
> made gigantic, where there stood a monolith, one hundred million
> years old, a seemingly infinite wilderness, a land of living fossils,
> occupied by a proud culture, linked to the dawn of man. A land where
> a city would be settled among sheltering coves, where a spectacular
> metropolis would wrap itself around a glistening harbour. Where a
> daring structure, perched on the waters, announced the none-too-
> subtle ambitions of a bold restless people.[24]

The Opening Ceremony was a key part of an overall strategy to develop
an appropriate 'face' of Australia that would attract both investment and
tourists. In fact, these celebrations were the culmination of a direct marketing campaign that sold 'Brand Australia' to an international audience
and were regarded as integral to the success of these promotional efforts:
'Key aspects of Brand Australia were evident throughout the Games, for
example the Opening and Closing Ceremonies emphasized Australia's natural environment and its free spirited and optimistic people.'[25] Links
between the Australian Tourist Commission and various members of the
Olympic family, including sponsors and host broadcasters, ensured that
Australia featured in news pieces, documentaries, feature stories and advertisements in key international markets in the years leading up to the Games.

Despite the use of landscape images that resonated with international
tourist markets, during the preparations for the Olympics Australia's repu-
tation as a natural environment was juxtaposed against the reality of its
highly urbanized culture. The enduring images of Australia's landscape
would certainly sell 'Brand Australia' to an international audience of
travellers, but the additional mission for the Sydney Games was to present
Australia as a desirable location for regional, if not global, corporate headquarters. Bid documents thus depicted Australia as a technologically competent nation capable of staging this and other global events. To satisfy the

demands of both the corporate and tourist industries, the nation was summarized as simply a land of contrasts between 'sand and sea, land and sky,
city and outback',[26] which continued through to SOCOG's official corporate
plan and which featured in the Opening Ceremony celebrations.

The Nature of Sport

It is no coincidence that images of nature, tamed as gardens or wild like the
Australian landscape, were embedded in the rhetoric of a sporting event.
Indeed, concerns about environmental degradation reinforce the primacy of
nature in modern sporting practices. Sport is predicated on an alleged
organic, or 'natural', origin as well as on human mastery over nature.[27]
Many organized sporting activities find their origins in the Romanticism of
the late eighteenth and early nineteenth century. At a time of emerging
industrialization, Romantics sought a greater commune with nature, which
was considered to be wild and untamed and was contrasted against the
rationality of industrial culture.[28] Nature was thus relegated to the 'margins
of modern industrial society'.[29] As such, the natural environment became a
refuge from the industrial city, and the countryside symbolized a return to
healthy, organic values. In this context, Kate Soper confirms:

> Untamed nature begins to figure as a positive and redemptive power
> only at the point where human mastery over its forces is extensive
> enough to be experienced as itself a source of danger and alienation. It
> is only a culture which has begun to register the negative conse-
> quences of its industrial achievements that will be inclined to return to
> the wilderness, or to aestheticize its terrors as a form of foreboding
> against further advances against its territory.[30]

The untouched natural world, while remaining on the margins of
'society', provides the promise of liberation from the highly manipulated and
exploited industrial landscape. In continental Europe, a range of gymnastic
movements, such as *Turnen* in Germany, emerged in the early nineteenth
century as a means to allow boys and men to 'return to nature', as a way of
allowing freedom of movement and expression.[31] The rise of organized sport
in Britain was also largely a result of a perceived need to 'escape' from the
industrial landscape. In Australia, the wild outback represented an avenue of
escape from the 'swollen' cities, an opportunity to retreat to and recreate in a
natural landscape.[32] The role of healthy play away from the belching smoke-
stacks of urban life confirmed the emancipatory capacity of the countryside.
Cindy Aron reveals that early vacations in both Europe and the United States
focused as much on restoring health as on pleasurable recreation.[33] The

wealthy middle classes sought refuge from disease and other threats of urban living in the fresh air of mountains and springs: 'Nature, many believed, could be enlisted in the cure and prevention of disease.'[34]

Sporting venues may represent something of a stylized retreat from the urban dangers of city life. Yet, 'untamed nature' may be missing from a stadium as the rational requirements of sport mean that the 'geographical "sameness" of sports space' must be retained if sporting events are to have any comparative value.[35] The only variable permitted to determine the outcome in an athletic contest must be human, uninfluenced by the vagaries of the environment. In this way, Homebush Bay does not represent 'untamed nature', but rather its conversion from a toxic, industrial site to a tamed 'garden' confirms Soper's argument: the emergence of 'Homebush Bay: Olympic Site' is a response to the industrial ravages wreaked upon 'Homebush Bay: Toxic Waste dump' by a society that 'has begun to register the negative consequences of its industrial achievements'.[36]

Given that the sportscape cannot be quite as 'untamed' as 'real' nature, yet still resembles it, it is of little surprise that sports stadiums and fields are often referred to as parks or gardens.[37] This metaphor reveals the garden to be an interface between nature and culture,[38] a 'natural' landscape that has been shaped and honed by the technologies of culture into a rational form that can be managed and replicated. Bale suggests that the sports stadium is caught between nature and culture, representing both the site of unbounded play and the strict regulation of codified sport.[39] Homebush Bay can thus be read as a liminal space, not quite wild, but not completely controlled either, and the ambiguity of the site is embedded in its name: Home/Bush Bay. 'Home' represents cultural spaces, 'a place of return, an original settlement where peace can finally be found and experienced',[40] which contrasts with the 'mysterious and undiscovered' Australian continent,[41] signified by the 'bush'. The 'bay', on the other hand, offers us a site where the two reside side by side, where a 'spectacular metropolis' is 'settled among [the] sheltering coves' of a 'glistening harbour'.[42]

The presentation of Homebush Bay as a safe 'home' for the Olympics was critical in efforts to reform the movement's ailing image. Throughout the 1990s, the movement had stumbled from one allegation of corruption to the next, from Vyv Simpson and Andrew Jennings' initial charges through to later investigations of improprieties within the bidding process.[43] The celebration of 'serenity', 'peace, harmony and understanding' in a restored natural wonderland was a welcome respite from these indictments.[44] Locating the Games in such a landscape provided the Olympic movement with an opportunity to regenerate from a corrupted movement to a pure and noble ideal, just as the site itself had been restored from industrial toxicity to unpolluted paradise. After years of turmoil, then, the Olympic movement is returned 'home' to a calm 'bay' and an unblemished 'bush'.

Restoring the Natural Athlete

It is precisely in a site such as Homebush Bay, where nature and culture collide, that athletic bodies come to perform and be viewed, scrutinized and
ultimately judged. Athletic bodies, like the Olympic site itself, are at once
artificially produced and biological reality, an imagined site where national,
political, economic and ecological interests can be inscribed. In particular,
the elite athlete is a landscape that is variously representative of nature and
wilderness, whilst at the same time it is controlled and regulated by human
intervention. In this sense, the landscape is both organic and architecture.
Yet, the public reception of these bodies is confused by the very nature of
the site that privileges both architectural spectacle and environmental
responsibility. On the one hand, spectators expect 'pure' human performances from their Olympic athletes, yet on the other, the record-breaking
efforts that are now routine can only result from extreme bodily discipline.
Whilst athletic training has gradually been redefined as a 'natural' way of
extending the body's capabilities, there remain some technologies that are
regarded as unequivocally 'unnatural' and, as such, are prohibited in elite
sport.[45] The irony here is that few recognize the fundamental contradiction
in admiring the architectural achievements of the built environment while
simultaneously rejecting the same 'built' quality of athletes.

Public cynicism about the validity of athletic performance confronted
Olympic officials and bureaucrats who implemented ever-increasing levels
of surveillance in order to detect and weed out 'cheats'. Most of these
efforts centred on performance-enhancing drugs and the desire to rid
Olympic sport of what many saw as a 'scourge'. Of course, most arguments
to detect and ban performance-enhancing drugs have relied on ever-vaguer
notions of 'fair play' and obtuse interpretations of the 'essence' of sport,
whilst 'pure performance' is privileged.[46] Such actions demand that the athletic body, like the Olympic site, be regarded as virgin territory, which,
though in need of conquering, taming and modifying, remains a natural site
nevertheless.

Privileging the natural world as a source of health and redemption is fundamental to the role of sport as an escape from the realities of 'real life',
although within elite sport, there is, of course, no such thing as 'untamed
nature'.[47] All participants have been 'shaped and honed' to elicit the greatest
possible physical output, a fact of which the public is all too aware.[48]
Despite clear evidence of deliberate human intervention, athletic prowess is
still regarded as something innate. An athlete is believed to possess a gift or
talent that is demonstrated on the playing field, and success is read as representative of this natural ability.[49] If we regard the elite athletic form as a
kind of industrial achievement, perhaps even as an industrial scape, then the
modified body itself may become a 'source of danger and alienation',[50] as

we recognize the 'negative consequences' of the technological innovation in sport and its impact on the human body.

Yet, fears about the alienated industrial body presuppose that nature is immutable, that either one can only be manipulated by direct human intervention, which is itself assumed to be necessarily detrimental. Soper, on the other hand, reveals that there is no such thing as 'untouched' nature.[51] Almost every landscape is in its present form because of human interference. Whilst the body is regarded to be 'of nature', its very form and function is a result of human intervention, and this is clearly observable within elite sport. Concerns about the 'unnatural' intrusion of performance-enhancing drugs into the athletic body rely on the assumption that it is a natural body in the first place, and yet every ability, capacity and achievement is the result of external intervention. As Soper states: 'If nature is too glibly conceptualized as that which is entirely free of human "contamination", then in the absence of anything much on the planet which might be said to be strictly "natural" in this sense of the term, the injunction to "preserve" it begins to look vacuous and self-deprecating.'[52] Trying to preserve the natural athletic body is thus equally vacuous as we neglect to realize that the elite athlete only exists as a result of human 'contamination'.

The desire to preserve the integrity of the athletic body has been a particular concern of the Australian sporting fraternity, and the national media consistently presents positive images of its own athletes, whilst competitors from other nations are assumed to be guilty of serious athletic misdemeanours.[53] The veracity of these claims and the inability to regard Australian athletes as anything other than unproblematically 'clean', has, I have suggested elsewhere, provided an insight into the way that sporting bodies are incorporated into the process of securing Australian identity.[54]

Just like the national geography, athletes are employed in the construction of Australian identity, and examining the relationship between these landscapes is salient. Athletes exist in a metonymic relationship with the nation: individual bodies stand in for the collective community and are clothed and swathed in state colours and emblems. Their bodies and costuming are interpreted in a socio-political context, and the public has become quite expert at reading the athletic body. Through a number of recent 'scandals', the Australian public have learned to identify 'unnatural' enhancement simply by gazing at the surfaces of bodies in what I have termed a 'postmodern phrenologic examination'.[55] Even during the Sydney Olympics, the public was reminded that illicit enhancement could be determined through a cursory examination of external contours. Andrea Raducan, the Romanian gymnast found guilty of ingesting performance-enhancing drugs, was regarded overwhelmingly by press and public alike as 'innocent', whilst the similarly accused US shot-putter, C.J. Hunter, was immediately condemned. The public, now quite versed in detection techniques, had learned that the size, sex, race and even the physical attractiveness of suspicious bodies provided clues as to their guilt or innocence.

Significantly, it is only the visible surface that must satisfy the viewer; any underlying contradictions remain obscured. Golf courses famously present themselves as a kind of manicured nature,[56] whilst just below the surface is a labyrinth of watering and drainage systems that are required to sustain the garden above. Below the surface of Homebush Bay throbs a similar level of toxicity, whilst athletic bodies are contained in a skin that elides the degree to which the human form has been chemically manipulated in its pursuit of sporting glory. In the case of Homebush Bay, the poisons that lie beneath the surface threaten to leach out and pollute the Olympic host. The skin of 'environmental restoration', which demarcates inside and out, is all that contains the contamination. Athletic bodies, by contrast, are regarded as 'natural' entities under threat from contamination from without; their skin represents the final line of defence in the vigilant maintenance of their athletic purity. Yet, at the same time, they resemble the Olympic site. Their skin is all that prevents the modern Olympic athlete from exposing the chemical and technological manipulation within.

Thus, the inverse relationship between Olympic athletic bodies and the host site remained hidden by a rhetoric that sought to privilege a culturally defined notion of the 'natural' while invoking a host of scientific, engineering, medical and psychosocial techniques to produce an event that is sold as both the epitome of technological progress and naturalistic play. Of course, these notions are undone by the presence of a range of impurities. Just as the Sydney Bid Committee tried to cover up knowledge of environmental contamination of the site prior to the IOC's final decision,[57] so too the 2000 Games were dubbed 'the most tested' Games in an effort to lay bare the bodies of Olympic competitors. At the same time that the built environment was projected as reclaiming the natural, the Sydney Games sought to recover the 'natural' athlete, free from drugs – though ironically not free from scientific manipulation, just as the environment was merely a mimesis of a statically defined 'natural habitat'. Throughout initial promotional efforts and certainly throughout the Games, the unity of 'nature' and the 'natural athlete' was reaffirmed in an attempt to restore Olympic innocence. Of course, within the Olympic arena, and certainly in terms of Australian athletes, such strategies were clearly at odds with the presence of one of the most efficient technological systems of elite sport training.

Conclusion

In a global marketplace, cities are increasingly indistinguishable in terms of their architecture, resources or production, and thus rely increasingly on engineering an image of the city as a site of conspicuous consumption to generate an identity independent of other similarly sized and resourced urban environments. As Helen Wilson points out, cities that desire the prefix 'world class' develop a range of investment and touristic strategies to confirm their place in regional and global hierarchies.[58] Sporting mega-events provide cities with opportunities to differentiate themselves and thereby attract international tourists as well as corporate investment. Thus, cities rely on staging grand spectacles that are designed to engender a greater global recognition as well as to develop a competitive advantage over other urban rivals.[59] The Olympics, with its image of wholesome sport contested between nations in a friendly atmosphere of 'fair play', is the jewel in the global crown of hallmark sporting events and, since the mid 1980s, cities have spent millions of dollars in the hopes of hosting the quad-rennial festival and lifting their profile as a result.

Physical, geographical, climatic, social and economic attributes are packaged by bid committees and Games organizers alike to appeal to both national and international audiences in a process that has been described as a 'sophisticated international marketing exercise', with the commodity being the host city itself.[60] At the same time, the Olympics must strike a balance between retaining their brand identity while being packaged to suit the national and regional specifics of the host city. In order to distinguish their Olympics from another, a host city often attaches epithets to the event to feature a desirable aspect of the Games. In the case of Sydney 2000, the Games were designated variously as the 'Athletes' Games' and the 'Green Games'. Whilst the two labels may seem disconnected, I argue that the link between the environment and athletes at the 2000 Olympics was explicit and useful in generating a coherent image of Australia, particularly for the international and domestic audiences.

At the heart of this analysis is a recognition that nature played a critical role in the construction of the Sydney 2000 Olympics. From the emphasis on natural landscapes to the promotion of natural athletes, nature was used to sell the Sydney Games. From the official image guidelines to the related advertising and tourism campaigns, the Australian landscape remained central to the promotion of the Olympics. An environmental haven within which the corrupted Olympic movement could regenerate was offered to the international audience, while assurances were made that those entering the hallowed site would retain their biological integrity. Purity in all land-scapes was thus guaranteed. Within these landscapes, it was thus possible to identify a relationship between the body, the Olympic site and the

Australian nation, such that the construction of an uncontaminated athletic body was mirrored in the manufactured 'nature' of Homebush Bay, which in turn was represented as a microcosm of the national environment. In doing so, this relationship revealed explicit tensions between culture and nature, artifice and environment, and inside and outside, which were reflected in both the body and the site of the 2000 Olympics.

Surf Lifesavers and Surfers: Cultural and Spatial Conflict on the Australian Beach[1]

DOUGLAS BOOTH

There has always been a division about surfboard riders [and lifesavers]. The surf-board riders don't care about the others. All they want to do is ride surfboards. They forget about the [safety] flags, they surf … through the flags. The surfboats go out and practise to save lives and they might get three or four waves a day so they're not interrupting anything. But the surfboard riders want it all for themselves and bugger everybody else. They should be out getting a job and working instead of being out on the surfboards.

(Surf Lifesaving Official)[2]

During the course of the twentieth century millions of harried Australians flocked to the beach to escape the stresses, strains and com-plexities of industrial and post-industrial life. The beach was a sanctuary, a place to abandon cares, to let down one's hair, remove one's clothes and lose one's inhibitions; a paradise where one could laze in peace, without guilt, drifting between the hot sand and warm sea, and seek romance. The beach was life at its most joyful and simplest. But underscoring this apparent haven lay a tension between human urges for unbridled pleasure and social demands for public discipline.[3]

The surf lifesaving movement assumed responsibility for mediating this tension. Surf lifesavers not only patrolled sand and surf to protect the unwary and innocent, they also served as moral watchdogs.[4] 'Thanks to the intervention of lifesavers', wrote the commentator on beach life Egbert Russell in 1910, 'it is rare … that anybody hears of an incident which might not receive the hearty endorsement of the whole Council of Churches'. Among the examples Russell recounted were a 'lifesaver sternly order[ing] a girl to cease from diving from the shoulders of her male escort' and another commanding two youths to 'desist [from] … dragging a third by his heels into the water'.[5] Fearing outbursts of wanton hedonism, the Surf Life Saving Association of Australia (SLSA) initially rejected surfboards as pleasure craft and supported municipal by-laws requiring men to cover their

chests at the beach. Interestingly, Association officials reversed their position on topless bathing for men in the mid 1930s when they realized that the
public gaze was as effective as coercive laws in disciplining beachgoers and
standardizing their behaviour. Recognizing the self-disciplining effects of
public surveillance, SLSA declared that 'it should be our aim to encourage
young men to take pride in their physique. This cannot be better encouraged
than the opportunity to expose their rippling muscles to sunshine, fresh air
and public eye.'[6]

The surf lifesaving movement established cultural hegemony on the
Australian beach in the 1920s and 1930s, but in the late 1950s a new threat
to its authority emerged – the independent surfboard rider, or surfer.
Ironically, boardriding developed in Australia between the two wars within
the ambit of SLSA, with surf lifesavers using boards to rescue bathers in
difficulty, in sporting competitions and as pleasure craft. But the philosophy, club-based structure and culture of the lifesaving movement emphasized discipline and teamwork via beach patrols and organized sporting
competitions; both involved inordinate amounts of military-style marching
and parading. As a result, the movement suppressed individualistic hedonistic tendencies. By contrast, modern surfers were pure hedonists. They
viewed riding boards as a stylized form of art and a communion with nature,
and they advocated relaxed, non-conformist and free-spirited 'beatnik'
philosophies. Lifesavers anchored their culture at the clubhouses that lord
over Australia's most popular beaches and are, for all intents and purposes,
their private domains. At the heart of surfing culture lies the 'surfari', a
wanderlust trip in search of perfect waves that connotes escapism, especially from authority. Despite the lifesaving movement's initial attempts to
accommodate surfers, the latter quickly forged a distinct culture with its
own language, humour, rituals, legends and dress. Relationships soon deteriorated. Surfers sniggered at lifesavers' conservative appearances (short
hair, Speedo bathing costumes, terry-towelling hats and zinc-cream), com-
paring them unfavourably with their casual board shorts, T-shirts and long
hair. Lifesavers were disdainful of surfers' attitudes, deriding them as gyp-
sies, drifters and bums. Lifesavers took pride in their neatness, social
responsibility and highly honed rescue skills; according to lifesavers,
surfers were scruffy and selfish.[7]

This chapter traces the emergence and development of Australian
surfing culture between the 1950s and 1970s in the context of broad social
changes. It examines the relationships between surfers and lifesavers and
attempts by the latter, in collaboration with municipal councillors, to discipline surfers. In the 1970s technological advances in surfing and lifesaving
equipment, combined with a partial institutionalization of surfing, helped
reduce animosities. But tensions still simmer between the two cultures and
occasionally bubble to the surface. However, as we shall see, by the

century's end the lifesaving movement had lost much of its former status, a fact that SLSA officials have failed to recognize.

Surfing: The Cultural Context

A specific set of economic, political and structural circumstances predisposed the emergence of modern surfing culture in the 1950s. Economic prosperity and the boom in consumer capitalism at the end of the Second World War produced a generation of 'overstimulated over-consumers' that looked for continuous thrills and fun.[8] This same generation was also the first freed from the working responsibilities of young adulthood and the first to benefit from an education system undergoing a liberal transformation. In part a consequence of the technological requirements of advanced industrial production, revamped education systems encouraged self-expression and self-actualization. Concomitantly, technological advances in materials, manufacturing and design precipitated the production of short (around nine feet), lightweight (twenty to thirty pounds), highly manoeuvrable and easy to ride Malibu surfboards. Not surprisingly, in the prevailing social climate of California where the new surfboards first emerged, they spawned a new flamboyant youth culture.

Californian surfing culture quickly diffused to Australia with visiting surfers, specialist films and magazines. A team of Californian and Hawaiian lifeguards, which included surfers Greg Noll, Tommy Zahn, Mike Bright and Bobby Moore, introduced Malibu boards to Australia in the summer of 1956/57. Invited by SLSA for a special Queen's International Carnival coinciding with the Olympic Games in Melbourne, the lifeguards demonstrated the new boards and riding styles to enthralled audiences. Australian surfing at that stage was, in Zahn's words, 'like nowhere. They were still going straight … [down the wave] on 16 ft paddleboards. The big trick was standing on one foot or putting their hands behind their backs.'[9] Pioneer American surf film cinematographer Bud Browne visited Australia two years later. Browne developed a rapport with local surfer Bob Evans, who screened the American's movies at surf lifesaving clubs in Sydney before producing over a dozen himself. Bob Evans also launched a surf magazine – *Surfing World* – as a vehicle to promote his films.[10]

Unlike their counterparts in California, surfing enthusiasts in Australia had to share the beach with a pre-existing institution that had established cultural hegemony decades earlier. Yet, SLSA did not initially oppose new surfing. On the contrary, SLSA sought accommodation, although it warned, as early as 1959, that rules and regulations governing the use of Malibus were pending. SLSA's accommodation is not surprising. Sugar-coated Hollywood beach films portrayed surfing in a positive light in the late

1950s and early 1960s. Gidget, the young surfer girl who launched a Hollywood genre of romantic beach musicals, was a 'folk angel', a well-groomed and normal teen who mixed with other 'sensible middle-class kids'.[11] Even the *Australian Women's Weekly* sanctioned surfing in a feature article in the summer of 1958/59; four years later it published a substantial dictionary of surfing terms.[12]

SLSA boarded the surfing train by sponsoring 'Miss Sydney Gidget' contests. The Sydney Branch of the national association organized 'special' Malibu surfing events at the New South Wales surf lifesaving championships in 1962/63 and formally proposed surfing as a national title the following summer. SLSA introduced the event to the Australian surf lifesaving championships in 1965/66. Individual lifesaving clubs attempted to entice surfers. Mona Vale, on Sydney's northern beaches, advertised free board storage, hot showers, cooking and overnight sleeping facilities; nearby North Steyne conducted surfing competitions as part of a 'look to the future' policy. To the south, Cronulla encouraged an independent surfers' lifesaving unit.[13]

Surfers, too, supported coexistence with SLSA. Bob Evan's *Surfing World*, first published in September 1962, reported results from lifesaving carnivals as late as 1964. At one point, Evans even proposed conducting the 1964 world surfing championships (see below) as a joint carnival with SLSA.[14] One aim of the Australian Surfriders Association (ASA), founded in August 1963, was to 'assist the SLSA in any way possible to help the public on the beaches'.[15]

Structural conditions explain continued close relations between surfers and lifesavers. Young surfers and lifesavers typically went to the same schools, socialized together and shared a sporting ethic. It is also easy to exaggerate the mobility of youth (while credit became cheaper and more accessible in the 1960s, it was not widespread). Surfaris outside the metropolitan areas still made surfing 'news' well into the decade. Moreover, Malibu boards were generally unwelcome on public transport. Many surfers thus remained shackled to lifesaving clubhouses. Entrepreneurs offered board storage, but only a minority of surfers could afford the monthly A$2 charge. Lastly, while some surfers left lifesaving 'to escape patrol duties', many others remained to enjoy a familiar camaraderie.

On the other hand, there was a general recognition of the very real dangers that Malibu boards, particularly those without riders, posed to bathers. In 1960, officials from Sydney's coastal municipalities and lifesaving branches met to formulate uniform regulations for surfboards.[16] The following summer, the councils introduced a registration scheme, charging non-lifesavers five shillings for an annual surfboard licence; lifesavers received free licences. The councils demarcated surfing zones with distinctive markers on the beaches and authorized inspectors to confiscate boards used in bathing areas.[17]

Surfing officials supported these initiatives. Indeed, they helped police riders who infringed bathing-only zones. The New South Wales Surf Riders Association recommended the appointment of club presidents as honorary rangers; Mid-Steyne Surf Riders Club suspended a member for encroaching on bathing zones; and the adjacent Manly Beach Surf Riders Club reprimanded two members.[18]

Much of the official support for surfing in the early 1960s derived from the fact that leading surfers defined themselves as sportspersons, a term that connoted structure and discipline. For example, editorials in surfing magazines implored surfers 'to preserve the images' of 'devoted and inconspicuous athletes' and of 'good, clean-living, average guys, out for a day's sport in the sun'.[19] Success in international competition enhanced surfing's credibility. Bernard 'Midget' Farrelly, from Manly, Sydney, won the Waikiki Surf Club's tenth International Surfing Championship at Makaha, Hawaii, on New Year's Day 1963. Manly Council feted him upon his return and the following summer Farrelly began a regular column in the *Sun Herald*. A Sydney newspaper praised surfers for their 'maturity' in organizing an association; they had, the *Manly Daily* declared, now earned 'the right to promote their sport'.[20]

Big business and vested political interests flocked to the sport of surfing. Sponsors of the first official world surfing championships at Manly Beach in May 1964 included Manly Council, Ampol (Petroleum) and TAA (Trans Australian Airways). They were blunt about their motives: 'Manly will get a lot of publicity from international television coverage of the event', said Mayor Bill Nicholas.[21] The championships were a phenomenal success – an estimated crowd of 65,000 watched Farrelly capture the crown. A senior Ampol representative described surfing as 'the fastest growing sport in Australia' and pledged his company's continued support.[22]

But even as a formally organized sport, surfing failed to arrest increasingly negative sentiments exemplified by the observer who described 'useless' surfers who 'cruise from beach to beach looking for the best surf' and 'pay no rates or fees of any kind, frequently not even parking fees'.[23] As the 1960s unfolded, these views coalesced into a social hysteria that portrayed surfers as subversive itinerants, nomads and wanderers. Moreover, surfers dispensed with all notions of social accommodation, branding themselves outlaws and revolutionaries.

Troublemakers on the Beach

In the absence of highly visible formal institutions, a wide variety of commentators viewed surfing as an unanchored cultural practice without social utility. The New South Wales Youth Policy Advisory Committee (chaired by Judge Adrian Curlewis, the longstanding president of SLSA) blamed misbehaviour and delinquency on 'unattached' and 'unclubbable' young people, a problem it attributed to a plethora of precipitating causes: 'cheap commercialized entertainment ... comics, radio and TV thrillers, sex-stimulating films and magazines, excessive mobility of population'.[24] Surfers added to these sentiments by transgressing sartorial and behavioural norms. One newspaper correspondent denounced 'long-haired' surfers who 'took over footpaths for their boards, public toilets for changing rooms, made unofficial headquarters of public facilities', and passed loud 'rude' and 'foul' remarks at girls. Another summed them up as 'the worst behaved section of the community'.[25] Councillor J. Illingworth was especially vociferous, condemning surfers' style and conduct: 'those there [at Manly] last weekend were badly dressed. Their hair was longer than that of Alderman Mrs A.M. Ambrose. They were drinking wine. They blocked the stairways from the beach and were hustling people on the promenade.'[26] The principal of a Sydney high school warned that surfing, along with 'the wearing of jeans, lumber jackets, gaudy sweaters and socks and casual footwear', could adversely affect boys.[27]

The authorities increasingly saw surfers as a law and order problem. Incidents such as the one where a crowd of surfing enthusiasts, queuing to watch a surfing film at ANZAC House in Sydney, smashed a glass mural monument to Australian soldiers killed at Gallipoli, did little to pacify concerns.[28] But rather than analyzing broader structural conditions and searching for new solutions, the authorities simply regurgitated past methods of control. Instead of implementing proper crowd-control procedures, the management of ANZAC House banned surfing films. Liberal Party MP Robin Askin called for more police to deal with surfer 'louts'.[29] The president of one life saving club said 'surfboards bring to the beach a hoodlum element which is causing members a great deal of concern ... and we feel if boards were banned this element would disappear and the beach would once more become ... [a] family gathering place'.[30] E. Wilson, the president of Warringah Shire Council (WSC – at the time one of two local authorities responsible for Sydney's northern beaches), accused 'violently abusive' 'non-resident boardriders' of reducing beaches to 'surfboard jungles'. He implored the government to restore law and order.[31] Manly councillor Bill Nicholas urged surfers and lifesavers to join forces against 'itinerant riders'.[32]

As noted above, municipal councils and SLSA made several efforts to tighten controls over surfing in bathing areas in the early 1960s. But surfers generally ignored municipal laws and their disregard prompted sterner efforts to quell a perceived social menace. In February 1964, police, beach inspectors and lifesavers joined forces in a military-style operation against surfers at Sydney's Bondi Beach.[33] Manly Council, after meeting with representatives of local surfing clubs at the end of summer 1965/66, declared it would prosecute future offenders.[34] Finally, in September 1966, the WSC, in consultation with officials from the local life saving branch, banned surfing at Freshwater Beach and demarcated permanent bathing areas on the shire's 17 other beaches.[35]

Councillors and lifesaving officials wanted to discipline surfers and force them to share responsibility for guarding the beaches. After promulgating the ban and restrictions, the WSC wrote to the ASA, asking it to formulate a policy to administer and control surfing in the shire.[36] Allan Fitzgerald, president of the Manly–Warringah Life Saving Branch, proposed that surfers and lifesavers work together to 'cover the whole beach', although he made it abundantly clear that the latter would assume final responsibility and authority: 'the board boys would have to get their bronze medallion, and they would have to show themselves capable of accepting responsibility'.[37] (The bronze medallion is SLSA's qualifying award, allowing members to patrol beaches.) It was an unrealistic strategy that ignored the practical implications of enforcing the measures and the broader socio-economic and political conditions that fostered independent hedonistic lifestyles.

Rigid rules further soured relations between surfers and lifesavers and exacerbated hostility. Shortly after the promulgation of the restrictions, a mêlée erupted between lifesavers and surfers. On Sunday 6 November 1966, scores of surfers sheltered from blustery conditions at Sydney's Palm Beach. Late in the morning, lifesavers demanded surfers leave the water while they conducted a bronze medallion test. Many surfers refused and the Palm Beach club captain sent two surfboats to clear the water. The sweep of one of the boats boasted, 'I creamed those surfers off wave after wave; I was like a road grader.' Lifesavers confiscated boards washed ashore during the fracas and a crowd of surfers congregated on the beach and then marched on the clubhouse. A furious argument ensued between the surfers and lifesavers. According to one participant, it went 'within a hair's breadth of an all-in brawl' before being defused by a local police sergeant.[38]

Surfers, board manufacturers and small businesses launched a campaign to fight the board ban campaign. They displayed 'share the surf' stickers on their cars, wore protest badges, signed petitions and wrote letters of protest. The ASA recommended surfers living on Sydney's northern beaches register their boards elsewhere to deprive the WSC of income. The New South Wales Amalgamated Independent Traders Association warned that the restrictions would 'divert commerce away from the shire' and 'jeopardise' business. Protesting surfers drove a large black surfboard through central Sydney streets and vandalized signs prohibiting surfboards. The ASA's vice-president, Dr Robert Spence, called the laws unjust, inequitable and unrealistic. He said surfing did not imperil public safety in winter and pointed to the absurdity of demarcating permanent zones for crowds of bathers that rarely appeared.[39]

The restrictions lasted one season. A fortuitous, albeit unsavoury, event precipitated the intervention of bureaucratic rationalism that overrode political dalliance. In April 1967, the New South Wales minister for local government dismissed the WSC following charges of soliciting and receiving bribes against councillors Denis Thomas and George Knight and their subsequent convictions.[40] The government appointed an assistant under-secretary in the Department of Local Government, Jack Barnett, as shire administrator. After conferring with local surfing and life saving officials, Barnett reintroduced flexible bathing areas and buffer zones between bathers and surfers. He also dispensed with the surfboard-licensing scheme, admitting that it 'serves no really useful purpose'. Investigations showed administrative costs exceeded revenue, that only a minority of surfers registered their boards, and that registration would not obviate a council's liability in the event of an accident.[41] Neighbouring municipalities followed suit.

But lifting the ban did not lighten cultural animosities between surfers and lifesavers. On the contrary, relationships deteriorated further under the impetus of new social, economic and political forces.

The Counter-culture and Soul-Surfing

In 1964, the first baby boomers, the oldest members of the wholesome Disney-entertainment and Gidget generation, entered a liberalized university system that encouraged them to think, probe, question and challenge. But the intellectual freedom they discovered in the rapidly expanding tertiary sector was double-edged: the freedom to explore was also the freedom to express dissatisfaction.[42] Education exposed what Andrew Milner calls the 'recurring apocalyptic motif' – a host of new fears, including nuclear annihilation, ecological catastrophe and social alienation, that contributed to a collective social anxiety and pessimism about the future.[43] John Lawton, for example, recalls the Cuban missile crisis in October 1963 provoking genuine terror that the world was about to end.[44] Maturing baby boomers also found mass consumption capitalism culturally alienating. On the one hand, precisely as older teenagers demanded new fashions, styles and products to express their individuality and distinctiveness, standardized mass production imposed blandness and conformity. On the other hand, they blamed the relations of production associated with mass consumption capitalism for fragmenting the family by luring mothers out of the home and into the workforce under the guise of satisfying needs for consumer durables. Lastly, new political events, notably decolonization, the war in Vietnam and civil rights protests in the USA, informed the social consciences of educated middle-class youth around the world.

Collectively these conditions inspired the educated middle-class baby boomers to forge new counter-cultures that would not simply challenge the old conformity but would 'invert' bourgeois society.[45] David Harvey sums up the logic and direction of the counter-culture in the following terms:

> Antagonistic to the oppressive qualities of scientifically grounded technical-bureaucratic rationality as purveyed though monolithic corporate, state and other forms of institutionalised power, the counter-cultures explored the realms of individualised self-realisation through a distinctive 'new left' politics, through the embrace of anti-authoritarian gestures, iconoclastic habits (in music, dress, language and lifestyle), and in the critique of everyday life.[46]

Soul-surfing – riding waves for 'the good of one's soul' – articulated this new politics and critique, and conjoined surfing with the counter-culture. Soul-surfers rejected high consumption, materialism and competition; and they expounded a form of 'fraternal' individualism that extolled creativity and self-expression within a cooperative environment. Soul-surfers applied esoteric interpretations to surfing: waves became dreams, playgrounds, podia and even asylums, and the search for perfect waves became an endless pursuit. Surfing signified self-expression, freedom and escape from the dictates, structures and norms of bourgeois society. Australian surfer Robert Conneeley described surfing as 'the ultimate liberating factor on the planet'; fellow traveller Ted Spencer happily admitted that when he surfed he 'dance[d] for Krishna'; and former world champion turned soul-surfer Nat Young believed that by the simple virtue of riding waves, surfers were 'supporting the revolution'.[47]

In this new environment relations between surfers and lifesavers continued to decline. 'Clubbies' embodied the values and attitudes that soul-surfers scorned. The cartoon surfer Captain Goodvibes (see Figure 8.1) who appeared in *Tracks*, an alternative monthly magazine for surfers, ridiculed and satirized lifesaver conservatism, which Tony Edwards, the strip's creator, depicted as fascism. In the first strip in June 1973, for example, Goodvibes appears 'cunningly disguised as a clubby on his afternoon patrol' having consumed '17 times his own weight in beer at lunch'. When a patrol member informs his Captain that '27 people have just been swept out to sea', Goodvibes replies, 'Oh that's all right Ron … they've gotta be poofters if they can't swim anyway'.[48] (Nor did lifesaving escape the prevailing Zeitgeist. Graffiti on a noticeboard at the Bondi Surf Life Saving Club, scrawled under a request for volunteers to fill a patrol, retorted: 'Not a chance Dad. We all want to get drunk'!.[49])

Counter-culture transgressed middle-class tolerance. According to the media, surfers' long hair and beards, and their supposedly unwashed and soiled bodies, signified lack of discipline, self-indulgence and decadence. Sydney's *Sun Herald* called them 'jobless junkies'.[50] Many surfers did consume drugs and some were members of drug networks of investors, organizers, traffickers and dealers.[51] Nonetheless, the media's depictions of surfers too often descended into gross caricatures.

The counter-culture was unsustainable. Yippie leader Jerry Rubin's immortal words, 'people should do whatever the fuck they want',[52] could not reconcile alternative independence with an interdependent society. Adherents of the counter-culture presented 'philosophical' environmentalism and Eastern mysticism as panaceas, but neither engaged the state nor addressed the problems of political economy. Drugs, a key source of counterculture enlightenment, might have given surfer Ted Spencer 'an insight and an appreciation of the energy of … underlying things', but, as David Caute points out, 'the claimed journeys to "inner truth" degenerate, on inspection, into puddles of vomit'[53] – or, in the case of several renowned

FIGURE 8.1

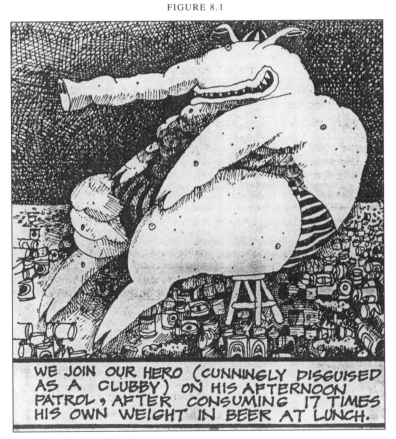

Captain Goodvibes. (Tony Edwards)

surfers, long periods of heroin addiction. Lastly, as the young aged they discovered new priorities, particularly after the resolution of major political issues, notably the withdrawal of troops from Vietnam and the end of conscription, and the onset of economic recession in the 1970s.

Overt hostilities between surfers and lifesavers receded in the mid 1970s along with the counter-culture and the long hair, scruffy, soul-surfing look. Two technological advances contributed significantly to the new climate. Firstly, surfers attached themselves to their boards with leg ropes. This simple cord largely removed the danger posed to bathers by unridden boards washing through swimming areas. Secondly, water-based highly manoeuvrable motorized IRBs (inflatable rescue boats) became the principal means of patrol and rescue in the lifesaving movement. They helped remove the domineering visual presence of lifesavers on the beach. In short, these two technologies radically changed traditional spatial arrangements among the two major users of the beach and increased the physical distances between them.

In addition, surfers established new structures to organize a professional surfing circuit. Paradoxically, the work-is-play philosophy of the counter-culture alerted a group of perspicacious surfers to professional competition as an avenue to eternal hedonism. Implicit in all professional sport is a system of embodied ethical values and attitudes which Bryan Turner calls 'managerial athleticism'.[54] In short, all professional athletes must carefully manage the public presentation of their bodies to convey acceptable images, especially to potential corporate sponsors. In particular, they must demonstrate that they are self-disciplined, hard working, conscientious and determined. Thus, in trying to achieve an 'image of authenticity and responsibility' among professional surfers, the new governing associations implemented codes of conduct that compelled members to put forward a good image to sponsors and the public. Consumption of recreational drugs in particular became taboo, much to the chagrin of some surfers who suddenly found themselves disciplined by peers who were also consumers. Nonetheless, it is no coincidence that many of the public criticisms directed at surfers quietly evaporated after they established institutional structures with explicit disciplinary functions and policies.

None of this means that surfers and surf lifesavers in Australia have reconciled their former antagonisms. As events in the small beach community of Avalon, north of Sydney, a quarter-of-a-century later testify, relationships between surfers and lifesavers remain fragile. When the film crew of 'Baywatch', a television adventure-drama series about Californian lifeguards, arrived in Avalon for 3½ days at the end of 1998, it rekindled cultural animosities between surfers and lifesavers. This time, however, the surfing community won the subsequent struggle and its victory demonstrated the waning credibility of the surf lifesaving movement.

Baywatch, Black Shirts and White Shorts

In November 1998, a 'Baywatch' crew arrived in Avalon to film a special episode entitled 'Baywatch Down Under'. Once boasting a regular audience of one billion people in 144 countries, stale and ludicrous story lines had begun to erode the show's popularity. The show's creator and executive producer, Greg Bonnan, thus proposed a new location to help revive the fortunes of a programme renowned for sculpted beach bodies wearing skimpy lycra swimwear. Unbeknown to all but a handful of colleagues and supporters, Bonnan intended 'Baywatch Down Under' as a prelude to an entire series at Avalon – a picturesque community with which he had a casual acquaintance stretching back several years. He also wanted a promotional vehicle to secure relocation costs from a Federal government eager to promote Australia as an international destination for film and television productions.

The 'Baywatch' film crew arrived in Avalon with 14 prime semi-trailers and commandeered the car park behind the Avalon Surf Life Saving Club (ASLSC). As well as providing parking space, the car park allows residents to safely unload and collect family members and friends, including school-age children, who use public transport. The appropriation of strategic community space shocked Avalon resident and local surfer Paul Morris when he arrived at the beach one morning. Security guards, dressed in intimidating black shirts, blocked his entrance and ordered him to leave. He returned later the same day and witnessed more disturbing scenes. Waiting patiently for the crew to complete filming at the tidal pool 'were two old ladies in their seventies or their eighties in their cossies with their towels over their arms wanting to get in for a swim'. As well as the car park, 'Baywatch' had appropriated the pool and denied access to two women, who, Morris surmised, had 'probably lived in the area all their lives ... paid rates' and seen their husbands fight in a war. Like other outraged residents, Morris saw the behaviour of the 'Baywatch' crew directly challenging and threatening the 'essence' of the Australian beach as a public resource.[55]

Furious local residents heaved a collective sigh of relief when 'Baywatch' departed. In addition to seizing the car park and the pool, 'Baywatch' crew had ordered surfers from the water and skateboarders from a dedicated area adjacent the car park, and had littered the headland with debris from a boat destroyed during a rescue scene. Their joy was short-lived. The next month, news leaked into the community that Bonnan planned to permanently relocate 'Baywatch'. Although 'Baywatch' required the permission of Pittwater Council to film at Avalon, sympathetic councillors and council staff imposed a veil of silence and refused to divulge any information. They claimed that until the producers lodged an official application to film, then the proposal was just that; and Bonnan was in no hurry to submit an official application while he was still negotiating relocation costs with the Federal government.

A small group of residents immediately formed the Save Avalon Beach Committee to lobby against 'Baywatch'. Over the following two months, they waged a political struggle that received the full attention of the national and the international media. Save Avalon Beach Committee and its supporters focused on lifestyle and cultural concerns and issues. Highly attuned to the nuances of Australian beach culture, they pointed out the incongruity of filming a Hollywood version of surf lifesaving on an urban Sydney beach. As one commentator put it, the show's star 'David Hasselhoff is to lifesaving what Popeye is to weightlifting'.[56] Avalon resident and former professional surfer Mark Warren was more blunt, dismissing 'Baywatch' as 'a bloody dinky operation' that 'misrepresents what we have as an Australian beach lifestyle'. 'The beach lifestyle that 'Baywatch' supposedly represents', he added, 'is so artificial and so far removed from the actual lifestyle of the people who do come down here to go swimming, or surfing or fishing or whatever, they don't bother to watch it because basically it's such a wank'.[57] Indeed, even American lifeguards 'laugh about the silliness quotient' and 'lament some of the misconceptions' that 'Baywatch' promotes. 'I can't remember the last time I chased a bank robber down the street', mocked Chris Linkletter, who works at California's Redondo Beach.[58] Others similarly condemned the sexist way that 'Baywatch' represented women.[59] Most of the opposition, however, came from residents determined to preserve their village and beach lifestyles from development and commercialization. In the words of journalist Deirdre Macken,

> even if 'Baywatch' can prove that it will buy all its sandwiches from local Avalon shops, there are some who will decide they can do without this extra tinkle in the till if it means that they can still surf whenever they choose. Avalon is full of people who have chosen less work, less-pressured jobs and lower incomes in return for time to enjoy their area. As one protester said, 'The beach is being treated by council as just another commodity but for the people it's part of their lives.'[60]

In contradistinction, the pro-'Baywatch' faction, who included the Australian film industry, the Federal and the New South Wales State governments, the Pittwater Council, the Avalon Chamber of Commerce and ASLSC, stressed the economic benefits. According to Greg Bonnan, 'Baywatch' would inject A$200 million a year directly into the regional economy and a further A$4.2 billion indirectly (calculated by the New South Wales government on the basis of 21 dollars generated for every one dollar spent).[61] Tourism New South Wales welcomed the 'anticipated benefits' of 'Baywatch'; music publisher Mark Beckhaus described it as 'an incredible opportunity for Australian workers'; local television producer

Hal McElroy concluded that 'the occasional inconvenience to the public is all worth it in economic terms'.[62] The single biggest direct beneficiary, however, was ASLSC. The production company repainted the surf lifesaving clubhouse for 'Baywatch Down Under' and paid the club A$4,400 to hire its hall; club members employed as IRB drivers and crew donated their fees, putting a further A$4,700 in the club's coffers.[63] The company also promised to spend A$40,000 renovating the clubhouse (including a new gymnasium and extensions to the main deck) in time for the 1999 filming season and offered an additional $200,000 over five years.[64] Understandably, club members accustomed to raising funds by selling raffle tickets and begging for money outside local shops welcomed 'Baywatch'.

The struggle climaxed at a public meeting in late February 1999. Called by the Save Avalon Beach Committee, and sanctioned by overconfident Pittwater councillors who erroneously believed that 'Baywatch' opponents constituted a vocal minority, the meeting attracted around 1,700 residents at Barrenjoey High School. Opponents outnumbered supporters three to one. Bonnan conceded 'some mistakes', including dressing security personnel in black shirts, and he promised to rectify these problems. 'We're not bad citizens, we're not bad guests', he pleaded, adding that 'we never have, and we never will, prevent anyone from using the beach. We never have and never will prevent surfers from surfing'.[65] Avalon resident Harvey Rose summed up the majority feeling with a simple rhetorical question: 'Is it not obvious, Mr Bonnan, that vast numbers of the people of Avalon do not want you here.'[66] (See Figure 8.2.)

Bonnan read the writing on the wall. Even before Pittwater Council made its final decision on 'Baywatch's' application, he had begun negotiations for an alternative beach. Shortly after he moved to Hawaii, where the government allegedly offered the producers a US$30 million package over four years.

'Baywatch' revived the 'cultural chasm' between surfers, who generally opposed the series and who were prominent members of the Save Avalon Beach Committee, and lifesavers who supported filming in their neighbourhood. But unlike the 1960s, when, in Mark Warren's words, 'problems like this were sorted out with a bit of biff on the beach',[67] the former carefully avoided attacking ASLSC while the latter 'maintained a façade of politeness'. But these were purely strategic positions and old animosities simmered beneath the surface; in the words of one prominent spokesperson for Save Avalon Beach Committee, things got 'nasty and personal' and, in some instances, even 'split families'.[68] 'Baywatch' rekindled Avalon surfers' long-standing distrust of the surf lifesaving movement and was a blatant reminder of 'an arrogant culture that simply assumed power'. The most obvious symbol of that arrogance was the black shirted 'Baywatch' staff. The colour may have been at the opposite end of the spectrum, but the

FIGURE 8.2

No 'Baywatch'. (Avalon Surf Life Saving Club)

similarities in the starched uniform-style of dress raised feelings of hatred in older surfers. They immediately remembered the white shorts, white shirts and white hats worn by 'little bastard officials' who served the life-saving movement after the Second World War.[69]

Conclusion

The Australian beach is a contested cultural terrain, a site where the rules of pleasure and discipline are continually negotiated. The history of lifesaving and surfing is a classic example of this process, as well as an illustration of how the balance of cultural power can shift over time. When modern surfing arrived in Australia in 1956 it confronted an association of surf life-savers who had established cultural hegemony and defined, in collaboration with municipal councils, the rules of pleasure and discipline at the beach. In short, SLSA and local councils sought to constrain unbounded hedonism. SLSA initially attempted to accommodate surfing but its moves were always destined to fail, premised as they were on the assumption that surfers would willingly conform to the Association's authority. Relations between surfers and surf lifesavers reached their nadir during the counter-culture as the former challenged institutionalized authority in all its guises. In the early 1970s, surfers attracted particularly adverse social comment.

The criticisms only evaporated as the counter-culture waned and as surfers created new institutional structures with an explicit disciplinary content. Discipline, paradoxically, was a fundamental prerequisite of eternal hedonism. Lastly, technological advances (leg ropes and IRBs) played a major role in spatially segregating the two cultures and lessening the chances of confrontation.

Two decades of relative peace on the Australian beach followed. But the 'Baywatch' saga at Avalon offers a potent reminder of the ongoing cultural tensions between surfers and surf lifesavers. More importantly, the 'Baywatch' controversy suggests a major decline in the cultural status of lifesavers. Once Australian icons, lifesavers are now viewed as just another interest group. In this climate it was perhaps not surprising that ASLSC officials maintained an uncharacteristically low profile during the 'Baywatch' dispute. While this could be interpreted as overconfidence and arrogance, officials may well have feared serious public debate about the lifesaving movement, its real role, its sources of funding, it expenditures, and its methods of operation. Why, for example, do patrols insist on herding bathers between safety flags when modern rescue equipment – notably IRBs and increasingly jet skis – allow lifesavers to effectively cover whole beaches? Given that lifeguards in California have no difficulty patrolling long sweeps of beach, it would appear that this method is a cultural legacy from when lifesavers assumed responsibility for disciplining beachgoers. And why does SLSA spend more than twice the amount of money on lifesaving sports than on lifesaving training and equipment? Lifesaving sports bear little relationship to rescue work. As a case in point, most of the 269 clubs in Australia own wooden surfboats, which cost around A$20,000 each; yet in 1998/99, surfboats were used a mere 25 times in 12,946 rescues.[70] (This statistic, of course, makes a mockery of the claims by the Avalon lifesaving official cited at the head of the chapter.) Not surprisingly, the lifesaving movement shies away from a frank discussion of these issues. But then again, burying its head in the sand has always been a hallmark of lifesaving culture.

Playing with Gravity:
Mountains and Mountaineering

PETER DONNELLY

At once humbling and uplifting, few sites in nature are as awe inspiring as mountains. But, too often, mountains are also perceived as remote from the day-to-day concerns of humankind. Nothing could be further from the truth. Mountains are home to communities worldwide and to important cultural traditions. They shelter vast reserves of biodiversity. They provide vital resources such as water and wood, contributing to the livelihoods of a significant portion of the world's population.[1]

Perhaps the most sacred place on earth is a mountain. Kailash, also known as Kang Rinpoche, is a 6,714-metre mountain in the part of the Himalayas known as the Internal Ranges of Tibet. It has no recorded ascent, and it is a central focus for at least four major religions: Bons (a pre-Buddhist religion in Tibet), Buddhists, Jains and Hindus (for whom it is the home of Shiva). Four of the great rivers of the Indian sub-continent, including the Indus and the Brahmaputra, have their source here. Of course, Kailash is a site of pilgrimage, and the *kora* or *parikrama* is a circumambulation of the mountain that covers a distance of 50 km at an altitude of over 5,000 m. Perhaps most astonishing in this feat of physicality is the fact that the *kora* is carried out as a series of prostrations – pilgrims literally measure out the path around the mountain in their body lengths.[2] 'For the Buddhists, the *parikrama* is equivalent to a cycle of birth and rebirth.'[3] But mountains represent far more than the spiritual, and this chapter is concerned with a different physicality. However, the case of Kailash, and the fact that there is no recorded ascent, is an important lesson to consider in the following analysis.

Kofi Annan, in the quote above, considers the significance of mountains in terms of their aesthetic appeal, their resources, and as human habitat; but he fails to make specific note of their recreational significance. This chapter focuses on mountains as playgrounds, as spaces where humans are able to play with gravity. In most of the well-known mountain activities – for example, the various forms of skiing and tobogganing, white water kayaking, and some of the so-called 'extreme' sports – the 9.75 m/s² force that can impel falling human bodies up to speeds of approximately 200 kilometres/hour is controlled only by friction and skill; the intent is to use gravity to attain speed. Other activities oppose the force to gain height – hiking, mountain running and mountain biking; but only mountaineers struggle against that force at the limits of friction, where a slip might mean injury or death.

This chapter considers the development of the social and material conditions in which it was possible for the sport of mountaineering to emerge. The following sections briefly consider: mountains before mountaineering; the changing aesthetic associated with both the Enlightenment and the emergence of the Romantic movement; the origins of mountaineering as a sport; and its development over the last 150 years. Implicit in this analysis is an understanding that the meanings of spaces are socially constructed, that such meanings vary by time and place, and that changing social and material conditions can result in the social reconstruction of such meanings. Also implicit is the idea that almost any space, even the most hostile environment, may be rendered meaningful for human play.

Mountains before Mountaineering

Global warming is revealing some unexpected aspects of human history. As the glaciers retreat, and their surfaces melt, bodies are appearing – first nations people from the sixteenth century in British Columbia, and even a Stone Age man in the Austrian Alps. 'The ice man', who died some 5,300 years ago, was found at 3,210 metres in the Ötztaler Alps.[4] Humans have probably been climbing mountains for the whole of human history. Certainly mountains were climbed in biblical and classical times. Arrowheads have been found at a summit in the Canadian Rockies, and a bronze spearhead was found at the summit of the Riffelhorn in the Swiss Alps. These events give the lie to Thoreau's comment that, 'Simple races, as savages, do not climb mountains – their tops are sacred and mysterious tracts never visited by them;'[5] and the comment certainly says more about Thoreau and his times than about actual events. The archaeological record now indicates that ancient peoples travelled at quite high altitudes in the mountains, and even visited some summits.

Mountains have both practical and spiritual significance to peoples living in mountainous areas. In practical terms mountains are landmarks; they can be used for both strategic and surveying purposes; and they are sites for the collection of resources (for example, hunting and mining). In spiritual terms mountains represent the homes of gods (such as Parnassus in ancient Greek cosmology; Shiva and Kailash in the example given above), and the pillars of the universe (e.g., the five sacred mountains – Sun Chan, Hua Chan, T'ai Chan, and two mountains named Heng Chan – in China). They are also the site of spiritual quests for peoples in many different parts of the world; and they have taken on mythological significance because of their shapes or their location (as in the naming of constellations). But while people have given meaning to mountains, mountains have also served to divide peoples. As objective entities, mountain ranges are natural barriers to travel and communication, and they often form regional, international, political, religious and linguistic boundaries. However, mountain people often become expert at mountain travel, and their work as miners, hunters, guides and traders was involved the development of early mountaineering skills, techniques and equipment. And while it is possible that some people probably climbed mountains for fun, or for adventure, or a dare,[6] there is no evidence that mountains were ever climbed systematically for such motives before the middle of the nineteenth century.

Most of the accessible written history of humans and mountains derives from Europe. There are clearly long traditions of mountain travel, and of mountain spirituality, in Asia and North and South America. For example, the Yamabushi society of monks in Japan have been mountain climbers for some 1,300 years. They combine Shinto and Buddhist traditions in making ritual ascents of mountains in the Japanese Alps.[7] But such records have not been incorporated into the predominantly Eurocentric history of mountaineering. Before the eighteenth century in Europe, mountains had little popular significance and were generally considered, by those who did not live among them, to be horrendous places. Between the fourteenth and seventeenth centuries there is a distinct ambivalence about mountains. Petrarch climbed Mont Ventoux[8] in Provence in 1355, and recorded his enjoyment of the experience. Paintings by Bellini, Titian and Van Eyck appear to show a genuine feeling for mountain beauty.[9] But Lunn, who notes this painterly feeling, also suggests that a return to some of the standards of classical Greek humanity resulted in the development of a taste for formal architecture and gardens (humans imposing their rule on nature) and the emergence of the term 'Gothic' (from Goths) to describe all things that were considered to be barbarian in taste – which included all wilderness, and especially mountains.

For those obliged to travel through the Alps, travellers were warned 'Here be dragons', and travellers' reports are full of the horrors of mountain travel. In his well-researched *Early Travellers in the Alps*, de Beer noted that:

> Unless he be a beggar or lunatic, nobody wanders about in the Alps unless he enjoys it. On the other hand, many have had to travel across

the Alps whether they liked it or not, which latter alternative was most usually the case in early times.[10]

Three principal types of traveller were identified. The first were those who had to travel through the Alps to reach their destination – soldiers, craftsmen and artists, merchants and scholars, and pilgrims, clergy and monarchs from Northern Europe on their way to and from Rome. The second were merchants and visitors to the baths and spas located in Alpine areas. The third were the early tourists, wealthy young men on the Grand Tour. One of the earliest recorded accounts was given by John de Bremble, an English monk who crossed the Alps in 1188 on his way to Rome:

> Lord, restore me to my brethren that I may tell them that they come not to this place of torment, where the marble pavement of the stony ground is ice alone, and you cannot set foot down safely.[11]

Such accounts were typical, and continued into the sixteenth century.

The changing aesthetic associated with the Enlightenment and the emergence of Romanticism was signalled in 1681 with the publication of Thomas Burnet's book, *Telluris Theoria Sacra (The Sacred Theory of the Earth)*.[12] Burnet reflected the dominant view at the time, noting that mountains:

> ... have neither Form not Beauty not Shape, nor Order ... they do not consist of any Proportion of Parts that is referrable to any Design, or that hath the least footsteps of Art or Counsel. There is nothing in Nature more shapeless and ill-figured than an old Rock or Mountain, and all that Variety that is among them, is but the various Modes of Irregularity.[13]

However, he went on to bridge the emerging science of geology with prevailing Christian religious principles by asking why God would create something as ugly as mountains?[14] His answer was a masterpiece of rationalization. The original, paradisaical earth had been a 'Mundane Egg,' smooth and unwrinkled, 'not a scar or fracture in all its body, no rock, Mountain nor hollow cavern'.[15] Thus, God had created perfection before the 'fall of man' – mountains were created by the geological consequences of the Great Flood, a part of God's punishment for the disobedience of Adam and Eve.[16] Biblical justification was found in the promise that the 'Mundane Egg' would reappear on the Day of Judgement: 'Every valley shall be exalted, and every mountain and hill shall be made low; and the crooked shall be made straight, and the rough places plain'.[17] This Christian and Eurocentric view should be contrasted with the existence of sacred mountains in Eastern cosmologies (for example, Kailash, and mountains in China and the Japanese Alps).

Changing Aesthetics

Mountains were not even named on maps of the European Alps before the seventeenth century, and even then there is some confusion as to whether a mountain or a pass is designated (although local people certainly had names for their mountains). 'M.', 'Mont', and 'Mons' meant both mountain and pass, and it is more likely that passes were designated since they were more important to travellers. However, the growth of science and the growth of tourism in the eighteenth century led to much more detailed maps and a growing interest in mountains. Burnet had been aware of the effects of water erosion in the creation of mountains, but growing interest in geology also led to a fascination with glaciers and glaciation, and fossils – especially the fossils of sea creatures that were found high in the mountains. The Enlightenment was also associated with interest in measurement (including the heights of mountains), collection and categorization (of plants, insects, animals, and minerals, including those found in the mountains), and phenomena such as the relationships between pressure, temperature and altitude.

The scientific and natural history societies that were formed at this time gave the gentlemen/amateur scientists a place to share and debate their findings, and provide motivation for the members to continue their work – a part of which involved travel to and in mountains to carry out observations and experiments. Interest in the heights of mountains grew in the latter part of the eighteenth century, with particular interest in what was believed to be the highest mountain in (Western) Europe, Mont Blanc (now known to be the highest, at 4,807 m). Horace Benedict de Saussure, a gentleman scientist from Geneva, had explored the glaciers on the French side of Mont Blanc in 1760, and was convinced the mountain could be climbed. He offered a reward for finding a route to the summit, and it was claimed by Dr Michel-Gabriel Paccard and the guide Jacques Balmat in 1786. The ascent was repeated by de Saussure the following year, and he made scientific observations on the summit.

The publicity attached to de Saussure's ascent had a double consequence. First, ascents were made on other mountains (although not necessarily to the summit) in order to collect specimens, and carry out scientific measurements and observations. Second, Mont Blanc itself began to become a tourist attraction, with growing numbers of Grand Tourists and other visitors travelling to Chamonix, and some even attempting ascents of the mountain. Trevelyan notes a rumour that there were some 40,000

English (both servants and masters) travelling or living in continental Europe in 1785.[18]

The increase in scientific and tourist travel was coincident with a vast improvement in communications during the eighteenth century. The introduction of maintained toll roads to facilitate wheeled traffic, including the stage-coaching system, and the construction of canals both began in the eighteenth century; although 'wheeled traffic did not appear on the [Alpine] passes until in 1775 Mr Greville drove his phaeton up the St Gotthard, to every one's amazement'.[19] Various elements (discussed below) began to emerge at the end of the eighteenth century which changed the whole meaning structure of mountains for urban Europeans. The British even became interested in their own mountains, in Wales, Scotland, and particularly in the English Lake District, 'though as yet no one but the shepherds went up the neighbouring mountains'.[20]

There is a tendency to assume that, because we find mountains an attractive aspect of scenery, they have always been considered in this way. But mountains, and other wild scenery, provide a perfect example of the social construction of taste.[21] Given the horror with which mountains were perceived until the second half of the eighteenth century, it is important to understand the aesthetic shift that occurred in order to facilitate the growing attraction of mountains in the latter part of the century. In 1739, Horace Walpole, son of the British Prime Minister, and the poet Thomas Gray visited the Alps as Grand Tourists and provided one of the earlier accounts of that 'oxymoron of agreeable horror',[22] a sensation that came to be described as 'the Sublime' (see, Edmund Burke's 1757 book, *Philosophical Inquiry into the Origin of Our Ideas of the Sublime and Beautiful*).[23] Their travels marked a distinct change in attitude from previous accounts: 'What they were interested in, along the high mountain passes, was … an experiment in sensation. Their journey was designed to take them close to the edge, to toy with disaster.'[24]

Notions of the 'sublime', of wild scenery and sensation, became the cornerstone of the Romantic movement, and tourists were increasingly attracted to mountains by Romantic ideals in the latter part of the eighteenth century. There was also a political/philosophical element to the movement which began to romanticize 'uncivilized' native populations whose simple and harmonious lifestyles in nature were held in contrast to the corrupt, polluted and effete life of European cities.[25] As the empires of European nations grew, this sentiment came to be manifested as the 'noble savage'. But it became evident that it was not necessary to look as far as Africa and the Americas – 'noble' and 'democratic' peasants lived much closer to home, in the Swiss mountains. This gave further impetus to travel, although the poverty and disease that were frequently discovered needed some reinterpretation to conform to Romantic ideals.

Two further trends, with origins in the eighteenth century, added to these emerging social, cultural and material conditions for the emergence of mountaineering. The first is a vigorous blend of athleticism and Empire in which mountains became another site of 'conquest'. Two years after Walpole and Gray travelled in the Alps, two other English 'gentlemen' visited the village of Chamonix (now a major mountaineering centre). Richard Pococke and 'Boxing' Windham represented the sporting and jingoistic aspects of Regency Britain, and they set out to explore/conquer the massive glacier now known as the Mer de Glace. Their writings about the event encouraged an active engagement with wild scenery rather than a more passive contemplation of the Sublime. The second is the initial stage of a democratization of the Grand Tour/travel experience as a result of more accessible transportation, and of the restructuring of social classes associated with the new wealth of industrialization.

All of these conditions continue into the nineteenth century, picking up again in the 1820s following a long hiatus associated with revolutionary France and the hostilities of the Napoleonic era. And, in keeping with the burgeoning of capitalism associated with the increasing mass production of goods (and related services), a commercial element was added to the conditions. Albert Smith produced a long-running and highly successful show in London in which he narrated and dramatized his ascent of Mont Blanc.[26] Also, the emergence and rapid spread of railroads revolutionized communications such that, by 1863, Thomas Cook organized his first tour from London to Switzerland only six years after the founding of the Alpine Club. Science, tourism, the Romantic movement, athleticism/Empire, democratization and commercialization all feature in the emergence of a sport that was to be called mountaineering. Mountains also became ideal sites for the expression of masculine character, a particular concern of elites in Victorian Britain.

The Emergence of Mountaineering[27]

In order for mountaineering to emerge as a sport, the meanings of mountains had to be socially re-constructed:

1. mountains had to be identified (named, measured, and mapped);
2. the summits of mountains had to achieve some significance;
3. reaching the summit, and recording the fact, had to become a meaningful activity.

The first occurred as a result of Romanticism; the second was associated with scientific measurement and imperialism; the third brought together athleticism and imperialism, competition and conquest, in the struggle to be first. This combination found its greatest expression in the 'character factories' of Victorian Britain – the British public (private) schools; and it is fitting that the British should claim to be, and are widely recognized as, the creators of 'mountaineering'.[28]

When were mountains first climbed for 'sport'? There is no clear answer to this question just as there is no clear answer for other sports such as rugby, ice hockey and baseball. However, as with those sports there is a foundational myth. Many histories of the sport report that mountain climbing (known as 'mountaineering' or, after its apparent origins, 'Alpinism') began in 1854.

The date of the first ascent of the Wetterhorn from Grindelwald – 17 September 1854 – is a red-letter day in the history of modern mountaineering – of mountaineering properly so called which is undertaken for its own sake, and entirely apart from the performing of some particular feat, or from some special scientific object ... Mr Justice Wills' [Sir Alfred Wills] ascent of the Wetterhorn was the first of a series of expeditions destined to become continuous and distinctly marked the commencement of systematic mountaineering. Hence it is that the anniversary of this ascent may well be termed the Founder's Day of our craft in its modern guise.[29]

There was a small controversy about this issue; some claimed that the Rev. John Frederick Hardy's (1826–88) ascent of the Finsteraarhorn (also in Switzerland) in 1857 marked the starting point, but consensus went to Wills. It should be pointed out, however, that neither of these ascents was the first ascent of the respective mountains.[30]

There was no way that Cunningham and Abney could have known if this was the first ascent 'undertaken for its own sake'. Coolidge was able to find records of 132 Alpine peaks in Western Europe being climbed before Wills' ascent of the Wetterhorn, and we have no means of knowing the motives for these recorded ascents, or knowing the number of, or motives for, unrecorded ascents.[31] The claim made for Wills is typical of the class and colonial arrogance of the period, best captured in the Thoreau quote noted previously: 'Simple races, as savages, do not climb mountains – their tops are sacred and mysterious tracts never visited by them.'[32]

The 1854 ascent marked the start of a period of sustained mountaineering activity in the Alps. In the ten years bracketed by the ascents of the Wetterhorn and the first recorded ascent of the Matterhorn (by the Englishman Whymper) in 1865, most of the major summits in the Alps were climbed for the first (*recorded*) time. Cunningham documents 57 major ascents, at least 60 per cent of which were made by British alpinists,[33] and refers to this period as the 'golden age' of mountaineering.[34] Our current view of the term 'golden age', often a period during our youth, was quite different from that of the classically trained British, who would have been well aware of its origins. The golden race of people, living in an idyllic 'golden age', was followed by silver, bronze and iron races/ages marked by increasing degeneracy, with the iron race the most degenerate of all. When Cunningham labelled the 'golden age', he also referred to the time of his writing (between 1865 and 1887) as the silver age of mountaineering. What at first seems to be just a little less significant (like an Olympic silver medal) is actually quite a biting criticism, applied by the (self-designated) golden agers to their followers who, they implied, had degenerated the sport from its initial purity.[35]

These are obviously major pieces of self-serving propaganda. At the height of imperial/Victorian Britain, with an all-conquering upper-middle class as the major engine of cultural production, it is to be expected that, given no other claimants, the British would claim the sport of mountaineering as their own invention. These individuals founded the first Alpine Club in 1857. The Club resembled the geographical and scientific societies that had been established since the mid eighteenth century. The Alpine Club started a journal (originally *Peaks, Passes and Glaciers*, soon changed to *Alpine Journal*) to record mountain exploration and scientific observation, and members came together to dine and read papers about their activities. Just as in science, priority was a matter of intense concern, and the *Alpine Journal* constituted a record of achievement in terms of first ascents – a matter of frequent dispute.

Despite these origins, and the claims regarding origins and purity of motives that are still repeated in histories of mountaineering, I will argue in the following section that the real 'sport' of mountaineering did not occur until after the so-called 'golden age'.

The Development of Mountaineering

The golden agers, in addition to ensuring their place in mountaineering history with this successful piece of self-serving propaganda, also attempted to ensure that *their* form/style of mountaineering became *the* form/style of the sport for the future. The first set of unwritten rules of the sport involved the following:

- climbers must be accompanied by guides;
- the only permitted equipment was ropes and ice axes;
- whatever number was right for a climbing team, two was wrong (and one was not even a consideration);
- the taking of risks was never acceptable, and these early climbers had a very clear sense of what was inappropriate or unacceptable in terms of choice of route, weather conditions, etc.;
- the form of the sport was to seek the easiest route to the summit of

significant new peaks – subsequent ascents were to follow the same route.

The fact that none of these rules any longer apply provides insights into the processes of cultural production, and limited reproduction, in this sport; the limits of 'playing with gravity' in these amazing physical spaces that were implied by these rules; and the transformation of this early form of mountain exploration into a sport.

If these rules had been followed, the only way for the sport to develop after 1865 was to complete the exploration of the Alps by climbing the few remaining major summits without recorded ascents, and to seek first ascents in other mountain ranges. This occurred, and this new Alpine form of mountaineering spread to the Caucasus, New Zealand, Africa, the Himalayas, North and South America, and other mountain ranges (New Guinea, Japan, etc.). Of course, the climbers took their European guides with them, and treated this form of mountaineering as a form of imperial conquest. This is best expressed in the anthropomorphic arrogance of Sir Francis Younghusband, a leading player of the 'Great Game' and Chair of the Everest Committee in the 1920s:

> Both man and mountains have emerged from the same original Earth and therefore have something in common between them. But the mountain is the lower in the scale of being, however massive and impressive in outward appearance. And man, the punier in appearance but the greater in reality, has that within him which will not let him rest until he has planted his foot on the topmost summit of the highest embodiment of the lower. He will not be daunted by bulk.[36]

However, if this was all that constituted the sport of mountaineering, there would be no sport:

- younger generations would have to go further and further afield in order to establish their reputations – limiting this possibility to a few wealthy individuals;
- at some point there would have been no new mountains left to climb, or so few that there would be no incentive (a situation that, if the original rules applied, we would have reached today);
- there is no sport in following in the footsteps of former climbers – it is a recreation, a pleasant physical activity, but it is not sport (faster ascents, which could have added an element of sport to the activity, were initially discouraged because they implied recklessness and danger; they were subsequently approved, but not for sport – faster ascents were safer because the risk of bad weather was avoided; speed was introduced as a sporting element by subsequent generations).

Thus, it is possible to argue that the sport did not really start until the second generation – the so-called 'silver age' of mountaineering. The second generation turned 'mountains into playgrounds',[37] not only developing the 'sport' of mountaineering but also institutionalizing other recreations such as downhill skiing (developed by Arnold Lunn, a member of the Alpine Club) and tobogganing (the Cresta Run). They changed the form and goals of mountaineering in various ways which ensured its future:

- some began climbing without guides, and developed their own mountaineering skills;
- ascents of minor peaks in the Alps (as well as major peaks in other regions), and the attribution of significance to the ascents of minor peaks (often technically more difficult and dangerous than the major peaks);
- seeking new routes (e.g., North Face, West Ridge, etc.) to the summits of already climbed peaks (almost always more difficult than the original route), and attribution of significance to these routes;
- recording variations such as first winter ascent, first women's ascent, etc.;
- an initial acknowledgement that it was sometimes necessary to take risks in order to accomplish a new route.

These changes were controversial, often resulting in condemnation from members of the older generation, but because of the particular structural form of the 'sport' the founders had created they were unable to prevent the changes (discussed below).

The essential changes that were made created a sustainable 'sport' of mountaineering. Being the first to stand on a previously (as far as is known) unclimbed summit remained significant, and it still is usually accepted as such. However:

- the innovation that made the sport is the 'route'; it is the only element that gives the sport any scope such that, not only is climbing still a sport, but it has seen an enormous increase in popularity in recent years;
- acceptance of the significance of the route, of increasing difficulty and the development of means to measure difficulty (grading systems), of (eventually) new equipment, and maintaining records of the first, the fastest, the most ethical ascents – all of these allowed the sport to branch out into rock climbing, ice climbing, and other forms.

Thus, whilst we accept that the first (known) ascent of Mount Temple in the Canadian Rockies was an achievement worth recording, we now also recognize that the first ascent of the difficult and dangerous North Face of Mount Temple some 70 years later was a highly significant achievement, even more worthy of recording.

Why were the first and subsequent generations of climbers not able to ensure the continuity of their form of mountaineering? The answer lies in the institutional structures of the sport. Since the earliest days of mountaineering, climbers have developed a consensus about the forms, values and goals of their activity. However, there was never a way to enforce the consensus. The size of mountains and mountain ranges were (and are) such that the activity is impossible to regulate. Any attempted restrictions would also fly in the face of the free spirit of discovery and exploration. Thus, since the earliest days of the gentlemen amateurs, climbers have trusted each other to act in ethical ways.[38]

These principles continue to dominate the sport which is, for the most part, governed by a socially constructed, socially reconstructed and socially sanctioned set of rules still known as 'ethics' among climbers. Such rules are unenforceable, relying on moral suasion. They are locally variable, and in the anarchic culture of climbers they are preferred over any codified set of rules. Changes and sanctions are debated in face-to-face interaction and in the climbing journals, but the only sanctions available are ridicule and the refusal to record a claimed achievement.

This does not mean that there is no regulation on the activity, or the spaces where it occurs. Climbing bans have been imposed in some areas, with varying degrees of success, and some national parks attempt to impose sign-in and sign-out procedures. Various suggestions have been heard which attempt to impose training and standard qualifications, and to restrict climbing to those so certified, but these have only been enforced for outdoor education and guiding purposes, and are widely rejected in other parts of the climbing community. The most regulated and institutionalized forms of mountaineering occurred in socialist societies. In the former Soviet Union, mass mountaineering was the norm with very large teams being led by more experienced climbers,[39] with all team members being registered and approved for specific ascents and routes. Moreover, speed climbing was developed as a formal competitive activity, and an attempt was made to promote it to the International Olympic Committee for inclusion in the 1980 Moscow Olympics. Mountaineering was also a part of the Soviet Master of Sport system.

Systems of enforceable rules in institutionalized sports ensure the cultural reproduction of those sports; changes occur slowly. Where ethics and moral suasion govern a sport, change is a constant as each new generation seeks new challenges and forms of expression in the sport. The second generation of climbers realized that, if they conformed to the standards of the first generation, there was very little left for them to do – a particularly frustrating condition when their climbing skills and equipment were better than their predecessors. As one second-generation mountaineer wrote, with reference to the first generation: 'They have picked out the plums and left us the stones'.[40] This clever pun refers to both the stones (pits) of fruit, and to the fact that the second generation began a move from easy angle snow and ice climbing to much more steep rock (stone) climbing.

Since that time, each new generation of climbers has had the capacity, if not always the inclination, to make changes in the form and meaning of mountaineering; this led to progressively more difficult ascents. They have engaged in a cultural struggle, which was at first intergenerational but by the 1930s had inter-class features, to determine the form and meaning of the sport. And each time there was such a change in the sport, the retiring generation condemned it. Each active generation of climbers, as it retired, claimed that it had reached the limits of what is possible in the sport – no further development of difficulty was conceivable without it being suicidal, or so flouting the prevailing ethics as to be cheating. Each subsequent active generation has proved its predecessors wrong. They have altered the rule structure while maintaining the sport (i.e., they have not cheated), and they have, in general, kept the death toll down.

In Raymond Williams' terms, mountaineering is a 'residual' activity, although the relatively new 'extreme' sport of 'sport climbing' may clearly be seen as 'emergent'.[41] It is residual in that its approximately 150-year history make it the exception that proves the rule – i.e., the rule about sports institutionalizing. It is also a model for alternate forms of sport. Institutionalization has a petrifying effect on sports, tending to freeze them at the moment the rules were written and enforced, and stifling the creativity of subsequent generations of participants. Try to imagine what ice hockey or soccer would look like today if each new generation of players had had the capacity to make changes in the form and meaning of the sports – to re-invent them.

Conclusion

There is a great deal of literature on mountaineering that describes endurance, effort, hardship, courage and risk. There is less on the sheer joy of confident movement in the vertical plane – playing with gravity – although all climbers that I have spoken to recognize it. This is an anarchic sport which leaves Kailash unclimbed (as far as we know) and in which those making the first ascent of Kanchenjunga (8,597 metres) in 1955 stopped two metres below the summit to respect a request from local Buddhist monks for whom it was a sacred summit that they did not wish to be violated.

Environmental and climatic changes, a rapid increase in the number of climbers in the last 30 years, the growing commercialization of the sport, and the neo-conservative notions of privatization and private property that have restricted access to some climbing sites all appear as threats to the sport in the early twenty-first century. It is fitting that 2002 was declared the International Year of Mountains (IYM), and the Union Internationale des Associations d'Alpinisme (UIAA) – an 'International Federation' which declares its membership in the IOC, but which can scarcely be considered a governing body – has captured these concerns with the publication of its *IYM Summit Charter 2002*.[42] The environment is the predominant feature of the Charter, but access, safety and commercialization are also addressed. A document such as this has no precedent in the sport, and it makes an appropriate conclusion to this consideration of the way in which humans have brought meaning and playful physicality to these amazing spaces.

In accordance with [the Charter], mountaineers, climbers and trekkers:

- Welcome the International Year of Mountains 2002 as signalling the importance of mountains and of mountain peoples; and of policies to enhance and sustain them.
- Believe that everyone should be free to enjoy the natural environment, including mountains and cliffs, with responsible access.
- Support the need for safeguards for wild and natural mountain terrain and cliffs, given their environmental value and fragility.
- Understand that mountaineering, climbing and trekking, practiced responsibly, are compatible with the natural environment.
- Know from experience that their activities contribute to the human spirit and to human endeavour, as freedom sports with human and social values;
- Accept the personal responsibility of the individual, supported by environmental awareness, codes of good practice, and training;
- Contribute to the growth in sustainable mountain tourism, with any charges for services and facilities to be reasonable and fair, bringing an economic benefit to local communities.
- Respect and uphold local culture, heritage and tradition;
- Propose adjustments to public policies, in line with these concepts, where equitable and beneficial.[43]

The Homoerotic Space of Sport in Pornography

BRIAN PRONGER

The places, traditions and icons of sport play a significant role in male pornography. Indeed pornography is one of several media genres that turn their gaze on sport alongside newspapers, television, Hollywood film and prose fiction. Pornography in general is far from a minor part of the entertainment industry. The *New York Times* estimates that in the USA alone it is a 10–14 billion dollar industry, which even at the lower estimate makes it a bigger business than professional football, basketball and baseball put together. In fact people spend more on pornography in America in a year than they do on cinema tickets, and more than they spend on all the performing arts combined.[1] While quantitatively sport plays a small role in the pornography industry, it does nevertheless play an important one in that genre of pornography which represents men only. Indeed the contexts of sport are frequently referenced in a range of pornographic media, including video, magazines, the Internet and prose fiction. In this type of pornography the spaces of sport, such as locker rooms and playing fields, the equipment of sport, such as uniforms, jock straps, weight training equipment and baseball bats, as well as the traditions of sport, such as initiation ceremonies and victory parties, establish the erotic context for the sexual activities that take place in the sports setting. This genre is often called gay male pornography, which suggests that it is produced by and for gay men. But a considered analysis of this material suggests that the producers and consumers of such pornography are not necessarily only gay men. It is better to avoid limiting these representations to sexual identity politics and consider them more simply as representations of men and that these representations can be read from a wide range of sexual sensibilities – and identity positions. It is worth noting that pornography that represents women very seldom features sport places, traditions and icons. Why this is the case will be considered later in this chapter.

To analyse pornographic sport spaces consider John Bale's idea of the landscapes of sport, which he calls 'sportscapes'. These are the human geographical configurations that provide the context and possibilities of sport experiences. Traditionally these would be the playing fields, stadia, swimming pools, gyms, locker rooms, parklands, cliff faces, etc. in which sporting activities are undertaken. The structures of sportscapes describe, inscribe and prescribe the spaces that realize sporting experiences. Eichberg and Bale have analysed the development of modern sportscapes, and similarly to Foucault's work on other architectural spaces, looked at the ways they developed as disciplinary spaces for physical activity, organizing the body according to modernist imperatives to rationality and linearity, for instance. Elsewhere, it can be argued that the socio-cultural space of same-sex sport functions as a disciplinary technology for sexuality that both explores homoerotic possibilities and restricts them.[2] It is also argued that sport disciplines desire more generally, which is to say it disciplines more than just sexual desire.[3] This chapter explores the ways in which the sportscape that is mobilized in pornography both disciplines desire and opens a space for difference.

Interestingly, the term 'landscape' entered the language as a technical term from painting, denoting the background – the spatial context for the subject of a picture. From its inception, the concept of the landscape has been embedded in methods of representation. Representation, then, has always been an important dimension in the idea of a landscape. So too representations of sport have relied on the spatial contexts of sport as the background for their intelligibility. The contexts of stadia, playing fields, ice surfaces, mountain slopes, running tracks and swimming pools make sense of the bodily activities that are represented by the media as occurring in those places. Whereas Bale's work on the sportscape has concentrated on the geographies of three-dimensional sport places and the ways in which they produce particular kinds of body cultures, considered here are the ways sportscapes form a context for reading *representations* of body cultures, specifically in pornography.

The pornographic sportscape is not independent of the mainstream, indeed it draws specifically on the places of mainstream sport as well as the emotional and political organization of their spatialization in a dynamic tension between homoeroticism and homophobia, for instance. While it may well be that the pornographic sportscape is marginal to the mainstream, as postmodernists and queer theorists have argued for over a decade now, we can learn a lot about the mainstream by studying the margins.

Bale points out that sportscapes include more than visual landscapes, such as the look of stadia and fields, but also the sounds and smells of these scapes. So the sportscape of a golf course, for instance, is not only the sight of lush greenery and manicured lawns, it is also the sound of water sprinklers, the thwack of the club and ball and the combined smell of fresh cut grass with human sweat. The sportscape also stimulates other senses, such as the oral, kinetic, and tactile: the taste of an opponent's sweat in contact sports,[4] the kinetic sensation of running over rough terrain on a cross-country run, or the feeling of body pressing against body in a rugby scrum.

Emotional senses are affected by the sportscape as well. The rules and traditions of different sports also contribute to the emotional experience of the sportscape. For instance there is considerable emotional difference between the space that is created in the martial art of Tai Chi and the space that is produced in freestyle wrestling, the former being an explicitly spiritual encounter, the latter being more instrumentally competitive for the production of the hierarchical difference between winner and loser. Rules and traditions have a profound effect on how the space of sport is produced. The sensory field of the sportscape, then, is multivalent, shaping visual, aural, oral, olfactory, kinetic, tactile and emotional experiences. All of these senses are affected by the sportscape's organization or production of embodied space.

The sportscape also includes complex culturally informed spatial senses of the body in terms of the boundaries that mark the difference between the internal and external body and the social rules that regulate what, when, where and how things enter and leave the inner space of the body. In baseball, for instance, spitting on the playing surface is de rigueur, in basketball it is not. These rules of inner and outer are very complex in the locker room where it is, for example, acceptable to publicly place one's fingers in one's anus in the shower for the sake of cleaning (but not for pleasure) but that is much less acceptable when standing at one's locker. (See Caroline Fusco's chapter on the locker room.) The ways in which sportscapes construct the boundaries of the inner and outer body are very important in sports porn, which often features the transgressions of such boundaries.

But our senses are not simply passive recipients of the sportscapes. Our senses are active in their appreciation of what they sense. Memory, for instance, informs how one experiences a sportscape. Certainly each time one enters a three-dimensional sportscape, such as a stadium or a locker room, one experiences the scape in the context of one's memories of previous experiences of such places as well as hope for future experiences. For example, a long-time fan of the Toronto Maple Leaf hockey team entering the old arena, Maple Leaf Gardens, for a 'sudden death' play-off, recalling the long-past years when the team won consecutive Stanley Cups, and the many subsequent years of disappointment, will enter the place with memories of these feelings and hopes for the future and will read the activities that take place in the context of these feelings. The historical place itself, some would say, arouses those memories and hopes and the ways that one experiences the place. (Indeed, it is the loss of memory that adds to the sadness of some sports fans when their teams are moved to new, more profitable venues.) In a similar fashion, memory goes to work when one sees or reads representations of sportscapes in newspapers, magazines, on television, or in a film. Memory and hope also inform the reading of pornographic representations of sportscapes. Just as a reader of the sports pages may wince in sympathy or even empathy at the sight of a picture of two hockey players slamming into each other, remembering, hoping for, or fearing such contact in their own experience, so too the reader of sports porn feels sympathy or empathy for the human encounter that is represented in the pornographic sportscape, recalling his experiences of and hopes (or fears) for similar sexual experiences of the sportscape. Representations of sportscapes invoke a full range of sensory experiences in order to invoke the feeling of these scapes and the relationships and experiences that might unfold in them. The *pornographic* representation of sporstcapes recalls visual, aural, oral, olfactory, kinetic, tactile, spatial embodiment and emotional experiences of actual sportscapes.

My analysis of the pornographic sportscape follows my ongoing concern for the fate of desire in the discourses of sport. Deleuze and Guattari posit desire as the flow of energy, the puissance, of human being/becoming/actuality, defining it as 'a process of production' in our capacity to connect, to affect and be affected.[5] Space is the opening that desire produces. Space, I suggest, is made by desire, and sportscapes contribute to the shape of desire. Sportscapes, in other words, open spaces for the actualization, realization or indeed production of desire. Understanding the spaces of desire involves considering power, not as a repressive force but as a productive one, as Foucault would say. How do sportscapes construct desire? How is desire actualized in the pornographic sportscape?

In the introduction to his anthology *Public Sex, Gay Space*, William Leap draws on the geographer Michel de Certeau, who makes a distinction between place and space in which place is understood as the planned (or natural) geographical and architectural structures in which human activity takes place.[6] These places are not realized until they are inhabited and used by people. It is in that use that place becomes space, a productive opening for actual living, becoming, desiring. 'Space emerges when practices are imposed on a given location, when forms of human activity impose meanings on a particular location, and transform "neutral" terrain into landscape, that is into a particular "way of seeing"[7] relevant to that particular locale.'[8] Following that logic, a sportscape is constituted by particular readings and uses of the places of sport; the ways that people use and understand a sportscape spatialize it, indeed give it life. Leap emphasizes that place and space are not 'static arrangements, but topics continually being constructed, negotiated, and contested'.[9] A shower room, for instance, may be designed with a particular limited sportscape in mind, for example as a space for getting clean after activity, and may indeed be spatialized that way as people clean themselves. But that sportscape may also simultaneously be a space for the exhibition and viewing of naked bodies. The space of a sportscape is not necessarily limited to hegemonic or traditional ways of seeing the place of sport or of actualizing it. The sportscape may be spatialized precisely in order to resist or transgress hegemonic ways of experiencing it. Indeed it is an erotic transgression of the hegemonic assumption of the heterosexuality of the sportscape that much of sporting pornography attempts to provoke.

Like three-dimensional sportscapes, various representational practices of sport read the sportscape in various ways. There are, for instance, the fan and business-oriented readings of the sportscape that occur on a daily basis in the sports pages of newspapers and other mainstream sport media. Quite different *academic* readings of sportscapes are offered in the scholarly world of critical sports studies, as in this volume. *Pornographic* readings of the sportscape offer another way of seeing the space of desire in sport. They play upon traditional ways of reading the sportscape, both challenging such readings and reinforcing them.

'Reading' Pornographic Sportscapes

Before proceeding to an analysis of pornographic sportscapes, comment should be made on 'reading' pornography. What does it mean to 'read' pornography?[10] While all reading opens imaginative spaces for readers, spaces which reader-response theorists have emphasized are profoundly influenced by the readers themselves, the imaginative space of porno-graphic reading has an important added dimension. In non-pornographic reading, the reader's body has a fairly passive physical role, normally sit-ting and reading a text, or watching a visual display. Reading books tends to be physically quite passive, with the occasional laugh or shedding of a tear being the extent of physical response to the text. Watching an action film may involve a sudden covering of the eyes. Watching a sporting repre-sentation of an exciting game on television, for example, may involve sudden bursts of physical excitement where the reader jumps from his or her seat, claps hands, shouts in support or disgust for a play that has just transpired. These are physical responses to an otherwise relatively passive physical act of reading. In pornographic reading, on the other hand, phys-ical stimulation – in the form of masturbation – is standard throughout the act of reading/viewing and it typically ceases either once climax occurs, or when the text is no longer inspirational. The point is that pornographic reading is directed at physically moving the interior space of the body by combining reading with the external manipulation of the body, exploring its surfaces and the openings to its interior. It is a reading practice that is not typically expected of sports representations, nor of actual three-dimensional sportscapes – one seldom sees men masturbating at hockey games or when

gathered around with their buddies watching the Superbowl on television –
but masturbation is the very pulse of reading all pornography, including
sporting pornography. 'Successful' pornographic readings of the sportscape
bring a physical, indeed erotic intensity to the experience of the sportscape
that is normally prohibited in such scapes, or at least kept under wraps. In
such a reading there is an explicit sexual tension and (sometimes) orgasmic
release that brings another sensory dimension to the experience of the
sportscape, in addition to the already mentioned senses of sight, sound,
smell and so on. And so, as we think about the multivalency of the senses
through which we read representations of the sportscape (oral, visual and so
on) in the case of the pornographic reading, we need to keep in mind that
one of the crucial perceptive abilities that is brought to bear on the representation is an erotic intensity that one desires to invoke as a way of experiencing the representation. While it is an intensity that does not always
come to pass, it is at least hoped for. Indeed that is the point of porn, and its
quality is determined by the extent to which it is able to produce an intense
erotic space. So the spatialization of the pornscape is the space of sexual
engagement, and in the representations that I am exploring here, the explicit
sexualization of the sportscape.

How does the sportscape inform the erotic spatialization of pornography? This question is answered having looked at some of the extensive
collection of pornography in the Sexual Representation Collection of the
University of Toronto, as well as a result of a wider study of sexual representation on the Internet. Readers of this analysis who are unfamiliar with
pornography may be surprised by the explicit and sometimes brutal language and images represented in the following. I believe it is important to
portray the phenomenon being described accurately; indeed to soften the
language to appeal to more delicate sensibilities would misrepresent the
sportscape, both pornographic and mainstream. Anyone who has spent any
time in men's locker rooms knows that the language and sexual references
are often far from subtle, and pornography frequently plays to similar
explicit language. Moreover, as I have argued elsewhere and will attempt to
illustrate here, sport is often a brutal form of social interaction in which
bodies intentionally collide and invade each other's spaces in the desire for
territorial conquest. Sport is also often intensely and explicitly homophobic
in ways that are frankly harsh and hurtful. The pornographic reading of the
sportscape often calls upon that brutality, telling us as much about sporting
desire as it does about the complexities of homoerotic desire and their intersections. So while the language here may appear harsh, it is because the
phenomenon being described is as well.

The first and perhaps overarching theme to be found is that the pornographic sportscape is an almost entirely male milieu. While there are count-
less examples of the sportscape in same-sex male videos, there are very few

that feature women and/or heterosexual sex. The exception to this is an extensive array of cheerleader pictures, with sites such as www.sexycheer-leaders.com. Cheerleading is frequently a clickable category on mainstream porn sites that depict women, such as at www.suckittome.com/cheer-leaders.htm. Any search under sex and cheerleaders will produce many hits. But it is worth noting that the cheerleader role of women in sports pornography reproduces the hegemonic place of women on the margins of the space of the male sportscape. There is also a limited number of representations of women that involve fitness facilities and equipment, reflecting sensibilities around fitness facilities as meat markets.

As numbers of feminist scholars have pointed out over the years, women are sexually represented in soft-porn issues of ostensibly non-sexual publications such as *Sports Illustrated*, the swimsuit issue being the flagship. Indeed the softcore porn sportscape is emerging as a feature of mainstream media representations of women athletes, as for example Brandi Chastain, USA World Cup champion soccer team member, appearing nude behind a soccer ball in *Gear* magazine or Olympic swimmer Jenny Thompson, represented shirtless in *Sports Illustrated*, her breasts covered only by her own clenched fists.[11] But these heterosexualized representations of women's sportscapes do not play a significant role in hardcore pornography, although a few are now making it into the celebrity porn web pages. Indeed if one searches for 'sexy women athletes porn' on the *Google* search engine, the lead hits are of academic articles critiquing the sexual representation of women athletes. On the other hand, if one searches for 'sexy male athletes porn' one is pointed to a multitude of hardcore porn sites that feature the sportscape in a wide variety of ways.

In so far as male-only representations dominate the hardcore pornographic sportscape, they reflect the gender divisions of the mainstream media sportscape. This should not be surprising. There is a much more interesting relationship between the mainstream media sportscape and its pornographic counterpart than simply the parallel between the two as male dominated. The pornographic sportscape plays upon nascent themes and transgressive possibilities of the mainstream. In so doing it opens spaces for readings of sportscapes that both conform to and transcend the mainstream.

A wide variety of themes in sports porn are worth comment, but only one – albeit a major one – will be commented upon here, identified as 'homoerotic slippage'.

It can be argued that the homophobia of men's sport serves the important structural function of maintaining the boundary between the homosociality of sport and its transgressive homoerotic potential. By promulgating fear of homoeroticism, homophobia prevents homoerotic slippage.[12] Homophobia is an important constituent in the sportscape's construction of desire, assumed as part of the emotional texture of the sportscape. Whereas in the mainstream sportscape homoerotic slippage is prevented by homophobia, in the pornographic sportscape it is actively pursued. Which is to say, the ostensibly straight and rule-bound sportscape becomes different. The disciplinary structure of the sportscape becomes especially dynamic, as homophobic control in one way or another dissipates under the pressure of homoerotic desire.

A popular version of this theme has ostensibly straight athletes having sex with each other. The locker room is a very popular place for this to happen. In the opening same-sex sexual scene of the video 'Sizing Up Before Your Very Eyes', a classic sports porn video directed by Matt Sterling in 1985 set at an international sports competition, boasts of heterosexual conquest and the macho banter of a group of young men in a team locker room establish the masculinist bravado of the traditional sportscape. That allows the homoerotic slippage theme to be established, not only in the context of the architectural place of the locker room but also in the traditional heterosexual appearance of the sportscape. In this scene, one of the traditional myths of sport performance – that it is best not to spend one's sexual energy before a competition – is reversed and functions to preserve some semblance of heterosexuality for one of the characters, which helps to maintain the ironic heterosexuality of the sportscape in the midst of its homoerotic subterfuge.

Once the rest of the team members have left the locker room to enter the stadium, two players are left. The first character sits on the bench and starts massaging his crotch through his jock strap, while watching from behind the second who bends over (in his jock strap) tying his shoes. The second is dismayed that one of the other players had just told everyone that he had sex with his girlfriend twice that morning, when he should have been saving his energy for the sport.

> First Character: Oh I don't know, sometimes all this tension makes me hornier than hell, it [having sex] really relaxes me. I know I'd be at my best out there if I could get my nut right now.
> Second Character: (Turns around shocked) Now?
> First Character: I'm so horny I could fuck anything that moves.

The first character's heterosexuality is ostensibly preserved in the instrumental reasoning of needing to have sex simply to perform his sport at his best. And his claim that he's so horny he 'could fuck anything that moves' suggests that it is not homosexual desire that is motivating him, but rather the traditional claim that masculine heterosexual desire is so powerful that even the gender of the sexual partner cannot undermine it. It's not the homosexual sex that he is interested in but his athletic performance that shouldn't be encumbered by his horniness. As the following lines show, the second character has helped out his team mate in this fashion before.

Second Character: You haven't changed you bastard, last time you fucked me I couldn't sit down for a fucking week.

First Character: You don't have to sit down to run the mile! Come on Marshall, we'll go out there full of piss and vinegar.

In that scene the heterosexual masculinity of the men's sportscape and its instrumentally rational approach to the body and desire, as well as all the masculine associations of the men's locker room, allows for a slide into homosexual sex that does not commit the characters to a gay identity. The place of the locker room and the emotional sportscape of heterosexual masculinity become the space for the expression of homoerotic desire that is simultaneously disavowed. The characters slip without slipping. This is a very popular theme in same-sex male pornography, straight guys getting it on with each other.

The male nude wrestling video is a staple of homosexual slippage. BG video has produced hundreds of them and before BG the Athletic Models Guild produced perhaps thousands from the 1960s to the late 1980s. It is argued in 'Outta My Endzone: Sport and the Territorial Anus', that competitive sport orders desire in the quest for spatial domination with a concomitant fear of penetration of space.[13] Which is to say that the competitive sportscape produces space in the tension between the domineering desire to penetrate the space of the other and the desire not to have one's own space penetrated. In field, court and ice sports such as football, basketball and hockey this territorial imperative is obvious. Sportsporn probes the often conflicted desire for and fear of penetration that is operative in the mainstream sportscape. The aggression of competitive sport, its intrinsic violence and the ambivalent interplay of homophobia and homoeroticism becomes itself an organization of sexual desire. The sportscape constructs an erotic space in which male bodies are both attracted to and repelled by each other, which is to say that sport makes it possible for men to touch each other and play the roles of penetrator and penetrated without admitting to the pleasure of male/male penetration.

In sportsporn, and especially in wrestling pornography, the aggression of the competitive sportscape, the mixture of love and hate, of attraction and repulsion, of homophilia and homophobia, are given a homoerotic masturbatory reading. Some wrestling videos, such as *Oiled, Grappled and Fucked* by BG video, render the implicit homoeroticism of the sporting relationship explicit by moving from the implicit sporting desire for penetration that finds its resolution only symbolically in points scored, to the explicit actual penile penetration of orifices in oral and anal fucking. Here the 'loser' gets fucked by the 'winner', an outcome which is not without irony from homoerotic perspectives in which being the penetrated is hardly an unwanted outcome. While the competitive sportscape produces a place for a contest that will determine who is the penetrator (winner) and who is the penetrated (loser), it is for the most part a symbolic space that is opened – the winner does not actually enter the interior physical spaces of the loser's body, thus maintaining the traditional boundaries that set the limits for exploration of the inner and outer spaces of the body in sport. In hardcore 'sportspornscapes', such as *Oiled, Grappled and Fucked*, however, the action moves from symbolic penetration to physical penetration of the interior oral and anal spaces of the body, thus transgressing the traditional homophobic limits on how deeply men can penetrate each other's bodies in the sportscape. For the masturbating reader of such sportspornscape, this presents a moment in which he can eroticize in his own body the slippage from the homophobic prohibition against men exploring the interior spaces of each other's body in the sportscape to the homoerotic licence to do precisely that. The implicit homoeroticism of the sportscape is explicitly realized in the masturbatory reading that the pornographic sportscape provides.

Many, indeed the majority of wrestling videos, however, do not go as far as representing penile penetration. Instead they explicitly sexualize the unresolved tension between homoeroticism and homophilia that is the very pulse of desire in the mainstream sportscape. In a BG video called *Michael Reuter vs Brent Denton* (BG II-1), for example, there is palpable anger and violence in the way they fight: hitting and clearly hurting each other with their faces looking very angry. Wrestling is represented as a tension between the potential desire for each other and the desire to hurt each other. One of the characters is a bit older than the other (perhaps 35 and 25 respectively), which adds the dynamics of age difference to the struggle. The video opens with the following friendly masculine dialogue, which can be read as both a traditional sporting taunt and a homoerotic come-on.

> Elder: 'Hey. I hear you got balls son.'
> Younger: 'I got more than balls.'
> Elder: 'Then let's see what you got.'

They then start slapping. And after some rough interplay, the elder says suggestively: 'Is that all you got?' To which the younger replies 'I'm not that kinda guy asshole.' At which point he grabs the elder by the pectoral muscles and lifts him off the ground and slams him into the wall several times. This obviously hurts the elder, and by his facial expression it is suggested that the violence of the attack has taken him by surprise. The younger says 'I'm going to make you suck my dick, you asshole.' And the elder replies 'You'll have a good time trying, buddy.'

This a particularly powerful video that represents in an almost *vérité* fashion a potent conflict for men's homoerotic desire to touch each other which is simultaneously attraction and repulsion for each other's body. These wrestling videos make explicit this conflicted erotic dynamic that is implicit in the energy of the kind of desire that the sportscape shapes. By making this desire explicit the pornographic sportscapes opens a space for homoerotic difference in the otherwise traditionally homophobic sportscape. But at the same time, in its invocation of the inherent violence of the sportscape it reproduces the hegemonic formation of sporting desire as a violent quest to penetrate with the concomitant fear of being penetrated. There is no homoerotic climax to this video, it simply ends with both wrestlers exhausted. This is a common format for the wrestling pornographic video. An accepting homoerotic conclusion such as that represented in *Oiled, Grappled and Fucked* is unusual in this genre of sports pornography.

Another very popular theme in sports pornography has the ostensibly straight man, with a bit of convincing, become homosexual. It represents a common experience of homosexuality in modern Euro-American culture, where homophobia that prevents homosexual expression eventually gives way. This is one of the cherished coming-out stories of modern lesbian and gay culture: people coming kicking and screaming out of the closet. The sportscape establishes the ostensible heterosexuality of the convert. Whereas the slippage in *Rendezvous with Jayson* represents homoerotic slippage as a gentle process, others represent it with a violence that parallels the violence of contact sports. For example, in a short story entitled *Repositioning the team: the Quarterback* by Cicero, a swashbuckling womanizing quarterback leaves the victory party after winning the Superbowl, and comes across two men having sex in a room in the stadium. The quarterback watches them for a bit, strangely disturbed by the phenomenon.

> Hell this was fucking far out! I couldn't breathe and tried to snap out of it by inhaling deeply. They must have heard me 'cause they both turned. As they did I could see the naked guy turn pale and his dick, which had been hard, wilted like a deflated balloon. He got to his feet, picked up a pile of clothes, and ran past me, leaving just me and the guy in the pants.
>
> 'Hey I know you' he said smiling as if nothing like what I saw had happened and we had just met in the street, 'You're the quarterback on the winning superbowl team. Hey man you were really hot.'
>
> Well, my mind's on what I had seen and how I'm hot to 'sack' that woman waiting for me [in the hotel] and [I wanted to] put behind me this strange feeling I had gotten watching them. Besides who has time for some faggot, 'get lost you dicksucker', I grumble. 'Go find your girlfriend.'
>
> 'Who do you think you are treating me like a punk!' he yells.
>
> 'Fuck you pussy, you're dealing with a real man.' I reply turning to walk away.

'Quarterback', he says 'since you ruined my fun I figure you owe me. Looks like you're my pussy tonight.'

Well, this really burns me. ME HIS PUSSY. Fuck him I'm the biggest cunt man in the league. I walk up to him ready to lay this faggot out. I swing, but he ducks and before I can reposition to swing again he throws a punch to my stomach so hard the air rushes out leaving me doubled over. As I'm gasping for air this guy then calmly lifts my face with his left hand so that I'm staring into these ice blue eyes and gives me a right uppercut that cleans my clock and spells lights out. When I awake I'm still in the room with my arms tied to overhead pipes. As the fog in my mind gets clearer I realize – HELL I'M NAKED !!

In the scene that follows the quarterback is bound and forced to have sado-masochistic sex, the very violence of which enables him to finally accept what he 'really' wanted. The quarterback falls in love with his new-found mentor and they become long-term boyfriends. The mentor turns out to be the invisible owner of the football team, and in subsequent stories the two of them throw lavish dinner parties for selected members of the team and help each one of them come out of the closet. This story plays to the popular gay myth that the most masculine of athletic sportscapes is really a well of repressed homosexuality that is just waiting to be released, which is to say that the homophobia of masculine sports is both mask and control for homoeroticism. Here the violence of sport is represented as requiring a con-comitantly violent rite of homosexual initiation.

Another example of homoerotic slippage can be seen in *Big Guns*, in which a hand gun shooting lesson gently slides into a homosexual sexual encounter. The juxtaposition of the exploding gun against the tenderness of homosexual touching, unlike the conflict of the wrestling video just described, moves to a non-homophobic, indeed positively gay resolution. The World Wide Web has many sites with prose pornographic fiction. www.nifty.org is an archive of gay-related fiction that lists stories in a variety of categories, such as 'first time', 'friendship' and 'athletics'. In a story entitled *Rendezvous with Jayson* by Jerome Moir (www.freegaysex.com/nifty/gay/athletics/rendezvous-with-jayson/ren-dezvous-with-jayson-1), those three themes conjoin as two late-teenaged fast-pitch softball players who have just won a game on a cool summer night set out from the stadium. Jayson follows Derrick home and Derrick, who wonders why, reluctantly allows him into his apartment after Jayson asks to come in for a drink of water. Derrick says that he is going to take a shower (a popular sportscape for homoerotic slippage) and Jayson asks if he can join him. Derrick refuses and tells Jayson to go and shower by him-self. Derrick desires Jayson, but has never had sex with a man before. After

Jayson showers, Derrick does so as well, but when he comes out of the bathroom he can't find Jayson, only to discover him naked on the bed. Still
reluctant, Derrick is taken in Jayson's arms, who says that he has always
wanted to hold him. 'This is unbelievable,' [Derrick] managed to say, as
[he] covered [his] face with [his] hands. There is an impassioned kiss that
melts Derrick's reluctance and he eventually gets fucked for the first time.
This is a story in which the masculinity and fit body culture of the sportscape is the backdrop for a gentle slide into a romantic homoerotic relationship. The slippage is also very physical as the first encounter of anal inter-
course is described as being of surprising ease and immediate, profoundly
enlightening pleasure. Jayson's athletcism plays a role here as well: 'Jayson
is an amazing softballer. But his rhythm in bed is even more impressive. I
know he can go the distance in a regular game, but he was into overtime in
my bed. I couldn't believe that he's been pumping in and out of me for so
long and it seems like he could go even longer.' And when Jayson orgasms,
'He was panting like he had just completed a hundred yards dash.' This
instalment of the story ends with a further confession of love from Jayson
and a wordless acceptance by Derrick that, 'As we drifted off to sleep, I
knew that this night was the beginning of a beautiful relationship.'

Throughout the story Derrick was reluctant to let himself slip, and tried
to resist, but could not persist, realizing in the end that he knew he was at
the beginning of a new life. The sportscape here is a relatively gentle context for the advent of male/male sexuality and love. Sometimes the slippage
is the product of homoerotic appropriation. Otherwise heterosexual sportscapes, by virtue of their placement in the homoerotic pornscape, become
spaces of homophilic desire, in which the ostensible heterosexuality of
sport maintains an uncompromised masculinity that is nevertheless available to the homosexual masturbating gaze. Sometimes this is simply a
matter of posting sports pictures – which then become softcore homoerotic
images: pictures that have been taken of mainstream sporting events are circulated as pornographic representations. This has become a popular genre
on the Internet. See for example www.straightlads.com. The slippage here
is that otherwise 'non-pornographic' images become homosexually pornographic. Here ostensibly straight images are subjected to homosexual masturbatory reading. And again the popular theme is of men's sport culture as
a well of barely repressed homosexual desire. Straightlads.com advertises
itself as showing: 'Straight boys taking their clothes off with each other just
for fun', or as part of an initiation by which they 'get to know the new boys
better'. The straight space of the traditional sportscape is re-spacialized as
the space of homosexual desire. Such pictures also play to the current popularity of 'reality' entertainment. The traditional heterosexuality of sport
and male-only rites constructs the sportscape for this reading.

The Space that (In)Difference Makes: (Re)Producing Subjectivities in/through Abjection – A Locker Room Theoretical Study

CAROLINE FUSCO

A whole history remains to be written of spaces – which would at the same time be the history of powers (both these terms in the plural) – from the great strategies of geo-politics to the little tactics of the habitat ... It is surprising how long the problem of space took to emerge as a historico-political problem.[1]

Why Space?

Harvey states that space, historically, was 'conceived of as something usable, malleable, and therefore capable of domination through human action' and that space came to be represented 'as abstract, objective, homogeneous, and universal in its qualities'.[2] Similarly, Soja, in *Postmodern Geographies*,[3] cites Foucault, who suggests that in the critical thought and discourse of modernity space tended to be treated as 'fixed, dead, undialectical; time as richness, life, dialectical ...'[4] Soja's aim is 'to open up and recompose the territory of the historical imagination through critical spatialization'.[5] Modernity, he says, has celebrated historical imagination while simultaneously inducing 'a growing submergence and dissipation of geographical imagination'.[6] And, as modernity proceeded, historical materialism dominated thought and erased sensitivity to human geographies. Modern geography, when it did emerge, was reduced primarily to the classification and accumulation of factual material. '[M]odern geography was theoretically asleep'.[7] With the introduction of Henri Lefebvre's work, Soja suggests that a type of postmodern critical human geography reasserted space in critical social theory. Lefebvre introduced the notion that 'social and spatial relations are dialectically inter-reactive, interdependent; that social relations of production are both space-forming and space contingent'.[8]

Lefebvre critiques the neglect of study about what space actually is by introducing his concept of 'social space'. From his perspective 'social space "incorporates" social actions', though he points out that social space is not a 'space "in itself"'. Nor is it … a mere 'frame', after the fashion of the frame of a painting, nor a form or container of a virtually neutral kind, designed simply to receive whatever is poured into it. On the contrary, social space 'is at once work and product – a materialization of "social being"'.[9]

> Space is a social morphology … To picture space as a 'frame' or a container into which nothing can be put unless it is smaller than the recipient, and to imagine that this container has no other purpose than to preserve what has been put in it – this is probably the initial error. But is it error or ideology? The latter, more than likely. If so who promotes it? Who exploits it? And why and how do they do so?[10]

For Lefebvre, societies 'secrete' space, producing and appropriating it as they go along. Yet in the modern era, he argues, this complexity of space has been reduced to an abstraction in order to be manipulated and homogenized for the purposes of power. It is drained of lived experience.[11] From Lefebvre onwards, theorists have posited that both human geographies and space are socially produced and intricately connected to the maintenance of power and the production of various subjectivities.[12]

For the purposes of this chapter I want to suggest that subjectivities are (re)produced in a physical education and sports space such as a recreational locker room. This is a complex space where, for example, discourses of public, private, hygiene, public health and the body prevail. My reading of locker rooms proceeds from a postmodern deconstruction of subjectivity and space.[13] My postmodern departure point refutes any claim that a complete story about locker rooms can be told. This constitutes a claim to 'presence' which is taken to be '… an indicator of authenticity, of experience of reality, of – simply put – being able to speak "the truth" about something or other'.[14] Given this acknowledgement I engage in a (figurative) (re)reading of a locker room space in order to speculate, theoretically, about how the promotion of certain kinds of subjectivities are enabled and constrained in locker rooms in, and through, a/the process of abjection which in turn ushers in the (re)production of respectable, normative and proper citizen-subjects. For the purposes of this chapter, my understanding of subjectivity is informed by post-structuralist and postmodern theories of subjectivity – subjectivity is socially constructed and consciousness is actively generated in/through cultural process and practices and psychic ambivalence.[15]

Why the Locker Room?

In sports, the sports sociology literature, 'the locker room' has been an/the object of study, yet writing about this space appears to reify the notion of locker rooms as fixed containers into and from which coherent subjects enter and exit.[16] The space per se, and its role in configuring subjectivities and events that occur there, has not been theorized. This is a modernist conception of space (something that can be filled up and manipulated) and identity (something that is autonomously created and that precedes and acts upon space). In a Lefebvrian sense, however, a locker room can be seen as dynamic space, one that (re)produces, and is (re)produced in/through the social. A locker room is not a space for the performance of already constituted identities but is made a space through various representations, thus enabling and/or constraining the configuration of subjectivities in the first place. As importantly, these subjectivities in turn, enable and/or constrain representations of locker room space. However, space has been theorized by a number of other sports studies scholars.[17] Van Ingen has recently examined the production of queer social space by a queer running group, and Unan has examined imperializing and colonizing aspects of gym space and fitness exercises.[18] Their ideas on a queer geographical imaginary and postcolonial spatializing in the study of sport and space inform my study of the production of subjectivities in a space such as a locker room along with excellent theorizing that has introduced a spatial analyses of the built environments of sport.[19] For example, Bale, Eichberg and Vertinsky separately show how the built environments of sport are particularly imbued with Foucauldian notions of power, discipline and governmentality.[20] Outside the discipline of sports studies the relationship between architecture (the built environment) and power has been a continual subject of discussion.[21] Lefebvre suggests that architects are mediators in discourses of power. He states:

> ... architects and city-planners offered – as an ideology in action – an empty space, a space that is primordial, a container ready to receive fragmentary contents, a neutral medium into which disjointed things, people and habitats might be introduced.[22]

Thus in modernity, Lefebvre would argue that architectural practices and building(s) have merely (re)organized and neutralized space through practices of order and regulation.[23] Space is (re)produced as homogeneous because modernist architectural practices work to eliminate particular differences or peculiarities. Architects (and architecture) offer(s) a neutral space into which new differences can be introduced and accentuated, enabling the exercise of power, and in doing so, close space off to heterogeneity and multiple possibilities. Locker rooms, architecturally, would appear to be a homogeneous space. Yet heterogeneity and difference prevail. The body, its fluids and excretions, its multiple differences, its smells and sounds, for example, are constant rem(a)inders of (in)difference. Body fluids drip or excrete from different pores and orifices. Such differences, however, are rendered fleeting because they are washed away from and off the body – the architectural arrangements help this cleansing process – peculiarities are eliminated in the interests of social hygiene (see Figure 11.1).

I argue that this hygienic regime, and the architectural arrangements in locker rooms, work to (re)organize, introduce and accentuate new differences (differences between clean/dirty, subject/abject, respectable/degenerate). These differences, and the binaries they establish, (con)strain to dominate and (re)produce locker room space as respectable, normative and homogeneous (see Figure 11.2).

(Re)Production of Subjectivity in/through Abjection of Degeneracy

My Locker Room Narrative

As I walk through my locker room I wonder about how this space is (re)produced and how I am (re)produced in/through it. In the space, that is (re)presented, and that (re)presents itself as 'locker room' (to us) there are bodies around m. In North American recreational and fitness centres these bodies are usually same-sex bodies that brush by me. There are many bodies that are (un)like me. There is body flesh, lots of it, bodies sweating, excreting and showering. My locker room is sens(e)ational. I smell sweat, odour, perfume and bleach. I see hairballs in the shower drains, sponges and towels that wash and dry Other bodies. Bathing suits hang and drip around me.

Sometimes I see a toilet that is out-of-order, or graffiti scrawled on a locker; a host of excrements are in my sights/sites. In my locker room I come into close contact, and even touch, the excreted bodily fluids and residues of others when I sit in a sauna or on a toilet seat or turn on a tap, open a toilet door. My feet touch and may get tangled up in hairs that linger on the shower room floor. I dry myself off with a towel that, before it was washed, previously touched someone else's body. But tacitly I know that I should not touch – directly – another's body in my locker room or touch myself for pleasure beyond the pleasure I get in washing my body. I hear water – flushing, dripping and sloshing – and chit-chat. I taste my sweat around my lips before it is washed away. This sens(e)sationality takes place amongst the various architectural arrangements – signs, mirrors, lockers, locks, weighing scales, garbage cans, showers, soap dispensers, water taps,

FIGURE 11.1

Locker room showers. (Author, courtesy University of Toronto)

FIGURE 11.2

Rules and regulations. (Author, courtesy University of Toronto)

drains and cubicles – that are part of a locker room. Outside the locker room – in my sports – I sweat, spit, blow mucus out of my nose – excretions predominate. I smell, touch and get soiled with grass, mud, water, blood and the bodily excretions and fluids from other bodies that touch me, the ball, the rackets, the weight machines, the exercise mats before I use them. If I am playing contact sports, I most definitely, and directly, touch other bodies. This mixing of bodily fluids and bodies is assumed to be appropriate to these discourses in designated sports spaces. Yet the bodily excretions that are on, and in, my body when I return to my locker room assume a(n) (in)different role. In my locker room my excretions mingle on the floors, on the toilet seats, on the doors or faucet handles with everyone else's excretions and fluids, yet here these mixtures of bodily fluids and excretions hover on the borders of inappropriateness. As they start to linger, they smell and grow stale. They 'must' be washed off me. So in my locker room, after my sports, I usually have a shower. I wash my body and my hair after my sport. In fact this, I am convinced, is one of the main reasons that I go to locker rooms. I lather up my hands and my sponge and then all my body parts with soaps and cleansers. I wash my body and the dirt off me under a warm water shower; I may sometimes even shave. I carry out all this activity in the full view of others; I clean off my excretions in public. These excretions flow from/off my body and mingle with all the other excretions that are making their way to the drains. Then I dry my body, my hair, put on creams, hair products and clean clothes. The wet, sweat-smelling clothes I worked out in are packed away to be washed later. The towel I use to cover my sweaty and 'dirty' body as I walk to the showers, that I use to rub all my body parts clean and dry, is thrown into a laundry basket with all the other towels that have touched other bodies. Someone then lifts these towels out of the basket and puts them in a washing machine from which the towels emerge clean and ready for their next body contact (see Figure 11.3). I cannot help but think that in this locker room space, in the midst of all these events, that my subjectivity (and that of Others) is (are) being (re)produced in that matter.

This personal narrative helps me think about how those of us who use locker rooms are encouraged to fit, for example, into particular discourses of social and public health and hygiene. These discourses, I believe, are (re)produced in, and through, locker room space. I argue that they are founded on the abjection of excess[24] and the desire to (re)produce a/the respectable, normative and proper subject. Locker room space and the spatial arrangements that are inherent to typical North American recreational centres are configured to enable and constrain certain excesses (e.g., sweat, excretions, eliminations – although these are managed in particular ways) while tacitly prohibiting others (e.g., infection, homoeroticism, co-ed mixing, voyeurism, sex acts). All these excesses, Bataille might suggest, are

FIGURE 11.3

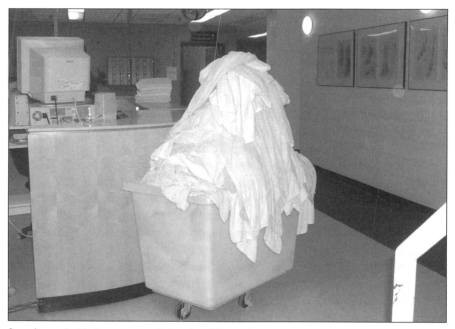

Laundry work. (Author, courtesy University of Toronto)

obscenities '… which upset the physical state associated with self-posses-sion, with the possession of a recognized and stable individuality'.[25] Likewise, Stallybrass and White might suggest that these excesses often figure as the 'recalcitrant Other to trouble the fantasy of an independent, separate, 'proper' identity'.[26]

The strategy for dealing with difference and excess and for maintaining a proper identity, with its bodily boundaries intact, is to abject excess (rep-resented in the locker room as dirt and/or disorder) because it disturbs sub-jectivity and the so-called civilized order.[27] Douglas's *Purity and Danger: An Analysis of the Concepts of Pollution and Taboo* examines how social taboos are established around disgust in order to maintain bodily boundaries and particular systems of exclusions in various non-western cultures. She suggests that '… pollution is a type of danger which is not likely to occur except where lines of structure, cosmic or social, are clearly defined'.[28] From her perspective, dirt and disorder are not isolated events but are by-products of a systematic classification of matter. Dirt, for instance, is matter out of place. Furthermore, attitudes around pollution are a reaction to the possible confusion of cherished classifications of order/disorder. Thus, Douglas's notions of purity and pollution are prefigured in the idea that there is a clear (and clean) separation between what is ordered and pure and what is not. Other authors have theorized how this clean/dirty binary is simultaneously constitutive of boundaries, not as a separate or absolute difference, as Douglas argues, but as differences that fold into one another, creating an ambivalent psychic attachment to abjection and dirt and disorder.[29] Maintaining purity and propriety of self, which is characteristic of the normative subject, is a never-ending battle against bodily residues – and it is a battle that has wider existential significance.[30]

Kristeva's *Powers of Horror* is important to a discussion of the concept of abjection in relation to the construction of discrete (psychic and social) subjectivity through exclusion and difference. Abjection here moves beyond the notion of merely making the already constituted body and subjectivity pure and proper. It founds subjectivity in the first place. Kristeva writes, 'I abject myself within the same motion through which "I" claim to establish myself ... I give birth to myself amid the violence of sobs, of vomit ... Such waste drops so that I might live.'[31] While the history of attitudes towards dirt and waste are founded on the idea(l) of expelling the abject, Kristeva suggests that what is troublesome to the subject, and by extension identity, is not a lack of cleanliness or health, it is anything that disturbs identity or the system of order. There is an attempt to expel the abject because it does not respect borders, positions, or rules. Rightly so, confirms Kristeva, since the abject is something to be scared of because 'excrement and its equivalents (decay, infection, disease, corpse, etc.) stand for the danger to identity that comes from without: the ego threatened by the non-ego, society threatened by its outside, life by death'.[32] The abject, therefore, is something that is designated as improper and unclean, something that the proper and clean subject throws away or refuses.[33] But the abject can never be completely expelled. Separations are never finally achieved because the abject is required for the subject to persist. The abject remains part of the subject though, as Kristeva writes, it hovers at the borders of the subject's identity threatening apparent unity and stability with disruption and possible dissolution.

Historically, attitudes towards excess, pollution, disgust, obscenity – and what or who is abjected – have been materially, and differently, constituted on particular bodies, thus enabling and/or constraining the (re)production of certain kinds of subjectivities.[34] Key to my discussion is the recognition that any threat to order establishes and accelerates not only the (re)production of bodily boundaries but the (re)production of spatial boundaries and methods of containment. The idea of the (re)production of spatial boundaries and methods of containment and their relation to the (re)production of subjectivities is not new, of course; it is a continual theme in the work of Foucault, particularly in relation to the construction of spaces to manage madness, criminality and sexual deviancy.[35] I suggest that the locker room is part of a system of social organization and spatialization that enables and constrains the abjection of excess, ensuring that proper bodies and objects, and those marked as non-proper, according to Butler, can come to matter at all.[36]

Proper subjectivity is one that is respectable and not degenerate. Although postmodern theorists have critiqued binarized conceptualizations (i.e., the notion of either/or), binaries do get (re)produced in, and through, social life. Bodies come to matter if they are respectable. They do not matter, or at least they matter in a different way, if they are degenerate. According to Fellows and Razack, respectability and degeneration are:

> ...descriptive term(s) for how the dominant group secures its position of dominance through the margins. How groups on the margins are positioned in relation to one another on the disrespectable, or more aptly, the degenerate side of the divide ...[37]

Discourses of respectability and degeneration and their impact on the production of subjectivities can be historically situated. The concept of degeneration was introduced by Morel into medical discourses and popular vocabulary in the nineteenth century.[38] Mosse states: degeneration is the antithesis of respectability, 'a term indicating "decent" and "correct"' manners and morals, as well as the proper attitude towards sexuality'. Respectability for Mosse was more than just decorum, it was constituted through the intersections of nineteenth-century European nationalism, aesthetic sensibilities, modesty, purity, the practice of virtue and European middle-class attitudes towards the human body.[39]

Historically, McClintock writes, degeneration was a necessary concept for the self-definition of the middle classes in nineteenth-century Europe. Discourses of degeneration were deployed to ensure regimes of discipline, whether that was hygienic or miscegenation, and were especially prevalent in Britain when imperial rivalry with Germany and the United States threatened Britain's status in colonial domination. The social power of degeneration cast various groups as contagious and pathological, describing them as foreign, non-indigenous, or of another race in opposition to the healthy and powerful imperial race.[40] Discourses of degeneration were concomitant with a fixation on sanitation; while acute diseases and unhygienic conditions did prevail, these discourses also served to rationalize and ritualize the policing and maintenance of spatial boundaries in European cities and in the colonies.[41] Aesthetic and hygienic sensibility was particularly linked with social hygiene in nineteenth-century Europe and was intricately connected not only with the (re)production of architectural boundaries, spatial confinements, and arrangements but to the manufacture of products such as soaps and detergents which were marketed as products that could bestow respectability on (particularly middle-class) users. These products are, of course, central to one's locker room experience. In the nineteenth century, soap promised salvation and regeneration to the 'threatened potency of the imperial body politic and the race'. Soap and bleach were also vividly embodied as products that could convert other(ed) cultures to civilization, 'the whitening agent of bleach promise(d) an alchemy of racial uplift'. The aesthetics of respectability, then, were linked to the imperial mission itself.[42] The colonial and racist links between notions of purity, cleanliness and whiteness in opposition to dirt and the defiled cannot be underestimated.[43] In the nineteenth century, clean and proper individuals, cleanliness and Victorian purifying rituals 'were peddled globally as the God-given sign of Britain's evolutionary superiority'.[44] Soap manufacture and discourses on hygiene flourished because they could 'pervasively mediate the Victorian poetics of racial hygiene and imperial progress'.[45] It is beyond the scope of this chapter, but I would suggest that these representations continue to prevail today. In fact, Dyer points out that still 'Non-white people are associated in various ways with the dirt that comes out of the body ... To be white is to have expunged all dirt, faecal or otherwise, from oneself: to be white is to look clean.'[46]

Fellows and Razack suggest that as these discourses of physical and moral health became linked to the survival of the European White nation in the nineteenth century the concept of degeneracy emerged as antithetical to health and the production of European bourgeois subjects. Furthermore, they suggest these notions of respectability and degeneracy continue today because they enable 'the boundaries between those who are included in the body politic and those who are not' to be established.[47] Respectability and degeneracy are thus spatialized. Razack argues that the identity-making processes, characteristic of the nineteenth-century bourgeois subject, which still occur today, require a 'containment of the Other' in order to engage in a 'making of the dominant self'. Spatial arrangements still '... establish who is respectable and who is not. Space determines who belongs to the nation state and who does not'.[48] The social and spatial organization of the locker room ensures that the locker room is a space where degenerate differences, peculiarities and 'Otherness' can be legitimately contained and expelled whether, for example, this is in the form of containing and monitoring the body, bodily excretions or who has access to the space and the consumption of leisure that it is part of. This containment may enable the continual (re)making of normative subjectivities in this space.

Locker Room Architecstructures – Technical Organizations of
Space and Subjectivity

Historically, Wigley shows that with the invention of personal privacy in the Enlightenment period, and the space it produced, architecture was established as a site of purification. He suggests that as the body itself emerged as a threat to the purity of space, architecture defended against the body by ordering it. A typical modern North American recreational locker room appears to enable this ordering. Technical strategies, like drains, attempt to control and organize the refuse of the body. They attempt to carry away 'the abject domain from the spatial representation of pure order'.[49]

> The smell gives away the presence of that which should be hidden. Like the other bodily functions in the bedroom, it must be doubly privatized. Architecture no longer simply reveals what it houses. This new sense of privacy was gradually produced throughout the following centuries by redefining the spaces of the house into a complex order of layered spaces and subdivisions of spaces that map a social order by literally drawing the lines between hierarchies of propriety ... Without such vigilant control of the surface, the disorder of the body can infect ethical, aesthetic, political, and juridical regimes.[50]

Similarly, Betsky states that for modernist architects such as Le Corbusier, 'the bathroom and plumbing held central place because of their ability to drain off the reality of the body as quickly, hygienically, and elegantly as possible'.[51] Locker rooms (and their early forerunners, such as dressing rooms in bathhouses or washhouses), and the spatial arrangements therein, like showers and toilets, appear to be designed specifically to drain off the peculiarities and waste, potential infections of/from the body. Thus, it may be theorized that locker rooms were/are intricately connected with the rise of modernity and the constitutive developments of social hygiene, public sanitation, the health and well-being of the social body and the private individual.

A postmodern reading of respectability, social hygiene and public sanitation would posit cleanliness as the modern project's supreme act.[52] Modernity has attempted to repress the abject and unclean – often defined as, but not confined to, excrement, putrefaction, dirt, semen and menses – through securing hygienic architecture that works to eliminate the abject through an overemphasis on visual cleanliness, proper plumbing and right angles. There is a compulsion to sustain hygienic efficiency, not only in the architecture (literally in the walls and surfaces of the locker room) but also in the very artifacts that (re)organize and (re)produce hygiene. For example, Braham points out that:

> Keeping dirt and water in their place and removing any trace of their presence is a strategy for preserving the artifacts conceived by the architectural imagination. ... These are material qualities by which the hygienic order is understood and exercised in everyday constructions like a tub.[53]

To this I might add artifacts like the shower, toilet and washbasins. In fact the aesthetics of many modern locker room facilities appear to (and are encouraged to) secure hygienic efficiency through their emphasis on clean, light pastel and brightly coloured paintwork, straight lines, rectangles and polished surfaces (see Figure 11.4).[54] Architectural and hygienic practices, I suggest, both combine to enable and constrain what, or who, is regarded as respectable and proper, and what, or who, is degenerate, abject and needs to be expelled. This process engenders locker room space and the subjects of/in space.

Probyn writes that 'space is a pressing matter and it matters which bodies, where and how, press up against it'.[55] If this is so then it is important to examine how architectural arrangements (re)configure locker room space in order to enable, and/or constrain, who or what presses up against us in that space. Changing and preparing for sport in a typical North American recreation and fitness centre cannot, and should not (according to particular guidelines), take place just anywhere; it takes place under standardized circumstances.[56] Preparation for, and cleansing after, sports must all occur in one particular place. The messy, sweaty, smelly, excreting bodies that move in and through the locker room are subjected to vigilant control. Although it appears there is some choice about whether to shower or not (i.e., to be or not to be clean), there is great pressure bearing down on individuals to wash and flush away the excretionsthat press against them in order to be hygienic. Locker room architectural arrangements appear to prioritize purification yet there is often a distinction between what is respectable purification and what is not. For instance, at the University of Toronto Athletic Centre locker room patrons can shower but are discouraged from other intimate personal hygiene activities (e.g., removing callouses and clipping toe-nails). Yet the locker room does allow patrons to openly deal with (the horror of) excreted fluids that they are prohibited from dealing with elsewhere in the athletic centre. For instance, if activities such as washing, walking around naked or going to the bathroom were carried on outside the locker room in the main athletic facility, then they would be deemed out of place and disgusting. There is an acknowledgment, then, of the unique kinds of corporeal activities that take place within the locker room walls; the space gives legitimacy, for example, to cleaning corporeal chaos and excretions but this chaos is constrained and managed in certain ways. And if the chaotic corporeality is not washed away, then there is always a cleaner or maintenance staff who comes into the locker room to hose the chaos further out of sight with an array of mops and cleansers (see Figure 11.5). This cleaner most often is a woman or man of colour, or a non Anglo-Canadian white immigrant.[57]

FIGURE 11.4

Locker room aesthetics. (Author, courtesy University of Toronto)

FIGURE 11.5

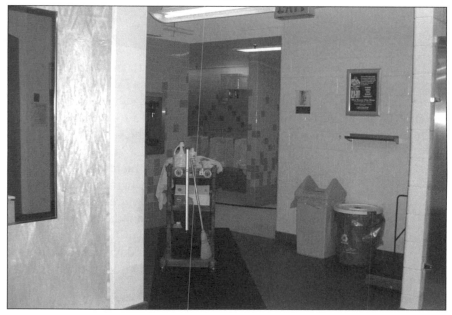

Cleaning corporeal chaos. (Author, courtesy University of Toronto)

The locker room (in conjunction with a gym) is where bodies are made to fit. Yet in the locker room there may be constant rem(a)inders of how unfit bodies may be. Unfit, not in terms of their muscularity, although this too is probably a source of constant anxiety, but in terms of what shape the body is in, for instance, when it is covered and dripping with the bodily residues of sporting activity. Sweat, dirt and some bodily fluid excretions are celebrated in sport for they are a mark of a hard workout (and often a mark of masculinity). One can see numerous advertisements with athletes' faces and clothes drenched in sweat or dripping *Gatorade* from their pores. There are also images of baseball players chewing and spitting tobacco and blood-drenched enforcer hockey players. Yet there is a point when all these fluids, excretions and dirt (if these are not expelled onto the ice and into the grass) have to be dealt with, particularly when they start to smell, linger on the athlete's body and mix with the fluids of others. This is when the (social) body is/may be pressed to send these uncanny corporeal fluids somewhere else. The architectural organization of my locker room, with its showers, toilets and saunas provides the body with a place to expel the threatening excessive and abject(ed) sweat, bodily fluids, waste and dirt from one's pores and orifices. While recognizing that there are social and hygienic reasons for dirt and bodily excrements to be cleaned away, the rites of purification that are engaged in in locker rooms, such as washing, wearing foot protection, avoiding soiled toilet seats and so on, not only protect against infection but protect the subject from becoming (materially and psychically) contaminated by polluting pseudo-objects (like sweat, hair, faeces and urine). They enable respectability and propriety to be (re)produced.

Sibley suggests that the urge to set up borders between clean and dirty, order and disorder, and to expel the abject is critical to an articulation of the identity of rational respectable, white, Westerners. Degeneracy, as suggested previously, is the threat that can unhinge the subject, so there is an attempt to avoid it. The anxiety that is expressed to expel the abject is particularly virulent in a locker room because, as Sibley states:

> ... the consciousness of dirt and disorder is increased and we can anticipate that a feeling of abjection will be particularly strong in those environments ... which are symbolically pure. It is the identification of numerous residues, to be expelled from the body, the home, the locality, which is the characteristic of the purification process. In such environments, difference will register as deviance, a source of threat to be kept out through the erection of strong boundaries, or expelled.[58]

In addition to the pressure exerted on the patrons in my locker room to clean themselves, there is also pressure not to press against other bodies, particularly same-sex bodies. This is tacitly understood. In such a way, not only are sweat, excrement and bodily fluids marked as abject and different, but Other(ed) bodies may be differently marked as abject and Other, and may be repudiated, for example, because of their class, sex, sexuality and colour.[59] Sibley argues that when interacting with Others' residues the 'fear of pollution can be a constant source of anxiety'.[60] In my locker room the bodily residues of everyone's bodies are in constant confrontation but the design and aesthetics of my locker room attempt to give the patrons a sense of distance from dirt and disorder and from Others, (e.g., the emphasis on bright paint colours, polished surfaces, individual shower stalls, privacy cubicles). However, discourses of social and public hygiene may still press the patrons to socially and psychically project degeneracy onto Other(ed) bodies, particularly those bodies that do not fit, or are outside the on-going body projects of modernity.[61] Butler suggests that the expulsion of these abject bodies is 'followed by a 'repulsion' that founds and consolidates culturally hegemonic identities along, for example, sex/race/sexuality axis of differentiation'. This process of socially regulating the body's borders is a mode by which 'Others become shit' and are made abject.[62]

The Space that Indifference Makes

The architectural arrangements of the locker room I use, with its toilets, showers, saunas, hand-basins and the discourses of public/private, for example, that prevail there enable and/or constrain the expulsion or containment of the abject. The architecture of the locker room (con)strains to emphasize sanitary conditions and coherent subjectivity yet the space can disrupt our imperial identities.[63] The borders between (my)self and abject objects (e.g., shit, hair-balls) and Others (e.g., non-normative bodies), are rendered incoherent at times. For example, although the locker room, on the surface, engenders a sense of hygiene and cleanliness, underneath the floor, behind the walls and in the piping, not so far from the surfaces I touch, smell and see, a labyrinth of sewers harbouring and flushing around, and out, my dirt, sweat and excrement (see Figure 11.6). Sometimes the excessive abject is not washed away and presents itself to me, however fleetingly, in the out-of-order toilet, the hairball in the shower drains, the smell of sweat, the dripping sponges that have touched Other(ed) bodies.

In the locker room, subjects and objects do collide, press and rub up against each other. In my locker room, for example, the previously used towels that were wrapped around sweaty bodies, that rubbed clean and dried the bodies of others, are cleaned and re-used. All around, flesh and excre-

FIGURE 11.6

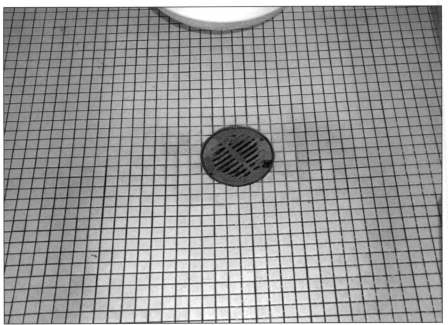

Dirt, disorder and drains. (Author, courtesy University of Toronto)

tions are colliding even though the space (con)strains to make clear the boundaries between respectability and degeneracy, proper and improper. Yet all the boundaries (i.e., those between bodies, bodies and excretions, surfaces and bodies) are subject to momentary collapse. Abject objects and Others, I have argued, are set up in opposition to the idea(l) of the respectable, clean, secure and coherent proper subject. These abject objects (and Others) may be established as repugnant and obscene only because they are a threat to the boundaries of the clean and proper subject. (Re)turning to Kristeva to (re)think abjection psychoanalytically, these uncanny, obscene abject objects and Others are required for the subject's (the Self's) existence, because it is their haunting and inhabiting of the ego that is simultaneously constitutive of its (the ego's) very identification. Although discourses of social hygiene, public sanitation and healthy and safe architecture constitute locker room space and establish the domain of the (re)presentable in locker rooms, even these discourses are inevitably, as Butler might suggest, 'bounded through the production of a constitutive outside: the unspeakable, the unsignifiable'. Butler writes that the 'posture of the adult subject consists precisely in the denial and reenactment of this dependency' on the unspeakable, and I would add that the representations of locker room space also depend on this prohibition.[64] Thus the subjects and discourses of locker room space are intimately bounded by and have an unspeakable ambivalent and indifferent attachment to, the abject.

In/Unconclusion

Can the binaries of respectability/degeneracy and subject/abject that set Other(ed) bodies and objects up as shit in locker room space be transgressed to engender new subjectivities? The point is not to prescribe the taking up/on of new and different identifications, for instance, to identify as degenerate or abject. Identifications that are conventionally disavowed cannot be suddenly avowed. Stallybrass and White argue that this appropriation is dangerous because it constitutes a discovery of bourgeois pleasures, dangers and desires under the sign of the Other, in the realm of the Other. This playful inversion is constitutive of the very formation of a normative and respectable identity in the first place.[65] Butler also cautions against taking on/in/up an Other(ed) identity position because it is an imperial gesture – in the sense of the imperial 'I':

> The ideal of transforming all excluded identifications into inclusive features – of appropriating all difference into unity – would mark the return to a Hegelian synthesis which has no exterior and that, in appropriating all difference as exemplary features of itself, becomes a figure for imperialism, a figure that installs itself by the way of a romantic, insidious, and all-consuming humanism.[66]

The task, then, is not to embrace abject objects or subjectivities, or to suddenly avow, or open up to, degeneracy because 'certain kinds of disavowals function as constitutive constraints, and they cannot be willed away'. In order to come to matter at all, there are 'exclusions that must be refused, identifications that must remain as refuse, as abjected' in order for coherent identifications to exist.[67]

The task is to recognize and re-cognize how subjectivities and space are (re)produced in physical education, sport and community health space(s). It is to (re)think the limits of the discourses that organize and spatialize. The system of social organization that enables and/or (con)strains to render locker room space and other physical education and sports space(s) homogenous in order to neutralize, cleanse and eliminate heterogeneity and difference(s) needs to be destabilized and thought (in)differently. The task is to show how the discourses that organize/render/(re)produce locker room space and locker room subjectivities – focused on refusing excessive and abject difference(s) – always already inevitably are failing as subjectivity and space that cannot be (re)produced or (re)presented without (in)difference and ambivalence. Exploring how this ambivalence and indifference is governed to maintain particular modes of social life, subjectivity and space is an on-going project.

Acknowledgements

The author wishes to thank the Faculty of Physical Education and Health at the University of Toronto for granting permission and access to take her photographs in the locker rooms. All photographs are copyright of the author.

For Pleasure? Or Profit
Or Personal Health?:
College Gymnasia as Contested Terrain

ROBERTA J. PARK

I could do for the young men at the University, that which would be of much
profit and pleasure to them ... if I would construct on the University grounds a
building to be used as a gymnasium, and on extra University occasions,
as an auditorium.

Letter from A.K.P. Harmon to the Board of Regents
of the University of California, 1879

Those associated with Cal who have roamed the southwest quadrant of the
Berkeley campus in recent weeks have conjured up images of the open-air Roman
Colosseum ... the deconstruction of Harmon Gymnasium, clearing the way for the
building of the Walter Haas, Jr. Pavilion, has been well under way for the past
several months.

The Promise of Berkeley, California Athletics Campaign, Winter 1998

In reviewing the events of the past year ... the most prominent object, and the one
that will confer the greatest benefit upon the whole body of the students, is the
Harmon Gymnasium. ... Every student ... feels himself daily growing physically
and mentally stronger under its health-giving stimulus.

1879 Blue and Gold

Cal's sports across the board stand to benefit from the higher revenues, the new
office space, and the ability to show off a wonderful building to new recruits. ...
How appropriate that the venue [Haas Pavilion] will open its doors with a brand-
new banner to raise, celebrating the Bears' 1999 NIT Championship.

Haas Pavilion: Dreams Do Come True, 1999

Introduction

The above statements, separated by 120 years, are indicative of changes that
have occurred with regard to those structures that we call gymnasiums, the
purposes for which they exist on a college campus and the activities that
take place within their premises. When in 1879 local businessman Albion

Keith Harmon used the word 'profit', did he intend the same thing as the attractive 1999 brochure *Dreams Do Come True* when it used the term 'revenues'? Or do different motivations now influence the building of college gymnasia?

Everyone knows – or thinks they know – what a gymnasium is, what kind of programmes are conducted therein, and for what purposes. Gymnasia have become such integral parts of the American college campus that it is easy to assume a kind of linear progression from the small building at Amherst College in the 1860s through the more grandiose Harvard Gymnasium of the 1890s to today's vast complexes with their special exercise rooms filled with Nautilus and other equipment, martial arts rooms, handball and squash courts, extensive training quarters, special amenities for athletic 'boosters' and huge basketball pavilions. However, when questions are asked about such things as their centrality or marginality (both physical and conceptual); their architectural style, their size, floor plans, and functionality; who uses what portions of the facility and under what conditions; which modality dominates – *hygeia* or *ludus*; and where in the hierarchical value structures of an institution do programmes whose focus is the exercising body stand, it becomes evident that realities are more complex.

Within the gymnasium many – and often conflicting – 'discourses' have been, and are, acted out. Here the body holds a commanding presence as it is freed of restrictive clothing and extends itself in contests and physical activities ranging from gymnastics to basketball to interpretive dance – and more. At the same time, within these same spaces and places the body has been and still is severely constrained and disciplined as it is subjected to prescribed exercise programmes and intense training regimens and evaluated by a host of methodologies ranging from the tape measure to oxygen uptake while exercising on a bicycle ergometer. Here values that coalesce in, construct and reinforce our conceptions of power, weakness, masculinity, femininity, and much more are, quite literally, 'acted out'. These complex – and often paradoxical – matters, which are infused with ever-present Cartesian dualisms, merit greater attention than they have received to date. This paper examines a constellation of such matters at one institution – the University of California, Berkeley.

'Place, Space and Purpose' – In the Beginning

Established by an act of the California State Legislature in 1868, the University of California (UC) began operation the following year with ten male faculty and 40 male students in the town of Oakland. Action by the Board of Regents made it possible for 17 women to register for classes in autumn 1870. Three years later, when South Hall (still standing) and North Hall were completed, the University moved to its present location in Berkeley. In the 1875–77 *Biennial Report of the Regents*, UC President John LeConte listed among his highest priorities for the campus a museum, a library and a building that would serve as a gymnasium, auditorium and military drill room.[1] (The Morrill Land Grant Act of 1862, under whose conditions the University had been established, required instruction in military training as well as agriculture and the mechanic arts.) Mathematics professor George Edwards (Class of 1873), who had married Harmon's daughter, prevailed upon him to offer $15,000. Harmon wrote to the Board of Regents, stating:

> [It has been] suggested to me by Mr George C. Edwards, that if I felt inclined, I could do for the young men at the University, that which would be of much profit and pleasure to them. … if I would construct on the University grounds a building to be used as a gymnasium, and on extra University occasions, as an auditorium.

In his letter Harmon specified that the 'prime object' of the building was to enable students to obtain 'a certain reasonable amount of exercise' and urged the University to secure the 'services of an excellent instructor'. In a statement that must be considered advanced for its time he also expressed hope that 'suitable hours' would be set aside for female students, who were to be supplied with equipment that would cultivate 'symmetry and strength'.[2]

The 21,200 sq. ft. octagonal wooden building (the third to be constructed on the Berkeley campus), completed in 1879, had rustic mouldings and a pitched roof adorned with a cupola. The tongue and groove redwood inner walls, to which racks of Indian clubs and a number of pulley weights would be affixed, were oiled and varnished to preserve the natural grain.[3] Within a short time a few hours had been set aside on Wednesday and Friday afternoons for the exclusive use of the 'co-eds'. Because the University had no auditorium, Harmon Gym (see Figure 12.1) was used for such functions as the Junior Prom and the annual football banquet. Benjamin Ide Wheeler, who became the eighth President in 1899, initiated the practice of holding University meetings there. (Among those who spoke during the early years were Frank Norris, Jack London and Booker T. Washington.)[4] Additions in 1903 more than doubled the building's size.

A voluntary class for 'young ladies wishing to share the same benefits' as the young men (who had been required to enroll when the Department of Physical Culture opened in 1888) was begun in 1889. Instruction was given by Mr Walter Magee, whose wife Genevra served as chaperone – later as Associate in Physical Culture.[5] Not satisfied with their limited opportunities, more than 200 current and former students petitioned the Board of

FIGURE 12.1

Harmon Gymnasium. (Hearst Gymnasium Historical Collection, University of California, Berkeley)

Regents in 1891, stating: 'A large number of young women in this University wish to take the course in physical culture, but are debarred by the want of a woman examiner [i.e., physician]. They thus suffer injustice, as members of the University, in being debarred from equal enjoyment of its advantages.'[6] The local chapter of the Association of Collegiate Alumnae (today's American Association of University Women) added its support. The University's great benefactress and first woman Regent, Phoebe Apperson Hearst, provided funds to make possible the appointment of Mary Bennett Ritter, MD (who already was serving on a voluntary basis). In 1893, ten hours were made available for their exclusive use and Dr Ritter began giving them lectures on hygiene, how the body functions, the benefits of healthful activity and how to care for the injured.[7]

The Creation of a Department of Physical Culture

In his 1882–84 *Biennial Report* William T. Reid (the University's fourth president) spoke enthusiastically about the new Harmon Gymnasium, noting the importance of providing students with systematic instruction in physical education. The section titled 'Gymnasium' followed that titled 'Health of Students' and in it Reid wrote: 'That physical education is of grave importance is becoming recognized by some of the best colleges in the country. Indeed, such satisfactory results have followed from systematic physical training, conducted upon sound physiological principles, that the gymnasium is rapidly assuming an importance almost, if not quite, co-ordinate with the many other branches of education.'[8]

During the last decades of the nineteenth century physical education was a topic of interest to an impressive number of educators, social reformers and medical doctors. Views similar to those articulated by Reid in his 1882–84 *Report* were expressed at meetings of the American Social Science Association and published in an array of journals ranging from the *Journal of the American Medical Association* and the *Pedagogical Seminary* (today's *Journal of Genetic Psychology*) to the widely circulated *North American Review*.[9] It might surprise today's reader to learn how much attention the *Boston Medical and Surgical Journal* (*BMSJ*, today's *New England Journal of Medicine*) devoted to the topic – or how many founders of the American Association for the Advancement of Physical Education (AAAPE) in 1885 held a medical degree.[10]

Reporting on the 1889 Boston Conference on Physical Training, which had been attended by 2,000 interested individuals, the *BMSJ* declared: '[W]e believe that a department of physical education should be given a place and voice in the regular curriculum … The mature, well-balanced adult of the future will probably look back with much satisfaction to the time devoted to this department of school and college work.'[11] Physical training, another *BMSJ* article observed, recently had been 'organized into a profession of considerable importance, involving and implying study, training, thought and research'. Luther Halsey Gulick (a graduate of the New York University Medical School and member of the young American Association for the Advancement of Physical Education) declared it to be a new profession 'involving for its fullest appreciation a profound knowledge of man through physiology, anatomy, psychology, history and philosophy'. There were, he maintained, few other fields that offered as many opportunities 'of greater value to the human race'.[12]

When UC's President Reid declared the purpose of physical education was to 'accompany the well balanced mental training of the college with an equally well balanced physical training', he had stipulated that athletics and physical education served quite different ends. The director of the gymnasium must be a man who had a thorough medical education and 'ha[d] made physical development a special study'. It was to be 'clearly borne in mind', Reid insisted, 'that it is not the purpose of a college gymnasium to make athletes'. He thanked Mr Harmon for providing a facility that was 'excelled by few other college gymnasiums' and ended this section of his *Report* by expressing hope that systematic physical training soon would be required of every student.[13]

Two years later the Board of Regents appropriated $3,000 for the establishment of a Department of Physical Culture. The Academic Senate thereupon voted 'that all male undergraduates, at least during the first two years' attendance at the University, be required to take five half hours per week of active exercise'.[14] When the Department of Physical Culture opened in 1888, Frank Howard Payne, MD, was named Director of the Gymnasium. His duties included overseeing the programme (instruction was given by Mr Magee), giving each man an annual medical examination, and providing lectures on physiology and hygiene. Payne reported on the progress of his department in the December 1890 *Pacific Medical Journal*, citing several instances in which the students' health had been improved. He also made the perceptive observation: 'Physical culture means far more than is suggested to the outside world.'[15]

Defining, Designing, Creating, and Controlling Places and Spaces

In his article Payne had stated: 'We shall gladly hail the time when some great hearted California millionaire will cause to be erected a suitable building for the purpose of a gymnasium and club-house for the young women.'[16] In 1899 Phoebe Hearst donated the 19,410 sq. ft. reception hall (see Figure 12.2) (designed by Bernard Maybeck to receive dignitaries during the judging of the international architectural competition for the Berkeley campus) that adjoined her home. The redwood shingle building with laminated Gothic arches was moved in sections to the campus, where it was converted into a gymnasium and social centre for women students. An outdoor basketball court surrounded by a high fence 'to prevent anyone from witnessing the game from the outside' was built; and a physical education 'requirement' for female students was initiated in 1901. An uncovered swimming pool, also surrounded by a high fence, was added in 1914.[17]

The 1901 *Occident* (Women's Edition) was dedicated to Mrs Hearst 'in heartfelt love and gratitude'. Whereas formerly the campus had been 'a spot where women had to contest for standing room', one commentator noted, now they had their own debating, journalism, and musical organizations, and their own rooters club. Moreover, thanks to Mrs Hearst's beneficence they finally had their own gymnasium – 'a source of real pleasure'.[18] That same year they created their own athletic association, Sports and Pastimes (renamed the Women's Athletic Association in 1921).

As the nineteenth century ended, the 245-acre campus consisted of about a dozen buildings (half of which were small and of a 'temporary' nature), a tennis court, cinder track and considerable open space where sports like baseball and other extracurricular activities took place. Increasing enrolments (approximately 1,500 by 1897) intensified the need for new buildings.[19] Bay Area leaders had already exhibited a desire to create 'a city

FIGURE 12.2

Hearst Hall, Berkeley. (Hearst Gymnasium Historical Collection, University of California, Berkeley)

FIGURE 12.3

Emil Bénard's winning entry for Berkeley campus development in 1899. International Competition for the Phoebe Hearst Architectural Plan for the University of California (1899)

of learning that could win international acclaim'; the founding of Leland Stanford Jr. University, some 50 miles to the south, provided an added impulse.[20] In his 1898 Charter Day Address, the President of the Associated Alumni spoke for many others when he declared that the task at hand was to create an institution that would produce 'the highest learning', serve the 'commonwealth' (i.e., state of California) and ensure that 'latent manhood and womanhood are developed to their fullness'.[21]

Maybeck (a graduate of the École des Beaux Arts), who had joined the Berkeley faculty in 1894, had already suggested to newly appointed Regent Jacob Reinstein an international competition to develop the campus; Phoebe Hearst provided the funds. The prospectus (published in English, French, Italian and German) included *gymnasia* under 'Provision for general and collective purposes common to all the departments'.[22] More than 100 submissions were received. Initial judging occurred in Antwerp; final judging took place at the Ferry Building in San Francisco on 1 September 1899. The largest element of Paris architect Emile Bénard's winning Beaux Arts plan (see Figure 12.3) – the part he chose to submit in detail – was a monumental complex consisting of two massive gymnasia joined by a colossal vaulted central structure adorned with stained glass windows, columns with Corinthian capitals, statues of cherubs on horses, and huge paintings depicting pastoral and other scenes.[23] Immediately to the west Bénard had situated a massive open space with viewing stands at both ends (each with its own columns and capitals) where military drills and athletic events were to take place. If Bénard's plan had been implemented Berkeley's male and female students would have had the most grandiose gymnasia in the nation. Their functionality might have been another matter! (The 'visions' of architects and those who work in physical education have often been at odds.)

Also never constructed was the men's gymnasium that was part of John Galen Howard's proposed 1914 plan. (Howard, also trained at the École des Beaux Arts, had been selected as University Architect and charged with adjusting the Bénard plan to the topography and needs of the campus.) This was to have been built to the west of Hearst Hall (the gymnasium donated by Mrs Hearst in 1899) and separated from it by the track (which had been moved from its earlier location near Harmon Gymnasium) and the 17,000-seat California Field (designed by Howard in 1905) on which the 'Golden Bears' played their football games.[24]

By 1921 California Field could no longer accommodate the throngs who wished to attend the annual 'Big Game'. Colleges and universities across the country – in part as memorials to men who had given their lives in the Great War – were building football stadia; Stanford's new 60,000-seat stadium was nearing completion. With the backing of the administration, the Associated Students of the University of California ((ASUC) who would control intercollegiate athletics until 1960) initiated a subscription drive and a Stadium Executive Committee, headed by Professor of Mining Frank H. Probert, was formed. The 77,000-seat, concrete-and-steel California Memorial Stadium (designed by Howard and built at a cost of $1,021,500) was completed in 1923 in time for the Cal–Stanford game.[25] The large attractive campaign brochure that had helped launch the project included statements from President David Barrows, Treasurer Robert Gordon Sproul (who would become President in 1930), Probert and George C. Edwards. Sproul's remarks most fully reflected the major forces that had brought the stadium into being. In addition to being a remembrance of 'those Californians who died in the War of Nations that civilization might not perish', more seats were needed to accommodate the ever-growing requests for football tickets. Intercollegiate contests 'more than any other single factor', Sproul declared, bound alumni 'to their Alma Mater'.[26] When the 21,000-seat Edwards Track Stadium was completed in 1932 Berkeley's male students had some of the finest athletic facilities in the nation.

Those available to women students were, in their own way, more impressive. In the early hours of 22 June 1922 Hearst Hall had burned to the ground.[27] An outdoor dancing platform was built and the department adjusted the curriculum to emphasize activities that could be carried on at the pool (which had been spared), tennis courts and playing fields. (Hastily constructed wooden 'shacks' served as offices and dressing rooms.) In addition to the required curriculum, an extensive programme of Women's Athletic Association activities was continued.[28]

Upon learning of the disaster, William Randolph Hearst Jr. telegraphed President Barrows indicating his intention to build a fireproof structure to replace the gymnasium 'given by my mother for the benefit of the girl undergraduates'.[29] (The Board of Regents even considered the possibility of creating a 'woman's quadrangle', where their social, recreational and physical education activities could be 'sufficiently removed from the common activities of the University as to give women independence and a certain seclusion'.)[30] Dean of Women Lucy Stebbins and departmental chairman Ruth Elliott thereupon sent the President an extensive list of needs and recommendations for the new building.

Hearst selected Maybeck as his architect. The original plans called for a grandiose complex of polychromatic buildings that included a 600-seat auditorium with a rotunda similar to that of the Palace of Fine Arts that Maybeck had designed for the 1915 Panama-Pacific International Exposition. Aware that these did not adequately provide for the needs of a gymnasium, Elliott and Stebbins urged William Campbell (who had just become President) to intercede. Campbell's letter to Maybeck was stark: 'I have examined the blue prints carefully, I have shown them to the representatives of the women connected with the University and to the Grounds

and Building and the Finance Committees of the Board of Regents. All of
these persons have commented unfavourably as to their meeting the
requirements of the situation.'[31]

Hearst was extremely dissatisfied that the needs of the women were not
being addressed and even considered withdrawing his proposal. Campbell
immediately assured him of the Regents' desire for a 'suitable memorial' to
his mother, stating that 'service facilities for women students' must be paramount.[32] Julia Morgan (UC 1894; École des Beaux-Arts; and architect of the
huge Mediterranean-style 'castle' that Hearst Sr. had built at San Simeon)
was engaged to design the interior and supervise the building's construction.[33] Concerned about escalating costs (ultimately $660,000), Hearst
informed her that 'the best thing to do' would be to 'build the utilitarian part
– gymnasiums, baths, etc. and to leave the Memorial Hall [the giant auditorium that had been part of the Maybeck plan] until funds accumulate'.[34]
(The auditorium was never built.)

Construction of the three-wing, reinforced-concrete-and-plaster semi-
monumental Phoebe A. Hearst Gymnasium for Women began in 1925 and
was completed in 1927. It included three gymnasia, each approximately 60
× 95 ft, for modern dance, basketball (too small by the 1960s) and
gymnastic exercises (equipment here included a horizontal ladder, climbing
ropes, travelling rings, and stall bars affixed to all four walls), as well as
three smaller gymnasia for other activities (see Figure 12.4). Large steel
casement windows, surrounded on the outside by copper columns and bas-
reliefs, emitted pleasing and ample light. A 33-yard white-and-black Italian
marble swimming pool (a smaller version of the magnificent one at San
Simeon) and two smaller marble pools made possible a wide range of
aquatic activities. Surrounding the main pool were cement ornamental urns
with sculpted lion heads, cherubs and nymphs in diaphanous garments similar to those at the Jardin de la Fontaine in Nîmes.[35] Exterior walls were
adorned with columns with Corinthian capitals and other classical orna-
mentation (see Figure 12.5). In addition to the usual functional facilities
(e.g., showers, dressing rooms, offices), the 142,000 sq. ft. building contained inner courtyards (one with a long reflecting pool), a library, a room
for 'rest', a laboratory for research and a kitchen where members of the
Women's Athletic Association (WAA) prepared food for the semi-annual
WAA banquet and the annual High School Sports Day. It was – and is – a
very pleasant place in which to work and play.

The spacious and well-appointed Phoebe Hearst Gymnasium for
Women was dedicated on 8 April 1927. Fencing and modern dance were
returned to the curriculum; tumbling, water safety instructor training and
other activities were added; and the President's office granted the women
exclusive use of four of the nine tennis courts.[36] Adroit insistence by Violet
Marshall (who had become Director when Elliott left to pursue doctoral

FIGURE 12.5

Hearst gymnasium for women, South façade, with small swimming pool. (Hearst Gymnasium Historical Collection, University of California, Berkeley)

studies at Columbia) that the women's playing fields must be close to their shower facilities (so that there would be no need to traverse the campus while wearing costumes 'appropriate only for the practice of sports') ensured that they would have their own outdoor space and not be forced to relinquish it to other programmes for many years.[37] Following a two-week visit by Margaret H'Doubler (the University of Wisconsin's modern dance authority), Berkeley's students formed their own Orchesis club in 1929 and soon were giving productions to which the general university community was invited.[38] Until the 1950s this would be one of those few instances when men were welcomed in the women's gym.[39]

Students were enthralled with their new building and delighted that the obligatory black bloomer suit had been replaced by a beige blouse of cotton broadcloth and a 'knicker' of brown fabric. For decades both departments furnished and laundered gymnasium attire. Hygiene was the major reason and a costume appropriate to the activity could be a matter of safety. As the years passed women were issued a white cotton (later nylon) blouse and blue shorts (white for those taking tennis) or a blue cotton leotard and short skirt for modern dance. Except on the rarest occasions (i.e., annual productions of the synchronized swimming club) no one was permitted in any of the Hearst pools except in a freshly laundered bathing suit obtained at the Service Centre. Male students wore department-issued trunks when entering their swimming pools. Until the 1960s, when it was replaced by a colourful T-shirt and boxer shorts, their gymnasium costume consisted of grey trousers (later twill shorts) and a sleeveless cotton jersey. Now students wear a vast array of colourful garments that they provide themselves.

When a new steel-and-concrete Men's Gymnasium – subsequently renamed Harmon Gymnasium – opened in early 1933, the old Harmon Gymnasium was demolished. The Spartan-appearing new facility, built at a cost of $1,000,000 ($485,000 from the estate of Ernest V. Cowell; $100,00 from the ASUC; the remainder from State funds), included special rooms for instruction in boxing, wrestling, fencing and gymnastics; squash courts; a research laboratory; and a room for rest. Space was divided among physical education (108,000 sq. ft.), military and naval science (25,000 sq. ft.), and the ASUC's athletic functions (15,000 sq. ft.). The central feature was a basketball arena, with seating for 5,000 spectators, located in a large rectangular block with chamfered corners and clerestory windows.[40] Marked across the main court's length were three courts that served the needs of physical education classes and intramural games. Immediately to the south of the building were two large outdoor pools (one for swimming, one for diving) used for classes, intramurals and competitive events. Six Art Deco bas-relief Greco-Roman athletic figures adorned the main entrance, which opened onto a large lobby with custom chandeliers. Here were displayed bronze plaques commemorating Harmon, Cowell, the State of California and the ASUC, as well as intercollegiate and intramural trophies. Above the entryway the Latin motto 'It is wonderful how the intellect is kept alert by the movement and action of the body' was inscribed.[41]

Of Which 'Body' Do We Speak?

Nearly 20 years ago sociologist John O'Neill explored different dimensions of what he referred to as the 'physical body' and the 'communicative body' and ways that these may 'aid us in our understanding of the larger issues of social order, conflict, and change'. O'Neill's Introduction contains the following quote from Maurice Merleau-Ponty's *Phenomenology of Perception*: 'The body is our general medium for having a world. Sometimes it is restricted to the actions necessary for the conservation of life, and accordingly it posits around us a biological world; at other times, elaborating upon these primary actions and moving from their literal to a figurative meaning, it manifests through them a core of new significance: this is true of motor habits such as dancing.'[42]

Modern and interpretive dance are examples of activities that we think of as 'freeing' the body, but here it also is 'disciplined'. In gymnastics the body must be severely disciplined, both for safety and as a consequence of the standards by which competitive judging is done. Yet, as the gymnast soars above the bar there can be a remarkable (if brief) sense of freedom.[43] Most gymnasts tend to be rather short in stature; a woman who is over six feet tall has a better chance of becoming the centre on a basketball team than does a much shorter individual. Moreover, words and phrases that are used to identify physical activities need to be appropriately situated in their historical contexts. Today one is likely to think of events like those included in the Olympic Games, but in the early 1900s 'gymnastics' typically referred to one of several systems of calisthenic exercises.

To what did the words 'systematic exercise' in Payne's 1890 *Pacific Medical Journal* article refer? Certainly not to intercollegiate athletics, which were rapidly attaining popularity with students, alumni and the general public. Nor did they refer to sports for the general student (soon to be called 'educational athletics'). In the late 1800s and early 1900s the physical education curriculum was dominated by various 'systems' of calisthenic exercises. The most popular were the Swedish, the German and that devised by Dudley Allen Sargent, MD, Director of the Harvard Gymnasium. At Berkeley physical culture for men included various aspects of the German 'system' as well several features advocated by Sargent (e.g., developing appliances). The women's course was especially informed by the Swedish 'system'.[44] The aim of such programmes was all-around development of the body, considered beneficial for physiological reasons and by extension the mind and 'will'.[45]

External form (symmetry was desired) was thought to reflect inner function. Shortly after his appointment, Payne, like most of his contemporaries, began collecting and recording quantities of information from each male student – height, weight, waist, thigh, knee, ankle and chest girth. (Thousands of these anthropometric charts remain today within the Hearst Gymnasium Historical Collections.) On the page following the section on 'Athletics' the 1892 *Blue and Gold* (UC's student yearbook) published 'average measurements' (lung capacity, girth of right forearm and left calf) of the class of 1888 and the class of 1890, noting that the latter showed considerable improvement and that in eight of 12 instances Berkeley's men were better than men at Amherst, Yale and Cornell.[46] (Competition is not limited to athletics!)

Why was anthropometry the major 'scientific' preoccupation of physical educators in the late nineteenth century? There were several influences. Attempts to rank races and populations and to find laws that governed inheritance – such as were reflected in Francis Galton's *Hereditary Genius* (1869) – surely were a factor. Anthropometry also resonated with tendencies in the 'sanitary sciences' (public health) to collect and correlate demographic information about such things as communicable diseases and with the rise of 'statistical thinking'[47] in medicine. It had intersections with comparative growth studies of children and youth such as those that Henry Pickering Bowditch, professor of physiology at Harvard University, and British physician Charles Roberts were conducting in the 1870s and 1880s.[48] The range and extent of such interest was reflected in the 117 citations in the 'Anthropometry' section of the 1893 *Publications of the American Statistical Association*. All these tendencies, and more, were incorporated into a paper that Edward Hitchcock (President of AAAPE), who had initiated anthropometric studies of college men at Amherst College in 1861), delivered at the 1887 AAAPE meeting. Interest in proportions of the human body, Hitchcock noted, was not new. The statue the 'Greeks called Doryhoros' had provided the model for the human figure; but the father of modern anthropometry was the Belgian mathematician Adolph Quetelet, who had given attention to 'actual measurements [and] ... means and averages deduced from them as the true scientific way of ascertaining human proportions'.[49]

Collection of data is one thing; assumptions that undergird that collection and what is done with the data are other matters. AAAPE member James Babbitt, MD, soon asked '[are we] possibly wasting too much time on [this] endless routine work?' At the 1901 AAAPE convention, anthropologist Franz Boas (who produced the first national standards for height and weight of North American children) acknowledged that some of the most valuable anthropometrical material had been collected by directors of gymnasia, but challenged the assumption that there was 'only one ideal type'.[50] Aware that one ideal standard could not adequately reflect the actual range of human bodies, contemporaries had already begun compiling 'averages' for men of different heights. Tests of strength, then agility, neuromuscular control, and other performance parameters would soon begin to displace – but not entirely eliminate – the collection of anthropometric measures.[51] According to Frank Kleeberger (Director of hysical Education for Men) 'physical ability' tests (jumping, wall-scaling, wrestling) rather than 'traditional methods of tape measurements' were initiated at Berkeley in 1914.[52]

Attention also was given to measuring female students. Information that Sargent obtained from 20 colleges was used by sculptor H.H. Kitson to create the statue of the Typical American Student (Female Composite) that was displayed at the 1893 World's Columbian Exposition. The report that Oberlin College's Dr Delphine Hanna prepared from examinations of 1,600 women[53] and Anne Barr's (University of Nebraska) collection of data from 1,500 women west of the Mississippi were probably the most extensive projects.[54] Measurements taken of female students at the University of California in the 1890s compared favorably (stronger, taller, greater lung capacity) with those of Oberlin women.[55]

Among female physical educators more attention would be given to assessing posture and attempting to ameliorate functional difficulties by means of 'corrective exercises'. Improper body alignment, which could be the result of diseases like rickets (the possibility of correction here was limited), was often discussed in turn-of-the-century medical journals.[56] Poor habits (especially correctable among the young) adversely affected nerves, viscera, and in the case of females the reproductive organs. For decades social reformers and some physicians had complained that women's fashion (long skirts, corsets) impaired health. Dr Eliza M. Mosher's 'The Influence of Habitual Posture on Symmetry and Health of the Body' (1892) is an early example of the type of work that female physical educators would pursue.[57]

The Swedish gymnastic system, favoured among female physical educators, gave considerable attention to proper body mechanics and alignment.[58] It was an essential part of the curriculum at the Boston Normal School of Gymnastics (BNSG, the nation's best training school for women before the 1930s), which became the Wellesley College Department of Hygiene and Physical Training in 1909.[59] Writing on the topic 'Anthropometry' for Wellesley's 1916/17 *Alumnae Bulletin*, Sarah R. Davis noted that 'measurements of girth, breadth and depth [were] becoming fewer' and that emphasis was moving to evaluations of functional measurements and posture.[60] Davis arrived at the University of California in 1919, the second in a long line of BNSG/Wellesley College graduates who joined the Department of Physical Education for Women, and for nearly four decades taught courses in kinesiology, massage, and corrective and remedial gymnastics.

Women trained in physical education had served as assistants to orthopaedic surgeons since the early 1900s. Following America's entry into the First World War, the Division of Physical Reconstruction (physiotherapy, occupational therapy) was created by the United States Army, and physical education schools were asked to expand relevant work.[61] A Reconstruction Aides programme (for physical education graduates and other qualified women) was initiated in 1918 at the University of California and placed under the direction of Elsie Blanchard, MD, a member of the Department of Physical Education for Women. The curriculum included

anatomy, physiology, kinesiology, physiotherapy, electrotherapy and remedial gymnastics. Clinical experiences were arranged at local hospitals.
(While knowledge in the neurosciences and other relevant areas has
expanded greatly, today's physical therapy programmes bear several
striking resemblances.)[62]

Women majoring in physical education at Berkeley in the 1920s studied
similar subjects as well as child health, public health, psychology, and the
history and theory of physical education. Those who planned to teach also
took classes in folk and classical dancing and the supervision of play and
'athletics'. Male physical education majors studied the same 'core' courses
as did the women. Those who intended careers in teaching or coaching (the
majority) were expected to complete 'methods' classes in baseball, basketball, football, track – and subsequently courts sports (e.g., tennis), swimming, and other activities.[63]

As at other colleges and universities, each entering woman was given an
examination in which female physicians from the Student Health Service
and the Department of Physical Education for Women cooperated. The
latter's task included recording posture details (lateral curvature of the spine
[scoliosis]; pelvic inclination).[64] (Many of these records still exist within the
Hearst Gymnasium Historical Collections.) Where possible, photographic
and schematographic records were taken. From the evaluation of these,
each student with special needs was assigned a prescribed series of exercises. Those with good posture and muscle tone were given more general
exercise regimens. In both instances flexibility, range of joint motion and
coordination as well as strength were emphasized.

Proper posture for males also received attention. *Body Mechanics and
Health* (1922) opened with the statement: 'Good body mechanics means correct poise and control of the body with the normal functioning of every
organ.' The general fitness and highest physical efficiency reflected 'in the
type of man chosen for competitive athletics' was then compared with the '80
per cent of the men in the freshman class ... [who] fall far below the normal
standard of development'.[65] *Preventive and Corrective Physical Education*
(1928), an example of a work directed explicitly to males, gave considerable
attention to posture and included chapters on proper diet, treatment of heart
disturbances by exercise, and the prevention of athletic injuries.[66]

Upon entering the University of California each male student was also
given a medical examination by Student Health Services physicians and a
postural examination by the men's physical education staff. Those who
showed 'organic weakness' – about 4 per cent – were immediately assigned
special corrective exercises. A battery of 'physical efficiency' tests, which
included agility (running, vaulting over obstacles), defence (wrestling,
boxing) and swimming was also administered. A man who failed the agility
portion was assigned to a gymnastic class best suited to his needs. If he

passed the agility portion but not the swimming or combative portions he was counselled that this would be necessary before he could enrol in a sport of his choice. Freshmen and sophomores who passed all categories moved from the 'novice' to the 'athletic' division. To encourage men to improve their skills, the Director posted every man's efficiency score![67]

Athletics – Educational and Otherwise

Plato, Galen and other philosophers and physicians of the classical world understood the difference between athletics (from *athlein* 'to contend for a prize') and physical education. The distinction seems to elude many people today. By 1900 intercollegiate athletics for men (baseball, crew, track and especially football) had become an intractable part of higher education. Within a short time games and sports (for reasons other than contest spectacle) would become an integral part of the physical education curriculum.

'Child study', which began in the United States in the 1880s, attracted the attention of important social scientists as well as educators, who saw play and games as essential in the development of children and youth. *The Pedagogical Seminary*, which psychologist G. Stanley Hall launched in 1891, was committed to such matters, publishing important contributions from prominent figures in anthropology, biology, education, psychology and sociology, as well as physical educators like Gulick. Hall's influential *Adolescence, Its Psychology and Its Relations to Physiology, Anthropology, Sociology, Sex, Crime, Religion and Education* (1904) is one example of the extensive literature concerning play and games in relation to psycho-motor and psycho-social development.

Athletics (rightly conceived, to be sure) was considered to be an extension of the same impulses that gave to play and games their educational merit. Too often, however, they were tainted by excess and commercialism. Prevailing attitudes were summarized in a 1905 paper by George Meylan, MD. While 'formal gymnastics have their corrective and educational value', Columbia University's Director of Physical Training stated, 'they can never take the place of outdoor sports to develop organic vigour'. Athletics developed self-reliance, judgment, self-control, respect for others, a sense of loyalty, and many other desirable qualities; but when newspaper notoriety and inducements to athletes and coaches prevailed they had no place in education.[68] The same issues, endlessly debated throughout the century, formed the core of the paper that James R. Day (Chancellor of Syracuse University) read at the 1909 meetings of the Intercollegiate Athletic Association of the United States (which was renamed the National Collegiate Athletic Association (NCAA) in 1910).[69] Concerns that led the Carnegie Foundation for the Advancement of Teaching to undertake several studies in the 1920s, the most influential of which was *American College Athletics* (1929), differ only in magnitude from those in the 1991 report of the Knight Foundation Commission on Intercollegiate Athletics.[70]

Between 1907, when Clark Hetherington's 'Analysis of Problems in College Athletics' was published in the *American Physical Education Review*, and 1922, when the National Amateur Athletic Federation (NAAF) was formed, large numbers of educators, physical educators and prominent Americans sought to implement a different model. Their goal was 'athletic sports for everybody', Elwood S. Brown (NAAF executive) told a group of YMCA, YHMA, American Legion and recreational leaders meeting in San Francisco in 1923. At the NAAF's 1926 annual meeting, Hetherington stressed the importance of distinguishing between 'educational athletics' ('organized for the enjoyment and education of the masses of youth') and 'spectator athletics', ('organized for a few skilled athletes under the domination of the spectator's interests and influence').[71]

The April 1923 Conference on Athletics and Physical Education for Women and Girls (called by Mrs Herbert Hoover at the suggestion of the NAAF) led to the creation of a Women's Division, the 'philosophy' of which exerted powerful control over college programmes for the next five decades. The Women's Division's 'Every girl in a sport/A sport for every girl' platform stressed intramural and 'interclass' events. As a result there were few opportunities for college women who might have enjoyed and benefited from opportunities similar to those their male counterparts might pursue. However, the situation was more complex than is suggested in most historical accounts. Female physical educators were well aware that their male counterparts were unable to exert control over intercollegiate athletics and that the lines between these and 'educational athletics' were often blurred. Many – probably most – believed that as educators they had a responsibility to uphold educational values. They also were cognizant of the fact that female physical educators typically accounted for the largest portion of the very few women on a co-educational campus. And they recognized that if they embraced the intercollegiate model most coaches likely would be men, who already had the requisite experience. (Acosta and Carpenter's recent findings of the marked decline of female coaches since the implementation of Title IX are suggestive!)[72]

Developments at Berkeley

As elsewhere in the United States, men's intercollegiate athletics at the University of California grew rapidly during the 1890s. The most significant stimuli were the establishment of Leland Stanford Jr. University (which made possible the first Cal–Stanford football contest on 19 March

1892) and the better-than-expected success of the 1895 'Golden Bears' track team, the first of any of it's athletic teams to compete in the east.[73] Women's sports developed differently. Shortly after the new game of basketball had been played at Smith College, Walter Magee introduced it to women at Berkeley, who engaged in the first contest to be played by their university (against Miss Head's School, a nearby private preparatory school for girls) on 18 November 1892. When they played a Stanford team at the San Francisco Page Street Armory four years later 500 female spectators enthusiastically watched. The only male present was the referee![74]

Although their participation was minuscule in comparison to that of male students, for the next eight years women enjoyed a very occasional 'intercollegiate' contest against Stanford, nearby Mills College, or the University of Nevada. This would change in 1914 when Maude Cleveland (a Berkeley graduate, who had played three years on the basketball team and attended the Boston Normal School of Gymnastics)[75] was named Assistant Professor of the newly created Department of Physical Education for Women. Frank Kleeberger (AB from Berkeley in 1908 and MA in 1915) was named Director of the now separate Department of Physical Education for Men. (Separate departments would continue until 1942.) The *Daily Californian* reported: 'Women's Athletics to Have New Start'. The emphasis now would be on 'interclass' competition (and soon intramural events) in such sports as basketball, swimming, track and rowing (in whaleboats at Oakland's Lake Merritt). Field hockey, a sport popular at a number of eastern women's colleges, was introduced in 1915. Unless it is recognized that in the United States few men played field hockey, it may be difficult to comprehend why conventional wisdom held that a 100-yard field posed little threat to a woman's health but a 100-foot basketball court, typically divided into two or three sections, did! (The fact that players in both sports were encumbered by heavy long black serge 'bloomer' costumes should call into question prevailing views of the 'frail female'.)[76]

The men's department also initiated intramural events (1,150 students participated in autumn 1919) and organized competitions in 'minor' varsity sports (boxing, wrestling, gymnastics) and 'weight' teams in basketball, football and baseball.[77] Upon completion of the Men's Gymnasium, several other activities were added. The 1933 Intramural Sports booklet set forth two objectives: (1) 'beneficial athletic competition for all'; (2) creation of new interest among 'students not skilled in sports, who had lost enthusiasm because of past emphasis on intercollegiate competition'.[78] During the Second World War, the men's department provided instruction for male students in the Army Specialized Training Programme, worked cooperatively with Chief Specialists to implement the Navy V-12 Programme, and organized Army, Navy and Air Force intramural leagues.[79] By the late 1940s intramural competitions were being offered in 22 individual and team sports. Various athletic clubs (volleyball, tennis) were arranging a 'ladies nite' at least once a month. So many intramural men's basketball teams were participating by 1960 that it was necessary to schedule games on Harmon's three courts as late as midnight. The Department of Physical Education's responsibility for intramural sports would continue until 1976, when a separate Department of Recreational Sports was created.

In addition to intramural and interclass events, Berkeley's female students might participate in the semi-annual field days that had been initiated following Cleveland's arrival. In 1922 student leaders and faculty from UC, Stanford and Mills College came together to propose 'intercollegiate interclass games' among their institutions. According to the Women's Athletic Association (WAA) President, these differed from 'varsity' teams in allowing more women to participate and decreasing 'nervous strain' (one of the assumed evils of varsity competition).[80] Known as Triangular Sports Day, these would continue until 1952 when other local colleges were included and the event was renamed Bay Area Sports Day.

Although the focus was sports, a Woman's Athletic Association (at Berkeley and elsewhere) did not exist solely 'for sport'. Developing leadership skills and giving service were also important components. Criteria for receipt of the Block 'C' (a rough equivalent of the men's varsity letter) required service to the organization as well as good skill in two sports. In 1924 the WAA held the first of its annual High School Sports Days. More than 400 young women from northern California high schools were attending by 1960. In 1961 the WAA Council added a third branch – 'extramural programme' – for those women who desired more competitive experiences.[81] This action preceded by six years the Commission on Intercollegiate Athletics for Women's announcement of national championships.[82]

Given the salience of the body in constructions of power, it is not surprising that athletics quickly became the standard bearer of Title IX, the 'Prohibition of Sex Discrimination' section of Public Law 92–318, enacted by the 92nd Congress of the United States in 1972. (The law pertained to 'any education programme or activity receiving Federal financial assistance'). At Berkeley a Co-ordinator of Women's Intercollegiate Sports (who reported to the chairman of the Department of Physical Education) was appointed in 1973, and the former WAA budget of $3,000 was raised to $42,500. Three years later an autonomous Department of Intercollegiate Athletics for Women was formed. This remained one of the few separate departments at a large institution until the men's and women's programmes were merged in 1991.[83]

By the mid-1950s, as the Berkeley student body was nearing 19,000, physical education faculty member Kooman Boycheff (who would subsequently be named Co-ordinator of Intramural Sports for Men and

Recreation) initiated efforts to secure additional facilities. A request was submitted to the Buildings and Campus Development Committee in 1958 urging the creation of an intramural-recreational gymnasium. Two and a half decades would ensue before this became a reality. The Regents subsequently authorized the conduct of an investigation concerning the feasibility of constructing an intramural facility. Of 18,580 students who responded to a May 1973 survey, nearly 53 per cent indicated that they would be willing to pay a special fee to help support 'a coeducational multipurpose recreation centre'. (Over 65 per cent of the faculty and staff responded in the affirmative.) By 1982 Harmon was in constant use from 6.00 a.m. until 2.00 a.m.[84]

Four possible sites were identified, one of which was on property owned by the University about ten blocks from the campus that had come to be known as 'People's Park'. It finally was decided to build immediately to the south of Harmon Gymnasium and Edwards Field (where the men's varsity baseball team played) and adjacent to the recently constructed 50 m Spieker Aquatics Complex (which had replaced Harmon's two old swimming pools). The 13.5 million dollar Intramural and Recreational Sports Facility (RSF), completed in 1984, consisted of two 11,000 sq. ft. gymnasia aligned along a 10,000 sq. ft. central atrium and a 21,000 sq. ft. field house where seating could be arranged for 800 (the small number reflects the emphasis on participation). It also included a large weight room with Nautilus and Universal machines, a spacious martial arts room, a combatives room and a dance studio. By remodelling those in Harmon Gymnasium and constructing others in the new facility there now were 17 handball and racquetball courts;[85] the central court was named for Kooman Boycheff, a small tribute for the man who had inspired it all.

Adequate field space is always a problem for an urban campus. In an effort to meet student needs, fields and tennis courts were constructed on the top of parking structures. By 1970, the once-popular men's touch football intramural leagues were declining in part due to lack of fields and in part a consequence of the 'New Games' movement and more gentle forms of sport.[86] It now is rare to see young men playing touch football – only an occasional, usually co-educational, frisbee game on a poorly maintained field. The once immaculately groomed turf 'pitch' on which the WAA field hockey team had played against Stanford and the University of the Pacific is now covered with 'temporary' buildings erected to house departments whose buildings are, or will be, under renovation. Perhaps this is a reason why so many students are to be found in the Recreational Sports Facility's weight room. More likely this usage reflects current intense interest in ideal 'body shapes'.[87]

By 1970 Hearst Gymnasium, used by some 7,500 students a year for instructional physical education classes – and many more for intramural sports, was in need of renovations. New structural design standards and technologies for earthquake-resistant structures (no small matter for a campus located adjacent to a major fault) required re-evaluations of the physical plant. Regulations promulgated by the Department of Health, Education and Welfare pursuant to Title IX, would require educational institutions to provide comparable athletic opportunities for females. In 1975 the Board of Trustees of the William Randolph Hearst Jr. Foundation approved $1,750,000 for renovations, noting in their transmittal letter 'the remarkable services' Hearst Gymnasium had provided students 'for more than half a century'.[88]

A number of much needed improvements were achieved, but thick concrete walls made it impossible to expand any of the three large gymnasia. When the hoped for new addition was not funded it became necessary to continue to schedule women's intercollegiate practices and games on the main court at Harmon. The growth of women's programmes had already decreased the hours available for physical education classes and forced changes in the men's intercollegiate schedule, a problem whose proportions would grow over the next decade. In the early 1980s the east wing of the lower floor of Hearst Gymnasium (formerly a enormous dressing room with several hundred individual booths) was converted into offices for the Department of Intercollegiate Athletics for Women, which had been separated (with both units' full approval) from the Department of Physical Education. Following the 1991/92 merger of the two athletic departments, personnel were distributed among the various offices that housed the men's programme. Four branches of the military services (which now enlist women) at present occupy the former WIA office area at Hearst Gymnasium – an arrangement that would have been unacceptable a few decades earlier. Their orderliness makes the military departments very welcome neighbours. Changes at Harmon would be more dramatic!

Intercollegiate basketball, like intercollegiate football, has become 'big business', as attested to by the costs of programmes and the massive arenas in which games are now played. The new 15,300-seat basketball arena at Michigan State University, which was featured in the *Athletic Business* Third Annual Architectural Showcase in 1990, is one example of the many changes that have been occurring at colleges and universities.[89] Although the intimacy of Harmon Gymnasium (where bleachers almost overlapped the sidelines) appealed to many fans, for many years basketball enthusiasts had expressed a desire for a larger and more modern facility. A Chancellor-appointed committee was formed in 1991 and a commitment was made to developing 'a facility suitable for hosting NCAA Division I games and tournaments at the regional and national level'. Several sites on and off the campus were considered. The Department of Intercollegiate Athletics formulated a plan to raise $28,000,000 from private donations (a goal it would exceed by more than $20,000,000) and a campaign was launched with an

11-million-dollar gift from Walter Haas Jr., whose generosity had already been of great benefit to the campus. Construction began in 1997 with the 'deconstruction' of Harmon Gymnasium, of which approximately one-third would remain when the Walter Haas Jr. Pavilion was completed in 1999. The ceiling was raised 37 feet and seating capacity for basketball was increased to 12,300 (of which 1,500 chairback seats were offered for a donation of $5,000 per seat).[90] The purpose of the striking new facility was made clear in the attractive brochure *Dreams Do Come True* that attended its dedication: 'The men's and women's hoop squads will share their home with other athletic programmes. Cal's sports across the board stand to benefit from the higher revenues, the new office space, (state-of-the-art training facilities, rooms where 'Old Blues will meet, greet, wine and dine'), and the ability to show off a wonderful building to new recruits'. Neither intramurals nor physical education activity classes enjoy any of the new facility's benefits.

The Rise and Demise[91] of Berkeley's Undergraduate Major and Graduate Programmes in Physical Education

Until it was 'disestablished' in 1997, Berkeley's was the oldest continuous physical education major programme at any American university. In 1890 Dr Payne had appraised Acting University President Martin Kellogg of the state's growing need for competent teachers. The Academic Council recommended a two-year course that could be taken by any man or woman who completed the four-year bachelor's programme. Begun in 1897/98, this consisted of four units of anatomy and 16 units of work provided by the Department of Physical Culture (anthropometry, human anatomy demonstrations, physiology of exercise, hygiene, physical examination and diagnosis, exercises adapted to public schools, acquired deformities).[92] Fifteen men and 21 women had graduated by 1903.[93]

Increasing public school enrolments and the growth of the high school created a continuing demand for qualified teachers, which was intensified by the playground movement of the early 1900s. Berkeley's first summer session courses in Physical Culture were offered in 1901; offerings in playground work (under the Department of Education) began in 1910. The following summer the two departments offered 25 courses. A group major for the AB degree in physical education was approved in 1914.[94] Assembly Bill 599, signed by the Governor on 26 May 1917, made physical education a requirement in the public schools[95] and increased the demand for teachers. Preparation for the AB major in 1945/46 included relevant courses in physiology, public health, psychology, zoology and nutrition. Required upper division courses were anatomy, kinesiology, exercise physiology, psychological bases of physical activity, educational psychology, history and principles of physical education, tests and measurements, community recreation and a course (selected with the approval of an adviser) dealing with 'the problems of society and human relations'. For those who planned teaching and similar careers, the department offered several 'professional' courses – e.g., rhythmic bases of dance, theory of group athletics, organization and administration of physical education, conditioning of athletes and care of injuries (men). A fifth year of postgraduate professional course work, required by state teacher certification regulations, was the responsibility of the Department of Education, which worked cooperatively with the Department of Physical Education.[96] A Master of Arts degree consisting of 20 units and a thesis was initiated in 1930.[97] However, as elsewhere the preparation of teachers for public schools, colleges and universities remained the central function, as reflected in Jack Hewitt's 1942 survey of advanced degree work in physical education (MA, MS, M.Ed, Ed.D. and/or Ph.D.).[98] This would change markedly, beginning in the 1960s.

For decades a small number of individuals who held faculty positions in departments of physical education had engaged in research. Following the Second World War more began to operate in ways that customarily have been associated with academic/scholarly communities. The 1960 volume *Science and Medicine of Exercise and Sports*, which assessed the state of research in the physiological, psychological, cultural, historical, therapeutic, nutritional, growth and development, and other aspects of exercise and sports, marks a major transition. In the Introduction, editor Warren Johnson likened physical education to medicine in that both had important and necessary intersections with many fields of investigation.[99]

Although discussions were occurring elsewhere, it was the seminal 1964 paper 'Physical Education – An Academic Discipline'[100] by Franklin Henry (Professor of Physical Education at UCB) that launched two decades of debates (often contentious) that moved physical education at research universities much closer to a scientific/scholarly enterprise.[101] Courses in anatomy, physiology, physics, and appropriate behavioural and social sciences, Henry declared, provided the foundations. Students majoring in physical education then needed to pursue specialized studies in kinesiology and biomechanics relevant to human movement, physiology of exercise, neuromuscular co-ordination, motor activity, the role of sports, dance and other physical activities in various cultures, and other areas that informed the field. This work, he believed, could not be achieved by interdisciplinary arrangements because traditional disciplines were not informed with respect to 'integrated knowledge of human motor behavior and capacity'. The proper model was a 'cross-disciplinary' programme within its own department. That department was physical education.

Both faculty and students had become increasingly dissatisfied with the joint Department of Physical Education/School of Education doctoral degree, which required too many professional courses. Mary Lou Norrie (who had become Chair in 1973) successfully petitioned the Academic Senate for a separate and much more academically oriented Ph.D. To facilitate interaction among faculty (and graduate students) the department asked that its exercise physiology, kinesiology, motor development, psychology (motor behaviour), and socio-cultural laboratories be relocated nearer each other in the north wing of Harmon Gymnasium.[102] During renovations Harmon's large collection of books and journals was moved to Hearst Gymnasium, where the library already contained several thousand volumes as well a vast assortment of annual reports of city recreation departments, reports of state directors of physical education (California and elsewhere) dating from the 1920s, and other materials of great value to historians and others interested in health, exercise, play, child development, sports, the Olympic Games, and more.

By 1980 the 50-department College of Letters and Science had been organized into four divisions: humanities, social sciences, physical sciences and biological sciences (which included the Department of Physical Education). Berkeley's several hundred biology faculty members were dispersed among 20 departments, half of which were in units like the College of Natural Resources and the School of Public Health. Each department was responsible for the recruitment of its own faculty. The absence of a medical school (that function having been located at the Toland Medical College – now the University of California at San Francisco – in the late 1800s) oriented biology toward cellular and sub-cellular 'visions'. Of particular consequence, research in the biological sciences was undergoing a revolution and Berkeley's 'rankings' in several fields had fallen since 1970. L and S Dean and soon-to-be Vice Chancellor Roderic Park (a professor of botany) initiated efforts to remedy the situation. Most important would be much needed new and renovated space and the creation of a Chancellor's Advisory Committee on Biology.[103]

The Advisory Committee's 3 December 1984 'first draft' report on 'Reorganization of the Biological Sciences' recommended that the 20 existing departments be reconfigured into two areas: (1) Studies in Molecular and Cellular Biology and (2) Studies in Organismal, Ecological and Evolutionary Biology. Although not directly stated, the report made it patently clear that the Department of Physical Education would cease to exist.[104] Upon receipt of the document, the chairman called the faculty together and charged its Ad Hoc Internal Review Committee with drafting a response, stating: 'The decisions which we all make in the next several weeks will be, I believe, the most consequential the Department of Physical Education has ever made.'[105]

The department's response, submitted in January 1985, cited the report's overwhelming orientation to molecular concerns, its failure to recognize 'the importance of studying intact functioning individuals', and a 'complete lack of knowledge … of the discipline of Physical Education'. Also cited was the fact that Berkeley's department had been a leader in the development of physical education as an academic discipline; that its many graduates were to be found in careers ranging from medicine and nursing to physical therapy to education and more; and that the Student Health Service long had recognized that its activity programme performed 'an important role in the immediate and long term health needs of the student body'.[106] Furthermore, compelling evidence now existed that physical activity was important for the maintenance of health. The department had a long history of 'providing leadership in the field of physical education for the people of the State of California': And it was the only department in the University of California system that offered degrees from the A.B. through the Ph.D. Therefore, it should 'be left intact'.[107]

Physical education was not the only department dissatisfied with the reorganization plans. Over the next six months several, often contentious, open meetings were held. The Vice Chancellor issued the Advisory Council on Biology's second iteration in July 1985, noting that because 'many objections had been raised … [t]he Physical Education Department will be the subject of a separate administrative committee review'.[108] The department responded that its current structure best ensured continuing contributions and pointed to the favorable report it had received from a duly constituted academic programme review in 1977.[109] In the end, it was not the administration but the Academic Senate (appropriately, as the Senate has authority over curricula) that conducted the review.

In early spring 1988 the extremely supportive review report (which called for an increase of professorial faculty) was sent to the department, where it was made available for comment to all faculty members and the graduate students who had prepared their portion of the original submission. In her response to the Graduate Dean, the chairman pointed to the Review Committee's endorsement of the cross/interdisciplinary nature of its degree programmes, especially the AB, noting that the committee had stated that Berkeley's major 'already is an intellectually rich and diverse human biology major, reflecting liberal education at its best'.[110]

Many factors – external as well as internal – influence decisions educational institutions make. Confronted with financial difficulties, the State markedly reduced its support in the early 1990s. A new campus administration urged the department to consider having its faculty assigned to other departments – a request which the chairman adamantly rejected.[111] Confronted with escalating deficits, the then Vice Chancellor created an Academic Programmes Working Group (with ten disciplinary area advisory panels) to evaluate course work across disciplines. Included among its major recommendations was 'greater co-ordination of curricula'.[112] This led to a 're-visitation' of the Department of Physical Education's recently completed review, and to a confirmation of the support that the Graduate Council had endorsed in 1989. In its assessment the 1992 Graduate Council declared that the department had 'a keen sense of the field (in research, scholarship and practice) and had made a compelling case for increasing its faculty'.[113]

Nonetheless, the administration continued to withhold support and it was becoming evident that physical education and three other small departments were in jeopardy.[114] In early August 1994 the recently retired chairman of the Department of Human Biodynamics (the name the Department of Physical Education had recently assumed) wrote to the new chairman, citing the repeated intransigence of the administration and noting that its willingness to ignore repeated endorsements by the Academic Senate (widely recognized as the strongest in the nation)[115] was tantamount to making 'a travesty of the notion of faculty governance'. Constant vigilance would be a necessity, she cautioned. Why might not the Department of Human Biodynamics be a 'centre of human/systems physiology on the campus'.[116] The promised faculty positions were not obtained and the department was disestablished in 1997, exactly 100 years after its foundations had been endorsed by action of the Academic Council.

As these matters were occurring, the American Academy of Kinesiology and Physical Education (AAKPE) was investigating reasons why departments with strong programmes were being downsized or eliminated. In the Introduction to 'Meeting the Challenges of the 21st Century in Higher Education', president-elect Jack Wilmore (who had chaired the AAKPE's special committee) made a number of very insightful observations. In addition to excellence in scholarship, respect for colleagues across subdisciplines and a commitment to both the disciplinary and professional aspects of the field were essential at the departmental level. More broadly, departmental administrators must be willing and able to 'promote and publicize the department's programmes and faculty on campus [and] ... have the courage to defend the department's programmes to top administrators'.[117]

Conclusion

Berkeley did have the wisdom to retain its exemplary instructional physical activity classes, now organized within a unit titled 'Physical Education Programme' and headed by a director who formerly had served as the Vice Chairman of the Department of Physical Education. Today, as in former years, hundreds of young women and men enrol each semester in classes ranging from aquatics, ballet and modern dance to martial arts and tennis, and more. Those who wish to combine 'academic' understandings of such things as cardiovascular function with practical applications (is this not the basic paradigm of medicine?) may do so in one of the other types of classes this programme offers. And what might Phoebe Apperson Hearst think about the scores of students who attend with such interest to their instructor's verbal- and visual-sequenced presentations of how to perform the backstroke or the forehand drive? Although she might be a bit surprised to find young men so engaged at the 'women's gymnasium', she doubtless would be pleased that the purposes for which she and her son had given facilities are still being fulfilled.

In October 1999 a *Daily Californian* headline declared: 'Top U.C. Berkeley officials and faculty announced plans yesterday to integrate several campus departments in a broad-ranging effort to improve the quality of health research.' It was anticipated that some 400 researchers from the biosciences, physical sciences, psychology, engineering and more would contribute to expanding 'the boundaries of teaching and research in the health sciences'. Moreover, the plan was to allow 'different departments to design interdisciplinary classes that are moulded to specialized majors'.[118] This, of course, was what the AB major in physical education had provided for most of the twentieth century! As scientific and clinical evidence continues to accumulate (in both the biological and psycho-social domains) in support of physical activity as an essential component of health, it is incongruous that there remains so little understanding of the true merits of physical education.

Notes

Series Editor's Foreword

1. Bertrand Russell, *History of Western Philosophy* (London: Allen and Unwin, 1955-5th impression), p. 90.

Introduction

1. Among introductions to places and spaces of sport are Phillip Wagner, 'Sport: Culture and Society', in A. Pred (ed.), *Time and Space in Geography* (Lund: Gleerup, 1981), pp. 85–108; John Bale, *Landscapes of Modern Sport*, (Leicester: Leicester University Press, 1994); Karl Raitz (ed.), *The Theater of Sport* (Baltimore, MD: Johns Hopkins University Press, 1995).
2. Paul Weiss, *Sport: A Philosophic Enquiry* (Carbondale: University of Southern Illinois Press, 1969).
3. Edward Relph, *Place and Placelessness* (London: Pion, 1976); Paul Virilio, *The Lost Dimension* (New York: Semiotext(e), 1991); Jean Baudrillard, *The Transparency of Evil* (London: Verso, 1993).
4. See, for example, Michael Jones, *Living Machines* (San Francisco, CA: Ignatius Press, 1995).
5. Christian Norberg-Schultz, *Genius Loci: The Phenomenology of Architecture* (New York: Rizzoli, 1979).
6. Yi-Fu Tuan, *Space and Place; The Perspective of Experience* (Minneapolis, MN: University of Minnesota Press, 1977).

Chapter 1

1. David Harvey reminds us that globalization is not exactly a new process but simply a new phase of the capitalist production of space where the re-jigging of the map of the earth's human cultures is proceeding apace (*Spaces of Hope* (Berkeley: University of California Press, 2000), pp. 54, 67).
2. Andrew Blake, *The Body Language: The Meaning of Modern Sport* (London: Lawrence and Wishart, 1996), p. 25.
3. Edward Relph, *Place and Placelessness* (London: Pion, 1976), p. 33.
4. Clifford Geertz, *The Interpretation of Cultures* (New York: Basic Books, 1973).
5. Karl Raitz, *The Theater of Sport* (Baltimore, MD: Johns Hopkins University Press, 1995), p. vi; Financier Leonard Asper completes the metaphor. Sports teams, he said recently, are really just a programme for such theatres. 'Take the 84 annual games of the Toronto Maple Leafs, multiply by three and you get 252 hours of television content'. *Vancouver Sun* (2 Aug. 2000), A3.
6. Henning Eichberg, 'Race-Track and Labyrinth: The Space of Physical Culture in Berlin', *The Journal of Sport History*, 17, 2 (1990), p. 245.

7. Michel de Certeau, *The Practice of Everyday Life* (Berkeley, CA: University of California Press, 1984), p. 117.
8. Meaghan Morris, 'Great Moments in Social Climbing: King Kong and the Human Fly', in Beatriz Colomina (ed.), *Sexuality and Space* (Princeton, NJ: Princeton Architectural Press, 1992), p. 3.
9. Linda McDowell, *Gender, Identity and Place: Understanding Feminist Geographers* (Minneapolis: University of Minnesota Press, 1999), p. 5.
10. Doreen Massey explains that if we think of space in terms of the ever-shifting geometry of social/power relations, then the spatial is both open to and a necessary element in politics in the broadest sense of the word. (*Space, Place and Gender* (Cambridge: Polity Press, 1994), p. 4.)
11. Heidi Nast and Steve Pile (eds), *Places Through the Body* (New York: Routledge, 1998), p. 4.
12. Massey, *Space, Place and Gender*, p. 154.
13. Dolores Hayden, *The Power of Place* (Cambridge, MA: MIT Press, 1995), p. 15.
14. Neil Smith and Cindy Katz, 'Grounding Metaphor. Towards a Spatialized Politics', in M. Keith (ed.), *Place and the Politics of Identity* (New York: Routledge, 1993), p. 87.
15. 'Ideas about space form a kind of philosophical palimpsest for descriptions of politics, epistemology and subjectivity.' Kathleen M. Kirby, *Indifferent Boundaries. Spatial Concepts of Human Subjectivity* (New York: The Guilford Press, 1996), p. 1.
16. Paul Gilroy, *The Black Atlantic: Modernity and Double Consciousness* (London: Verso, 1993).
17. Michel Foucault, 'Of Other Spaces', (trans. Jay Miskowiee), *Diacritics*, 16 (1986), p. 22. The reduction of time (history) to place (geography) was Nietzsche's philosophical defence of the utopia of eternal return. What was lost in history, he said, will return as place. He further suggested that 'the entire earth will be … a sum of health centres' – that is to say the places of our well-being and health, i.e., a proposed cure for the nation. See R. Dainotto, 'All the Legions Do Smilingly Revolt: The Literature of Place and Region', *Critical Inquiry*, 22, 3 (1996), p. 495.
18. Don Mitchell, *Cultural Geography, A Critical Introduction* (Oxford: Blackwell Press, 2000), pp. xiii–xiv.
19. Postmodernism and post-colonial approaches have pressed us to move beyond Eurocentric thinking and old Enlightenment certainties about progress, understanding and single truths to the celebration of multiple perspectives and mediated realities. Mitchell, *Cultural Geography*, p. 57.
20. De Certeau, *The Practice of Everyday Life*, p. ix.
21. Anthony Giddens, *Modernity and Self-Identity* (Cambridge: Polity Press, 1991), p. 2. For him, modernity is a juggernaut which crushes all who resist it in a world where tradition has lost its privileged status. Individuals create their social contexts through manufactured risk, even while being constrained by them.
22. M. Castells, 'The Information Age', *The Rise of the Network Society*, Vol. 1 (Oxford: Blackwell, 1996); S. Lash and J. Urry (eds), *Economies of Signs and Space* (London: Sage, 1993), p. 283.
23. John Bale, *Landscapes of Modern Sport* (Leicester: Leicester University Press, 1994), p. 101. Bale uses Ralph's 1976 view that many modern landscapes are characterized by placelessness, which refers to both a form of, and an attitude towards, the cultural landscape. An airport, says Augé is a classic example of a non-place where people interact as autonomous individuals with a technological object or employee, who deals with them as statistics in an anonymous flow-through. See M. Augé, *Non-Places: The Anthropology of Super-Modernity* (London: Verso, 1996).
24. Raitz, *The Theater of Sport*, p. xiv.
25. Henry Lefebvre, *The Production of Space*, tr. D. Nicholson-Smith (Oxford: Blackwell, 1991), p. 49. This is not to say, however, that sports places do not vary in their degree of placelessness. There is a great deal of ambiguity in the strictly ordered world of many rigidly defined geometrical and ordered sports places. See John Bale, 'Parks and Gardens as Places of Sport', in David Crouch (ed.), *Leisure/Tourism Geographies* (New York: Routledge, 1999), p. 54.
26. Far from resulting in homogenization, therefore, globalization constantly creates new spaces and places for the mixing and clashing of cultures. See Lash and Urry, *Economies of Signs and Space*. More subtly, Santos Boaventura de Sousa suggests that there is not one globalization but many. Globalization is the process by which a given local condition, or entity, succeeds in extending its reach over the globe and by doing so, develops the capacity to designate a rival social condition or entity as local. (*Towards a New Commonsense* (London: Routledge, 1995), p. 216.)
27. McDowell, *Gender, Identity and Place*, pp. 2–29.
28. Comments from Roland Robertson's lecture 'The Limits and Opportunities for Opposition to Globalization', Syracuse University, 19 Feb. 1999, quoted in Mitchell, *Cultural Geography*, p. xiii.

29. Henning Eichberg, 'New Spatial Configurations of Sport. Experiences from Danish Alternative Planning', *International Review of Sociology of Sport*, 28 (1993), pp. 245–61.
30. Massey, *Space, Place and Gender*, p. 149.
31. For a full discussion see Patricia Vertinsky, *The Eternally Wounded Woman: Women, Doctors and Medicine in the Late Nineteenth Century* (Champaign, IL: University of Illinois Press, 1994).
32. Bale, *Landscapes of Modern Sport*, p. 76.
33. Gillian Rose, *Feminism and Geography: The Limits of Geographical Knowledge* (Minneapolis, MN: University of Minnesota Press, 1993).
34. Mitchell, *Cultural Geography*, p. 215.
35. David Harvey, *The Condition of Postmodernity: An Inquiry into the Origins of Cultural Change* (Oxford: Blackwell, 1990), p. 234.
36. Ibid., p. 233.
37. Quoted in Hayden, *The Power of Place*, p. 30.
38. Massey, *Space, Place and Gender*, p. 154.
39. For an excellent example of functional/cultural space in a unique college building in Denmark see Jørn Hansen and Søren Nagbøl, 'Ollerup College of Physical Education – 'Living Space – Culture of Movement and Social Identity', in Henning Eichberg and Jørn Hansen (eds), *Bewegungs-Räume. Körperanthropologische Beiträge* (Institut International d'Anthropologie: Afra Verlag, 1996), pp. 147–86.
40. Raphael Samuel, 'Theatres of Memory', in *Past and Present in Contemporary Culture*. Vol. 1 (London: Verso, 1994), p. 27.
41. Leslie Roman, 'Opening Remarks, The University as/in Contested Space', UBC Conference, The Discipline/Space Collective, Vancouver, 1 May 1998.
42. Franklin M. Henry, 'Physical Education. An Academic Discipline', *Journal of Health, Physical Education and Recreation*, 35, 7 (1964), pp. 31–3, 69.
43. Eichberg, 'Race-track and Labyrinth', p. 246.
44. Sherry McKay, 'Designing Disciplines: The Architecture of a Gymnasium', in Patricia Vertinsky and Sherry Mckay (eds), *Disciplining Bodies in the Gymnasium: Memory, Monument, Modernism* (London: Frank Cass, 2004).
45. Marco Diani and Catherine Ingraham, Introduction, *Edifying Projects: Restructuring Architectural Theory* (Evanston, IL: Northwestern University Press, 1989), p. 2.
46. Kent C. Bloomer and Charles W. Moore, *Body, Memory and Architecture* (New Haven, CT: Yale University Press, 1977), p. 59.
47. J. Carsten and J. Hugh Jones (eds), *About the House: Levi Strauss and Beyond* (Cambridge: Cambridge University Press, 1995), p. 2.
48. J. Ormonde-Hall, 'Speaking Editorially', *Graduate Chronicle*, 2, 3 (1948), pp. 34–6.
49. Jani Scandura and Michael Thurston (eds), 'Modernism Inc.', in *Body, Memory, Capital* (New York: New York University Press, 2001), p. 5.
50. It is important to note here that modernism had many different hues and meanings depending upon its location. As David Harvey points out, modernism internationalized its own maelstrom of ambiguities, contradictions and pulsating aesthetic changes at the same time as it sought to affect the aesthetics of daily life. The particularities of daily life put a distinctive stamp on the diversity of the modernist effort. High modernism that became hegemonic after 1945 exhibited a much more comfortable relation to the dominant power centres in society. Harvey, *The Condition of Modernity*, pp. 25, 35.
51. Rhodri Windsor-Liscombe, *The New Spirit: Modern Architecture in Vancouver, 1938–63* (Douglas and McIntyre, Vancouver: Canadian Centre for Architecture, 1997), p. 22.
52. *The Ubyssey*, 15 Jan. 1953, p. 3.
53. Tecton was a large modernist architectural firm in London headed by Berthold Lubetkin, whose members were all enamoured of Le Corbusier. See John Allan, *Berthold Lubetkin: Architecture and the Tradition of Progress* (London: RIBA Publications Ltd 1992), p. 109.
54. Windsor-Liscombe, *The New Spirit*, p. 84.
55. The original design of the gym included four floors crammed with facilities for sport, recreation and training; a steam room, sun room, physiotherapy facilities, massage room, individual activities room and six bowling alleys. There was locker accommodation for 2,500, along with team rooms, a 42-seat snack bar and a small gymnasium for tumbling, wrestling and boxing. Space was allocated for the Physical Education Department, the Men's Athletic Directorate, the Memorial Lobby and the gymnasium proper – designed as a classic basketball gymnasium with roll-in glass backboards at each end and seating for almost 7,000.

56. Windsor-Liscombe, *The New Spirit*, p. 86.
57. 'UBC Now Has One of the Finest College Gyms on the Continent', *Alumni Chronicle*, Dec. 1950, p. 8.
58. 'Best Rec Building', *The Ubyssey*, 15 Jan. 1953, p.3; 'Recreation Buildings', *RAIC Journal*, 30, 1 (1953), pp. 24–7.
59. Samuel, *Theatres of Memory*, p. 59.
60. Ruth Morrow, 'Architectural Assumptions and Environmental Discrimination: The Case for More Inclusive Design in Schools of Architecture', in David Nicol and Simon Pilling (eds), *Changing Architectural Education: Towards a New Profession* (London and New York: E. and F. N. Spon, 2000), p. 43.
61. Edward Relph, 'Modernity as the Reclamation of Place', in David Seamon (ed.), *Dwelling, Seeing and Designing* (New York: SUNY Press, 1993), p. 26.
62. See Robert W. Connell, *Which Way is Up? Essays on Sex, Class and Culture* (Sydney: Allen and Unwin, 1983), pp. 19, 27–8.
63. Colomina, *Privacy and Publicity*, p. 136; Le Corbusier, *The Decorative Art of Today* (London: Architectural Press, 1925).
64. William J. R. Curtis, *Le Corbusier: Ideas and Forms* (London: Phaidon Press, 1986).
65. Rob Imrie, 'The Body, Disability and Le Corbusier's Conception of the Radiant Environment', in Ruth Butler and Hester Parr (eds), *Mind and Body Spaces: Geographies of Illness, Impairment and Disability* (New York: Routledge, 1999), p. 135.
66. Luis E. Carranza, 'Le Corbusier and the Problems of Representation', *Journal of Architectural Education*, 48, 2 (1994), pp. 70–81.
67. Beatriz Colomina, 'The Split Wall. Domestic Voyeurism', in Colomina, *Sexuality and Space*, pp. 104, 113.
68. Le Corbusier, *The City of Tomorrow and Its Planning*, tr. from *Urbanisme* by Frederick Etchells (New York: Dover Publications, 1925), p. 22.
69. Kate Bornstein, *Gender Outlaw* (New York: Routledge, 1994), p. 27. See also Rosa Ainley (ed.), *New Frontiers of Space, Bodies and Gender* (New York: Routledge, 1998) and Neil Smith, 'Homeless/Global: Scaling Places', in J. Bird, B. Curtis, T. Putnam, G. Robertson and L. Tickner (eds), *Mapping the Futures: Local Cultures and Global Change* (London: Routledge, 1993).
70. Henning Eichberg's post-1980 view on sport, space and place are discussed by John Bale and Chris Philo (eds), in *Body Culture: Essays on Sport, Space and Identity: Henning Eichberg* (London: Routledge, 1997). See also John Bale. *Sport, Space and the City* (London: Routledge, 1993).
71. Le Corbusier, *The City of Tomorrow*, pp. 5, 13.
72. Michel Foucault, *Discipline and Punish* (London: Harmondsworth, 1975).
73. Le Corbusier, *When the Cathedrals Were White; A Journey to the Country of Timid People* (London: Routledge, 1925), p. 141.
74. Pierre Bourdieu, *Distinction: A Social Critique of the Judgement of Taste* (London: Routledge, 1984), p. 474.
75. Fred Hume in *The Point*. Just as I have noted with 'place', the term 'home' is also 'one of the most loaded words in the English language – indeed in many languages'. McDowell, *Gender, Identity and Place*, p. 71. Heidegger argued that home is that place where a special unity exists between humans and things. See Bachelard who called home 'a key element of the development of people's sense of themselves or belonging to a place. By remembering places like home we learn to abide within ourselves. (G. Bachelard, *The Poetics of Space* (Boston: Beacon Press, 1969).)
76. The idea of home is always attached to a relationship between the participants involved and the unique circumstances in question. Thus it is contingent, a mark of what Clifford Geertz calls local knowledge: a contextualized and specific knowledge that is attached to local conditions and circumstances. (*Further Essays in Interpretive Anthropology* (London: Fontana Press, 1993), p. 167.)
77. McDowell, *Gender, Identity and Place*, p. 5.
78. The sceptre of 'evil lesbianism' has haunted female athletics and physical education in Canada as elsewhere. Susan Cahn has documented the contradictory relationship between athleticism and womanhood in North America that has seen advocates of women's sports over the last century seeking numerous and competing strategies to avoid the charge of masculinization. (*Coming on Strong: Gender and Sexuality in Twentieth Century Women's Sport* (New York: The Free Press, 1994), especially chapter 7.)
79. Elspeth Probyn, 'Sporting Bodies: Dynamics of Shame and Pride', *Body and Society*, 6, 1 (2000), p. 27.

80. Letter from Bob Osborne to Ned Pratt, 3 Aug. 1949, Department of Physical Education and Athletics.
81. In the years preceding the building of the War Memorial Gym, women students had time and again been denied both co-educational opportunities and places of their own, a subject which I cannot expand on here but which can be found discussed in a number of excellent works on women and sport in the twentieth century. See for example at UBC, Lee Stewart, *It's Up to You. Women At UBC in the Early Years* (Vancouver: UBC Press, 1990); and in Canada, Helen Lenskyj, *Out of Bounds: Women, Sport and Sexuality* (Toronto: The Women's Press, 1986), and M. Ann Hall, 'Creators of the Lost and Perfect Game', in Philip White and Kevin Young (eds), *Sport and Gender in Canada* (Oxford: Oxford University Press, 1999), pp. 5–23.
82. Flanked by outdoor tennis courts and playing fields, it housed several clubrooms, a central 60 ×100 ft gymnasium with limited spectator space, and a well-equipped kitchen.
83. Elizabeth Grosz, 'Women, Chora, Dwelling', in Sophie Watson and Katherine Gibson (eds), *Postmodern Cities and Spaces* (Oxford: Blackwell, 1995), p. 56.
84. Larry Owens, 'Pure and Sound Government: Laboratories, Playing Fields and Gymnasia in the Nineteenth Century Search for Order', *ISIS*, 76 (1985), pp. 182–94.
85. Helen Gurney, *Girls' Sports: A Century of Progress in Ontario High Schools* (Don Mills, ON: OFSAA Publications, 1979).
86. Martha H. Verbrugge, 'Recreating the Body: Women's Physical Education and the Science of Sex Differences in America, 1900–1940', *Bulletin of the History of Medicine*, 71, 2 (1997), p. 275.
87. Patricia Vertinsky, 'Reclaiming Space, Revisioning the Body: The Quest for Gender Sensitive Physical Education', *Quest*, 44 (1992), p. 172.
88. Bloomer and Moore, *Body, Memory and Architecture*, p. 107.
89. Judith Okely, *Own or Other Culture* (London: Routledge, 1996), p. 144.
90. Brian Pronger, 'Outta My End Zone: Sport and the Territorial Anus', *Journal of Sport and Social Issues*, 23, 4 (1999), p. 375.
91. Owens, 'Pure and Sound Government', p. 186.
92. Relph, *Place and Placelessness*.
93. Massey, *Space, Place and Gender*.
94. Daniel R. Williams and Bjorn P. Kaltenborn, 'Leisure Places and Modernity', in Crouch (ed.), *Leisure Tourism/Geographies*, pp.214–37.
95. Grosz, 'Women, Chora, Dwelling', p. 135.
96. Walter Benjamin, 'Paris, Capital of the Nineteenth Century', *Reflections*, tr. Kent Edmund Jephcott (New York: Schoken Books, 1986), pp.155–6.
97. Linda McDowell, 'Spatializing Feminism', in Nancy Duncan (ed.), *Body Space* (New York: Routledge, 1996), p. 31.
98. Arjun Appadurai, *Modernity at Large* (Minneapolis: University of Minnesota Press, 1996).

Chapter 2

1. Paul Weiss, *Sport: A Philosophic Enquiry* (Carbondale: University of Southern Illinois Press, 1969), p. 105.
2. John Bale, 'Virtual Fandoms: Futurescapes of Football', in A. Brown (ed.), *Fanatics: Power, Identity and Fandom in Football* (London: Routledge, 1988), pp. 265–78. The term 'placelessness' is dealt with in E. Relph, *Place and Placelessness* (London: Pion, 1976).
3. John Bale, *Landscapes of Modern Sport* (London: Leicester University Press, 1994).
4. John Bale, 'Space, Place and Body Culture: Yi-Fu Tuan and a Geography of Sport', *Geografiska Annaler*, 78B, 3 (1996), pp. 163–71.
5. On the senses, see P. Rodaway, *Sensuous Geographies* (London: Routledge, 1994).
6. Yi-Fu Tuan, *Space and Place: The Perspective of Experience* (Minneapolis, MN: University of Minnesota Press, 1997), p. 11.
7. Ibid., p. 10.
8. J. Urry, *The Tourist Gaze* (London: Routledge, 1990), pp. 71–2.
9. S. Zukin, *Landscapes of Power* (Berkeley, CA: University of California Press, 1991), p. 219.
10. Urry, *The Tourist Gaze*, pp. 80–1.
11. M. Foucault, *Discipline and Punish: The Birth of the Prison* (London: Penguin, 1977). Probably the most detailed application of 'the gaze' in a football context is J. Tomkins, 'Football Gazes and Spaces: A Foucauldian History of the Present', unpublished doctoral thesis, University of

Brighton, 1995. See also H. Eichberg, 'Stadium, Pyramid, Labyrinth: Eye and Body on the Move', in J. Bale and O. Moen (eds), *The Stadium and the City* (Keele: Keele University Press, 1995), pp. 323–47.
12. Tuan, *Space and Place*, p. 14.
13. Bale, 'Virtual Fandoms'.
14. Tuan, *Space and Place*, p. 15.
15. Bale, 'Virtual fandoms'.
16. Note, especially, chapter 2 in L. Back, T. Crabbe and J. Solomos, *The Changing Face of Football: Racism, Identity and Multiculture in the English Game* (Oxford: Berg, 2001).
17. Tuan, *Space and Place*, p. 14.
18. Ibid., p. 58.
19. Ibid., p. 12.
20. G. Rail, 'Seismography of the Postmodern Condition: Three Theses on the Implosion of Sport', in G. Rail (ed.), *Sport and Postmodern Times* (Albany, NY: State University of New York Press 1998), p. 149.
21. Bill Buford, *Among the Thugs* (New York: Norton 1992).
22. Ibid.
23. Ibid., p. 166.
24. www.thediamondangle.com/crank/20000822.html
25. John Bale, *Sport, Space and the City* (Caldwell, NJ: The Blackburn Press, 2001), p. 71.
26. I. Plenderleith, www.dottwo.co.uk/usa/grounds.html (2001).
27. It should be noted that stadium menus are frequently reflective of regional diets. For example, at the Ballpark in Arlington, Texas, one finds 'bar-b-que' sandwiches, tacos and margaritas on sale while in New England one can find Samuel Adams and clam chowder. The most popular food at Lusitano Stadium (a small Division III stadium in Ludlow, Massachusetts) is Portuguese sausage. Examining the food and drink on sale at any stadium can provide perspective on regional diet. Additionally, the pricing, size, and variation of alcoholic beverages is significant in the analysis of the culture of stadiums. At the same time, micro-geographic variations in food consumption inside the stadium also exist, usually based on social class differences. The allusion to the over-emphasis in the late modern stadium of 'prawn sandwiches' in the executive block at Old Trafford, Manchester, is a well-known UK example.
28. Eichberg, 'Stadium, Pyramid, Labyrinth', p. 323.
29. Bale, *Sport, Space and the City.*
30. Y.-F. Tuan, *Topophilia* (Englewood Cliffs, NJ: Prentice-Hall, 1974).
31. Urry, *The Tourist Gaze*, p. 83.
32. N.K. Nielsen, 'The Stadium in the City', in J. Bale and O. Moen (eds), *The Stadium and the City* (Keele: Keele University Press, 1995), p. 34.
33. Urry, *The Tourist Gaze*, p. 81.
34. Buford, *Among The Thugs*, p. 184.
35. Tuan, *Space and Place*, p. 64.
36. Buford, *Among the Thugs*, p. 167.
37. Tuan, *Space and Place*, p. 18.
38. J. Maguire, 'Sport, the Stadium and Metropolitan Life', in Bale and Moen (eds), *The Stadium and the City*, p. 47.
39. Tuan, *Space and Place*, p. 9.
40. J. Baudrillard, *The Transparency of Evil* (London: Verso, 1993), p. 80.

Chapter 3

1. M. Foucault, *Surveiller et punir* (Paris: Gallimard, 1975).
2. D. Denis, *Le Corps enseigné* (Paris: Ed. Universitaires, 1974).
3. On this topic, see the complementary analyses by G. Vigarello, *Le Corps redressé* (Paris: Delages, 1978), A. Rauch, *Le Souci du corps* (Paris: PUF, 1983), and P. Arnaud, *Le Militaire, l'écolier, le gymnaste* (Lyon: PUL, 1991).
4. I have already discussed some of these aspects in T. Terret, 'L'eau, l'école et l'espace: Normes scolaires et pratiques de la natation au XXème siècle', in P. Arnaud and T. Terret (eds), *Le Sport et ses espaces: XIXème–XXème Siècles* (Paris: Ed. du Comité des Travaux Historiques et Scientifiques, Ministère de l'Education Nationale, de l'Enseignement Supérieur et de la Recherche, 1998).

5. At the end of the nineteenth century, public baths were officially defined as 'the places, apartments, establishments open to the persons who want to bath, i.e. to plunge their body, partly or totally, in water or in another fluid, for pleasure, cleaning or health'. (E. Picard and N. D'Offschmidt, 'Pandectes Belges', *Encyclopédie de législation, de doctrine et de jurisprudence Belges* (Bruxelles: Larcier, 1884), Vol. 12, p. 550 ff., article 'Bains et lavoirs publics'. Due to the multiplication of notions, used in later documents (therme, swimming pool, bath, swimming establishment, swimming school ...) and despite clear differences between them, I will adopt a very broad definition of swimming pool as 'an aquatic space built or structured by men, in order to bathe for various purposes and using various physical modalities'.

6. G. Vigarello, *Le Propre et le sale* (Paris: Seuil, 1985).

7. T. Terret, *Evolution des besoins et transformation des espaces aquatiques: Approche historique et sociologique*, Proceedings of the IVth 'Congreso de actividades acuàticas', Barcelona, 20–22 October 1995.

8. M. Girard, 'Sur les établissements de bains publics à Paris depuis le VIème siècle jusqu'à nos jours', *Annales d'hygiène* (Paris, 1852); Dr Napias, *Les Établissements de bains froids* (Paris, 1877).

9. A. Campbell, *Report on Public Baths and Wash-Houses in the U.K.* (Edinburgh, 1918), p. 2.

10. Ibid., p. 3, as well as A. Sinclair and W. Henry, *Swimming* (London: Sinclair and Henry, 1893), p. 413.

11. Sinclair and Henry, *Swimming*, p. 413.

12. A.W. Cross, *Public Baths and Wash-Houses* (London: Batsford, 1906).

13. F. Sachs, *The Complete Swimmer* (London: Methuen, 1912), p. 234.

14. Such as the famous Parisian 'Bains Deligny' on the Seine, which, strangely, sank a few years ago.

15. Cuisin, *Les Bains de Paris et des principales villes des quatre parties du monde ou le Neptune des Dames* (Paris: Verdière, 1822); E. Briffault, *Paris dans l'Eau* (Paris: Hetzel, 1844); E. Chapus, *Le Sport à Paris* (Paris: Hachette, 1854).

16. Such as to learn how to carry things, how to save people, etc.

17. For the North of France, see for example *La Gazette d'Armentières*, (8 July 1892) and Archives Municipales de Tourcoing, M1F/3.

18. It has to be said that, at the end of the nineteenth century, swimming as a sport did not really exist in France (nor in a large part of Europe), as was the case in England. When swimming races began to be organized, the conditions often favoured open water. Until WWI, most of the European swimming championships still used rivers, sea coasts, natural baths and lakes. On this point, see T. Terret, *Naissance et développement de la natation* (Paris: L'Harmattan, 1994).

19. N. Estran, *Réalisation, gestion, animation des piscines, 1890–1990*, mémoire de maîtrise en STAPS, (Master's degree, Lille, 1992); T. Terret, 'Hygienisation: Civic Baths and Body Cleanliness in late Nineteenth Century France', *The International Journal of the History of Sport*, 3 (1993), pp. 396–408.

20. Like in Lyon and Bordeaux. See Dr Merry-Delabost, *Sur les bains-douches de propreté...* (Le mans, 1890); A. E. Hausser, *L'Oeuvre des bains-douches à bon marché* (Paris: 1902); T. Terret, 'La Politique Lyonnaise en matière d'Installations balnéaires (XIX–XX siècles)', *STAPS*, 33 (1994), pp. 89–102.

21. P. Augé, 'La Natation', in P. Moreau and G. Voulquin (eds), *Les Sports modernes illustrés* (Paris: 1905).

22. Gymnastics was often taught by soldiers and firemen (active or retired). See P. Arnaud, *Le Militaire*, or Y. Leziart, 'Les Premiers Enseignants de Gymnastique Scolaire: Histoire d'une profession qui se constitue', *STAPS*, 32 (Oct. 1993).

23. These points are developed in T. Terret, 'La Natation scolaire à la fin du XIX siècle: Réalités et difficultés d'une intégration', *STAPS*, 39 (Feb. 1996).

24. Ministère de l'Instruction Publique et des Beaux-Arts, *Manuel d'exercices gymnastiques et de jeux scolaires* (Paris: Imp. Nationale, 1891) and, more generally, P. Pelayo and T. Terret, 'Savoirs et enjeux relatifs à la natation dans les instructions et programmes officiels (1877–1986)', *STAPS*, 33 (1994).

25. C. Defrançois, *La Locomotion dans l'eau: Manuel de gymnastique théorique et pédagogique* (Paris: Dumaine, 1886); A. Lemoine, *Traité d'éducation physique* (Gand: Jacqmain, 1857); E. Couvreur, *Les exercices du corps: Le Développement de la force et de l'adresse* (Paris: Baillière, 1890).

26. J. Wallon, *Notice sur les exercices physiques* (Amiens, 1884).

27. A. Aignan, and V. Guillard, *Notions élémentaires sur la mer, la navigation, la pêche, suivies de*

leçons sur la gymnastique et la natation à l'usage des écoles primaires du littoral (cours moyens 1ère et 2ième années) (Paris: Gedulge, 1902).

28. *Enseignement de la gymnastique: Rapport et programme*, 1889, p. 39. See also J. Thibault, *Sport et éducation physique* (Paris: Vrin, 1972), p. 33.

29. Dr Mangenot, *Les Bains et la natation dans les écoles primaires communales de Paris* (Paris: Masson, 1892), pp. 16-7.

30. G. Vigarello, 'Pratiques de natation au XIX siècle: Représentation de l'eau et différenciations socials', *Sport et Société* (St Etienne: CIEREC, 1981), p. 190.

31. T. Terret, *Naissance et diffusion de la natation sportive* (Paris: L'Harmattan, 1994).

32. A. Poulaillon, *La Natation, les bains et piscines: Exposé de la situation présentée au Comité d'Initiative de l'Union des Sociétés Sportives Lyonnaises*, Minutes of the meeting of 8 July 1904 (Lyon: Impr. Decléris, 1904), p. 7.

33. For the example of the City of Bègles, see J.P. Callède, 'Notes d'architecture sportive: le Socialisme municipal des années trente à Bègles', *Annales du Midi,* 102, 192 (Oct.–Dec. 1990), and, for those of the city of Lyon, T. Terret, 'La Politique Lyonnaise'.

34. On the normalization of swimming between the two World Wars, see T. Terret, *L'Institution et le nageur: Histoire de la Fédération Française de Natation. 1919–1939* (Lyon: Presses universitaires de Lyon, 1998).

35. To take a shower before entering the pool became compulsory in 1930. (L. Martin, G. Brouardel, and R. Dujarric de la Rivière, *Traité d'hygiène* (Paris: Baillière, 1930).)

36. Circulaire No. 8 ES-DS/3/670, 29 May 1943, Ministère de la Santé publique et de la Population, *Réglementation de l'hygiène des piscines et autres lieux de baignades* (Paris: Imprimerie nationale, 1947).

37. *Annuaire des plages et piscines du continent: Année 1931* (Paris, 1931).

38. *Le Miroir des sports,* 316 (2 June 1926). This description was given again in E.G. Drigny, *La natation: Natation élémentaire et natation sportive* (Nancy-Paris-Strasbourg: Berger-Levrault, 1921), p. 79. See also: F. Kopp, *Des Piscines de jadis aux piscines de demain* (Rouen: Desrages, 1934), p. 10.

39. See the arguments developed by Drigny to build summer aquatic facilities and the example of the pool of a famous Toulouse swimming club, called TOEC (*Le Miroir des Sports*, 330 (11 Aug. 1926) and 434 (29 June 1928)).

40. As testified by an investigation supervised by a member of the French Parliament, Duclos, in Sept. 1933.

41. *Mémoire concernant les résultats obtenus dans l'armée de terre et de mer par l'application du système de natation de P.L.A. Le chevallier du Havre.* (Paris: Beaulé, 1852).

42. P. Beulque and A. Descarpentrie, *Méthode de natation* (Tourcoing, 1922), pp. 25–6.

43. Ibid., pp. 19–20.

44. P. Pelayo and Paul Beulque. 'Les Origines de l'enseignement collectif de la natation scolaire', *Sciences et Motricité* (1990).

45. M. Berlioux, *La Natation* (Paris: Flammarion, 1947), p. 47.

46. E. Schoebel, *Précis de natation scolaire* (Paris: Bourrelier, 1957).

47. Beulque and Descarpentrie, *Methode de natation*, p. 74.

48. Ibid.

49. M. Amar, *Nés pour courir: Sport, pouvoir et rebellion* (Grenoble: PUG, 1987).

50. J.P. Callède, *Histoire des politiques sportives en France* (Paris: Economica, 2000).

51. See 'Paris, le petit bain d'une école de natation' (imprint Crafty, Musée Carnavalet), Moeurs 81 bis, quoted in Délégation à l'action artistique de la ville de Paris, *Deux Siècles d'Architecture Sportive* (Paris: 1984), p. 24.

52. It was the case in the city of Lyon. Cf. Arch. mun. of Lyon I-1-120.

53. *Le Miroir des Sports*, 330 (11 Aug. 1926).

54. *Villeurbanne. 1924–1934. 10 Ans d'administration* (Villeurbanne, 1934) (Arch. municipale de Villeurbanne).

55. Interview with M. Degueurce, 11 Jan. 1990.

56. It was on this last basis that the congress of the Association Générale des Hygiénistes et Techniciens Municipaux agreed in 1936, in a text which was used again in 1942 by the Commissariat Général à l'Education Générale et Sportive. (Mariage *et al.*, Commissariat Général à l'EGS, *Les Piscines et l'hygiène*. Rapports présentés au congrès de l'Association générale des hygiénistes et techniciens municipaux à Dijon, du 1er au 5 juillet 1936 (Paris: Imp. Nationale, 1942), p. 7.)

57. 'The current establishments must offer as far as possible, baths for teaching with progressive depths, using a beach with a soft slope, or especially arranged; a bath for sport, with deep water, being 50 meters or 25 meters long ... for training on all distances, like a track for swimmers; in the main facilities, a bath for water polo, as distinct from the previous one; finally, a reserved space to dive, set in front of the diving boards', L.A. Grenet, *Principes de la natation* (Paris: Susse, 1946), p. 152.
58. Haut Comité des Sports, *La Sécurité dans les piscines*. Report presented by M. Gerville-Réache (Paris: Institut Pédagogique National, 1964).
59. *Circulaires* of 19 Jan. 1965, 15 Sept. 1965 and 18 Sept. 1965.
60. *Circulaires* of 23 Dec. 1971 and 9 June 1972.
61. Interview with J.B. Grosborne, 26 Feb. 1991.
62. J.B. Grosborne, 'Une Solution intéressante au problème des baignades', *EPS*, 7 (Oct. 1951).
63. Archives Fédération Française de Natation.
64. Grosborne, 'Une Solution intéressante au problème des baignades'.
65. Archives Fédération Française de Natation.
66. Ibid.
67. *EPS*, 20 (April 1954), p. 30.
68. In 1956, the same company, still supported by the Ministry of Education, created a 'summer bath for terrestrial sites', with a tank inside the 'domineaux' which allowed the teaching space to became clearly distinct from recreational or sport space. See Les bassins-école, in *EPS*, 30 (April 1956), p. 41. The homologation by the services of Youth and Sports was officially achieved in November 1955 (Letter from the *Services Techniques de l'Équipement* to the company SES, 26 Nov. (1955), Archives FFN).
69. Literally 'Moving Teaching Bath'.
70. *Aquamobile. Le Bassin d'apprentissage mobile. techniques et loisirs,* plaquette technique, no date, Archives Direction Départementale Jeunesse et Sport du Rhône.
71. For an analysis of these sport politics, see J.P. Callède, *Histoire des politiques sportives en France* (Paris: Economica, 2000).
72. Letter from the *Secrétaire d'Etat Chargé de la Jeunesse, des Sports et des Loisirs* to the *Préfets de Région* and *Recteurs* (24 March 1970), Archives Direction Départementale Jeunesse et Sport du Rhône.
73. A second generation of BAM was created after 1975 along with some Fixed Teaching Baths (BAF), thanks to the initiative of the Director of Youth and Sport in the Loiret Department. See Conseil Général du Loiret, *Bassins d'apprentissage fixes de natation* (1983), and SARECO-Ministère du Temps Libre, *La Conception et l'exploitation des bassins d'apprentissage* (Paris, 1984).
74. 'It is obvious that a large bath is necessary to improve the already existing bases and to check the effectiveness of the exercises in the whole aquatic medium.' (J. Vivensang, *Pédagogie moderne de la natation* (Paris: Chiron, 1981).
75. Secrétariat d'Etat Jeunesse, Sport et Loisir, *Concours Nationaux sur le thème des piscines. Présentation des projets privés*, no date (*c.* 1970).
76. Vivensang (1965), p. 477.
77. R. Catteau and G. Garoff, *L'Enseignement de la natation* (Paris: Vigot, 1968), p. 272.
78. Ibid., p. 99.
79. A. Vadepied, *Les Eaux troublées* (Paris: Ed. Scarabée, 1978), pp. 135–6.
80. See the *Essai de Réponse* published by both the Ministry of Education and the Ministry for Sport and Leisure: *Activités aquatiques à l'école maternelle* and *La natation à l'école élémentaire*.
81. Vadepied used many neologisms whose translation cannot give the exact meaning (*Les Eaux troublées*, p. 249).
82. CPD du Rhône, *Nager, réussir et comprendre* (video and accompanying document) (ARIP-CRDP Lyon, 1989).
83. See for example D. Maillard and P. Pelayo, 'Natation et APPN: le test Pechomaro', *EPS*, 250 (Nov.–Dec. 1994). These types of tests recently became very successful in France.
84. B. Vignal, S. Champely and T. Terret, 'Swimming and Forms of Practice in Lyon', *International Review for Sport Sociology* (Dec. 2001).
85. In the case of Paris, see C. Rouca, 'Les Piscines Parisiennes: Pratiques et espaces. La Vogue de l'eau' (Diss., Univ. Paris VII, 1999).
86. On the history of such practices, see T. Terret, *A History of Aquatic Fitness* (Miami, FL: Report to the AEA, 2001).
87. C. Rouca, *Les Piscines Parisiennes*.

88. Sixteen out of 21. Cf. *Le Progrès*, 17 Sept. 2000 (Lyon is the second-largest city in France after Paris). Caroline Rouca observed the same trends in Paris.
89. J.B. Trpkov, *Organisation du travail et culture professionnelle dans le secteur de la forme: Analyse de la situation dans le Rhône* (Master's thesis, Lyon, 2000).
90. C. Carrier, 'La Subaquathérapie', *EPS*, 246 (March–April 1994).
91. There were about 40 of these establishments in the UK at the beginning of the 1990s.
92. It has to be assumed that many of these 'innovations' are not so modern and unusual. Some have existed for a long time, like artificial waves – which were already used at the beginning of the last century.
93. N. Gal, L. Ria, C. Sève and M. Durand, La 'file indienne' en natation: un dispositif de déplacement des élèves jouant le rôle d'artefact cognitif, Proceedings, 'L'intervention en EPS et en sport', Antibes (16–18 Dec. 1998).
94. C. Dubois and J.P. Robin, *Natation: De l'École ... aux associations* (Paris: Ed. review, *EPS*, 1985).
95. M.L. Palmer, *Science de l'enseignement de la natation* (Paris: Vigot, 1985), p. 18.
96. Terret, *Naissance et diffusion de la natation sportive*.
97. The pedagogical uses of aquatic leisure space were developed in T. Terret, 'Savoir Nager. Une Histoire des pratiques et des techniques de la natation', in P. Goirand and J. Metzler (eds), *Histoire technique et culture scolaire* (Paris: Ed. review, *EPS*, 1996). See also, *APPN et EPS, Actes de l'université d'été sur le développement des activités physiques de pleine nature dans l'enseignement de l'éducation physique et sportive* (Grenoble, 1992).
98. J. Eisenbeis and Y. Touchard, *L'Éducation à la sécurité* (Paris: Ed. review, *EPS*, 1994).

Chapter 4

1. D. Massey, *Space, Place and Gender* (Oxford: Blackwell, 1994), p. 4.
2. G. Davis, *Frostiana or A History of the River Thames in a Frozen State* (London, 1814), p. 124.
3. I. Wendl, *Eis mit Stil* [Ice with Style] (München: Jugend & Volk, 1979), p. 16.
4. See, for instance: R. Jones, *A Treatise on Skating: Founded on Certain Principles Deduced from Many Years Experience; by which that Noble Exercise is now Reduced to an Art* (London: J. Ridley, 1772); F. Swift and M.R. Clark, *The Skater's Textbook* (New York, 1868); H. Winzer, 'Geschichte des Eiskunstlaufs', [History of Figure Skating] in C. Diem, A. Mallwitz, and E. Neuendorff (eds), *Handbuch der Leibesübungen* [Handbook of Physical Exercises], Vol. 8, *Eissport* [Ice Sport] (Berlin: Veidmannsche Buchhandlung, 1925), pp. 33–61.
5. J. Lewis, *Skating and the Philadelphia Skating Club* (Philadelphia: Philadelphia Skating, 1895).
6. G. Anderson, *The Art of Skating with Illustrations, Diagrams and Plain Directions for the Acquirement of the most Difficult and Graceful Movements*, 4th edn (London: Horace Cox, 1880).
7. Jones, *A Treatise on Skating*, p. 10.
8. Alfonse Lamartine, cited in G. Vail, *L'Art du patinage* (Paris, 1886).
9. Matthias Hampe, *Stilwandel im Eiskunstlauf: eine Ästhetik und Kulturgeschichte* (Changing Styles in Figure Skating: An Aesthetic and Cultural History) (Frankfurt am Main: Lang, 1994), p. 28.
10. Cited in M. Elliot, 'The Edinburgh Skating Club, 1778–1966', in *The Book of the Old Edinburgh Club*, Vol. 33, Pt 2 (Edinburgh, 1971), p. 96.
11. Ibid., p. 101.
12. The Skating Club, *Historical Sketch of the Club and Description of the Rink and Pavilion* (London: The Skating Club, 1909), p. 3.
13. M. Monier-Williams, *Figure Skating* (London: A.D. Innes, 1898), p. 30.
14. Ibid., p. 31.
15. H.E. Vandervell and T. Maxwell Witham, *A System of Figure Skating*, 2nd edn. (London: Horace Cox, 1874), p. 16.
16. Ibid., p. 19.
17. The Skating Club, *Historical Sketch*, p. 12.
18. H. Eichberg, 'The Enclosure of the Body: the Historical Relativity of 'Health', 'Nature' and the Environment of Sport,' in John Bale and Chris Philo (eds), *Body Cultures: Essays on Sport, Space and Identity* (London: Routledge, 1998), p. 50.
19. D. Brailsford, *British Sport: A Social History* (Cambridge: Butterworth, 1992).

20. R. Hutchinson, *Empire Games: The British Invention of Twentieth-Century Sport* (London: Mainstream, 1996), p. 144.
21. The Skating Club, *Historical Sketch*, p. 19.
22. Anderson, *The Art of Skating*, p. 9.
23. Ibid., p. v.
24. Monier-Williams, *Figure-Skating*, pp. 21–2.
25. E.F. Benson, *English Figure Skating: A Guide to Theory and Practice of Skating in the English Style* (London: George Bell and Sons,1908), p. 4.
26. E.F. Benson, *Winter Sports in Switzerland* (New York: Dodd, Mead and Company, 1913), p. 31.
27. Ibid., p. 24.
28. N. Brown, *Ice-Skating: A History* (London: Sportsman's Press, 1960), p. 140.
29. J.M. Heathcote, H. Elligton, E. Syers, and M.S. Monier-Williams, *A History of the National Skating Association of Great Britain, 1879–1901* (London: National Skating Association, 1902), p. 38.
30. Monier-Williams, *Figure-Skating*, p. 33.
31. M. Vinson, 'Gay Blades', typescript (Colorado Springs: Vinson Diaries, World Figure Skating Museum, 1933), p. 13.
32. The number of indoor rinks in Canada is 3,350; in the United States it is 2,500. In the rest of the world the total number of indoor rinks is 1,576. See: International Ice Hockey Federation, 'Canada leads all hockey nations in rinks and players' (News Archives, 3 July, http://db2.iih f.com/cgi-bin/db2wwwexe./news/news.d2w/archive).

Chapter 5

1. I. Opie and P. Opie, *The Lore and Language of Schoolchildren* (Oxford: Oxford University Press, 1959).
2. P. Blatchford, *Social Life in School: Pupils' Experiences of Breaktime and Recess from 7 to 16 Years* (London: Falmer Press, 1998), p. 1; P. Blatchford, *Playtime in the Primary School: Problems and Improvements* (London: NFER-Nelson, 1989); P. Blatchford et al., 'Playground Games and Playtime: The Children's View', *Educational Research Journal*, 32, 3 (1990), pp. 163–4; P. Blatchford and S. Sharp (eds), *Breaktime and the School: Understanding and Changing Playground Behaviour* (London: Routledge, 1994); P. Blatchford and C. Sumpner, 'What do we Know About Breaktime? Results from a National Survey of Breaktime and Lunchtime in Primary and Secondary Schools', *British Educational Research Journal*, 24, 1 (1998), p. 79 ff.
3. A. Pellegrini and P.K. Smith, 'School Recess: Implications for Education and Development', *Review of Educational Research*, 63, 1 (1993), pp. 51–67; J. Evans, and A. Pellegrini, 'Surplus Energy Theory: An Enduring but Inadequate Justification for School Break-Time', *Educational Review*, 49, 3 (1997); Blatchford and Sumpner, 'What do we Know About Breaktime?'; M. Sleap and P. Warburton, 'Physical Activity Levels of 5–11 year Old Children in England as Determined by Continuous Observation' *International Journal of Sports Medicine*, 17 (1996), pp. 248–53.
4. K. Blakely, 'Parents' Conceptions of Social Dangers to Children in the Urban Environment', *Children's Environments*, 11, 1 (1994), pp. 16–25; M. Hillman et al., *One False Move: A Study of Children's Independent Mobility* (London: Policy Studies Institute, 1990); A. Davis and L. Jones 'The Children's Enclosure', *Town and Country Planning* (Sept. 1996), pp. 233–5; G. Valentine, 'Angels and Devils: Moral Landscapes of Childhood', *Environment and Planning D*, 14 (1996), pp. 581–99; G. Valentine and J. McKendrick, 'Children's Outdoor Play: Exploring Parental Concerns about Children's Safety and the Changing Nature of Childhood', *Geoforum*, 28, 2 (1997), pp. 219–23.
5. J. McKendrick, M. Bradford and A. Fielder, 'Time for a Party! Making Sense of the Commercialisation of Leisure Space for Children', in S. Holloway and G. Valentine (eds), *Children's Geographies, Playing, Living, Learning* (London, Routledge, 2000), pp.100–16; F. Smith and J. Barker 'Out of School, In School: A Social Geography of Out of School Childcare', in S. Holloway and G. Valentine (eds), *Children's Geographies, Playing, Living, Learning* (London: Routledge, 2000), pp. 245–56. P. Adler and P. Adler, 'Social Reproduction and the Corporate Other: The Institutionalisation of After School Activities', *The Sociological Quarterly*, 35, 2 (1994), pp. 309–28.
6. J. Evans, *Children at Play: Life in the School Playground* (Deakin: Deakin University Press,

1989); A. Pellegrini, 'Outdoor Recess: Is it Really Necessary?' *Principal*, 70, 5 (1991), p. 40; B. Sutton-Smith, 'School Playground as Festival', *Children's Environments Quarterly*, 7, 2 (1990), pp. 3–7; T. Jambor 'School Recess and Social Development', *Dimensions of Early Childhood*, 23, 1 (1994), pp. 17–20 (Internet accessed 10 June 1998); Blatchford, *Playtime in the Primary School*; Blatchford, *Social Life in School*.

7. M. Foucault, *Discipline and Punish: The Birth of the Prison* (London: Penguin, 1977).

8. R.D. Sack, *Human Territoriality: Its Theory and History* (Cambridge: Cambridge University Press, 1986).

9. Foucault, *Discipline and Punish*.

10. Blatchford, *Social Life in School*.

11. Sutton-Smith, 'School Playground as Festival'.

12. McKendrick *et al.*, 'Time for a Party!', pp. ???

13. K. Rousmaniere, 'Questioning the Visual in the History of Education', *History of Education*, 30, 2 (2001), pp. 109–16.

14. Ibid.

15. S. Holloway and G. Valentine, 'Children's Geographies and the New Social Studies of Childhood', in S. Holloway and G. Valentine (eds), *Children's Geographies, Playing, Living, Learning* (London: Routledge, 2000), pp. 1–26; S. James, 'Is There a "Place" for Children in Geography?' *Area*, 22, 3 (1990), p. 281.

16. B. Simpson, 'Regulation and Resistance: Children's Embodiment During the Primary–Secondary School Transition', in Alan Prout (ed.), *The Body, Childhood and Society* (London: Macmillan, 2001), pp. 60–78; D. Kirk, *Schooling Bodies* (London: Leicester University Press, 1998); Rousmaniere, 'Questioning the Visual in the History of Education'; B. Eggermont, 'The Choreography of Schooling as Site of Struggle: Belgian Primary Schools, 1880–1940', *History of Education*, 30, 2 (2001), pp. 129–40; S. Fielding, 'Walk on the Left! Children's Geographies and the Primary School' in S. Holloway and G. Valentine (eds), *Children's Geographies, Playing, Living, Learning* (London: Routledge, 2000), pp. 230–44; Foucault, *Discipline and Punish*; M.J. Gore, 'Disciplining Bodies: On the Continuity of Power Relations' in R.E Paechter *et al.* (eds), *Learning, Space and Identity* (London: Paul Chapman Publishing, 2001), pp. 167–81.

17. Rousmaniere, 'Questioning the Visual in the History of Education', p. 115.

18. Ibid.

19. H. Silver (ed.), *Robert Owen on Education* (Cambridge: Cambridge University Press, 1969), p. 102.

20. D. Stow, *National Education, Supplement to Moral Training and the Training System, with Plans for Erecting and Fitting up of Training Schools* (Glasgow: W.R. M'Phun, 1839).

21. Quoted in H.C. Barnard, *A History of English Education from 1760* (London: University of London Press, 1947).

22. Quoted in C. Birchenough, *History of Elementary Education in England and Wales from 1800 to Present Day* (London: University Tutorial Press Ltd, 1938).

23. *Oxford Illustrated Dictionary* (London: Oxford University Press, 1962), p. 714.

24. E. Kelly, 'Racism and Sexism in the Playground', in Blatchford and Sharp (eds), *Breaktime and the School*.

25. Blatchford, *Playtime in the Primary School*; Blatchford, *Social Life in School*.

26. Personal conversation with Roger Hart at 'Designing Modern Childhoods: Landscapes, Buildings and Material Culture'. An International, Interdisciplinary Conference, Berkeley USA, 2002.

27. Y.-F. Tuan, 'Thought and Landscape: The Eye and the Mind's Eye', in D. W. Meinig (ed.), *The Interpretation of Ordinary Landscapes* (New York: Oxford University Press, 1979), p. 99.

28. W. Lucas, 'The Power of School Grounds: The Philosophy and Practice of Leaving Through Landscapes', in Blatchford and Sharp (eds), *Breaktime and the School*.

29. J. McKendrick and M. Bradford, 'Organised Spaces for Leisure: A New Departure in the Institutionalisation of Children's Leisure?' Paper presented to the Nordic–British Conference on Children, Norway, 1999.

30. News broadcast on BBC 'News at One', British Broadcasting Corporation, 1999.

31. B. Russell, 'Old Games are More than Child's Play', *Independent* (3 June 1999).

32. Sutton-Smith, 'School Playground as Festival', p. 6.

33. S. Thomson, 'No One Played Marbles': The Changing Dimension of School Playground Activities (Unpublished undergraduate dissertation, Keele University, 1998); S. Thomson, 'Playground or Playpound? The Contested Terrain of the Primary School Playground'. Paper presented at the British Educational Research Association Conference, Cardiff University, 2000.

34. Opie and Opie, *The Lore and Language of Schoolchildren*; and Blatchford, *Playtime in the Primary School*.
35. James, 'Is there a "Place" for Children in Geography?', p. 282.
36. Simpson, 'Regulation and Resistance', p. 77.
37. J. Bale, *Landscapes of Modern Sport* (London: Leicester University Press, 1994), p. 125.

Chapter 6

1. 'Girls Marching Teams in New Zealand Arouse Controversy and Draw Crowds', *New York Times* (25 Feb. 1958), p. 3.
2. Ibid. Marching teams were also part of the capital city, Wellington's, welcome to the Queen Mother (*Dominion* (7 Feb. 1958), p. 11).
3. See also *Quick March*, March, April, May, nos. 82–4, 1958; Editorial, *Dominion* (27 Feb. 1958), p. 10; *Evening Post*, 1 March 1958, p. 12; 28 Feb. 1958, p. 9, 'Not Just Strutters, Say Marching Girls', p. 10; N. Mangos and J. Stayt, *Marching Down Under* (Wellington: New Zealand Marching Association, 1984), p. 3.
4. Bruce Mason, 'Stepping it Out, Stepping it High', *New Zealand Listener*, 82, 1899 (1 May 1976), pp. 9–10; Linda Brady, 'Whatever Happened to Marching Girls?', *Thursday* (16 Oct. 1969), pp. 59–61; Matt Philp, 'March Past', *New Zealand Listener*, 165, 3040 (15 Aug. 1998), pp. 30–1.
5. William H. McNeill, *Keeping Together in Time: Dance and Drill in Human History* (Cambridge, Mass: Harvard University Press, 1995).
6. For a recent discussion of American cheerleading, see Mary Ellen Hanson, *Go! Fight! Win! Cheerleading in American Culture* (Bowling Green: Bowling Green State University Popular Press, 1995). In 1961 the *New Zealand Listener* reported American visitors comments that New Zealand's marching girls were 'much superior' as a major attraction than their Drum Majorettes, H.W. Orsman (ed.), *The Dictionary of New Zealand English* (Auckland: Oxford University Press, 1997), p. 483b.
7. Elaine Tyler May, 'Explosive Issues: Sex, Women and the Bomb', in L. May (ed.), *Recasting America: Culture and Politics in the Age of the Cold War* (Chicago and London: University of Chicago Press, 1989), p. 154.
8. 'Marching Teams', A.H. McLintock (ed.), *Encyclopaedia of New Zealand* (Wellington: Government Printer, 1966), p. 490; Jill Williams, Val Browning and Charlotte Macdonald, 'New Zealand Marching Association', in Anne Else (ed.), *Women Together: A History of Women's Organisations in New Zealand* (Wellington: Daphne Brasell Associates with Historical Branch, Department of Internal Affairs, 1993), pp. 437–9; Sandra Coney, *Standing in the Sunshine: A History of New Zealand Women Since they Won the Vote* (Auckland: Viking/Penguin, 1993), pp. 250–1; Mangos and Stayt, *Marching Down Under*; *Women in Sport*, 1, 7 (Aug. 1948), *Women in Sport*, 8 (Sept. 1948), *Women in Sport*, 11 (Dec. 1948); *New Zealand Sportswoman*, 1 (1949).
9. *New Zealand Official Yearbook 1993* (Wellington: Department of Statistics, 1993), p. 63.
10. See, for example: Capt. H.N. Fearnley, a veteran of two world wars, who was the coach of the Otaki marching teams (Edna Snowdon, 'Girl's Marching', *Otaki Historical Society: Historical Journal*, 9 (1986), pp. 21–6); Russell Sissons served overseas in WWI, joined the temporary army headquarters staff in WWII serving for six years as instructor with the Home Guard and school cadets (obit. *Northern Advocate*, (14 Jan. 1997), p. 9); Geo Austad and pen portraits in Mangos and Stayt, *Marching Down Under*, pp. 19–29.
11. Arthur Morgan, 'The Girls are Marching', *New Zealand Magazine*, 1 (1951), p. 5a.
12. Orsman, *The Dictionary of New Zealand English*, p. 483c.
13. See, for example, Otaki teams, Snowdon, 'Girl's Marching', pp. 21–6.
14. The march plan for 1947/8 consisted of 24 different sequences beginning with the following: 'A' Ready to fall in. (1) Fall-in, inspection. (2) End of quickstep course. (3) Double retreat countermarch. (4) Right form. (5) Left form and form echelon. (6) Right incline. (7) Left turn. (8) Right incline. (9) About-turn countermarch. (Mangos and Stayt, *Marching Down Under*, p. 5.)
15. NZ Marching Association papers, MS 856, Auckland Public Library; *Quick March* (Nov. 1951–Oct. 1963); *Quick Step* (1978–94); *New Zealand on the March*, 1994; Mangos and Stayt, *Marching Down Under*; 'Marching off to Edinburgh', *New Zealand Woman's Weekly* (20 June 1977), pp. 16–8; 'Lochiel Girls Thrill Crowd', *Evening Post* (17 Sept. 1983). The Lochiel Marching Team has had a long involvement with the Edinburgh Tattoo, performing in the Tattoo

on a number of occasions. The connection endures: the Lochiel Team performed in the first Edinburgh Tattoo staged outside Scotland. This took place in Wellington, New Zealand, in March 2000, complete with replica castle built and installed in brand new sports stadium, which was the venue for performances. The Tattoo was immensely popular and sold out months in advance. There is an interesting racial dimension to this point. Maori as well as Pakeha (New Zealanders of European descent) girls and young women were involved in marching but there is little sign of Maori names or cultural symbols being used in marching teams or uniforms. In this sense the sport was consistent with the prevailing assimilationist view of race relations at this time. The predominant view was that all New Zealanders were 'one people' who enjoyed some of the best race relations in the world, despite the considerable disparities in wealth, education, health and life span between Maori and non-Maori peoples. This view of race relations was seriously challenged by a resurgent Maori political and social activism from the late 1960s.

16. For New Zealanders the popularity and significance of the new reign was intensified by the coincidence of the coronation with the 'conquest' of Mt Everest by New Zealand climber Edmund Hillary and Nepali Sherpa Tenzing Norgay, followed by the six-week-long tour of the country undertaken by Queen Elizabeth and Prince Phillip over the summer (Dec./Jan.) of 1953/54 (the first major overseas tour by the new monarch). (Jock Phillips, *Royal Summer: The Visit of Queen Elizabeth II and Prince Philip to New Zealand 1953–54* (Wellington: Historical Branch, Department of Internal Affairs/Daphne Brassell Associates Press, 1993).)

17. David Cannadine, 'The Context, Performance and Meaning of Ritual: The British Monarchy and the 'Invention of Tradition', c. 1820–1977', in Eric Hobsbawm and Terence Ranger (eds), *The Invention of Tradition* (Cambridge: Cambridge University Press, 1983), pp. 101–64.

18. W.D. McIntyre, 'Imperialism and Nationalism', and 'From Dual Dependency to Nuclear Free', in Geoffrey W. Rice (ed.), *Oxford History of New Zealand* (Auckland: Oxford University Press, 1992, 2nd edn.); Malcolm McKinnon, *Independence and Foreign Policy in New Zealand: New Zealand in the World since 1935* (Auckland: Auckland University Press, 1993). Domestically, the insecurities of the cold war were also evident in New Zealand's political and social fabric. A major industrial dispute closed the country's docks for 151 days from February to June 1951. In the highly polarized political climate of the time, the workers were seen as the red enemy within. Emergency Regulations invoked during the dispute gave the government draconian powers over freedom of speech and liberty of movement. Members of the Communist Party (CP), or activists suspected of being members of the CP, were placed under special surveillance.

19. Tammy M. Proctor, '(Uni)Forming Youth: Girls Guides and Boy Scouts in Britain, 1908–39', *History Workshop Journal*, 45 (Spring 1998), pp. 103–34.

20. See May, 'Explosive Issues'; Margot Hendrikson, *Dr Strangelove's America: Society and Culture in the Atomic Age* (Berkeley: University of California Press, 1997); also Helen May, *Minding Children, Managing Men: Conflict and Compromise in the Lives of Postwar Pakeha Women* (Wellington: Bridget Williams Books, 1992) on individual control, exercise of restraint and psychological training in an educational and social context.

21. Finlay Macdonald, *The Game of Our Lives* (Auckland: Penguin/Viking, 1996); Jock Phillips, *A Man's Country: The Image of the Pakeha Male – A History* (Auckland: Penguin, 1996); Tim Chandler and John Nauright (eds), *Making Men: Rugby and Masculine Identity* (London: Frank Cass, 1996).

22. See May, 'Explosive Issues' and Hendrikson, *Dr Strangelove's America*.

23. Julie Glamuzina and Alison Laurie, *Parker and Hulme* (Auckland: New Women's Press, 1991). The 'Parker–Hulme' case, as it became known, shattered the calm surfaces of suburban Christchurch/New Zealand, revealing troubled marriages, adultery, tumultuous parent-child relations, a friendship depicted as of pathological obsession and dangerous fantasy extending to the suggestion of sexually intimate relationship between the two girls. (The case became the core of Peter Jackson's 1994 film *Heavenly Creatures*.)

24. Redmer Yska, *All Shook Up: The Flash Bodgie and the Rise of the New Zealand Teenager in the Fifties* (Auckland: Penguin, 1993). In part, blame was placed at the door of working mothers who were absent from home – and therefore unable to supervise their teenage children's behaviour outside school hours. (Bowlby's influence is clear.) But the causes of such moral laxity and social pathology were also traced more broadly to a too great materialism in the society, to a lack of moral and social leadership as well as to practical factors such as the absence of leisure facilities for young people in the Valley.

25. John Dix, *Stranded in Paradise* (Wellington: Paradise Publications, 1988); Yska, *All Shook Up*; Roger Watkins, *When Rock Got Rolling* (Christchurch: Hazard Press, 1989) and *Hostage to the*

Beat (Auckland: Tandem Press, 1995). The film was viewable only by those over the age of 16 and then only after initial resistance by the leading cinema chain owner who feared his movie houses would be destroyed by youthful movie watchers rendered uncontrollable by the film.

26. Ian Pool, *Te Iwi Maori: A New Zealand Population Past, Present and Projected* (Auckland: Auckland University Press, 1991); Joan Metge, *A New Maori Migration*, (London: Athlone Press, 1964); Ranginui Walker, 'Maori People Since 1950', *Oxford History of New Zealand* (Auckland: Oxford University Press, 1992, 2nd edn); Ranginui Walker, *Ka Whawhai Tonu Matou – Struggle Without End* (Auckland: Penguin, 1990).

27. Graeme Dunstall, 'The Social Pattern', *Oxford History of New Zealand*, 2nd edn (Auckland: Oxford University Press, 1992.

Chapter 7

1. R. McGeoch, *The Bid: How Australia Won the 2000 Games* (Melbourne: William Heinemann Australia, 1994).
2. Sydney Olympic Games Committee (SOGC), *Sydney Olympics 2000* (Sydney: SOGC, 1991).
3. N. Smith, 'The Production of Nature', in G. Robertson, M. Mash, L. Tickner, J. Bird, B. Curtie and T. Putnam (eds), *Future Natural: Nature, Science, Culture* (London: Routledge, 1996), p. 41.
4. P. Groth, 'Frameworks for Cultural Landscape Study', in P. Groth and T.W. Bressi (eds), *Understanding Ordinary Landscapes* (New Haven, CT: Yale University Press, 1997), p. 1.
5. N. Lovell, 'Introduction. Belonging in Need of Emplacement?', in N. Lovell (ed.), *Locality and Belonging* (London: Routledge, 1998), p. 6.
6. J. Bale, *Landscapes of Modern Sport* (Leicester: Leicester University Press, 1994), p. 13.
7. T.R. Dunlap, *Nature and the English Diaspora. Environment and History in the United States, Canada, Australia, and New Zealand* (Cambridge: Cambridge University Press, 1999).
8. Sydney Olympics 2000 Bid Limited (SOBL), *Sydney 2000. Share the Spirit. Volume 2 Olympic Information* (Sydney: SOBL, 1993), p. 354.
9. J.B. Hirst, 'The Pioneer Legend', in J. Carroll (ed.), *Intruders in the Bush: The Australian Quest for Identity* (Melbourne: Oxford University Press, 1992), pp. 14–37.
10. SOCOG, *Sydney 2000 Olympic Games Image Guidelines* (Sydney: SOCOG, 1998), n.p.
11. J. Weirick, 'Urban Design', in R. Cashman and A. Hughes (eds), *Staging the Olympics: The Event and its Impact* (Sydney: University of New South Wales Press, 1999), pp. 70–82.
12. Weirick, 'Urban Design', pp. 70–82.
13. Greenpeace, *Environmental Report*. Retrieved 10 Nov. 2000 from the Internet: www.greenpeace.com.au.
14. H. Cantelon and M. Letters, 'The Making of the IOC Environmental Policy as a Third Dimension of the Olympic Movement', *International Review for the Sociology of Sport*, 35, 3 (2000), pp. 294–308; H. Lenskyj, *Inside the Olympic Industry: Power, Politics, and Activism* (Albany: SUNY Press, 2000).
15. L. Allison, 'Sport as an Environmental Issue', in L. Allison (ed.), *The Changing Politics of Sport* (Manchester: Manchester University Press, 1993), pp. 207–32.
16. Lenskyj, *Inside the Olympic Industry*.
17. P. Hoffie, 'Landscape and Identity in the 1980s', in G. Levitus (ed.), *Lying About the Landscape* (Sydney: Craftsman House, 1997), p. 69.
18. Dunlap, *Nature and the English Diaspora*; G. Turner, *National Fictions: Literature, Film and the Construction of Australian Narrative* (Sydney: Allen & Unwin, 1986).
19. Turner, *National Fictions*.
20. Dunlap, *Nature and the English Diaspora*.
21. Ibid.; Hoffie, 'Landscape and Identity in the 1980s'.
22. Dunlap, *Nature and the English Diaspora*.
23. D. Godwell, 'The Olympic Branding of Aborigines: The 2000 Olympic Games and Australia's Indigenous Peoples', in K. Schaffer and S. Smith (eds), *The Olympics at the Millennium. Power, Politics and the Games* (New Brunswick: Rutgers University Press, 2000), pp. 243–57; D. MacCannell, *Empty Meeting Grounds: The Tourist Papers* (London: Routledge, 1992).
24. NBC, *Telecast of the Opening Ceremony of the Games of the XXVIIth Olympiad*, 15 Sept. 2000.
25. Australian Tourist Commission, 'The Olympic Effect'. *ATC-On-line – Tourism Industry Essentials*. Retrieved 4 April 2002 from the Internet: http://www.atc.net.au/brand.asp? art=672.
26. SOCOG, *Sydney 2000 Olympic Games Image Guidelines*.

27. Bale, *Landscapes of Modern Sport*.
28. B. Adam, *Timescapes of Modernity. The Environment and Invisible Hazards* (London: Routledge, 1998).
29. P. Macnaghten and J. Urry, *Contested Natures* (London: Sage, 1998), p. 13.
30. K. Soper, 'Nature/"Nature"', in Robertson, Mash, Tickner, Bird, Curtie and Putnam (eds), *Future Natural*, p. 25.
31. H. Eichberg, J. Bale and C. Philo (eds), *Body Cultures: Essays on Sport, Space and Identity* (London: Routledge, 1998).
32. Dunlap, *Nature and the English Diaspora*.
33. C. Aron, *Working at Play. A History of Vacations in the United States* (Oxford: Oxford University Press, 1999).
34. Aron, *Working at Play*, p. 18.
35. Bale, *Landscapes of Modern Sport*, p. 63.
36. Soper, 'Nature/'Nature"', p. 25.
37. Bale, *Landscapes of Modern Sport*.
38. M. Crozier, 'After the Garden?', *The South Atlantic Quarterly*, 98, 4 (1999), pp. 625–31.
39. Bale, *Landscapes of Modern Sport*.
40. Lovell, 'Introduction. Belonging in Need of Emplacement?', pp. 2–3.
41. SOBL, *Sydney 2000. Share the Spirit. Volume 2 Olympic Information* (Sydney: SOBL, 1993), p. 6.
42. NBC, *Telecast of the Opening Ceremony of the Games of the XXVIIth Olympiad*, 15 Sept. 2000.
43. V. Simpson and A. Jennings, *The Lords of the Rings* (Toronto: Stoddart, 1992); Lenskyj, *Inside the Olympic Industry*.
44. SOBL, Sydney 2000 Presentation to the IOC Executive Board, ANOC, Acapulco, Nov. 1992, p. 19.
45. See J. Hoberman, *Mortal Engines: The Science of Performance and the Dehumanization of Sport* (New York: The Free Press, 1992).
46. Australian Federal Minister for Sport, Jackie Kelly, held an international conference on doping entitled 'Pure Performance' in 1999.
47. Perhaps the closest exponent would be Eric Moussambani, the Equatorial Guinean swimmer whose lack of training was apparent as he struggled down the two lengths of the Olympic pool in Sydney. See J. Nauright and T. Magdalinski (in press), '"A Hapless Attempt at Swimming": Framing Eric Mousambani through the Western Press', *Critical Arts*.
48. C. Shilling, *The Body and Social Theory* (London: Sage, 1993), p. 5.
49. An excellent example on the belief in 'natural talent' rather than hard work is Tiger Woods. His 'natural ability' is constantly acclaimed, even though he has been playing golf since he was 18 months old. When does natural talent end and training begin?
50. Soper, 'Nature/"Nature"', p. 25.
51. Ibid., p. 24.
52. Ibid.
53. T. Magdalinski, 'Drugs, Sport and National Identity in Australia', in W. Wilson and E. Derse (eds), *Doping in Elite Sport: The Politics of Drugs in the Olympic Movement* (Champaign, Ill: Human Kinetics, 2001), pp. 189–202; T. Magdalinski, '"Excising the Cancer": Drugs, Sport and the Crisis of Australian Identity', *AVANTE*, 6, 3 (2000), pp. 1–15.
54. Magdalinski, 'Drugs, Sport and National Identity in Australia'.
55. T. Magdalinski, 'Drugs Inside Sport: The Rehabilitation of Samantha Riley', *Sporting Traditions*, 17, 2 (2001), p. 18.
56. See Bale, *Landscapes of Modern Sport*.
57. See Lenskyj, *Inside the Olympic industry*.
58. H. Wilson, 'What is an Olympic City? Visions of Sydney 2000', *Media, Culture and Society*, 18 (1996), pp. 603–18.
59. Godwell, 'The Olympic Branding of Aborigines'; G. Waitt, 'Playing Games with Sydney: Marketing Sydney for the 2000 Olympics', *Urban Studies*, 36, 7 (1999), pp. 1055–77; Wilson, 'What is an Olympic City?'.
60. McGeoch, *The Bid*, p. 66.

Chapter 8

1. The material in this chapter focuses on the popular urban beaches in Sydney. They were the epicentres of both surf lifesaving and surfing in Australia. Limited material from other urban centres, notably Queensland's Gold Coast and Perth, suggests that conditions in Sydney were not unique.

2. 'Baywatch Unplugged', producer Nick Franklin, 'The Morning Show', Triple J (Sydney 105.7fm), 26 March 1999.

3. Chris Rojek analyses leisure within a framework of the 'legitimating rules of pleasure and [discipline]'. According to Rojek, mass consumer capitalism created the conditions under which the middle classes revised traditional ideas about leisure as an adjunct of work; leisure became an autonomous social practice based on individually chosen lifestyles. But while consumer capitalism promoted greater freedom and tolerance in leisure, it also raised concerns about 'correct' behaviour. Chris Rojek, *Capitalism and Leisure Theory* (London: Tavistock, 1985), p. 181. (While Rojek uses the term 'unpleasure', the context suggests he means discipline.)

4. Sydney surfbathers formed clubs at local beaches early in the twentieth century to challenge Victorian rectitude that banned bathing in daylight hours. In 1907, the clubs coalesced as the Surf Bathing Association of New South Wales, which became the Surf Life Saving Association of Australia (SLSA) in 1923. Surf lifesavers represented the business and health interests of the middle classes and, contrary to arguments by early historians of SLSA, were not social rebels. For a detailed history of the founding of the lifesaving movement, see Douglas Booth, *Australian Beach Cultures: the History of Sun, Sand and Surf* (London: Frank Cass, 2001), pp. 67–75.

5. Egbert Russell, 'Australia's Amphibians', *Lone Hand* (Jan. 1910), p. 265.

6. Editorial, *Surf in Australia*, 1 Jan. 1937, p. 1.

7. Kent Pearson, *Surfing Subcultures of Australia and New Zealand* (Brisbane: University of Queensland Press, 1979); Craig McGregor, *Profile of Australia* (London: Hodder & Stoughton, 1966).

8. John Lawton, *1963: Five Hundred Days* (London: Hodder & Stoughton, 1992), p. 220.

9. *The History of Australian Surfing*, producer Nat Young (CBS/Fox, 1986), videocassette; Malcolm Gault-Williams and Gary Lynch, 'Pulling Seaward: Tommy Zahn', *The Surfer's Journal* (late Spring 2000), p. 83.

10. Albie Thoms, *Surfmovies: The History of Surf Film in Australia* (Sydney: Shore Thing Publishing, 2000), especially pp. 69–81 and pp. 89–94.

11. Jon Stratton, 'Youth Subcultures and their Cultural Contexts', *Australian and New Zealand Journal of Sociology*, 21, 2 (1985), p. 211; Gary Morris, 'Beyond the Beach: Social and Formal Aspects of AIP's Beach Party Movies', *Journal of Popular Film and Television*, 21, 1 (1993), pp. 2–11; R.L. Rutsky, 'Surfing the Other: Ideology on the Beach', *Film Quarterly*, 52, 4 (1999), pp. 12–23.

12. '"Doggers" of the Surf', *Australian Women's Weekly*, 3 Dec. 1958, p. 3; 'Surf–Riders' Dictionary', *The Teenagers' Weekly*, suppl. to *Australian Women's Weekly*, 24 Oct. 1962, p. 3.

13. 'Mona Vale Surf Club Seeks Members', *Manley Daily* (*MD*), 6 Nov. 1965; 'North Steyne SLSC president retires', *MD*, 30 Sept. 1965; Lionel Ford, Letters to the editor, *Sydney Morning Herald* (*SMH*), 18 Feb. 1965.

14. 'Title Contest for Australia', *SW* (Feb. 1963), p. 9.

15. 'ASA Formation', *Surfing World* (*SW*), Dec. 1963), p. 1.

16. Report of the Conference to Discuss the Standardization of Methods of Control of Surf Craft Riding in the Metropolitan Area (22 July 1960), Warringah Shire Council (WSC), file 20A.

17. Report of the Meeting of the Committee of Implementation Set Up to Deal with Details Relating to the Regulation and Control of Surf Craft in the Metropolitan Area, (26 Aug. 1960), WSC file 20A; 'Manly Council will Tighten Control of Surf Boards and Surf Skis', *MD*, 1 Oct. 1960; 'Uniform Surf Craft Control', *MD*, 16 Nov. 1960.

18. 'Appeal for Boardriders Discipline Plan', *MD*, 23 April 1966.

19. Editorial, *Surfabout* (Summer 1967), p. 3.

20. 'Early Problems', *MD*, (15 May 1964).

21. 'World Surfboard Titles at Manly, May 16–17', *MD*, 16 April 1964.

22. 'Manly's Record Sporting Crowd Sees Farrelly's Board Win', *MD*, 19 May 1964.

23. Letter, John Titchen to WSC, 14 March 1966, WSC file 20A.

24. Youth Policy Advisory Committee, Report 41/1962/3 (Sydney: New South Wales Government, 1963), pp. 23–4.

25. Letter, 'Observer', *MD*, 15 Oct. 1965; Letter, R. McKinnon, *Daily Telegraph* (*DT*), 13 Feb. 1964.

26. '"Hoodlum Packs" Sleep on Beach: Council Plans Action', *MD*, 7 Oct. 1965.
27. T. Monoghan, 'Balgowlah Boys' High School Ended a Year of Scholastic Achievement', *MD*, 18 Dec. 1962.
28. Thoms, *Surfmovies*, p. 77.
29. New South Wales Parliamentary Debates, Legislative Assembly, 5 March 1963, p. 2970.
30. Letter, R. M. Brown to WSC, 17 Jan. 1966 0, WSC file 20A.
31. 'Surfboard Riders Criticised', *SMH*, 6 March 1963.
32. 'Surfrider Offenders. "Last Warning"'; 'Prosecute', *MD*, 25 March 1966.
33. 'Police Impound 54 Surfboards in Raid', *SMH*, (6 Feb. 1964); 'Police "Raid" Boardriders', *DT*, 6 Feb. 1964.
34. 'Surfrider Offenders.'
35. Designation of surfcraft areas, Item 39, Parks and Reserves Committee Report, 13 Sep. 1966, WSC file 20A.
36. WSC, Minutes of the Ordinary Meeting, 31 Oct. 1966, p. 6; Letter, WSC to ASA, 11 Nov. 1966, WSC file 20A.
37. 'The Surf Lifesaving Movement: Executives Out of Step with an Unsquare Age', *SMH*, 12 Feb. 1965.
38. Interviews: Mick Mabbott (surfer), 26 Oct. 1992) Alex McTaggart (surfer), 10 March 1993, John Windshuttle (boat sweep), 10 March 1993; 'Board and Surf Men in Clash', *SMH*, 7 Nov. 1966.
39. Murray Trembath, 'Far Places Calling', *Sun*, (30 Sept. 1966); Letter, The Amalgamated Independent Traders' Association to WSC, (22 Sept. 1966), WSC file 20A; 'Board Ban may be Eased', *MD*, 29 Sept. 1966; 'Beach warnings ripped', *Sun Herald* (*SH*), 9 Oct. 1966; 'No Man's Land' in Surf Riders' Plan', *MD*, 8 Oct. 1966.
40. 'Warringah Council Dismissed', *MD*, 4 April 1967.
41. Shire Clerk's Special Report presented to the Ordinary Meeting, 17 July 1967, WSC file 20A.
42. Lawton, *1963*, p. 32; John Clarke, Stuart Hall, Tony Jefferson and Brian Roberts, 'Subcultures, Cultures and Class', in Hall and Jefferson (eds), *Resistance Through Rituals* (London: Hutchinson,1976), p. 67.
43. Andrew Milner, 'On the Beach: Apocalyptic Hedonism and the Origins of Postmodernism', in Ian Craven, *Australian Popular Culture* (Cambridge: Cambridge University Press, 1994), p. 199.
44. Lawton, *1963*, p. 12.
45. Clarke *et al.*, 'Subcultures, Cultures and Class', p. 62.
46. David Harvey, *The Condition of Postmodernity: An Inquiry into the Origins of Cultural Change* (Oxford: Blackwell, 1990), p. 38.
47. Robert Conneeley, 'Interview', *Tracks* (April 1978), p. 18; Ted Spencer, 'Interview', *Tracks* (Aug. 1974), p. 10; Letter, Nat Young, *Tracks* (Oct. 1970), p. 7.
48. 'Absence of apostrophes as per original', *Tracks* (June 1973), p. 4.
49. Gavin Souter, 'A Golden Lure Along the Rim of the City', *SMH*, 17 Dec. 1960.
50. 'Jobless Junkies Roaming Beaches', *SH*, 19 April 1971.
51. Phil Jarratt, *Mr Sunset: The Jeff Hakman Story* (London: General Publishing, 1997), pp. 70–3, 78–84; Drew Kampion, *Stoked: A History of Surf Culture* (Los Angeles: General Publishing, 1997), pp. 127–32.
52. Irwin Silber, *The Cultural Revolution: A Marxist Analysis* (New York: Times Change Press, 1970), p. 58.
53. Spencer, 'Interview', p. 9; David Caute, *Sixty-Eight: The Year of Barricades* (London: Hamish Hamilton,1988), p. 40.
54. Bryan Turner, *The Body and Society* (Oxford: Basil Blackwell, 1984), pp. 111–12.
55. 'Baywatch Unplugged'.
56. Deirdre Macken, 'We Must Fight them on the Beaches', *SMH*, 25 Feb. 1999.
57. 'Baywatch Unplugged'; 'Today', Channel Nine (Sydney), 25 Feb. 1999.
58. Mary Blaich, 'Women for All Seasons', "Wahine", 3, 1 (1997), p. 32.
59. 'Baywatch Unplugged'.
60. Macken, 'Fight Them on the Beaches'.
61. 'Today'.
62. 'Fears of a Tourist Invasion', *MD*, (20 Feb. 1999); 'Too Good to Pass Up', *MD*, 24 Feb. 1999.
63. Treasurer's Report, ASLSC Annual Report 1998–99, p. 12.
64. 'Club in *Baywatch* Deal', *MD*, (23 Feb. 1999).
65. 'Baywatch Unplugged'; 'Today'.
66. 'A Current Affair', Channel Seven (Sydney), 25 Feb. 1999.

67. 'Baywatch Unplugged'.
68. Interview, McTaggart.
69. Ibid.
70. SLSA Annual Report 1999, p. 37.

Chapter 9

1. From the message of Secretary-General Kofi Annan for the United Nations Year of Mountains (2002), www.unis.unvienna.org/iym/en/launch.
2. For those interested in body culture and feats of physicality, a study of devotional physicality is waiting to be carried out. Pilgrimages to shrines, many in the mountains or at the summits of mountains, often involve striking feats of endurance and exposure to pain – whether it is the long distance hike to Santiago, or an ascent of the stairs to a shrine on one's knees. The *parikrama* involves both.
3. T.S. Blakeney, 'Kailas: A Holy Mountain', in M.C. Tobias and H. Drasdo (eds), *The Mountain Spirit* (Woodstock, NY: The Overlook Press, 1979), pp. 149–59; J. Saili, *Himalayan Mysteries* (New Delhi, India: Roli Books, 2001), p. 36.
4. K. Spindler, *The Man in the Ice: The Discovery of a 5,000 Year Old Body Reveals the Secrets of the Stone Age* (New York: Harmony Books, 1994).
5. H.D. Thoreau, *The Maine Woods* (Boston: Tichnor and Fields, 1864).
6. Anthropologist Mike Thompson contrasted the risk-taking and risk-accepting attitudes of Buddhists in Tibet and Nepal with the risk-avoiding attitudes of Hindus. Those Buddhist attitudes were expressed historically in running trade routes through the Himalayas, but are now most evident in the Sherpa mountain guides working for foreign expeditions in the Nepal Himalaya. M.Thompson, 'The Aesthetics of Risk', in J. Perrin (ed.), *Mirrors in the Cliffs* (London: Diadem Books, 1983), pp. 561–73.
7. H.B. Earhart, 'Sacred Mountains in Japan: Shugendo as 'Mountain Religion'', in Tobias and Drasdo (eds), *The Mountain Spirit*, pp. 107–16.
8. At 1909 m, Mont Ventoux, in Provence, represents a significant climb, although there is now a road to the summit which is regularly on the route of the Tour de France cycle race. Other early ascents for pleasure were made by Conrad Gesner, who climbed Mount Pilatus (Switzerland) in 1555; Placidus á Spescha, who climbed Velan in 1779, and Clément de Champéry, who climbed the Dent du Midi in 1784.
9. A. Lunn, *A Century of Mountaineering, 1857–1957* (London: Allen and Unwin, 1957).
10. Sir Gavin de Beer, *Early Travellers in the Alps* (New York: October House, 1967), p. vii.
11. Cited by de Beer, *Early Travellers in the Alps*, p. 12.
12. Thomas Burnet, *Telluris Theoria Sacra (The Sacred Theory of the Earth)* (Londini: Typis R.N. impensis Gualt, 1681).
13. Cited by Lunn, *A Century of Mountaineering*, p. 18.
14. M.H. Nicolson, *Mountain Gloom and Mountain Glory: The Development of the Aesthetics of the Infinite* (Ithaca, NY: Cornell University Press, 1959).
15. S. Schama, *Landscape and Memory* (Toronto: Random House, 1995), p. 451.
16. See Nicolson, *Mountain Gloom and Mountain Glory*, and Schama, *Landscape and Memory*, for additional discussions of the mountain aesthetic in the seventeenth century.
17. Isaiah 40:4.
18. G. Trevelyan, *Illustrated Social History of England* (Harmondsworth, UK: Penguin, 1964).
19. de Beer, *Early Travellers in the Alps*, p. 12.
20. Trevelyan, *Illustrated Social History*, p. 160. The British Library has a large collection of tourist pamphlets for the English Lake District published in the latter part of the eighteenth century.
21. A. Brandt, 'Views', *Atlantic Monthly* (July 1977), asks, 'why [is] Colorado full of viewpoints but Kansas ... has none. The answer only *seems* obvious: Kansas is flat and boring, Colorado vertical and spectacular .... Are such preferences immutable characteristics of human nature, or are they merely episodes in the history of human taste, soon to be superceded by new trends in aesthetic sensibility?' (p. 47). His answer supports the latter.
22. Schama, *Landscape and Memory*, p. 450.
23. Edmund Burke, *Philosophical Inquiry into the Origin of Our Ideas of the Sublime and Beautiful* (London: R. and J. Dodsley, 1757).
24. Schama, *Landscape and Memory*, p. 449.

25. See J.J. Rousseau's *Émile, ou de l'éducation* (Amsterdam: J. Néaulme, 1762).
26. P. Hansen, 'Albert Smith, the Alpine Club and the Invention of Mountaineering in Mid-Victorian Britain', *Journal of British Studies* 34 (1995), pp. 300–24.
27. Parts of this, and the following section, are adapted from P. Donnelly, 'the Invention of Tradition and the (Re)Invention of Mountaineering', in K. Wamsley (ed.), *Sport History and Social Theory* (Dubuque, IA: Brown and Benchmark, 1995), pp. 235–43.
28. See for example, P. Hansen, 'British Mountaineering, 1850–1914' (unpublished doctoral thesis, Harvard University, 1991); D. Robbins, 'Sport, Hegemony and the Middle Class: The Victorian Mountaineers', *Theory, Culture and Society*, 4 (1987), pp. 579–601.
29. C.D. Cunningham and W. de W. Abney, *Pioneers of the Alps* (London: Sampson Low, 1887), p. 1.
30. Despite Cunningham's claim, the ascent was not the first from Grindelwald – it seems likely to have been the third from Grindelwald, and the fifth overall – although 'a conspiracy of silence in Grindelwald regarding earlier ascents' may have been in place in order to make the ascent more attractive to Wills, and to the financial advantage of the local guides (W. Unsworth, *Hold the Heights: The Foundations of Mountaineering* (Seattle: The Mountaineers, 1994), pp. 376–7) the historical record clearly indicates that some of these ascents were made for pleasure – i.e., for their own sake.
31. W.A.B. Coolidge, *The Alps in Nature and History* (London: Methuen, 1908).
32. This arrogance is mirrored in the act of claiming the ascent as a 'conquest' and naming or re-naming the mountain (e.g., Denali was renamed Mount McKinley; Chomolungma/ Sagarmatha was renamed Mount Everest).
33. Cunningham and Abney, *Pioneers of the Alps*, p. 14.
34. Unsworth, *Hold the Heights*, p. 70, claims that 140 ascents were made in this period, almost half by British alpinists. It should be noted that all of these ascents were made with the assistance of local people who guided, cajoled, or pushed and pulled the climbers to the summits, and did most of the additional physical labour (step cutting, carrying loads, cooking, etc.). P. Donnelly, 'Who's Master, Who's Man?: Guide Client Relationships in 19th Century Mountaineering', Seward Staley Address presented to the Annual Conference of the North American Society for Sport History, Banff, Canada, 2000.
35. Even worse, and still with classical understanding, was the designation of the period between the World Wars as the iron age – a clever pun since it is generally assumed to refer to the widespread growth in the use of pitons and other aids by mountaineers in the Alps and other regions. But the implication is that the sport was by then at its most degenerate, according to the more conservative members of previous generations.
36. Sir Francis Younghusband, *The Epic of Mount Everest* (London: Arnold, 1926), p. ????
37. L. Stephen, *The Playground of Europe* (London: Longmans, 1871); J. Ruskin, *Sesame and Lilies* (London: Everett, 1916).
38. P. Donnelly, 'Take My Word For It: Trust in the Context of Birding and Mountaineering', *Qualitative Sociology*, 17 (1994), pp. 215–41.
39. Interestingly, similar mass ascents occurred in the Western United States in the early part of the twentieth century, under the leadership of groups such as the Sierra Club and Mazamas.
40. C.T. Dent, 'Two Attempts on the Aiguille de Dru', *Alpine Journal*, 7 (1876), pp. 65–79.
41. P. Donnelly, 'The Great Divide: Sport Climbing vs. Adventure Climbing', in S. Sydnor and R. Rinehart (eds), *To the Extreme: Alternative Sports Inside and Out* (Albany, NY: Suny Press, 2002), in press; R. Williams, *Marxism and Literature* (Oxford: Oxford University Press, 1977).
42. IYM *Summit Charter 2002* (www.uiaa.ch/iym).
43. http://www.uiaa.ch

Chapter 10

1. F. Rich, 'Naked Capitalists: There's No Business Like Porn Business', *New York Times Magazine*, 20 May 2001.
2. John Bale, *Landscapes of Modern Sport* (Leicester and London: Leicester University Press, 1994); Henning Eichberg, 'New Spatial Configurations of Sport? Experiences from Danish Alternative Planning', *International Review of the Sociology of Sport*, 28 (1993), pp. 245–61. B. Pronger, *The Arena of Masculinity: Sports, Homosexuality and the Meaning of Sex*, 2nd edn (Toronto: University of Toronto Press, 1992); 'Fear and Trembling: Homophobia in Men's

Sport', in P. White and K. Young (eds), *Sport and Gender in Canada* (Toronto: Oxford University Press, 1999); 'Outta My Endzone: Sport and the Territorial Anus', *Journal of Sport and Social Issues*, 23, 4 (1999), pp. 373–89; 'Homosexuality and Sport: Who's Winning?', in J. Mckay, M. Messner and D. Sabo (eds), *Masculinities and Sport* (London: Sage, 2000).

3. B. Pronger, 'Post-sport: Transgressing Boundaries in Physical Culture', in G. Rail (ed.), *Sport and Postmodern Times: Culture, Gender, Sexuality, the Body and Sport* (Buffalo: Suny Press, 1998).

4. I thank Ted Norman for this observation.

5. G. Deleuze and F. Guattari, *A Thousand Plateaus:Capitalism and Schizophrenia*, tr. B. Massumi (Minneapolis, MN: University of Minnesota Press, 1987), p. 154.

6. W. Leap (ed.), *Public Sex, Gay Space* (New York: Columbia University Press, 1999); M. de Certeau, *The Practice of Everyday Life*, tr. Steven Randall (Berkeley, CA: University of California Press, 1984).

7. See D. Cosgrove, *Social Formation and Symbolic Landscape* (London: Croom Helm, 1984).

8. Leap, *Public Sex*, p. 7.

9. Ibid.

10. The term 'reading' here includes viewing visual materials such as still photos, films and videos.

11. *Sports Illustrated* 2000; *Gear*, 1999.

12. Pronger, *The Arena of Masculinity*; 'Fear and Trembling'; 'Outta My Endzone'; 'Homosexuality and Sport'.

13. Pronger, 'Outta my EndZone'.

Chapter 11

1. M. Foucault, *Power/Knowledge: Selected Interviews and Other Writings, 1972–1977*, tr. C. Gordon (New York: Pantheon Books, 1980), p. 149.

2. David Harvey, *The Condition of Postmodernity: An Inquiry into the Origins of Social Change* (Oxford: Blackwell, 1990), pp. 176–7.

3. E. Soja, *Postmodern Geographies* (New York: Verso, 1989).

4. Foucault, *Power/Knowledge*, p. 11.

5. Soja, *Postmodern Geographies*, p. 12.

6. Ibid., p. 31.

7. Ibid., p. 38.

8. Ibid., p. 81.

9. H. Lefebvre, *The Production of Space*, tr. D. Nicholson-Smith (Oxford: Blackwell, 1991), pp. 33, 90, 93–4.

10. Ibid., p. 94.

11. Forty writes that Lefebvre's concept of abstract space 'is the form into which social space has been rendered by capitalism; its fundamental feature is the separation of mental space from "lived" space … the result is that consciousness of space occurs not through it being lived, but via representations of it, always thin and reductive, that are provided through the intellectual disciplines and other ideological practices of capitalism'. See A. Forty, *Words and Building: A Vocabulary of Modern Architecture* (London: Thames & Hudson Ltd, 2000), p. 274.

12. For a selection of work that focuses on space and the body, see H. Nast, and S. Pile (eds), *Places Through the Body* (New York: Routledge, 1998); S. Razack, 'Making Canada White: Law and the Policing of Bodies in the 1990's', *Canadian Journal of Law & Society* 14, 1 (1999), pp. 159–84; on space and gender, see S. Best, 'Sexualizing Space', in E. Grosz and E. Probyn (eds), *Sexy Bodies: The Strange Carnalities of Feminism* (New York: Routledge, 1995); L. Bondi, 'Gender Symbols and Urban Landscapes', *Progress in Human Geography*, 16, 2 (1992), pp. 157–70; N. Duncan, 'Renegotiating Gender and Sexuality in Public and Private Spaces', in N. Duncan (ed.), *Body Space: Destabilizing Geographies of Gender and Sexuality* (London: Routledge, 1996); D. Massey, 'Masculinity, Dualisms and High Technology', in Duncan, *Body Space*; L. McDowell, and J. Sharpe (eds), *Space, Gender, Knowledge: Feminist Readings* (London: Arnold, 1997); J. Rendell, B. Penner and I. Borden (eds), *Gender, Space, Architecture* (London: Routledge, 2000); M. Wigley, 'Untitled: The Housing of Gender', in B. Colomina (ed.), *Sexuality & Space* (New York: Princeton Papers on Architecture, Princeton Architectural Press, 1992); on space and sexuality, see D. Bell, J. Binne, J. Cream and G. Valentine, 'All Hyped Up and No Place to Go', *Gender, Place & Culture*, 1 (1994), pp. 31–47; D. Bell and G. Valentine

(eds), *Mapping Desire: Geographies of Sexualities* (London: Routledge, 1995); V. Blum, 'Ladies and Gentlemen: Train Rides and Other Oedipal Stories', in Nast and Pile, *Places Through the Body*; Colomina, *Sexuality & Space*; T. DeLauretis, 'Perverse Desire: The Lure of the Mannish Lesbian', in Nast and Pile, *Places Through the Body*; E. Grosz, *Space, Time and Perversion* (New York: Routledge, 1995); C. Ingraham, 'Initial Properties: Architecture and the Space of the Line', in Colomina, *Sexuality & Space*, pp. 255–71; L. Mulvey, 'Pandora: Topographies of the Mask and Curiosity', in Colomina, *Sexuality & Space*, pp. 53–71; S. Munt, 'The Lesbian *Flaneur*', in Bell and Valentine, *Mapping Desire*, pp. 114–25; E. Probyn, 'Lesbians in Space: Gender, Sex and the Structure of the Missing', *Gender, Place & Culture,* 2, 1 (1995), pp. 77–84; G. Valentine, '(Re)negotiating the 'Heterosexual Street'. Lesbian Productions of Space,' in Duncan, *Body Space*, pp. 146–53; and space, race and colonialism, see M. Mohanram, *Black Body: Women, Colonialism, and Space* (Minneapolis, MN: University of Minnesota Press, 1999); S. Razack, 'Race, Space and Prostitution', *Canadian Journal of Women and the Law*, 19, 2 (1998), pp. 338–76; S. Razack, 'From the "Clean Snows of Petawawa": The Violence of Canadian Peacekeepers in Somalia', *Cultural Anthropology*, 15, 1 (2000), pp. 127–63; S. Razack, 'Gendered Racial Violence and Spatialized Justice: The Murder of Pamela George', *Canadian Journal of Law & Society*, 15, 2 (2000).

13. Postmodern theoretical positions are concerned with tasks of deconstructing predictable versions of reality. Deconstruction, a type of postmodern and post-structuralist methodology, takes various texts apart in order to reveal their underlying assumptions and contradictions. According to Patti Lather in *Getting Smart: Feminist Research and Pedagogy With/In the Postmodern* (New York: Routledge, 1991), the focus of deconstruction is on disruption and the setting up of procedures to continuously demystify the realities that are created, as well as challenging the tendency for knowledge categories to congeal.

14. N. Fox, *Postmodernism, Sociology and Health* (Toronto: University of Toronto Press, 1994), p. 8.

15. S. Phelan, *Getting Specific: Postmodern Lesbian Politics* (Minneapolis, MN: University of Minnesota Press, 1994); C. Weedon, *Feminist Practice and Poststructuralist Theory* (Oxford: Blackwell, 1997); Judith Butler, *Bodies That Matter: On the Discursive Limits of 'Sex'* (New York: Routledge, 1993); Judith Butler, *The Psychic Life of Power: Theories in Subjection* (Stanford: Stanford University Press, 1997).

16. See for example, T. Bruce, 'Postmodernism and the Possibilities for Writing "Vital" Sports Texts', in G. Rail (ed.), *Sport and Postmodern Times* (Albany, NY: SUNY, 1998), pp. 3–20; G. Clarke, 'Crossing Borders: Lesbian Physical Education Students and the Struggle for Sexual Spaces', in S. Scraton and B. Watson (eds), *Sport, Leisure Identities and Gendered Spaces* (Brighton: LSA Publications, University of Brighton, 2000), pp. 75–94; T. Curry, 'Fraternal Bonding in the Locker Room: A Profeminist Analysis of Talk About Competition and Women', *Sociology of Sport Journal*, 8, 2 (1991), pp. 119–35; C. Fusco, 'Lesbians and Locker Rooms: The Subjective Experiences of Lesbians in Sport', in Rail, *Sport in Postmodern Times*, pp. 87–116; P. Griffin, *Strong Women, Deep Closets: Lesbians and Homophobia in Sport* (Champaign, IL: Human Kinetics, 1998), M. J. Kane, and L. Disch, 'Sexual Violence and the Reproduction of Male Power in the Locker Room: The "Lisa Olsen Incident"', *Sociology of Sport Journal*, 10 (1993), pp. 331–52; B. Pronger, *The Arena of Masculinity: Sports, Homosexuality and the Meaning of Sex* (New York: St Martin's Press, 1990); N. Theberge, 'Gender, Sport, and the Construction of Community: A Case Study from Women's Ice Hockey', *Sociology of Sport Journal*, 12, 4 (1995), pp. 389–402.

17. C. Aitchison and F. Jordan (eds), *Gender, Space and Identity: Leisure, Culture and Commerce* (Brighton: LSA Publications, University of Brighton, 1998); K. Cachy, 'Sports and Environment: Sports for Everyone – Room for Everyone?' *International Review for the Sociology of Sport*, 28, 2–3 (1993), pp. 311–23; J. Camy, E. Adamkiewics and P. Chantelat, 'Sporting Uses of the City: Urban Anthropology Applied to the Sports Practices in the Agglomeration of Lyon', *International Review for the Sociology of Sport*, 28, 2–3 (1993), pp. 159–74; J. Hughson, 'Soccer, Support and Social Identity', *International Review for the Sociology of Sport*, 33 (1998), pp. 403–9; N. Puig, J. Martinez del Castillo, P. Pellegrino and C. Lambert, 'Sports Facilities as a Revealing of Society,' *International Review for the Sociology of Sport*, 28, 2–3 (1993), pp. 203–22; S. Scraton, and B. Watson, 'Gendered Cities: Women and Public Leisure Space in the "Postmodern" City', *Leisure Studies*, 17, 2 (1998), pp. 123–37.

18. J. Unan, 'The Spatiality of Sporting Environments', paper presented at The Society for Philosophy and Geography, Towson, MD, 2000; J. Unan, 'Imperial Gyms: The Colonization of

Movement', paper presented at the North American Society for the Sociology of Sport Conference, Colorado Springs, 2000; C. Van Ingen, 'Exploring Alternative Terrain's of Resistance – Spatializing Resistance in the "Frontrunners'", paper presented at The Society for Philosophy and Geography, Towson, MD, 2000); C. Van Ingen, 'A Nomadic Inquiry into Spaces of Resistance', paper presented at the North American Society for the Sociology of Sport Conference, Colorado Springs, 2000).

19. J. Bale, *Sport and Place* (London: Hurst, 1982); J. Bale, 'The Spatial Development of the Modern Stadium', *International Review for the Sociology of Sport*, 28, 2–3 (1993), pp. 121–34; J. Bale, *Landscapes of Modern Sport* (London: Leicester University Press, 1994); J. Bale and C. Philo (eds), *Body cultures: Essays on Sport, Space and Identity* (London: Routledge, 1998); H. Eichberg, 'New Spatial Configurations of Sport? Experiences from Danish Alternative Planning', *International Review for the Sociology of Sport*, 28 (1993), pp. 245–61; L. Johnson, 'Reading the Sexed Bodies and Spaces of Gyms', in Nast and Pile, *Places Through the Body*, pp. 244–62; S. Nagbol, 'Enlivening and Deadening Shadows', *International Review for the Sociology of Sport*, 28, 2–3 (1993), pp. 265–80; J. Rendell, 'West End Rambling: Gender Architectural Space in London 1800–1830', *Leisure Studies*, 17, 2 (1998), pp. 108–22; P. Vertinsky, 'Space, Place and the Gendered Disciplining of Bodies: The Case of the War Memorial Gym', paper presented at the ISHPES Conference, Budapest, Hungary, 1999.

20. Foucault's notion of governmentality is '… conceived as a subtle, comprehensive management of life …' which includes '… the domination of others and of the self'. See Fox, *Postmodernism, Sociology and Health*, p. 32.

21. Forty, *Words and Building*; Ingraham, 'Initial properties'; N. Leach, (ed.), *Rethinking Architecture: A Reader in Cultural Theory* (London: Routledge, 1997); T. Markus, *Buildings and Power: Freedom and Control in the Origin of Modern Building Types* (London: Routledge, 1993).

22. Lefebvre in Forty, *Words and Buildings*, p. 275.

23. For the purposes of this chapter my understanding of modernity and modernist social theory is adapted from Fox, *Postmodernism, Sociology and Health*, p. 7. For Fox '… modernity and modernism are thought of as coinciding with philosophical commitments, to "truth", "rationality" and "progress", with the belief that scientific analysis is the mean by which the world will come to be known, and with "humanism" – the centring of the human subject as the wellspring of knowledge and good'.

24. Here excess means both the extra/superfluous body fluids and excretions that are produced by the body that is in the locker room and, in G. Bataille's *Eroticism, Death and Sensuality* (San Francisco, CA: City Lights, 1986), sense, obscene excess, what he calls eroticism, which is non-productive expenditure, outside reason, and as such disrupts the self.

25. Ibid., pp. 17–8.

26. P. Stallybrass, and A. White, *The Politics and Poetics of Transgression* (Ithaca, NY: Cornell University Press, 1986), p. 148.

27. M. Douglas, *Purity and Danger: An Analysis of the Concepts of Pollution and Taboo* (London: Routledge, 1966); N. Elias, *The Civilising Process* (Massachusetts: Blackwell, 2000); S. Freud, *Civilization, Society and Religion* (London: Penguin Books, 1985); J. Kristeva, *Powers of Horror: An Essay on Abjection* (New York: Columbia University Press, 1982); W. Miller, *The Anatomy of Disgust* (Cambridge, MA: Harvard University Press, 1997); Ibid.

28. Douglas, *Purity and Danger*, p. 114.

29. Kristeva, *Powers of Horror*; D. Sibley, *Geographies of Exclusion* (London: Routledge, 1995).

30. Sibley, *Geographies of Exclusion*.

31. Kristeva, *Powers of Horror*, p. 3.

32. Ibid., p.71.

33. M. Taylor, *Altarity* (Chicago, IL: University of Chicago Press, 1987), p. 160.

34. For links between abjection and gender, see Kristeva, *Powers of Horror*; for theories about pollution and the (re)production of classificatory categories such as class, see Elias, *The Civilising Process*; Sibley, *Geographies of Exclusion*; Stallybrass and White, *The Politics and Poetics of Transgression*; and on race, see A. McClintock, *Imperial Leather: Race, Gender, and Sexuality in the Colonial Contest* (New York: Routledge, 1995); Mohanram, *Black Body*.

35. M. Foucault, *Madness and Civilization: A History of Insanity in the Age of Reason* (New York: Vintage Books, 1965); M. Foucault, *Discipline and Punish: The Birth of the Prison* (New York: Vintage Books, 1977); M. Foucault, *The History of Sexuality: Volume I: An Introduction* (New York: Vintage Books, 1978).

36. Butler, *Bodies that Matter*.
37. M.L. Fellows and S. Razack, 'Race to Innocence. Confronting Hierarchical Relations Among Women', *The Journal of Gender, Race and Justice*, 1, 2 (1998), p. 336.
38. Razack, 'Gendered Racial Violence' uses the term 'degeneracy' 'to denote those groups whom Foucault describes as the "internal enemies" of the bourgeois male – women, racial others, the working class, people with disabilities, in short all those who would weaken the vigorous bourgeois body and state' (5–6, n. 7). These so-called degenerates are often classified as Other (than Self). See also, S. Gilman, *Difference and Pathology: Stereotypes of Sexuality, Race, and Madness* (Ithaca, NY: Cornell University Press, 1985), and G. Mosse, *Nationalism and Sexuality: Respectability and Abnormal Sexuality in Modern Europe* (New York: Howard Fertig, 1985).
39. Mosse, *Nationalism and Sexuality*, p. 1.
40. McClintock, *Imperial Leather*, p. 48.
41. Ibid.; Sibley, *Geographies of Exclusion*; L.A. Stoler, *Race and the Education of Desire: Foucault's History of Sexuality and the Colonial Order of Things* (Durham, NC: Duke University Press, 1995).
42. McClintock, *Imperial Leather*, pp. 211, 220. I must make it clear here that I am not suggesting that only white Western Europeans were/are concerned with hygiene. In Douglas, *Purity and Danger*, for instance demonstrates, in great detail, that non-Western cultures have extensive rituals of cleanliness, hygiene and purification. However, the discourses of cleanliness that emerged with colonial expansion – in the eighteenth and nineteenth centuries – appear to have been politicized in a particular ways. Cleanliness and hygienic practices, if one follows the arguments set out by McClintock and Stoler, for instance, were turned into features associated with a/the dominant European race. Hygienic practices were seen as essential to European racial purity. Particular hygienic practices of non-Western peoples were subjected to a Western hierarchy and, in such a way, the colonized were/are read as not being clean even though they may participate extensively in their own hygienic rituals.
43. Sibley, *Geographies of Exclusion*.
44. McClintock, *Imperial Leather*, p. 207.
45. Ibid., p. 209.
46. R. Dyer, *White* (London: Routledge, 1997), pp. 75–6.
47. Fellows and Razack, 'Race to Innocence', p. 349.
48. Razack, 'Race, Space and Prostitution', p. 367.
49. Wigley, 'Untitled', p. 344.
50. Ibid., p. 345.
51. A. Betsky, *Architecture and Same-Sex Desire* (New York: W. Morrow & Company, 1997), p. 103.
52. N. Lahiji and D. Friedman (eds), *Plumbing: Sounding Modern Architecture* (New York: Princeton Architectural Press, 1997).
53. W. Braham, 'Siegfried Giedion and the Fascination of the Tub', in Lahiji and Friedman (eds), *Plumbing*, p. 219.
54. See American College of Sports Medicine's Health and Fitness Facility Standards and Guidelines (2nd edn, Human Kinetics 1997).
55. Probyn, 'Lesbians in Space', p. 81.
56. American College of Sports Medicine's Health and Fitness Facility Standards and Guidelines.
57. Here I want to suggest that there is a link between the cleaning and maintenance of locker rooms and, historically, the colonial organization of bourgeois household spaces in the nineteenth century (this racialized organization of labour in households, hotels and other institutions that retain domestic cleaning staff still occurs today). Servants and housemaids, inevitably working-class and racialized as Black, had/have to confront white dirt, clean it away in order to maintain the respectability of the bourgeois household/spaces. These individuals literally and figuratively absorb(ed) 'white' dirt onto and into their bodies. For the purposes of my work I acknowledge that there is a clear distinction between who can practise and engage in leisure and be respectable, and who must clean away the by-products of that leisure, all the time enabling bourgeois respectability.
58. Sibley, *Geographies of Exclusion*, p. 78.
59. I do acknowledge that not all Others are repudiated or abjected. For some patrons it is imperative to make contact and press up against others in locker rooms, particularly if the locker room is construed as sexual space (see Pronger, *The Arena of Masculinity*). Generally, in North American recreational centre locker rooms this erotic and sexual activity is tacitly prohibited. In this case, Others and their behaviour may end up being abjected.

60. Sibley, *Geographies of Exclusion*, p. 56.
61. Other(ed) bodies that are often established as degenerate and disordered are often those that are marked as too muscular, too fat, excessively thin, too queer, too Black, too old, too young, too dirty, too disabled.
62. J. Butler, *Gender Trouble: Feminism and the Subversion of Identity* (New York: Routledge, 1990), p. 170.
63. Architectural design of spaces for cleansing disordered bodies was, and possibly remains, an 'imperial' project. Here I am using imperial in the broadest sense of the word. Fellows and Razack, 'Race to Innocence', use it to denote the (un)marked imperial and colonial bourgeois subject of the nineteenth century. I use it according to their sense of imperial as well but extend it to incorporate the imperial 'I', the self-conscious subject on whom the speculative economy of philosophy is based (Taylor, *Alterity*).
64. Butler, *The Psychic Life of Power*, p. 194.
65. Stallybrass and White, *The Politics and Poetics of Transgression*.
66. Butler, *Bodies That Matter*, p. 116.
67. Ibid., p. 116.

Chapter 12

1. *Biennial Report of the Regents of the University of California for the Year 1875–77*, pp. 56–7.
2. Letter of Mr Harmon, Oakland, 20th, 1879 to the Honorable, Board of Regents of the University of California, 380g P18 V.1-pamphlets (University Archives, University of California, Berkeley; hereafter University Archives).
3. 'Harmon Gymnasium', *The San Francisco Mirror*, 16 Nov. 1878.
4. 'Historic Gym Once Campus Social Center', *Daily Californian*, 13 Jan. 1933.
5. Like her husband, Mrs Magee does not seem to have had any college training, which was not unusual for the time. Following the creation of separate departments for men and for women in 1914 (each headed by an individual who held a master's degree and had training in physical education), the Magees' connections with the University were soon severed.
6. 'Communication: To the Honorable Board of Regents of the University of California', Regents' Records, 1891, CU-1, 25, 9 (University Archives. All CU citations are from these archives).
7. Mary Bennett Ritter, *More Than Gold in California, 1849–1933* (Berkeley, CA: The Professional Press, 1933), pp. 202–4.
8. *Biennial Report of the President of the University of California on Behalf of the Board of Regents, 1882–84*, pp. 34–5.
9. See Roberta J. Park, 'Physiologists, Physicians, and Physical Educators: Nineteenth Century Biology and Exercise, Hygienic and Educative', *Journal of Sport History*, 14 (1987), pp. 28–60.
10. See for example, Roberta J. Park, 'Science, Service, and the Professionalization of Physical Education, 1885–1905', *Research Quarterly for Exercise and Sport*: Special Centennial Issue (1985), pp. 7–20; Roberta J. Park, 'Health, Exercise, and the Biomedical Impulse, 1870–1914', *Research Quarterly for Exercise and Sport*, 61 (1990), pp. 126–40.
11. 'The Boston Conference on Physical Culture', *Boston Medical and Surgical Journal*, 121 (1889), pp. 566–7.
12. 'Physical Education', *Boston Medical and Surgical Journal*, 122 (1890), pp. 382–3; Luther H. Gulick, 'Physical Education: A New Profession', *Proceedings of the 5th Annual Meeting of the American Association for the Advancement of Physical Education* (Ithaca, NY: Andrus and Church, 1890), pp. 59–66. Gulick's article was also published in *Physique: Journal of Physical Education, Domestic, School and Personal Hygiene, Gymnastics, Athletics, Games and Sports*, published by Britain's National Union of Physical Training Teachers.
13. *Biennial Report of the President of the University of California on Behalf of the Board of Regents, 1882–84*.
14. *Academic Senate, 1887–89*, Regents' Records, CU-1: 6–2.
15. F[rank] H. Payne, 'Physical Culture at the University of California', *Pacific Medical Journal*, 33 (1890), pp. 705–10.
16. Ibid.
17. See Roberta J. Park, 'A Gym of Their Own: Women, Sports, and Physical Culture at the Berkeley Campus', *Chronicle of the University of California*, 1 (1998), pp. 21–47.

18. *Occident* (Women's Edition), 22 Feb. 1901, p. 106.
19. Martin Kellogg, 'A Year's Review', *University of California Chronicle*, 1 (1898), p. 25.
20. Roy Lowe, *'A Western Acropolis of Learning': The University of California in 1897* (University of California, Berkeley: Center for Studies in Higher Education and Institute of Governmental Studies, 1996), p. 25.
21. William E. Ritter, 'The University, Its Graduates, and the State', *University of California Chronicle*, 1 (1898), pp. 97–103.
22. 'Historical Account of the International Competition for the Phoebe A. Hearst Architectural Plan', *The International Competition for the Phoebe Hearst Plan for the University of California* [1899], p. 12.
23. 'The Ph[o]ebe Hearst Architectural Plan', *University of California Chronicle*, 1 (1898), pp. 469–72.
24. Loren W. Partridge, *John Galen Howard and the Berkeley Campus: Beaux-Arts Architecture in the 'Athens of the West'* (Berkeley Architectural Heritage Publication Series, No. 2, 1988), pp. 46–7.
25. Verne A. Stadman (ed.), *The Centennial Record of the University of California* (Berkeley, CA: University of California Printing Department, 1967), p. 53.
26. *California's Memorial Stadium* [brochure], CU-291, Box 1.
27. 'Hearst Hall Burnt; Loss Over $150,000', *Berkeley Daily Gazette*, 21 June 1922.
28. Henceforth, sports and dance would comprise the larger part of the curricular offerings of the Department of Physical Culture for Women. Upon joining the faculty in 1928, Anna Espenschade (MS degree from Wellesley; Ph.D. in psychology from the University of California) recalled with evident pleasure that she had taught her 'last class in gymnastics.' See Roberta J. Park, 'Time Given Freely to Worthwhile Causes: Anna S. Espenschade's Contributions to Physical Education', *Research Quarterly for Exercise and Sport*, 71 (2000), pp. 99–115.
29. William Randolph Hearst to David P. Barrows, 21 June 1922, President's Records, CU-5, 1922, p. 1281.
30. 'W.R. Hearst to Rebuild Women's Gymnasium Given by His Mother', *Daily Californian*, 24 June 1922.
31. W.W. Campbell to Mr Maybeck, 23 October 1923, President's Records, CU–5, (1923), p. 259.
32. William R. Hearst to William W. Campbell, 27 Jan. 1924; William W. Campbell to William R. Hearst [telegram], 2 Feb. 1924, President's Records, CU-5-Ser. 2:1924, p. 319.
33. 'Memorandum on Conference Between Mr William Randolph Hearst and President Campbell This Afternoon', 16 November 1923, Bernard Maybeck Papers, Documents Collection, College of Environmental Design, University of California; Dean Walter M. Hart to Julia Morgan and Julia Morgan to Walter Hart, 13 March 1924, President's Records, CU-5, (1924), p. 319.
34. William Randolph Hearst to Julia Morgan, 12 April 1924, President's Records, CU-5-Ser. 2 (1924), p. 319.
35. Harvey Helfand, *The Campus Guide, University of California, Berkeley: An Architectural Tour and Photographs* (New York: Princeton Architectural Press, 2002), pp. 204–8.
36. 'Annual University Day Celebrations to Include Many Colorful Events', *Daily Californian*, 8 April 1927; 'Greek Theater [and] Hearst Memorial Gymnasium', ibid. (Special Supplement).
37. Violet Marshall to W.W. Campbell, 27 Nov. 1924, President's Records, CU-5, ser. 2 (1924), p. 819.
38. 'Women Get Four Tennis Courts by President's Grant', *Daily Californian*, 22 Jan. 1923; 'Miss H'Doubler's Extension Class – 1929' (Hearst Gymnasium Historical Collections (HGHC)).
39. Although exceptions could be found, until the 1950/60s women's college gymnasia typically were physical as well as ideological 'separate spheres'. In those instances when male and female students shared the same facility, opportunities for women were considerably more limited and more cloistered.
40. Helfand, *An Architectural Tour*, pp. 173–4. Movable bleachers made it possible to accommodate another 2,000.
41. 'Gymnasium at U. C. Will Be Dedicated Friday', *Berkeley Daily Gazette*, 11 January 1933; 'All-Day Ceremonies, Basketball Will Dedicate New Gymnasium' and 'Dedication of Gymnasium Is Attended by 5000', *Daily Californian*, 13 Jan. 1933, ibid.
42. John O'Neill, *Five Bodies: The Human Shape of Modern Society* (Ithaca, NY: Cornell University Press, 1985), pp. 16–25.
43. I attempt to explore this in 'Cells or Soaring?: Historical Reflections on "Visions" of the Body,

Athletics, and Modern Olympism', *Olympika: The International Journal of Olympic Studies*, 9 (2000), pp. 1–24.

44. 'Physical Culture', *University of California Register, 1898–99*, pp. 236–7.
45. For example, in his opening remarks at the 1889 Boston Conference of Physical Training, United States Commissioner of Education William T. Harris observed that the new physical education sought to 'discover whereby the vital organs – the lungs, the heart ... in short all the functions that are involuntary in their action may be assisted and influenced by voluntary action and motion' and spoke of the value of calisthenics in exercising the will. In *Physical Training: A Full Report of the Papers and Discussions of the Conference Held in Boston in November, 1889* (Boston: George H. Ellis, 1899), pp. 3–4.
46. 'Department of Physical Culture', *1892 Blue and Gold*, p. 90.
47. Theodore M. Porter, *The Rise of Statistical Thinking, 1820–1900* (Princeton, NJ: Princeton University Press, 1986); James H. Cassedy, *American Medicine and Statistical Thinking, 1800–1860* (Cambridge, MA: Harvard University Press, 1984).
48. See J.M. Tanner, *A History of Human Growth* (Cambridge: Cambridge University Press, 1981).
49. Edward Hitchcock, 'Anthropometry', Paper Read at the Second Annual Meeting of the AAAPE, Brooklyn, NY, 26 Nov. 1887 (Brooklyn, NY: Rome Brothers, 1887).
50. James A. Babbitt, 'Present Condition of Gymnastics and Athletics in American Colleges', *American Physical Education Review*, 8 (1903), pp. 280–3; Franz Boas, 'Statistical Study of Anthropometry', *American Physical Education Review*, 6 (1901), pp. 174–80.
51. For example, John F. Bovard and Frederick W. Cozens, *Tests and Measurements in Physical Education* (Philadelphia: W.B. Saunders Co., 1930).
52. *Annual Report of the President of the University of California, 1919–1920*, pp. 47–51.
53. Reported in Ellen W. Gerber, *Innovators and Institutions in Physical Education* (Philadelphia: Lea & Febiger, 1971), p. 329.
54. Anne L. Barr, 'Some Anthropometric Data of Western College Girls', *American Physical Education Review*, 8 (1903), pp. 245–8.
55. *Official Guide to the World's Columbian Exposition in the City of Chicago ...* (Chicago: The Columbian Guide Co., 1893), pp. 37–38; 'Here's More Glory for California University Girls', *San Francisco Examiner*, 30 Jan. 1897.
56. For example, Robert W. Lovett, 'Round Shoulders and Faulty Attitudes: A Method of Observation and Record, With Conclusions as to Treatment', *American Physical Education Review*, 7 (1902), pp. 169–87. (Reprinted from the *Boston Medical and Surgical Journal* (6 Nov. 1902).)
57. See Alison M. Wrynn, *Contributions of Women Researchers to the Development of a Science of Physical Education*, Ph.D. dissertation, University of California, 1996, pp. 98–103.
58. See for example, William Skarstrom, *Gymnastic Kinesiology: A Manual of the Mechanism of Gymnastic Movement* (Springfield, MA: American Physical Education Association, 1909), especially pp. 87–100.
59. Betty Spears, 'The Influential Miss Homans', *Quest*, 29 (1978), pp. 46–59.
60. Sarah R. Davis, 'Anthropometry', *Mary Hemenway Alumnae Association of the Department of Hygiene Wellesley College Bulletin, 1916–17*, pp. 7–11.
61. Glenn Gritzer and Arnold Arluke, *The Making of Rehabilitation: A Political Economy of Medical Specialization, 1890–1980* (Berkeley: University of California Press, 1985), chapter 3; Mary McMillan, *Massage and Therapeutic Exercise* (Philadelphia: W. B. Saunders Co., 1921), pp. 9–12.
62. For example, *Columbia University Bulletin, The Faculty of Medicine Program in Physical Therapy, 1994–1995*; *Programs in Physical Therapy, Northwestern University Medical School*, (1994).
63. Physical Education for Women', *Annual Report of the President of the University of California, 1918–1919*, pp. 41–3; University of California, *Announcement of Courses, 1924–25*, pp. 228–30.
64. See, for example, Lillian Curtis Drew, *Adapted Group Gymnastics* (Philadelphia: Lea & Febiger, 1927).
65. Leah C. Thomas and Joel E. Goldthwait, *Body Mechanics and Health* (Boston: Houghton Mifflin Co., 1922), pp. 13–26.
66. George T. Stafford, *Preventative and Corrective Physical Education* (New York: A.S. Barnes and Co., 1928).
67. F[rank] L. Kleeberger, 'Physical Efficiency Tests As a Practical Method of Popularizing

Physical Education at the University of California', *The American Turner*, 5 (1917), pp. 1428–37; *Annual Report of the President of the University of California, 1918–19*, pp. 37–40; University of California, *Announcement of Courses, 1924–25*, pp. 222–7. A statement that Kleeberger made in a study of data obtained from 15,000 students from 1915 to the early 1930s made his 'philosophy' abundantly clear. A man must possess two fundamental things: 'a body skilled in natural and usable activities, and a soul filled with that spirit of play, joy, and chivalry which comes only through fierce but generous competition'. (In 'Physical Efficiency as Measured at the University of California', *Research Quarterly*, 3 (1932), pp. 151–72.)

68. George Meylan, 'Athletics', *American Physical Education Review*, 10 (1905), pp. 157–63; Clark W. Hetherington, 'Analysis of Problems in College Athletics', *American Physical Education Review*, 12 (1907), pp. 154–81.

69. James R. Day, 'The Function of College Athletics', *Proceedings of the 14th Annual Convention of the Intercollegiate Athletic Association of the United States, December 28, 1909*, pp. 34–43.

70. See, for example, John R. Thelin, *Games Colleges Play: Scandal and Reform in Intercollegiate Athletics* (Baltimore, MD: Johns Hopkins University Press, 1994); Andrew Zimbalist, *Unpaid Professionals: Commercialism and Conflict in Big-Time College Sports* (Princeton, NJ: Princeton University Press, 1999).

71. 'Athletic Sports for Everybody Is Federation's Aim', *Oakland Tribune*, 27 July 1923; Clark W. Hetherington, 'The Federation Movement – Its Objectives and Ideals', paper presented at the Third Annual Meeting, May 1926 [printed booklet].

72. Vivian Acosta and Linda J. Carpenter, 'As the Years Go By – Coaching Opportunities in the 1990s', *Journal of Physical Education, Recreation, and Dance*, 63, 3 (1992), pp. 36–41.

73. Roberta J. Park, 'From Football to Rugby – and Back, 1906–1919: The University of California-Stanford University Response to the "Football Crisis of 1905"', *Journal of Sport History*, 11 (1984), pp. 5–40; J.R.K. Kantor, 'The First 'Golden Bears": The Transcontinental Tour of Cal's Track Team; 1895', *Chronicle of the University of California*, 4 (2000), pp. 13–16.

74. 'Used Baskets As Goals', *San Francisco Examiner*, 19 November 1892; 'Waterloo for Berkeley Girls', *San Francisco Examiner*, 5 April 1896. See also Lynne F. Emery and Margaret Toohey-Costa, 'Hoops and Skirts: Women's Basketball on the West Coast, 1892–1930s', in Joan S. Hult and Marianna Trekell (eds), *A Century of Women's Basketball: From Frailty to Final Four* (Reston, VA: American Alliance for Health, Physical Education, Recreation, and Dance, 1991), pp. 137–54.

75. The Boston Normal School of Gymnastics, founded in 1889, called upon faculty from Harvard and MIT to instruct such courses as physiology and psychology. In 1909, the School became the Department of Hygiene and Physical Education of Wellesley College and carried on its tradition of leadership into the 1930s, when graduate work was offered by an increasing number of colleges and universities. See: Betty Spears, *Leading the Way: Amy Morris Homans and the Beginnings of Professional Education* (New York: Greenwood Press, 1986).

76. The most informative source on such matters is Patricia Vertinsky, *The Eternally Wounded Woman: Women, Exercise and Doctors in the Late Nineteenth Century* (Manchester: Manchester University Press, 1990).

77. *Annual Report of the President of the University of California, 1919–20*, pp. 47–51.

78. University of California, *Intramural Sports* [1933 Brochure] (HGHC).

79. Report of the Department of Physical Education for the Biennium, 1 July 1942 to 30 June 1944 (HGHC).

80. 'High School Sports Day at California' and 'A New Plan', *Newsletter of the Athletic Conference of American College Women, April 1, 1925*, pp. 36–7; 'Women Confer to Plan Games' and 'W.A.A. Discourages Varsity Contests', *Daily Californian*, 6 October 1922.

81. WAA Sports Club Board, Advisor's Report of 1962. (HGHC).

82. The CIAW was transformed into the Association of Intercollegiate Athletics for Women in 1971–72. See Joan S. Hult, 'The Philosophical Conflicts in Men's and Women's Intercollegiate Athletics', *Quest*, 32 (1980), pp. 77–94.

83. Roberta J. Park, 'Athletics at Berkeley at the Turn of Both Centuries', *Chronicle of the University of California*, 4 (2000), pp. 175–88.

84. University of California Berkeley Campus, Capital Improvement Program, 'Project Planning Guide: Intramural Sports Facility' (Sports and Recreation Facility), Account No. 910800; Task Force Report, Sports and Athletic Facilities, Prepared as Part of the Berkeley Campus Space Plan, May 1982 (HGHC).

85. 'New Sport Facility – 14 Years of Planning', *University of California, Planning News*, Feb. 1984; Fact Sheet: Recreational Sports Facility [1984]; 'A Place of Their Own', *Athletic Business*, 12 Dec. 1985, pp. 24–7.

86. For example, Andrew Fluegelman (ed.), *The New Games Book* (San Francisco: Headlands Press, 1976); George Leonard, *The Ultimate Athlete: Re-Visioning Sports, Physical Education, and the Body* (New York: Viking Press, 1975).

87. For example, 'The Men in the Mirror', *The Chronicle of Higher Education*, 27 Sep. 2002, pp. A53–4.

88. Hearst Gymnasium, University of California, 26 Sep. 1975 [prepared by the campus Office of Architects and Engineers]; Charles L. Gould to Chancellor Albert Bowker, 22 Dec. 1975 (HGHC).

89. 'Jack Breslin Student Events Center Michigan State University East Lansing, MI', *Athletic Business*, 14 (June 1990), p. 58. Words used when describing the new facility at the University of California, Irvine reflect these modern tendencies: 'intercollegiate/entertainment/cultural'. (In 'Bren Events Center University of California, Irvine, CA', *Athletic Business*, 13 (Nov. 1989), p. 26.)

90. *The Promise of Berkeley – California Athletics Campaign*, 3, 1 (Summer 1997); *The Promise of Berkeley – California Athletics Campaign*, 3, 2 (Winter 1998); 'Setting Plan for Full Bowl Floor Plan, Walter A. Haas, Jr. Pavilion: The Expansion & Remodeling of Harmon Gymnasium', U. C. Project No. 912740 [Archictural Drawing], (HGHC); Helfand, *An Architectural Tour*, p. 173; 'Haas Pavilion: The House that Haas Built', *Daily Californian* (Special Supplement), 15 Oct. 1999.

91. See Roberta J. Park, 'The Rise and Demise of Harvard's B. S. Program in Anatomy, Physiology, and Physical Training: A Case of Conflicts of Interest and Scarce Resources', *Research Quarterly for Exercise and Sport*, 63 (1992), pp. 1–15. Scare resources and conflicts of interest were also factors in the demise at Berkeley.

92. 'Teachers Course in Physical Culture', Regents' records, 11 Feb. 1897, CU-1, 25, 8; 'Special Recommendations in Physical Culture', *1897–98 Register*; 'Teachers Course in Physical Culture', University of California, *Annual Announcement of Courses of Instruction for the Academic Year, 1898–99*, pp. 119–22.

93. Delphine Hanna, 'Present Status of Physical Training in Normal Schools', *American Physical Education Review*, 8 (1903), pp. 293–7. According to Hanna this was the first four-year programme in the United States. A professional course for teachers of physical education was also created at the University of Nebraska in 1897, but its existence was not continuous, according to Ruth Elliott, in *The Organization of Professional Training in Physical Education in State Universities* (New York: Teachers College, Columbia University, 1927), chapter 2.

94. 'Majors in (A) Colleges of General Culture: Revised Requirements for the Recommendation for the High School Certificate', Academic Senate, CU-9, 1914, 11, 13; *Annual Report of the President of the University of California, 1915–16*, p. 61.

95. California was the second state to enact such legislation. The Secretary of the California Committee to Promote Physical Education, which had a role in fostering it, was Maude Cleveland. A 1866 School Law, which specified 'Instruction shall be given in all grades of schools, and in all classes, during the entire school course, in manners and morals, and the laws of health, and due attention shall be given to such physical exercises for the pupils as may be conducive to health and vigor of the body', was still in effect but neither adequate nor widely implemented.

96. University of California, *General Catalogue*, 1945/6, pp. 72–3, 340–5.

97. University of California, *Announcement of the Graduate Division, Physical Education*, Nov. 1930.

98. Jack E. Hewitt, 'The Graduate Major in Physical Education', *Research Quarterly*, 13 (1942), pp. 252–6.

99. Warren R. Johnson (ed.), *Science and Medicine of Exercise and Sports* (New York: Harper and Brothers, 1960).

100. Franklin M. Henry, 'Physical Education – An Academic Discipline', *Journal of Health, Physical Education, and Recreation*, 35, 7 (1964), pp. 32–3; 69. (Henry was describing the AB major in physical education at the University of California as it was constituted in 1964 – a fact many individuals have not realized.) See also the more detailed Franklin M. Henry, 'The Academic Discipline of Physical Education', *Quest*, 29 (1978), pp. 13–79.

101. Various issues of *Quest*, the journal of the National Association for Physical Education in

Higher Education, are especially informative regarding these matters.

102. Mary Lou Norrie to Ted Chenoweth, 25 Jan. 1978 (HGHC).

103. Especially useful are the analyses provided by Martin Trow, *Leadership and Academic Reform: Biology at Berkeley*, Working Paper 99–8, Institute of Governmental Studies, University of California, Berkeley [1999].

104. To Chancellor Michael Heyman and Vice Chancellor Roderic Park from Chancellor's Advisory Council on Biology, 3 Dec. 1984 (HGHC).

105. To Professors Bredemeier, Brooks, Lehman; Ms. Scott, Mr Cutino and Dr. Frey from Roberta J. Park, 11 Dec. 1984 (HGHC).

106. George A. Brooks (Acting Chairman) and Roberta J. Park (Chairman) to Vice Chancellor Roderic B. Park, 22 Jan. 1985 (HGHC).

107. Vice Chancellor Roderic B. Park to Berkeley Biology Faculty, 19 July 1985. (To this is attached the Joint Report of the Chancellor's Advisory Committee on Biology and Subcommittee for Second Iteration: Reorganization of the Life Sciences, 15 July 1985.)

108. Roberta J. Park to Vice Chancellor Roderic B. Park, 30 Aug. 1985 (HGHC).

109. Roberta J. Park to Dean Joseph Cerny, Re: Statement Regarding Response to the Report of Committee to Review the Department of Physical Education, 25 April 1988 (HGHC). The Review Committee also stated: 'The faculty of Berkeley's Department of Physical Education contradict [the] common perception'

110. Roberta J. Park to Provost Carol T. Christ and Dean David R. Bentley, 23 Sept. 1991 (HGHC).

111. Jack McCurdy and William Trombley, *On the Brink: The Impact of Budget Cuts on California's Public Universities*. A Report from the California Higher Education Policy Center, Aug. 1993.

112. Report of the Academic Programs Working Group based on the reports of the Disciplinary Advisory Panels, May 1994.

113. Graduate Council Report on the Review(s) of the Department of Physical Education, 18 May 1992 (HGHC).

114. In the end these three units, each of which had a smaller faculty compliment and smaller faculty/student ratio, were retained – either as a department or in a slightly reconfigured form.

115. In the Introduction to Angus E. Taylor, *The Academic Senate of the University of California: Its Role in the Shared Governance and Operations of the University of California* (University of California, Berkeley: Institute of Governmental Studies Press, 1998) former UC President and Berkeley Chancellor Clark Kerr has written: 'I think the academic success of the university is based more on the contributions of the Academic Senate than any other factor' (p. xiii).

116. Roberta J. Park to Timothy P. White, 8 Aug. 1994 (HGHC).

117. Jack H. Wilmore, 'Building Strong Academic Programs for Our Future', *Quest*, 50 (1998), pp. 103–7. It is not insignificant that most heavily impacted were state-supported institutions in Arizona, California, Oregon and Washington. Administrators do talk with each other!

118. 'U.C. to Integrate Some Departments: Goal to Improve Health Research', *Daily Californian*, 7 Oct. 1999.

Bibliography

Acosta V. and Carpenter, L.J., 'As the Years Go By – Coaching Opportunities in the 1990s', *Journal of Physical Education, Recreation, and Dance*, 63, 3 (1992), pp. 36–41.

Adam, B., *Timescapes of Modernity: The Environment and Invisible Hazards* (London: Routledge, 1998).

Adler, P. and Adler, P., 'Social Reproduction and the Corporate Other: The Institutionalisation of After School Activities', *The Sociological Quarterly*, 35, 2 (1994), pp. 309–28.

Aignan, A. and Guillard, V., *Notions élémentaires sur la mer, la navigation, la pêche, suivies de leçons sur la gymnastique et la natation à l'usage des écoles primaires du littoral (Cours moyens 1ère et 2ième années)* (Paris: Gedulge, 1902).

Ainley, R. (ed.), *New Frontiers of Space, Bodies and Gender* (London: Routledge, 1998).

Aitchison, C. and Jordan, F. (eds), *Gender, Space and Identity: Leisure, Culture and Commerce* (Brighton: LSA Publications, University of Brighton, 1998).

Allan, J., *Berthold Lubetkin: Architecture and the Tradition of Progress* (London: RIBA Publications Ltd, 1992).

Allison, L., 'Sport as an Environmental Issue', in L. Allison (ed.), *The Changing Politics of Sport* (Manchester: Manchester University Press, 1993), pp. 207–32.

Amar, M., *Nés pour courir: Sport, pouvoir et rebellion* (Grenoble: PUG, 1987).

Anderson, G., *The Art of Skating with illustrations, diagrams and plain directions for the acquirement of the most difficult and graceful movements*, 4th edn (London: Horace Cox, 1880).

Appadurai, A., *Modernity at Large* (Minneapolis: University of Minnesota Press, 1996).

Arnaud, P., *Le Militaire, l'écolier, le gymnaste* (Lyon: PUL, 1991).

Arnaud, P. and Terret, T. (eds), *Le Sport et ses espaces: XIXème–XXème Siècles* (Paris: Ed. du Comité des Travaux Historiques et Scientifiques, Ministère de l'Education Nationale, 1998).

Aron, C., *Working at Play: A History of Vacations in the United States* (Oxford: Oxford University Press, 1999).

Augé, M., *Non-Places: The Anthropology of Super-Modernity* (London: Verso, 1996).

Augé, P., 'La Natation', in P. Moreau and G. Voulquin (eds), *Les Sports modernes illustrés* (Paris: 1905).

Augustin, J.P., *Sport, Géographie, Management* (Paris: Nathan, 1995).

Babbitt, J.A., 'Present Condition of Gymnastics and Athletics in American Colleges', *American Physical Education Review*, 8 (1903), pp. 280–3;

Bachelard, G., *The Poetics of Space* (Boston: Beacon Press, 1969).

Back, L., Crabbe,T. and Solomos, J., *The Changing Face of Football: Racism, Identity and Multiculture in the English Game* (Oxford: Berg, 2001).

Bale, J., *Sport and Place* (London: Hurst, 1982).

Bale, J., 'Virtual Fandoms: Futurescapes of Football', in A. Brown (ed.), *Fanatics: Power, Identity and Fandom in Football* (London: Routledge, 1988).

Bale, J., 'The Spatial Development of the Modern Stadium', *International Review for the Sociology of Sport,* 28, 2–3 (1993), pp. 121–34.

Bale, J., *Landscapes of Modern Sport* (Leicester: Leicester University Press, 1994), p. 13.

Bale, J., 'Space, Place and Body Culture: Yi-Fu Tuan and a Geography of Sport', *Geografiska Annaler*, 78B, 3 (1996), pp. 163–71.

Bale, J., *Sport, Space and the City* (London: Routledge, 1993, and Caldwell, NJ: Blackburn, 2001).

Bale, J. and Philo C. (eds), *Body Cultures: Essays on Sport, Space and Identity* (London: Routledge, 1998).

Barnard, H.C., *A History of English Education from 1760* (London: University of London Press, 1947).

Barr, A.L., 'Some Anthropometric Data of Western College Girls', *American Physical Education Review*, 8 (1903), pp. 245–8.

Bataille, G., *Eroticism, Death and Sensuality* (San Francisco: City Lights, 1986).

Baudrillard, J., *The Transparency of Evil* (London: Verso, 1993).

Bell, D. and Valentine, G. (eds), *Mapping Desire: Geographies of Sexualities* (London: Routledge, 1995).

Bell, D., Binne, J., Cream J. and Valentine, G., 'All Hyped Up and No Place to Go', *Gender, Place & Culture,* 1 (1994), pp. 31–47.

Benjamin, W., 'Paris, Capital of the Nineteenth Century', *Reflections*, tr. Kent Edmund Jephcott (New York: Schoken Books, 1986).

Benson, E.F., *English Figure Skating: A Guide to Theory and Practice of Skating in the English Style* (London: George Bell and Sons, 1908).

Benson, E.F., *Winter Sports in Switzerland* (New York: Dodd, Mead and Company, 1913).

Berlioux, M., *La Natation* (Paris: Flammarion, 1947).

Best, S., 'Sexualizing Space', in E. Grosz and E. Probyn (eds), *Sexy Bodies: The Strange Carnalities of Feminism* (New York: Routledge, 1995), pp. 181–94.

Betsky, A., *Architecture and Same-Sex Desire* (New York: W. Morrow & Company, 1997).

Beulque P. and Descarpentrie, A., *Méthode de natation* (Tourcoing, 1922).

Birchenough, C., *History of Elementary Education in England and Wales from 1800 to Present Day* (London: University Tutorial Press Ltd, 1938).

Blake, A., *The Body Language: The Meaning of Modern Sport* (London: Lawrence and Wishart, 1996).

Blakely, K., 'Parents' Conceptions of Social Dangers to Children in the Urban Environment', *Children's Environments*, 11, 1 (1994), pp. 16–25.

Blakeney, T.S., 'Kailas: A Holy Mountain', in M.C. Tobias and H. Drasdo (eds), *The Mountain Spirit* (Woodstock, NY: The Overlook Press, 1979), pp. 149–59.

Blatchford, P., *Playtime in the Primary School: Problems and Improvements* (London: NFER-Nelson, 1989).

Blatchford, P., *Social Life in School: Pupils' Experiences of Breaktime and Recess from 7 to 16 years* (London: Falmer Press, 1998).

Blatchford, P. and Sharp, S. (eds), *Breaktime and the School: Understanding and Changing Playground Behaviour* (London: Routledge, 1994).

Blatchford, P. and Sumpner, C., 'What do we Know About Breaktime? Results from a National Survey of Breaktime and Lunchtime in Primary and Secondary Schools', *British Educational Research Journal*, 24, 1 (1998), pp. 79–94.

Blatchford P. *et al.*, 'Playground Games and Playtime: The Children's View', *Educational Research Journal*, 32, 3 (1990), pp. 163–74.

Bloomer, K.C. and Moore, C.W., *Body, Memory and Architecture* (New Haven: Yale University Press, 1997).

Blum, V., 'Ladies and Gentlemen. Train Rides and Other Oedipal Stories', in J. Nast and S. Pile (eds), *Places Through the Body* (New York: Routledge, 1998), pp. 263–79.

Boas, F., 'Statistical Study of Anthropometry', *American Physical Education Review*, 6 (1901), pp. 174–80.

Boaventura de Sousa, S., *Towards a New Commonsense* (London: Routledge, 1995).

Bondi, L., 'Gender Symbols and Urban Landscapes', *Progress in Human Geography*, 16, 2 (1992), pp. 157–70.

Booth, D., *Australian Beach Cultures: The History of Sun, Sand and Surf in Australia* (London: Frank Cass, 2001).

Bornstein, K., *Gender Outlaw* (New York: Routledge, 1994).

Boston Conference on Physical Culture, *Boston Medical and Surgical Journal*, 121 (1889), pp. 566–7.

Bourdieu, P., *Distinction: A Social Critique of the Judgement of Taste* (London: Routledge, 1984).

Bovard, J.F. and Cozens, W.F., *Tests and Measurements in Physical Education* (Philadelphia: W.B. Saunders Co., 1930).

Brady, L., 'Whatever Happened to Marching Girls?', *Thursday* (16 Oct. 1969), pp. 59–61.

Braham, W., 'Siegfried Giedion and the Fascination of the Tub', in N. Lahiji and D. Friedman (eds), *Plumbing: Sounding Modern Architecture* (New York: Princeton Architectural Press 1997), pp. 200–24.

Brailsford, D., *British Sport: A Social History* (Cambridge: Butterworth Press, 1992).

Brandt, A., 'Views', *Atlantic Monthly* (July 1977), pp. 46–9.

Briffault, E., *Paris dans l'eau* (Paris: Hetzel, 1844).

Brown, N., *Ice-Skating: A History* (London: Sportsman's Press, 1960).

Bruce, T., 'Postmodernism and the Possibilities for Writing "Vital" Sports Texts', in G. Rail (ed.), *Sport and Postmodern Times* (Albany NY: SUNY, 1998), pp. 3–20.

Buford, B., *Among the Thugs* (New York: Norton, 1992).

Burke, E., *Philosophical Inquiry into the Origin of Our Ideas of the Sublime and Beautiful* (London: R. and J. Dodsley, 1757).

Burnet, T., *Telluris Theoria Sacra (The Sacred Theory of the Earth)* (Londini: Typis R.N. impensis Gualt, 1681).

Butler, J., *Gender Trouble: Feminism and the Subversion of Identity* (New York: Routledge, 1990).

Butler, J., *Bodies that Matter: On the Discursive Limits of 'Sex'* (New York: Routledge, 1993).

Butler, J., *The Psychic Life of Power: Theories in Subjection* (Stanford: Stanford University Press, 1997).

Cachy, K., 'Sports and Environment: Sports for Everyone – Room for Everyone?' *International Review for the Sociology of Sport*, 28, 2–3 (1993).

Cahn, S., *Coming on Strong: Gender and Sexuality in Twentieth Century Women's Sport* (New York: The Free Press, 1994).

Callède, J.P., *Histoire des politiques sportives en France* (Paris: Economica, 2000).

Callède, J.P., 'Notes d'architecture sportive: le Socialisme municipal des années trente à Bègles', *Annales du Midi*, 102, 192 (Oct.–Dec. 1990).

Campbell, A., *Report on Public Baths and Wash-Houses in the U.K.* (Edinburgh, 1918).

Camy, J., Adamkiewics, E. and Chantelat, P., 'Sporting Uses of the City: Urban Anthropology Applied to the Sports Practices in the Agglomeration of Lyon', *International Review for the Sociology of Sport*, 28, 2–3 (1993), pp. 159–74.

Cannadine, D., 'The Context, Performance and Meaning of Ritual: The British Monarchy and the "Invention of Tradition" c.1820–1977', in E. Hobsbawm and T. Ranger (eds), *The Invention of Tradition* (Cambridge: Cambridge University Press, 1983), pp. 101–64.

Cantelon H. and Letters, M., 'The Making of the IOC Environmental Policy as a Third Dimension of the Olympic Movement', *International Review for the Sociology of Sport*, 35, 3 (2000), pp. 294–308.

Carranza, L.E., 'Le Corbusier and the Problems of Representation', *Journal of Architectural Education*, 48, 2, (1994), pp. 70–81.

Carrier, C., 'La Subaquathérapie', *EPS*, 246 (March–April 1994).

Carsten, J. and Hugh-Jones, J. (eds), *About the House: Levi Strauss and Beyond* (Cambridge: Cambridge University Press, 1995).

Cassedy, J.H., *American Medicine and Statistical Thinking, 1800–1860* (Cambridge, MA: Harvard University Press, 1984).

Castells, M. 'The Information Age', *The Rise of the Network Society,* Vol. 1 (Oxford: Blackwell, 1996).

Catteau, R. and Garoff, G., *L'Enseignement de la natation* (Paris: Vigot, 1968).

Caute, D., *Sixty-Eight: The Year of Barricades* (London: Hamish Hamilton, 1988), p. 40.

Chandler, T. and Nauright, J. (eds), *Making Men: Rugby and Masculine Identity* (London: Cass, 1996).

Chapus, E., *Le Sport à Paris* (Paris: Hachette, 1854).

Clarke, G., 'Crossing Borders: Lesbian Physical Education Students and the Struggle for Sexual Spaces', in S. Scraton and B. Watson (eds), *Sport, Leisure Identities and Gendered Spaces* (Brighton: LSA Publications, University of Brighton, 2000), pp. 75–94.

Clarke, J., Hall, S., Jefferson T. and Roberts, B., 'Subcultures, Cultures and Class', in S. Hall and T. Jefferson (eds.), *Resistance Through Rituals* (London: Hutchinson, 1976), p. 67.

Clément, J.P., Defrance, J. and Pociello, C., *Sport et pouvoirs au XXième siècle, enjeux culturels, sociaux et politiques des éducations physiques, des sports et des loisirs dans les sociétés industrielles* (Grenoble: Presses universitaires de Grenoble, 1994).

Colomina, B. (ed.), *Sexuality & Space* (New York: Princeton Papers on Architecture, Princeton Architectural Press, 1992).

Colomina, B., *Privacy and Publicity: Modern Architecture as Mass Media* (Cambridge MA: MIT Press, 1994).

Coney, S., *Standing in the Sunshine: A History of New Zealand Women Since they Won the Vote* (Auckland: Viking/Penguin, 1993).

Connell, R.W., *Which Way is Up? Essays on Sex, Class and Culture* (Sydney: Allen and Unwin, 1983).

Conseil Général du Loiret, *Bassins d'apprentissage fixes de natation* (Orléans: Conseil Général du Loiret, 1983).

Coolidge, W.A.B., *The Alps in Nature and History* (London: Methuen, 1908).

Cosgrove, D., *Social Formation and Symbolic Landscape* (London: Croom Helm, 1984).

Couvreur, E., *Les Exercices du corps: Le développement de la force et de l'adresse* (Paris: Baillière, 1890).

CPD du Rhône, *Nager, réussir et comprendre* (video and accompanying document), (ARIP-CRDP Lyon, 1989)

Cross, A.W., *Public Baths and Wash-Houses* (London: Batsford, 1906).

Crouch, D. (ed.), *Leisure/Tourism Geographies* (New York: Routledge, 1999).

Crozier, M., 'After the Garden?', *The South Atlantic Quarterly*, 98, 4 (1999), pp. 625–31.

Cuisin, *Les Bains de Paris et des principales villes des quatre parties du monde ou le Neptune des Dames* (Paris: Verdière, 1822).

Cunningham, C.D. and Abney, W. de W., *Pioneers of the Alps* (London: Sampson Low, 1887).

Curry, T., 'Fraternal Bonding in the Locker Room: A Profeminist Analysis of Talk About Competition and Women', *Sociology of Sport Journal*, 8, 2 (1991), pp. 119–35.

Curtis, W.J.R., *Le Corbusier: Ideas and Forms* (London: Phaidon Press, 1986).

Dainotto, R.M., 'All the Legions do Smilingly Revolt: The Literature of Place and Region', *Critical Inquiry*, 22, 3 (Spring 1996), pp. 486–505.

Davis, A. and Jones, L., 'The Children's Enclosure', *Town and Country Planning* (Sept. 1996), pp. 233–5.

Davis, G., *Frostiana or A History of the River Thames in a Frozen State* (London: Printed and published on the River Thames, 5 Feb. 1814).

Davis, S.R., 'Anthropometry', *Mary Hemenway Alumnae Association of the Department of Hygiene Wellesley College Bulletin*, 1916–17, pp. 7–11.

Day, J.R., 'The Function of College Athletics', *Proceedings of the 14th Annual Convention of the Intercollegiate Athletic Association of the United States*, (28 Dec. 1909), pp. 34–43.

de Beer, Sir G., *Early Travellers in the Alps* (New York: October House, 1967 [1930]).

de Certeau, M., *The Practice of Everyday Life*, tr. Steven Randall, (Berkeley, CA: University of California Press, 1984).

Defrançois, C., *La Locomotion dans l'eau: Manuel de gymnastique théorique et pédagogique* (Paris: Dumaine, 1886).

DeLauretis, T., 'Perverse Desire: The Lure of the Mannish Lesbian', in H. Nast and S. Pile (eds), *Places Through the Body* (New York: Routledge, 1998), pp. 230–43.

Délégation à l'Action Artistique de la Ville de Paris, *Deux Siècles d'Architecture Sportive* (Paris: Catalogue de l'exposition 'Deux siècles d'architecture sportive', Délégation à l'Action artistique de la Ville de Paris, 1984).

Deleuze, G. and Guattari, G., *A Thousand Plateaus: Capitalism and Schizophrenia*, tr. B. Massumi (Minneapolis, MN: University of Minnesota Press, 1987).

Denis, D., *Le Corps enseigné* (Paris: Ed. Universitaires, 1974).

Dent, C.T., 'Two Attempts on the Aiguille du Dru', *Alpine Journal*, 7 (1876), pp. 65–79.

Diani, M. and Ingraham, C., *Edifying Projects: Restructuring Architectural Theory* (Evanston, IL: Northwestern University Press).

Dix, J., *Stranded in Paradise* (Wellington: Paradise Publications, 1988).

Donnelly, P., 'Take My Word for It: Trust in the Context of Birding and Mountaineering', *Qualitative Sociology*, 17 (1994), pp. 215–41.

Donnelly, P., 'The Invention of Tradition and the (Re)Invention of Mountaineering', in K. Wamsley (ed.), *Sport History and Social Theory* (Dubuque, IA: Brown & Benchmark, 1995), pp. 235–43.

Donnelly, P., 'Who's Master, Who's Man: Guide–Client Relationships in 19th Century Mountaineering', Seward Staley Address presented at the annual conference of the North American Society for Sport History, Banff, Canada, 2000).

Donnelly, P., 'The Great Divide: Sport Climbing vs. Adventure Climbing', in S. Sydnor and R. Rinehart (eds), *To the Extreme: Alternative Sports Inside and Out* (Albany, NY: State University of New York Press, 2002).

Douglas, M., *Purity and Danger: An Analysis of the Concepts of Pollution and Taboo* (London: Routledge, 1966).

Drew, L.C., *Adapted Group Gymnastics* (Philadelphia: Lea & Febiger, 1927).

Drigny, E.G., *La Natation: Natation élémentaire et natation sportive* (Nancy-Paris-Strasbourg: Berger-Levrault, 1921).

Dubois, C. and Robin, J.P., *Natation: De l'École ... aux Associations* (Paris: Ed. Review, *EPS*, 1985).

Duncan, N., 'Renegotiating Gender and Sexuality in Public and Private Spaces', in N. Duncan (ed.), *Body Space: Destabilizing Geographies of Gender and Sexuality* (London: Routledge, 1996), pp. 127–45.

Dunlap, T.R., *Nature and the English Diaspora: Environment and History in the United States, Canada, Australia, and New Zealand* (Cambridge: Cambridge University Press, 1999).

Dunstall, G., 'The Social Pattern', in *Oxford History of New Zealand*, 2nd edn (Auckland: Oxford University Press, 1992).

Dyer, R., *White* (London: Routledge, 1997).

Earhart, H.B., 'Sacred Mountains in Japan: Shugendo as "Mountain Religion"', in M.C. Tobias and H. Drasdo (eds), *The Mountain Spirit* (Woodstock, NY: The Overlook Press, 1979), pp. 107–16.

Eggermont, B., 'The Choreography of Schooling as Site of Struggle: Belgian Primary Schools, 1880–1940', *History of Education*, 30, 2 (2001), pp. 129–40.

Eichberg, H., 'Race-track and Labyrinth: The Space of Physical Culture in Berlin', *The Journal of Sport History*, 17, 2 (1990), pp. 245–60.

Eichberg, H., 'New Spatial Configurations of Sport. Experiences from Danish Alternative Planning', *International Review of Sociology of Sport*, 28 (1993), pp. 245–61.

Eichberg, H., 'Stadium, Pyramid, Labyrinth: Eye and Body on the Move', in J. Bale and O. Moen (eds), *The Stadium and the City* (Keele: Keele University Press, 1995), pp. 323–47.

Eichberg, H., 'The Enclosure of the Body: the Historical Relativity of "Health", "Nature" and the Environment of Spor', in J. Bale, and C. Philo (eds), *Body Cultures: Essays on Sport, Space and Identity* (London: Routledge, 1998), pp. 47–67.

Eichberg, H. and Hansen, J. (eds), *Bewegungs-Räume. Körper-anthropologische Beiträge* (Institut International d'Anthropologie: Afra Verlag, 1996).

Eisenbeis, J. and Touchard, Y., *L'Éducation à la sécurité* (Paris: Ed. Review, *EPS*, 1994).

Elias, N., *The Civilising Process* (Massachusetts: Blackwell, 2000).

Elliot, M., 'The Edinburgh Skating Club, 1778–1966', in *The Book of the Old Edinburgh Club*, Vol. 33, Pt 2 (Edinburgh: The Edinburgh Club, 1971), pp. 96–136.

Elliott, R., *The Organization of Professional Training in Physical Education in State Universities* (New York: Teachers College, Columbia University, 1927).

Emery, L.F. and Toohey-Costa, M., 'Hoops and Skirts: Women's Basketball on the West Coast, 1892–1930s', in J.S. Hult and M. Trekell (eds), *A Century of Women's Basketball: From Frailty to Final Four* (Reston, VA: American Alliance for Health, Physical Education, Recreation, and Dance, 1991), pp. 137–54.

Estran, N., *Réalisation, gestion, animation des piscines 1890–1990*, STAPS (Master's Degree, Lille, 1992).

Evans, J., *Children at Play: Life in the School Playground* (Geelong: Deakin University Press, 1989).

Evans, J., 'Children's Attitudes to Recess and the Changes Taking Place in Australian Primary Schools', *Research in Education,* 56 (1997), pp. 49–56.

Evans, J. and Pellegrini A., 'Surplus Energy Theory: An Enduring but Inadequate Justification for School Break-Time', *Educational Review,* 49, 3 (1997).

Fellows, M.L. and Razack, S., 'Race to Innocence: Confronting Hierarchical Relations Among Women', *The Journal of Gender, Race and Justice,* 1, 2 (1998), pp. 335–52.

Fielding, S., 'Walk on the Left! Children's Geographies and the Primary School', in S. Holloway and G. Valentine (eds), *Children's Geographies, Playing, Living, Learning* (London: Routledge, 2000), pp. 230–44.

Fluegelman, A. (ed.), *The New Games Book* (San Francisco: Headlands Press, 1976).

Forty, A., *Words and Buildings: A Vocabulary of Modern Architecture* (London: Thames & Hudson Ltd, 2000).

Foucault, M., *Madness and Civilization: A History of Insanity in the Age of Reason* (New York: Vintage Books, 1965).

Foucault, M., *Surveiller et Punir* (Paris: Gallimard, 1975), pub. in English as *Discipline and Punish: The Birth of the Prison* (London: Penguin Books, 1977).

Foucault, M., *The History of Sexuality: Volume I: An Introduction* (New York: Vintage Books, 1978).

Foucault, M., *Power/Knowledge: Selected Interviews and Other Writings, 1972–1977,* tr. C. Gordon (New York: Pantheon Books, 1980).

Foucault, M., 'Of Other spaces', tr. Jay Miskowiee, *Diacritics,* 16 (1986), pp. 22–7.

Fox, N., *Postmodernism, Sociology and Health* (Toronto: University of Toronto Press, 1994).

Freud, S., *Civilization, Society and Religion* Vol. 12 (London: Penguin Books, 1985).

Fusco, C., 'Lesbians and Locker Rooms: The Subjective Experiences of Lesbians in Sport', in G. Rail (ed.), *Sport in Postmodern Times* (Albany, NY: SUNY Press, 1998), pp. 87–116.

Gal, N., Ria, L., Sève, C. and Durand, M., La 'file indienne' en natation: un dispositif de déplacement des élèves jouant le rôle d'artefact cognitif, Proceedings, 'L'intervention en EPS et en sport', Antibes (16–18 Dec. 1998).

Geertz, C., *Further Essays in Interpretive Anthropology* (London: Fontana Press, 1993).

Geertz, C., *The Interpretation of Cultures* (New York: Basic Books, 1973).

Gerber, E.W., *Innovators and Institutions in Physical Education* (Philadelphia, PA: Lea & Febiger, 1971), p. 329.

Giddens, A., *The Consequences of Modernity* (Cambridge: Polity Press, 1990).

Giddens, A., *Modernity and Self-Identity* (Cambridge: Polity Press, 1991).

Gilman, S., *Difference and Pathology: Stereotypes of Sexuality, Race, and Madness* (Ithaca, NY: Cornell University Press, 1985).

Gilroy, P., *The Black Atlantic: Modernity and Double Consciousness* (London: Verso, 1993).

Girard, M., 'Sur les établissements de bains publics à Paris depuis le VIème siècle jusqu'à nos jours', *Annales d'Hygiène* (Paris, 1852).

Glamuzina, J. and Laurie, A., *Parker and Hulme* (Auckland: New Women's Press, 1991).

Godwell, D., 'The Olympic Branding of Aborigines: The 2000 Olympic Games and Australia's Indigenous Peoples', in K. Schaffer and S. Smith (eds), *The Olympics at the Millennium. Power, Politics and the Games* (New Brunswick: Rutgers University Press, 2000), pp. 243–257

Goirand P. and Metzler, J. (eds), *Histoire technique et culture scolaire* (Paris: Ed., *EPS*, 1996).

Gore, M. J., 'Disciplining Bodies; On the Continuity of Power Relations', in R.E. Paechter *et al.*, *Learning, Space and Identity* (London: Paul Chapman Publishing, 2001), pp. 167–81.

Greenpeace, *Environmental Report*. Retrieved 10 Nov. 2000 from: www.greenpeace.com.au.

Grenet, L.A., *Principes de la natation* (Paris: Susse, 1946).

Griffin, P., *Strong Women, Deep Closets: Lesbians and Homophobia in Sport* (Champaign, IL: Human Kinetics, 1998).

Gritzer, G. and Arluke, A., *The Making of Rehabilitation: A Political Economy of Medical Specialization, 1890–1980* (Berkeley: University of California Press, 1985).

Grosborne, J.B., 'Une Solution intéressante au problème des baignades', *EPS*, 7 (Oct. 1951).

Grosz, E., *Space, Time and Perversion* (New York: Routledge, 1995).

Grosz, E., 'Women, Chora, Dwelling', in S. Watson and K. Gibson (eds), *Postmodern Cities and Spaces* (Oxford: Blackwell, 1995), pp. 203–31.

Groth, P., 'Frameworks for Cultural Landscape Study', in P. Groth and T.W. Bressi (eds), *Understanding Ordinary Landscapes* (New Haven, CT: Yale University Press, 1997), p. 1.

Gulick, L.H., 'Physical Education: A New Profession', *Proceedings of the 5th Annual Meeting of the American Association for the Advancement of Physical Education* (Ithaca NY: Andrus and Church, 1890), pp. 59–66.

Gurney, H., *Girls' Sports. A Century of Progress in Ontario High Schools* (Don Mills: OFSAA Publications, 1979).

Hall, M.A., 'Creators of the Lost and Perfect Game', in P. White and K. Young (eds), *Sport and Gender in Canada* (Oxford: Oxford University Press, 1999), pp. 5–23.

Hampe, M., *Stilwandel im Eiskunstlauf: eine Ästhetik und Kulturgeschichte* [Changing Styles in Figure Skating: An Aesthetic and Cultural History] (Frankfurt am Main: Lang, 1994).

Hanna, D., 'Present Status of Physical Training in Normal Schools', *American Physical Education Review*, 8 (1903), pp. 293–7.

Hansen, J. and Nagbøl, S., 'Ollerup College of Physical Education – Living Space – Culture of Movement and Social Identity', in H. Eichberg and J. Hansen (eds), *Bewegungs-Räume: Körperanthropologische Beiträge* (Institut International d'Anthropologie: Afra Verlag, 1996), pp. 147–86.

Hansen, P.H., 'Albert Smith, the Alpine Club, and the Invention of Mountaineering in Mid-Victorian Britain', *Journal of British Studies*, 34 (1995), pp. 300–24.

Hansen, P.H., 'British Mountaineering, 1850–1914' (unpublished doctoral thesis, Harvard University, 1991).

Hanson, M.E., *Go! Fight! Win! Cheerleading in American Culture* (Bowling Green: Bowling Green State University Popular Press, 1995).

Harris, W.T., in *Physical Training: A Full Report of the Papers and Discussions of the Conference Held in Boston in November, 1889* (Boston: George H. Ellis, 1899), pp. 3–4.

Hart, R., 'Personal Conversation at Designing Modern Childhoods: Landscapes, Buildings and Material Culture', Paper presented at an International, Interdisciplinary Conference, Berkeley, USA, 2002.

Harvey, D., *The Condition of Postmodernity: An Inquiry into the Origins of Cultural Change* (Oxford: Blackwell, 1990).

Harvey, D., *Spaces of Hope* (Berkeley: University of California Press, 2000).

Hausser, A.E., *L'Oeuvre des bains-douches à bon marché* (Paris: 1902).

Haut Comité des Sports, *La Sécurité dans les piscines* (Paris: Institut Pédagogique National, *c*.1964).

Hayden, D., *The Power of Place* (Cambridge: MIT Press, 1995).

Heathcote, J.M., Elligton, H., Syers, E. and Monier-Williams, M.S., *A History of the National Skating Association of Great Britain, 1879–1901* (London: National Skating Association, 1902).

Helfand, H., *The Campus Guide, University of California, Berkeley: An Architectural Tour and Photographs* (New York: Princeton Architectural Press, 2002), pp. 204–8.

Hendrikson, M., *Dr Strangelove's America: Society and Culture in the Atomic Age* (Berkeley: University of California Press, 1997).

Henry, F.M., 'Physical Education. An Academic Discipline', *Journal of Health, Physical Education and Recreation*, 35, 7 (1964), pp. 31–3, 69.

Henry, F.M., 'The Academic Discipline of Physical Education', *Quest*, 29 (1978), pp. 13–79.

Hetherington, C.W., 'Analysis of Problems in College Athletics', *American Physical Education Review*, 12 (1907), pp. 154–81.

Hetherington, C.W., 'The Federation Movement – its Objectives and Ideals', paper presented at the Third Annual Meeting, May 1926 [booklet].

Hewitt, J.E., 'The Graduate Major in Physical Education', *Research Quarterly*, 13 (1942), pp. 252–6.

Hillman, M. *et al.*, *One False Move: A Study of Children's Independent Mobility* (London: Policy Studies Institute, 1990).

Hirst, J.B., 'The Pioneer Legend', in John Carroll (ed.), *Intruders in the Bush: The Australian Quest for Identity* (Melbourne: Oxford University Press, 1992), pp. 14–37.

Hitchcock, E., 'Anthropometry', Paper read at the Second Annual Meeting of the AAAPE, Brooklyn, NY, 26 Nov. 1887 (Brooklyn: Rome Brothers, 1887).

Hoberman, J., *Mortal Engines: The Science of Performance and the Dehumanization of Sport* (New York: The Free Press, 1992).

Hoffie, P., 'Landscape and Identity in the 1980s', in G. Levitus (ed.), *Lying About the Landscape* (Sydney: Craftsman House, 1997), p. 69.

Holloway, S. and Valentine, G., 'Children's Geographies and the New Social Studies of Childhood', in S. Holloway and G. Valentine (eds), *Children's Geographies, Playing, Living, Learning* (London: Routledge, 2000), pp. 1–26.

Hughson, J., 'Soccer, Support and Social Identity', *International Review for the Sociology of Sport*, 33 (1998), pp. 403–9.

Hult, J.S., 'The Philosophical Conflicts in Men's and Women's Intercollegiate Athletics', *Quest*, 32 (1980), pp. 77–94.

Hutchinson, R., *Empire Games: The British Invention of Twentieth-Century Sport* (Edinburgh and London: Mainstream Publishing, 1996).

Imrie, R., 'The Body, Disability and Le Corbusier's Conception of the Radiant Environment', in R. Butler and H. Parr (eds), *Mind and Body Spaces: Geographies of Illness, Impairment and Disability* (New York: Routledge, 1999) pp. 25–45.

Ingraham, C., 'Initial Properties: Architecture and the Space of the Line', in B. Colomina (ed.), *Sexuality & Space* (New York: Princeton Papers on Architecture, Princeton Architectural Press, 1992), pp. 255–71.

International Ice Hockey Federation, 'Canada Leads All Hockey Nations in Rinks and Players', News Archives, http://db2.iihf.com/cgi-bin/db2 wwwexe./news/news.d2w/archive (3 July 2001).

Jambor, T., 'School Recess and Social Development', *Dimensions of Early Childhood*, 23, 1 (1994), pp. 17–20.

James, A. *et al.*, *Theorising Childhood* (Cambridge: Polity Press, 1998).

James, S., 'Is There a "Place" for Children in Geography?', *Area*, 22, 3 (1990), p. 281.

Jarratt, P., *Mr Sunset: The Jeff Hakman Story* (London: General Publishing, 1997), pp. 70–3, 78–84.

Jerome, J., *On Mountains* (New York: McGraw-Hill, 1978).

Johnson, L., 'Reading the Sexed Bodies and Spaces of Gyms', in H. Nast and S. Pile (eds), *Places Through the Body* (New York: Routledge, 1998), pp. 244–62.

Johnson, W.R. (ed.), *Science and Medicine of Exercise and Sports* (New York: Harper and Brothers, 1960).

Jones, M., *Living Machines* (San Francisco, CA: Ignatius Press, 1995).

Jones, R., *A Treatise on Skating: Founded on Certain Principles Deduced From Many Years Experience; By Which That Noble Exercise is Now Reduced to an Art* (London: J. Ridley, 1772).

Kampion, D., *Stoked: A History of Surf Culture* (Los Angeles: General Publishing, 1997), pp. 127–32.

Kane, M.J. and Disch, L., 'Sexual Violence and the Reproduction of Male Power in the Locker Room: The "Lisa Olsen Incident"', *Sociology of Sport Journal* 10 (1993), pp. 331–52.

Kantor, J.R.K., 'The First "Golden Bears": The Transcontinental Tour of Cal's Track Team, 1895', *Chronicle of the University of California*, 4 (2000), pp. 13–16.

Kellogg, M., 'A Year's Review', *University of California Chronicle*, 1 (1898), p. 25.

Kelly, E., 'Racism and Sexism in the Playground', in P. Blatchford and S. Sharp (eds), *Breaktime and the School: Understanding and Changing Playground Behaviour* (London: Routledge, 1994).

Kirby, K.M., *Indifferent Boundaries: Spatial Concepts of Human Subjectivity* (New York: The Guilford Press, 1996).

Kirk, D., *Schooling Bodies* (London: Leicester University Press, 1998).

Kleeberger, F.L., 'Physical Efficiency Tests as a Practical Method of Popularizing Physical Education at the University of California', *The American Turner*, 5 (1917), pp. 1428–37.

Kleeberger, F.L., 'Physical Efficiency as Measured at the University of California', *Research Quarterly*, 3 (1932), pp. 151–72.

Kopp, F., *Des Piscines de jadis aux piscines de demain* (Rouen: Desrages, 1934), p. 10.

Kristeva, J., *Powers of Horror: An Essay on Abjection* (New York: Columbia University Press, 1982).

Lahiji, N. and Friedman, D. (eds), *Plumbing: Sounding Modern Architecture* (New York: Princeton Architectural Press, 1997).

Lash, S. and Urry, J., *Economies of Signs and Space* (London: Sage, 1993).

Lather, P., *Getting Smart: Feminist Research and Pedagogy With/In the Postmodern* (New York: Routledge, 1991).

Lawton, J., *1963: Five Hundred Days* (London: Hodder & Stoughton, 1992), p. 220.

Le Bas, A., *Architectures du Sport* (Paris: Ed. connivences, 1991).

Le Corbusier, *The City of Tomorrow and its Planning*, tr. of *Urbanisme* by Frederick Etchells (New York: Dover Publications, 1925).

Le Corbusier, *The Decorative Art of Today* (London: Architectural Press, 1925).

Le Corbusier, *When the Cathedrals Were White: A Journey to the Country of Timid People* (London: Routledge, 1925).

Leach, N. (ed.), *Rethinking Architecture: A Reader in Cultural Theory* (London: Routledge, 1997).

Leap, W. (ed), *Public Sex, Gay Space* (New York: Columbia University Press, 1999).

Lefebvre, H. *The Production of Space*, tr. D. Nicholson-Smith (Oxford: Blackwell, 1991).

Lemoine, A., *Traité d'éducation physique* (Gand: Jacqmain, 1857).

Lenskyj, H., *Out of Bounds: Women, Sport and Sexuality* (Toronto: The Women's Press, 1986).

Lenskyj, H., *Inside the Olympic Industry: Power, Politics, and Activism* (Albany, NY: SUNY Press, 2000).

Leonard, G., *The Ultimate Athlete: Re-Visioning Sports, Physical Education, and the Body* (New York: Viking Press, 1975).

Lewis, J.F., *Skating and the Philadelphia Skating Club* (Philadelphia: Philadelphia Skating Club, 1895).

Leziart, Y.,'Les Premiers enseignants de gymnastique scolaire: Histoire d'une profession qui se constitue', *STAPS*, 32 (Oct. 1993).

Lovell, N., 'Introduction. Belonging in Need of Emplacement?', in N. Lovell (ed.), *Locality and Belonging* (London: Routledge, 1998), p. 6.

Lovett, R.W., 'Round Shoulders and Faulty Attitudes: A Method of Observation and Record, with Conclusions as to Treatment', *American Physical Education Review*, 7 (1902), pp. 169–87. (Reprinted from the *Boston Medical and Surgical Journal*, 6 Nov. 1902).

Lowe, R., '*A Western Acropolis of Learning': The University of California in 1897* (University of California, Berkeley: Center for Studies in Higher Education and Institute of Governmental Studies, 1996), p. 25.

Lucas, W., 'The Power of School Grounds: The Philosophy and Practice of Learning Through Landscapes', in P. Blatchford and S. Sharp (eds), *Breaktime and the School: Understanding and Changing Playground Behaviour* (London: Routledge, 1994).

Lunn, A., *A Century of Mountaineering, 1857–1957* (London: Allen & Unwin, 1957).

MacCannell, D., *Empty Meeting Grounds: The Tourist Papers* (London: Routledge, 1992).

Macdonald, C., 'The Unbalanced Parallel: Organizations in Sport, Recreation and Leisure', in A. Else (ed.), *Women Together: A History of Women's Organizations in New Zealand* (Wellington: Daphne Brasell with Historical Branch, Department of Internal Affairs, 1993), pp. 402–44.

Macdonald, F., *The Game of Our Lives* (Auckland: Penguin/Viking, 1996).

Macnaughten, P. and Urry, J., *Contested Natives* (London: Sage, 1998).

Magdalinski, T., '"Excising the Cancer": Drugs, Sport and the Crisis of Australian Identity', *AVANTE*, 6, 3 (2000), pp. 1–15.

Magdalinski, T., 'Drugs Inside Sport: The Rehabilitation of Samantha Riley', *Sporting Traditions*, 17, 2 (2001), p. 18.

Magdalinski, T., 'Drugs, Sport and National Identity in Australia', in W. Wilson and E. Derse (eds), *Doping in Elite Sport: The Politics of Drugs in the Olympic Movement* (Champaign, IL: Human Kinetics, 2001), pp. 189–202.

Maguire, J., 'Sport, the Stadium and Metropolitan Life', in J. Bale and O. Moen (eds), *The Stadium and the City* (Keele: Keele University Press, 1995), pp. 45–58.

Maillard D. and Pelayo, P., 'Natation et APPN: le test Pechomaro', *EPS*, 250 (Nov.–Dec. 1994).

Mangenot, Dr, *Les Bains et la natation dans les écoles primaires communales de Paris* (Paris: Masson, 1892), pp. 16–17.

Mangos, N. and Stayt, J., *Marching Down Under* (Wellington: New Zealand Marching Association, 1984), p. 3.

Mariage, P. *et al.*, *Les Piscines et l'Hygiène* (Paris: Imp. Nationale, 1942).

Markus, T., *Buildings and Power: Freedom and Control in the Origin of Modern Building Types* (London: Routledge, 1993).

Martin, J.L., *La Politique de l'Éducation Physique sous la Vie République*, Vol.1: *L'élan gaullien. 1958–1969* (Paris: Presses universitaires de France, 1999).

Martin, L., Brouardel, G. and Dujarric de la Rivière, R., *Traité d'hygiène* (Paris: Baillière, 1930).

Mason, B., 'Stepping it Out, Stepping it High', *New Zealand Listener*, 82, 1899 (1 May 1976), pp. 9–10.

Massey, D., 'Masculinity, Dualisms and High Technology', in N. Duncan (ed.), *Body Space: Destabilizing Geographies of Gender and Sexuality* (London: Routledge, 1996), pp. 109–26.

Massey, D., *Space, Place and Gender* (Oxford: Blackwell, 1994).

May, H., *Minding Children, Managing Men: Conflict and Compromise in the Lives of Postwar Pakeha Women* (Wellington: Bridget Williams Books, 1992).

May, T.E., 'Explosive Issues: Sex, Women and the Bomb', L. May (ed.), *Recasting America: Culture and Politics in the Age of the Cold War* (Chicago and London: University of Chicago Press, 1989), p. 154.

McClintock, A., *Imperial Leather: Race, Gender, and Sexuality in the Colonial Contest* (New York: Routledge, 1995).

McCurdy, J. and Trombley, W., *On the Brink: The Impact of Budget Cuts on California's Public Universities*. A Report from the California Higher Education Policy Center (Aug. 1993).

McDowell, L. and Sharpe, J. (eds), *Space, Gender, Knowledge: Feminist Readings* (London: Arnold, 1997).

McDowell, L., *Gender, Identity and Place: Understanding Feminist Geographers* (Minneapolis: University of Minnesota Press, 1999).

McDowell, L., 'Spatializing Feminism', in N. Duncan (ed.), *Body Space* (New York: Routledge, 1996).

McGeoch, R., *The Bid: How Australia Won the 2000 Games* (Melbourne: William Heinemann Australia, 1994).

McGregor, C., *Profile of Australia* (London: Hodder & Stoughton, 1966).

McIntyre, W.D., 'From Dual Dependency to Nuclear Free', in G.W. Rice (ed.), *Oxford History of New Zealand*, 2nd edn (Auckland: Oxford University Press, 1992).

McIntyre, W.D., 'Imperialism and Nationalism', in G.W. Rice (ed.), *Oxford History of New Zealand*, 2nd edn (Auckland: Oxford University Press, 1992).

McKay, S., 'Designing Disciplines: The Architecture of a Gymnasium', in P. Vertinsky and S McKay (eds), *Disciplining Bodies in the Gymnasium: Memory, Monument, Modernism* (London: Frank Cass, 2004).

McKendrick, J. and Bradford, M. 'Organised Spaces for Leisure: A New Departure in the Institutionalisation of Children's Leisure?' Paper presented to the Nordic–British Conference on Children, Norway, 1999.

McKendrick, J., Bradford, M. and Fielder, A. 'Time for a Party! Making Sense of the Commercialisation of Leisure Space for Children', in S. Holloway and G. Valentine (eds), *Children's Geographies, Playing, Living, Learning* (London: Routledge, 2000), pp. 100–16.

McKinnon, M., *Independence and Foreign Policy in New Zealand: New Zealand in the World Since 1935* (Auckland: Auckland University Press, 1993).

McMillan, M., *Massage and Therapeutic Exercise* (Philadelphia, PA: W.B. Saunders Co., 1921), pp. 9–12.

McNeill, W.H., *Keeping Together in Time: Dance and Drill in Human History* (Cambridge, Mass: Harvard University Press, 1995).

Merry-Delabost, Dr, *Sur les bains-douches de propreté* (Le mans, 1890).

Metge, J., *A New Maori Migration* (London: Athlone Press, 1964).

Meylan, G., 'Athletics', *American Physical Education Review*, 10 (1905), pp. 157–63.

Miller, W., *The Anatomy of Disgust* (Cambridge, MA: Harvard University Press, 1997).

Milner, A. 'On the Beach: Apocalyptic Hedonism and the Origins of Postmodernism', in Ian Craven (ed.), *Australian Popular Culture* (Cambridge: Cambridge University Press, 1994), p. 199.

Ministère de l'Instruction Publique et des Beaux-Arts, *Manuel d'exercices gymnastiques et de jeux scolaires* (Paris: Imp. Nationale, 1891).

Mitchell, D., *Cultural Geography, A Critical Introduction* (Oxford: Blackwell Press, 2000).

Mohanram, M., *Black Body: Women, Colonialism, and Space* (Minneapolis, MN: University of Minnesota Press, 1999).

Monier-Williams, M.S., *Figure-Skating* (London: A.D. Innes, 1898).

Morgan, A., 'The Girls are Marching', *New Zealand Magazine*, 1 (1951), p. 5a.

Morris, G., 'Beyond the Beach: Social and Formal Aspects of AIP's Beach Party Movies', *Journal of Popular Film and Television*, 21, 1 (1993), pp. 2–11.

Morris, M. 'Great Moments in Social Climbing: King Kong and the Human Fly', in Beatriz Colomina (ed.), *Sexuality & Space* (New York: Princeton Papers on Architecture, Princeton Architectural Press, 1992), pp. 1–52.

Morrow, R., 'Architectural Assumptions and Environmental Discrimination: The Case for More Inclusive Design in Schools of Architecture', in D. Nicol and S. Pilling (eds), *Changing Architectural Education: Towards a New Profession* (London and New York: E. and F.N. Spon, 2000).

Mosse, G., *Nationalism and Sexuality: Respectability and Abnormal Sexuality in Modern Europe* (New York: Howard Fertig, 1985).

Mulvey, L., 'Pandora: Topographies of the Mask and Curiosity', in B. Colomina (ed.), *Sexuality & Space* (New York: Princeton Papers on Architecture, Princeton Architectural Press, 1992), pp. 53–71.

Munt, S., 'The Lesbian *Flaneur*', in D. Bell and G. Valentine (eds), *Mapping Desire: Geographies of Sexualities* (London: Routledge, 1995), pp. 114–25.

Nagbol, S., 'Enlivening and Deadening Shadows', *International Review for the Sociology of Sport* 28, 2–3 (1993), pp. 265–80.

Napias, Dr, *Les Établissements de bains froids* (Paris, 1877).

Nast, H. and Pile, S. (eds), *Places Through the Body* (London and New York: Routledge, 1998).

NBC, 'Telecast of the Opening Ceremony of the Games of the XXVIIth Olympiad' (15 Sept. 2000).

Nicolson, M.H., *Mountain Gloom and Mountain Glory: The Development of the Aesthetics of the Infinite* (Ithaca, NY: Cornell University Press, 1959).

Nielsen, N.K., 'The Stadium in the City', in J. Bale and O. Moen (eds), *The Stadium and the City* (Keele: Keele University Press, 1995), pp. 21–57.

Norberg-Schultz, C., *Genius Loci: The Phenomenology of Architecture* (New York: Rizzoli, 1979).

O'Neill, J., *Five Bodies: The Human Shape of Modern Society* (Ithaca, NY: Cornell University Press, 1985), pp. 16–25.

Okely, J., *Own or Other Culture* (London: Routledge, 1996).

Opie, I. and Opie, P., *The Lore and Language of Schoolchildren* (Oxford: Oxford University Press, 1959).

Ormonde-Hall, J., 'College Architecture', *The Graduate Chronicle*, (2 Oct. 1948), pp. 17–36.

Ormonde-Hall, J., 'Speaking Editorially', *Graduate Cronicle*, 2, 3 (1948), pp. 34–6.

Orsman, H.W. (ed.), *The Dictionary of New Zealand English* (Auckland: Oxford University Press, 1997), p. 483b.

Owens, L., 'Pure and Sound Government: Laboratories, Playing Fields and Gymnasia in the Nineteenth Century Search for Order', *ISIS*, 76 (1985), pp. 182–94.

Palmer, M.L., *Science de l'enseignement de la natation* (Paris: Vigot, 1985).

Park, R.J., 'From Football to Rugby – and Back, 1906–1919: The University of California-Stanford University Response to the "Football Crisis of 1905"', *Journal of Sport History*, 11 (1984), pp. 5–40;

Park, R.J., 'Science, Service, and the Professionalization of Physical Education, 1885–1905', *Research Quarterly for Exercise and Sport*. Special Centennial Issue (1985), pp. 7–20.

Park, R.J., 'Physiologists, Physicians, and Physical Educators: Nineteenth Century Biology and Exercise, Hygienic and Educative', *Journal of Sport History*, 14 (1987), pp. 28–60.

Park, R.J., 'Health, Exercise, and the Biomedical Impulse, 1870–1914', *Research Quarterly for Exercise and Sport*, 61 (1990), pp. 126–40.

Park, R.J., 'The Rise and Demise of Harvard's B.S. Program in Anatomy, Physiology, and Physical Training: A Case of Conflicts of Interest and Scarce Resources', *Research Quarterly for Exercise and Sport*, 63 (1992), pp. 1–15.

Park, R.J., 'A Gym of Their Own: Women, Sports, and Physical Culture at the Berkeley Campus', *Chronicle of the University of California*, 1 (1998), pp. 21–47.

Park, R.J., 'Athletics at Berkeley at the Turn of Both Centuries', *Chronicle of the University of California*, 4 (2000), pp. 175–88.

Park, R.J., 'Cells or Soaring?: Historical Reflections on "Visions" of the Body, Athletics, and Modern Olympism', *Olympika: The International Journal of Olympic Studies*, 9 (2000), pp. 1–24.

Park, R.J., 'Time Given Freely to Worthwhile Causes: Anna S. Espenschade's Contributions to Physical Education', *Research Quarterly for Exercise and Sport*, 71 (2000), pp. 99–115.

Partridge, L.W., *John Galen Howard and the Berkeley Campus: Beaux-Arts Architecture in the 'Athens of the West'* (Berkeley Architectural Heritage Publication Series, No. 2, 1988), pp. 46–7.

Payne, F.H., 'Physical Culture at the University of California', *Pacific Medical Journal*, 33 (1890), pp. 705–10.

Pearson, K., *Surfing Subcultures of Australia and New Zealand* (Brisbane: University of Queensland Press, 1979).

Pelayo P. and Beulque, P., 'Les Origines de l'Enseignement Collectif de la Natation Scolaire', *Sciences et Motricité* (1990).

Pelayo, P. and Terret, T., 'Savoirs et enjeux relatifs à la natation dans les instructions et programmes officiels (1877–1986)', *STAPS*, 33 (1994).

Pellegrini, A., 'Outdoor Recess: Is it Really Necessary?', *Principal*, 70, 5 (1991), p. 40.

Pellegrini, A., and Smith, P.K., 'School Recess: Implications for Education and Development', *Review of Educational Research*, 63, 1 (1993), pp. 51–67.

Pernderleith, I., www.dottwo.co.uk/usa/grounds.html (2001).

Phelan, S., *Getting Specific: Postmodern Lesbian Politics* (Minneapolis, MN: University of Minnesota Press, 1994).

Phillips, J., *A Man's Country: The Image of the Pakeha Male – A History* (Auckland: Penguin, 1996).

Phillips, J., *Royal Summer: The Visit of Queen Elizabeth II and Prince Philip to New Zealand 1953–54* (Wellington: Historical Branch, Department of Internal Affairs/Daphne Brassell Associates Press, 1993).

Philp, M., 'March Past', *New Zealand Listener*, 165, 3040 (15 Aug. 1998), p. 30–1.

Picard, E. and D'Offschmidt, N., 'Pandectes Belges'; 'Bains et lavoirs publics'; *Encyclopédie de Législation, de Doctrine et de Jurisprudence Belges*, Vol. 12 (Bruxelles: Larcier, 1884).

Pociello, C., *Les Cultures sportives* (Paris: Presses universitaires de France, 1995).

Pool, I., *Te Iwi Maori: A New Zealand Population Past, Present and Projected* (Auckland: Auckland University Press, 1991).

Porter, T.M., *The Rise of Statistical Thinking, 1820–1900* (Princeton, NJ: Princeton University Press, 1986).

Poulaillon, A., *La Natation, les bains et piscines: Exposé de la situation présentée au Comité d'Initiative de l'Union des Sociétés Sportives Lyonnaises*, Minutes of the meeting of the 8th July 1904 (Lyon: Impr. Decléris, 1904), p. 7.

Pred, A. (ed.), *Time and Space in Geography* (Lund: Gleerup, 1981).

Prior, L., 'The Architecture of the Hospital', *British Journal of Sociology*, 39 (1988), pp. 110.

Probyn, E., 'Lesbians in Space: Gender, Sex and the Structure of the Missing', *Gender, Place and Culture*, 2, 1 (1995), pp. 77–84.

Probyn, E., 'Sporting Bodies: Dynamics of Shame and Pride', *Body and Society*, 6, 1 (2000), pp. 13–28.

Proctor, T.M., '(Uni)Forming Youth: Girls Guides and Boy Scouts in Britain, 1908–39', *History Workshop Journal*, 45 (Spring 1998), pp. 103–34.

Proger, B., 'Fear and Trembling: Homophobia in Men's Sport', in P. White and K. Young (eds), *Sport and Gender in Canada* (Toronto: Oxford University Press, 1999).

Pronger, B., 'Homosexuality and Sport: Who's Winning?', in J. McKay, M. Messner and D. Sabo (eds), *Masculinities and Sport* (London: Sage, 2000).

Pronger, B., 'Post-sport: Transgressing Boundaries in Physical Culture', in *Sport and Postmodern Times: Culture, Gender, Sexuality, the Body and Sport* (Buffalo: SUNY Press, 1998).

Pronger, B., 'Outta My End Zone: Sport and the Territorial Anus', *Journal of Sport and Social Issues*, 23, 4 (1999), pp. 373–89.

Pronger, B., *The Arena of Masculinity: Sports, Homosexuality and the Meaning of Sex* (New York: St. Martin's Press, 1990).

Prout, A. (ed.), *The Body, Childhood and Society* (London: Macmillan, 2000).

Puig, N., Martinez del Castillo, J., Pellegrino, P. and Lambert, C., 'Sports Facilities as a Revealing of Society', *International Review for the Sociology of Sport* 28, 2–3 (1993), pp. 203–22.

Pyatt. E., *The Guinness Book of Mountains & Mountaineering Facts & Feats* (London: Guinness Superlatives, 1980).

Rail, G., 'Seismography of the Postmodern Condition: Three Theses on the Implosion of Sport', in G. Rail (ed.), *Sport and Postmodern Times* (Albany, NY: State University of New York Press, 1998).

Raitz, K. (ed.), *The Theater of Sport* (Baltimore, MD: Johns Hopkins University Press, 1995).

Rauch, A., *Le Souci du corps* (Paris: PUF, 1983).

Razack, S. 'Race, Space and Prostitution', *Canadian Journal of Women and the Law* 19, 2 (1998), pp. 338–76.

Razack, S., 'Making Canada White: Law and the Policing of Bodies in the 1990's', *Canadian Journal of Law & Society* 14, 1 (1999), pp. 159–84.

Razack, S., 'From the "Clean Snows of Petawawa": The Violence of Canadian Peacekeepers in Somalia', *Cultural Anthropology* 15, 1 (2000), pp. 127–63.

Razack, S., 'Gendered Racial Violence and Spatialized Justice: The Murder of Pamela George', *Canadian Journal of Law and Society* 15, 2 (2000).

Relph, E., *Place and Placelessness* (London: Pion, 1976).

Relph, E., 'Modernity as the Reclamation of Place', in David Seaman (ed.), *Dwelling, Seeing and Designing* (New York: SUNY Press, 1993).

Rendell, J., 'West End Rambling: Gender Architectural Space in London 1800–1830', *Leisure Studies* 17, 2 (1998), pp. 108–22.

Rendell, J., Penner, B. and Borden, I. (eds), *Gender, Space, Architecture* (London: Routledge, 2000).

Rice, G.W. (ed.), *The Oxford History of New Zealand*, 2nd edn, (Auckland: Oxford University Press, 1992).

Rich, F., 'Naked Capitalists: There's No Business Like Porn Business', *New York Times Magazine*, 20 May 2001.

Richards, E.L., 'College Athletics', *Popular Science Monthly*, 24 (1884), pp. 446–53.

Ritter, M.B., *More Than Gold in California, 1849–1933* (Berkeley, CA: The Professional Press, 1933), pp. 202–4.

Ritter, W.E., 'The University, Its Graduates, and the State', *University of California Chronicle*, 1 (1898), pp. 97–103.

Robbins, D., 'Sport, Hegemony and the Middle Class: The Victorian Mountaineers', *Theory, Culture and Society*, 4 (1987), pp. 579–601.

Robertson, R., *Globalization: Social Theory and Global Culture* (London: Sage, 1992).

Rodaway, P., *Sensuous Geographies* (London: Routledge, 1994).

Rojek, C., *Capitalism and Leisure Theory* (London: Tavistock, 1985).

Roman, L., 'Opening Remarks. The University as/in Contested Space' (Vancouver: UBC Conference, Vancouver, May 1998).

Rose, G., *Feminism and Geography: The Limits of Geographical Knowledge* (Minneapolis: University of Minnesota Press, 1993).

Rouca, C., 'Les Piscines parisiennes: Pratiques et espaces. La Vogue de l'eau' (Diss., Univ. Paris VII, 1999).

Rousmaniere, K., 'Questioning the Visual in the History of Education', *History of Education*, 30, 2 (2001), pp. 109–16.

Rousseau, J.J., *Emile, ou de l'éducation* (Amsterdam: J. Néaulme, 1762).

Roy, R., *Sherwood Lett. His Life and Times* (Vancouver: UBC Alumni Association, UBC, 1991).

Ruskin, J., *Sesame and Lilies* (London: Everett, 1916).

Russell, B., 'Old Games are More than Child's Play', *Independent*, 3 June 1999.

Russell, E., 'Australia's Amphibians', *Lone Hand* (Jan. 1910), p. 265.

Rutsky, R.L., 'Surfing the Other: Ideology on the Beach', *Film Quarterly*, 52, 4 (1999), pp. 12–23.

Sachs, F., *The Complete Swimmer* (London: Methuen, 1912).

Sack, R.D., *Human Territoriality, its Theory and History* (Cambridge: Cambridge University Press, 1986).

Saili, J., *Himalayan Mysteries* (New Delhi, India: Roli Books, 2001).

Samuel, R., 'Theatres of Memory', in *Past and Present in Contemporary Culture*, Vol.1 (London: Verso, 1994).

SARECO-Ministère du Temps Libre, *La Conception et l'exploitation des bassins d'apprentissage* (Paris, 1984).

Scandura, J. and Thurston, M., 'Modernism Inc.', in J. Scandura and M. Thurston (eds), *Body, Memory, Capital* (New York: New York University Press, 2001).

Schama, S., *Landscape and Memory* (Toronto: Random House, 1995).

Schoebel, E., *Précis de natation scolaire*, 2nd edn (Paris: Bourrelier, 1957).

Scraton, S. and Watson, B., 'Gendered Cities: Women and Public Leisure Space in the "Postmodern" City', *Leisure Studies,* 17, 2 (1998), pp. 123–37.

Shilling, C., *The Body and Social Theory* (London: Sage, 1993), p. 5.

Sibley, D., *Geographies of Exclusion* (London: Routledge, 1995).

Silber, I., *The Cultural Revolution: A Marxist Analysis* (New York: Times Change Press, 1970), p. 58.

Silver, H. (ed.), *Robert Owen on Education* (Cambridge: Cambridge University Press, 1969).

Simpson, B., 'Regulation and Resistance: Children's Embodiment during the Primary–Secondary School Transition', in A. Prout (ed.), *The Body, Childhood and Society* (London: Macmillan, 2000), pp. 60–78.

Simpson, V. and Jennings, A., *The Lords of the Rings* (Toronto: Stoddart, 1992).

Sinclair, A. and Henry, W., *Swimming* (London: Sinclair and Henry, 1893).

Skarstrom, W., *Gymnastic Kinesiology: A Manual of the Mechanism of Gymnastic Movement* (Springfield, MA: American Physical Education Association, 1909).

Skating Club, *Historical Sketch of the Club and Description of the Rink and Pavilion* (London: The Skating Club, 1909).

Sleap, M. and Warburton, P., 'Physical Activity Levels of 5–11 Year Old Children in England as Determined by Continuous Observation', *International Journal of Sports Medicine,* 17 (1996), pp. 248–53.

Smith, F. and Barker, J., 'Out of School, In School: A Social Geography of out of School Childcare', in S. Holloway and G. Valentine (eds), *Children's Geographies, Playing, Living, Learning* (London: Routledge, 2000), pp. 245–56.

Smith, N., 'The Production of Nature', in G. Robertson, M. Mash, L. Tickner, J. Bird, B. Curtie and T. Putnam (eds), *FutureNatural: Nature, Science, Culture* (London: Routledge, 1996), p. 41.

Smith, N. and Katz, C., 'Grounding Metaphor. Towards a Spatialized Politics', in M. Keith (ed.), *Place and the Politics of Identity* (New York: Routledge, 1993), pp. 67–83.

Snowdon, E., 'Girls Marching', *Otaki Historical Society Historical Journal*, 9 (1986), pp. 21–6.

Soja, E., *Postmodern Geographies* (New York: Verso, 1989).

Soper, K., 'Nature/Nature', in Robertson, Mash, Tickner, Bird, Curtie and Putnam (eds), *FutureNatural: Nature, Science, Culture* (London: Routledge, 1996), p. 25.

Spears, B., *Leading the Way: Amy Morris Homans and the Beginnings of Professional Education* (New York: Greenwood Press, 1986).

Spears, B., 'The Influential Miss Homans', *Quest*, 29 (1978), pp. 46–59.

Spindler, K., *The Man in the Ice: The Discovery of a 5,000 Year Old Body Reveals the Secrets of the Stone Age* (New York: Harmony Books, 1994).

Stadman, V.A. (ed.), *The Centennial Record of the University of California* (Berkeley, CA: University of California Printing Department, 1967), p. 53.

Stafford, G.T., *Preventative and Corrective Physical Education* (New York: A.S. Barnes and Co., 1928).

Stallybrass, P. and White, A.. *The Politics and Poetics of Transgression* (Ithaca, NY: Cornell University Press, 1986).

Stephen, L.. *The Playground of Europe* (London: Longmans, 1871).

Stewart, L., *It's Up to You: Women At UBC in the Early Years* (Vancouver: UBC Press, 1990).

Stoler, L. A., *Race and the Education of Desire: Foucault's History of Sexuality and the Colonial Order of Things* (Durham, NC: Duke University Press, 1995).

Stow, D., *National Education, Supplement to Moral Training and the Training System, with Plans for Erecting and Fitting up of Training Schools* (Glasgow: W.R. M'Phun, 1839).

Stratton, J., 'Youth Subcultures and their Cultural Contexts', *Australian and New Zealand Journal of Sociology*, 21, 2 (1985), p. 211.

Sutton-Smith, B., 'School Playground as Festival', *Children's Environments Quarterly,* 7, 2 (1990), pp. 3–7.

Swift, F. and Clark, M.R., *The Skater's Textbook* (New York, 1868).

Sydney Olympic Bid Ltd, Sydney 2000. Share the Spirit. Olympic Information, Vol. 2 (Sydney: SOBL, 1993).

Sydney Olympic Games Committee, *Sydney Olympics 2000* (Sydney: SOGC, 1991).

Tanner, J.M., *A History of Human Growth* (Cambridge: Cambridge University Press, 1981).

Taylor, A.E., *The Academic Senate of the University of California: Its Role in the Shared Governance and Operations of the University of California* (Berkeley, CA: University of California, Institute of Governmental Studies Press, 1998)

Taylor, M., *Alterity* (Chicago: University of Chicago Press, 1987).

Terret, T., 'Hygienisation: Civic Baths and Body Cleanliness in late Nineteenth Century France', *The International Journal of the History of Sport*, 3 (1993), pp. 396–408.

Terret, T., *Naissance et diffusion de la natation sportive* (Paris: L'Harmattan, 1994).

Terret, T., 'La Politique Lyonnaise en matière d'installations balnéaires (XIX–XX siècles)', *STAPS*, 33 (1994), pp. 89–102.

Terret, T., *Evolution des besoins et transformation des espaces aquatiques: approche historique et sociologique*, Proceedings of the IVth Congreso de actividades acuàticas, Barcelona, 20–22 October 1995.

Terret, T. (ed.), *Histoire des Sports* (Paris: L'Harmattan, 1996).

Terret, T., 'La Natation scolaire à la fin du XIX siècle: Réalités et difficultés d'une intégration', *STAPS,* 39 (Feb. 1996).

Terret, T., 'Savoir Nager. Une Histoire des Pratiques et des Techniques de la Natation', in P. Goirand and J. Metzler (eds), *Histoire technique et culture scolaire* (Paris: Ed. EPS, 1996).

Terret, T., 'L'Eau, l'école et l'espace: Normes scolaires et pratiques de la natation au XXème Siècle', in P. Arnaud and T. Terret (eds), *Le Sport et ses Espaces: XIXème-XXème Siècles* (Paris: Ed. du Comité des Travaux Historiques et Scientifiques, Ministère de l'Education Nationale, de l'Enseignement Supérieur et de la Recherche, 1998).

Terret, T., *L'Institution et le nageur: Histoire de la Fédération Française de Natation. 1919–1939* (Lyon: Presses universitaires de Lyon, 1998).

Terret, T., *A History of Aquatic Fitness* (Miami, FL: Report to the AEA, 2001).

'The Surf Lifesaving Movement: Executives Out of Step with an Unsquare Age', *Sydney Morning Herald*, 12 Feb. 1965.

Theberge, N., 'Gender, Sport, and the Construction of Community: A Case Study from Women's Ice Hockey', *Sociology of Sport Journal*, 12, 4 (1995), pp. 389–402.

Thelin, J.R., *Games Colleges Play: Scandal and Reform in Intercollegiate Athletics* (Baltimore, MD: Johns Hopkins University Press, 1994).

Thibault, J., *Sport et éducation physique* (Paris: Vrin, 1972), p. 33.

Thomas, L.C. and Goldthwait, J.E., *Body Mechanics and Health* (Boston: Houghton Mifflin Co., 1922), pp. 13–26.

Thompson, M., 'The Aesthetics of Risk', in J. Perrin (ed.), *Mirrors in the Cliffs* (London: Diadem Books, 1983), pp. 561–73.

Thoms, A., *Surfmovies: The History of Surf Film in Australia* (Sydney: Shore Thing Publishing, 2000).

Thomson, S.J., 'No One Played Marbles': The Changing Dimension of School Playground Activities' (unpublished undergraduate dissertation, Keele University, 1998).

Thomson, S.J., ' Playground or Playpound? The Contested Terrain of the Primary School Playground'. Paper presented at the British Educational Research Association Conference, Cardiff University, 2000.

Thoreau, H.D., *The Maine Woods* (Boston: Ticknor and Fields, 1864).

Tomkins, J., 'Football Gazes and Spaces: A Foucauldian History of the Present' (unpublished doctoral thesis, University of Brighton 1995).

Trevelyan, G., *Illustrated Social History of England* (Harmondsworth, UK: Penguin, 1964).

Trow, M., 'Leadership and Academic Reform: Biology at Berkeley', Working Paper 99–8. Institute of Governmental Studies, University of California, Berkeley (1999).

Trpkov, J.B., *Organisation du travail et culture professionnelle dans le secteur de la forme: analyse de la situation dans le Rhône* (Master thesis, Lyon, 2000).

Tuan, Yi-Fu, *Topophilia* (Englewood Cliffs, NJ: Prentice-Hall, 1974).

Tuan, Yi-Fu, *Space and Place: The Perspective of Experience* (Minneapolis: University of Minnesota Press, 1977).

Tuan, Yi-Fu, 'Thought and Landscape: The Eye and the Mind's Eye', in D.W. Meinig (ed.), *The Interpretation of Ordinary Landscapes* (New York: Oxford University Press, 1979), pp. 89–102.

Turner, B., *The Body and Society* (Oxford: Basil Blackwell, 1984).

Turner, G., *National Fictions. Literature, Film and the Construction of Australian Narrative* (Sydney: Allen and Unwin, 1986).

Unan, J., *'Imperial Gyms: The Colonization of Movement'*, Paper presented at the North American Society for the Sociology of Sport Conference, Colorado Springs, 2000.

Unan, J., *'The Spatiality of Sporting Environments'*, paper presented at The Society for Philosophy and Geography, Towson, MD, 2000.

Unsworth, W., *Hold the Heights: The Foundations of Mountaineering* (Seattle: The Mountaineers, 1994).

Urry, J., *The Tourist Gaze* (London: Routledge, 1990).

Vadepied, A., *Les Eaux troublées* (Paris: Ed. Scarabée, 1978).

Vail, G., *L'Art du patinage* (Paris, 1886).

Valentine, G. 'Angels and Devils: Moral Landscapes of Childhood', *Environment and Planning D*, 14 (1996), pp. 581–99.

Valentine, G., '(Hetero) sexing Space: Lesbian Perceptions and Experiences of Everyday Spaces', in L. McDowell and J. Sharpe (eds), *Space, Gender and Knowledge* (London: Arnold, 1997), pp. 284–300.

Valentine, G., '(Re)negotiating the 'Heterosexual Street. Lesbian Productions of Space', in N. Duncan (ed.), *Body Space: Destabilizing Geographies of Gender and Sexuality* (London: Routledge, 1996), pp. 146–53.

Valentine, G. and McKendrick, J., 'Children's Outdoor Play: Exploring Parental Concerns about Children's Safety and the Changing Nature of Childhood', *Geoforum, 28*, 2 (1997), pp. 219–23.

Van Ingen, C. '*A Nomadic Inquiry into Spaces of Resistance*', Paper presented at the North American Society for the Sociology of Sport Conference (Colorado Springs, 2000).

Van Ingen, C., 'Exploring Alternative Terrains of Resistance – Spatializing Resistance in the "Frontrunners", paper presented at The Society for Philosophy and Geography, Towson, MD, 2000).

Vandervell, H.E. and Witham, T.M., *A System of Figure Skating*, 2nd edn (London: Horace Cox, 1874).

Verbrugge, M.H., 'Recreating the Body: Women's Physical Education and the Science of Sex Differences in America, 1900–1940', *Bulletin of the History of Medicine, 71*, 2 (1997), p. 275.

Vertinsky, P., *The Eternally Wounded Woman: Women, Exercise and Doctors in the Late Nineteenth Century* (Manchester: Manchester University Press, 1990).

Vertinsky, P., 'Reclaiming Space, Revisioning the Body: The Quest for Gender Sensitive Physical Education', *Quest*, 44 (1992), p. 172.

Vertinsky, P., *The Eternally Wounded Woman: Women, Doctors and Medicine in the Late Nineteenth Century* (Champaign, IL: University of Illinois Press, 1994).

Vertinsky, P., 'Space, Place and the Gendered Disciplining of Bodies: The Case of the War Memorial Gym', paper presented at the ISHPES Conference, Budapest, Hungary, 1999.

Vigarello, G., *Le Corps redressé* (Paris: Delages, 1978)

Vigarello, G., 'Pratiques de natation au XIX siècle: Représentation de l'eau et différenciations socials', *Sport et Société* (St Etienne: CIEREC, 1981).

Vigarello, G., *Le Propre et le sale* (Paris: Seuil, 1985).

Vignal, B., Champely, S. and Terret, T., 'Swimming and Forms of Practice in Lyon', *International Review for Sport Sociology*, Dec. 2001.

Vigneau F., *Les Espaces du sport* (Paris: Presses universitaires de France, 1998).

Vinson, M., 'Gay Blades', typescript (Colorado Springs: Vinson Diaries, World Figure Skating Museum, 1933).

Vivensang, J., *Pédagogie moderne de la natation*, 4th edn (Paris: Chiron, 1981).

Waitt, G., 'Playing Games with Sydney: Marketing Sydney for the 2000 Olympics', *Urban Studies*, 36, 7 (1999), pp. 1055–77.

Walker, R., *Ka Whawhai Tonu Matou – Struggle Without End* (Auckland: Penguin, 1990).

Wallon, J., *Notice sur les exercices physiques* (Amiens, 1884).

Warringah Shire Council, File 1966–8. Parks and Baths 20A.

Watkins, R., *When Rock Got Rolling* (Christchurch: Hazard Press, 1989).

Watkins, R., *Hostage to the Beat* (Auckland: Tandem Press, 1995).

Weedon, C., *Feminist Practice and Poststrucuralist Theory* (Oxford: Blackwell, 1997).

Weirick, J., 'Urban Design', in R. Cashman and A. Hughes (eds), *Staging the Olympics: The Event and its Impact* (Sydney: University of New South Wales Press, 1999), pp. 70–82.

Weiss, P., *Sport: A Philosophic Enquiry* (Carbondale: University of Southern Illinois Press, 1969).

Wendl, I., *Eis mit Stil* [Ice with Style] (München: Jugend & Volk, 1979).

Wigley, M., 'Untitled: The Housing of Gender', in B. Colomina (ed.), *Sexuality & Space* (New York: Princeton Papers on Architecture, Princeton Architectural Press, 1992), pp. 327–89.

Wilderspin, S., 'On the Importance of Educating the Infant Children of the Poor' (London, 1823), in H.C. Barnard (ed.), *A History of English Education – From 1760* (London: University of London Press, 1947).

Williams, D.R. and Kaltenborn, Bjorn P., 'Leisure Places and Modernity', in David Crouch (ed.), *Leisure Tourism/ Geographies* (New York: Routledge, 1999), pp. 214–37.

Williams, J., Browning, V. and Macdonald, C. 'New Zealand Marching Association', in A. Else (ed.), *Women Together: A History of Women's Organisations in New Zealand* (Wellington: Daphne Brasell Associates with Historical Branch, Department of Internal Affairs, 1993), pp. 437–39.

Williams, R., *Marxism and Literature* (Oxford: Oxford University Press, 1977).

Wilmore, J.H.,'Building Strong Academic Programs for Our Future', *Quest*, 50 (1998), pp. 103–7.

Wilson, H., 'What is an Olympic City? Visions of Sydney 2000', *Media, Culture and Society*, 18 (1996), pp. 603–18.

Windsor-Liscombe, R., *The New Spirit: Modern Architecture in Vancouver 1938–1963* (Douglas and McIntyre, Vancouver: Canadian Centre for Architecture, 1997).

Winzer, H., 'Geschichte des Eiskunstlaufs' [History of Figure Skating], in C. Diem, A. Mallwitz and E. Neuendorff (eds), *Handbuch der Leibesübungen* [Handbook of Physical Exercises], Vol. 8, Eissport [Ice-sport] (Berlin: Veidmannsche Buchhandlung, 1925), pp. 33–61.

Wrynn, A.M., *Contributions of Women Researchers to the Development of a Science of Physical Education* (Ph.D. dissertation, University of California, 1996), pp. 98–103.

Younghusband, F. *The Epic of Mount Everest* (London: Arnold, 1926).

Youth Policy Advisory Committee, Report 41/1962–3 (Sydney: New South Wales Government, 1963).

Yska, R., *All Shook Up: The Flash Bodgie and the Rise of the New Zealand Teenager in the Fifties* (Auckland: Penguin, 1993).

Zimbalist, A., *Unpaid Professionals: Commercialism and Conflict in Big-Time College Sports* (Princeton, NJ: Princeton University Press, 1999).

Zukin, S., *Landscapes of Power* (Berkeley: University of California Press, 1991).

Notes on Contributors

Mary Louise Adams is an Associate Professor in the School of Physical and Health Education and the Department of Sociology at Queen's University in Kingston, Canada. She is currently working on a gender history of figure skating and is the author of *The Trouble With Normal: Postwar Youth and the Making of Heterosexuality* (University of Toronto Press, 1997).

John Bale obtained degrees from the University of London and currently shares his time teaching and researching between Aarhus University, Denmark, and Keele University, UK. He has been a visiting professor at the University of Jyvaskyla, Finland, the University of Western Ontario, Canada, and the University of Queensland, Australia. Among his books are *Sport, Space and the City*, *Landscapes of Modern Sport*, *Kenyan Running* (with Joe Sang) and *Imagined Olympians*.

Douglas Booth teaches at the University of Otago, New Zealand. His primary research covers the broad area of sport as a form of popular culture with a particular emphasis on political relationships and processes. Within this framework, specific areas of investigation have included racism in South African sport, sport policy in Australia and surfing as an extreme cultural practice. He is the author of *The Race Game: Sport and Politics in South Africa* (1998), *Australian Beach Cultures: The History of Sun, Sand and Surf* (2001) and, with Colin Tatz, *One-Eyed: A View of Australian Sport* (2000). He is book reviews editor of *International Sports Studies* and serves on the editorial boards of several journals, including *Journal of Sport History*, *Sport History Review* and *The International Journal of the History of Sport*.

Peter Donnelly is currently Director of the Centre for Sport Policy Studies and a Professor in the Faculty of Physical Education and Health at the

University of Toronto. He studied Physical Education as an undergraduate, and was a schoolteacher for several years before moving to the United States, where he completed undergraduate studies in New York City, and Master's and Ph.D. degrees in Sport Studies at the University of Massachusetts. In 1976 he moved to Canada, where he taught at the University of Western Ontario and McMaster University. His research interests include sport politics and policy issues (including the area of children's rights in sport), sport subcultures, and mountaineering (history). He has published numerous scholarly articles on those and other topics. Recent books include *Taking Sport Seriously: Social Issues in Canadian Sport* (1997; 2nd edn, 2000), and *Inside Sports* (with Jay Coakley, 1999).

Caroline Fusco received her undergraduate degree and teaching certification at the University of Ulster in 1986 and taught for four years in the public school system in Northern Ireland. After moving to Canada in 1990 she completed a Master of Science degree at the University of Manitoba and then taught there for three years. She has recently finished her Ph.D. in Community Health at the University of Toronto. Her dissertation, *The (Re)Production of Subjectivities Cultures of Work and Working Out*, is concerned with how power/knowledge and desire are organized in, and through, space(s).

Chris Gaffney is currently a Ph.D. student in geography at the University of Texas at Austin. His research on stadiums has covered North America, Europe, Asia and South America. Gaffney's dissertation study is focused on the cultural geography of the stadiums of Buenos Aires, Argentina. He received his MS in geography from the University of Massachusetts at Amherst, and a BA in history and philosophy from Trinity University (TX).

Charlotte Macdonald is Head of History at Victoria University of Wellington, New Zealand. She completed a Ph.D. at the University of Auckland and the London School of Economics and has since published in the area of women's and gender history. Her work includes *A Woman of Good Character: Single Women as Immigrant Settlers in Nineteenth-Century New Zealand* (Allen & Unwin, 1990); *The Book of New Zealand Women/Ko Kui Ma te Kaupapa* (with Merimeri Penfold and Bridget Williams (Bridget Williams Books, 1991)); *My Hand Will Write What My Heart Dictates* (with Frances Porter (Auckland University Press, 1996)), and two collections of women's history essays (edited with Barbara Brookes and Margaret Tennant). She was the President of the New Zealand Historical Association in 1997/98 and is the New Zealand coordinator for the International Federation for Research in Women's History.

Tara Magdalinski is Senior Lecturer in the Faculty of Arts and Sciences at the University of the Sunshine Coast, Australia. She has published widely in the area of sports studies, focusing most recently on the cultural construction of performance enhancement. In addition, she examines the role of 'nature' in the bodies and site of the Sydney 2000 Olympics, the cultural reception of 'Fastskin' and the corporate motives of Olympic education. She has co-edited a book with Timothy Chandler, *With God on their Side: Sport in the Service of Religion* (London: Routledge, 2002), and is currently writing a book on performance enhancement.

Roberta J. Park is Professor Emeritus, Department of Integrative Biology, University of California, Berkeley, where she has been a faculty member for more than 40 years. Her research has focused upon health, hygiene, education and exercise from the seventeenth to the twentieth centuries, and more recently upon various aspects of the history of sports medicine and exercise science. Editor of numerous books and articles, she was Chair of the Department of Physical Education from 1982–1992. She has served on several editorial boards, such as the *International Journal of the History of Sport,* and has been an officer in a number of organizations, including Vice-President of the International Society for the History of Physical Education and Sport and President of the American Academy of Kinesiology and Physical Education.

Brian Pronger is Associate Professor of Philosophy at the Faculty of Physical Education and Health, University of Toronto. He has published extensively on sexuality and desire in sport and physical education. His books include *Body Fascism: Salvation in the Technology of Physical Fitness* (University of Toronto Press, 2002) and *The Arena of Masculinity: Sport, Homosexuality and the Meaning of Sex* (University of Toronto Press, 1992).

Thierry Terret is a Professor of Sport History at the University of Lyon, where he manages an interdisciplinary institute research centre for sport science. He is the current President of the *International Society for the History of Physical Education* (ISHPES) and the former President of the *French Association for Sport Science* (AFRAPS). After several years spent on the history of aquatic sports his main fields of interest are now the historical diffusion of sport, both nationally and internationally, sport history and health, and sport history and gender. He has published many articles and is the author, co-author or editor of 22 books, including a recent essay on the Inter-allied Games of 1919 in which he investigates the way a sport event can be simultaneously affected by military, political, religious and sport stakes.

Sarah Thomson is completing her doctoral degree at Keele University, UK. Her research interests lie in the area of children's play and play spaces and she focuses on areas of surveillance, litigation and risk. She has published papers on risk and litigation and its effects on children's play, and has lectured in Britain and North America.

Patricia Vertinsky is Professor of Human Kinetics at the University of British Columbia, Canada. A social and cultural historian of the body, she is the author of *The Eternally Wounded Woman: Women, Doctors and Exercise in the late 19th Century* (1994), and co-author of *Physical Activity, Aging and Stereotypes* (1996) and *Memory, Monument and Modernism: Disciplining the Body in the Gymnasium* (2003). She is a past-president of the North American Society of Sports History, Vice-President of the International Society of the History of Sport and Physical Education and is on the editorial boards of the *Journal of Sport History*, the *International Journal of the History of Sport, International Sport Studies, The Sports Historian* and *Sporting Traditions*.

Index